# The Maoris of
# New Zealand
## Rautahi

# The Maoris of New Zealand
# Rautahi

Joan Metge

Routledge & Kegan Paul
London, Henley and Boston

*First published in 1967*
*This revised edition first published in 1976*
*by Routledge & Kegan Paul Ltd,*
*39 Store Street,*
*London WC1E 7DD*
*Broadway House,*
*Newtown Road,*
*Henley-on-Thames,*
*Oxon RG9 1EN and*
*9 Park Street, Boston, Mass. 02108, USA*
*Set in 'Monotype' Times New Roman*
*and printed in Great Britain by*
*W & J Mackay Limited, Chatham*

*ISBN 0 7100 8352 1 (c)*
*ISBN 0 7100 8381 5 (p)*

*Royalties from the sale of this book are paid into the Joan Metge*
*Charitable Trust and disbursed for Maori purposes, especially*
*education.*

To

Paihana Taua, Reihana Matiu, Rarawa Kerehoma, Miriama Taylor,
Mika Nathan, Tiki Walters and Waata Te Pania of Te Rarawa
Sue Te Tai and Rīpeka Te Paa of Ngāpuhi
Rangitaua Tāpara of Waikato
Kingi Wētere of Ngāti Maniapoto
Maharaia Winiata and Mīria Hōtere of Ngāti Ranginui
Rāniera Kingi and Hōhepa Tāepa of Te Arawa
Pita Tāpene of Ngāti Tūwharetoa
Hirini Tāwhai, Mani Waititi and Hoani Waititi of
Te Whānau-ā-Apanui
Te Oenuku Rēne of Ngāti Toa and Ngāti Raukawa

*Ki a koutou, ki ngā mātua mē ngā whaea*
*e moe mai nā i Tua-whakarere*
*nā koutou nei ahau i atawhai, i whāngai, i penapena—*
*inā te taonga nei,*
*nāku, otirā nā tātou ngātahi.*
*Nāu te rourou, nāku te rourou,*
*kā kī te kete.*

The work is not mine but ours.

# Contents

# Plates

*Photographs are by John Miller unless otherwise indicated*

# Tables

# Figures

*The figures were all drawn by Mrs Barbara Winchester of Wellington*

# Introduction

This book had its beginnings in Kaitaia in 1959 when Matiu Te Hau, Maori Tutor-Organizer for the Department of Adult Education at the University of Auckland and a long-time personal friend, asked me to give four weekly lectures on 'Maori society today' at Kaitaia College. The series was attended by Maoris and Pakehas in roughly equal numbers. The Pakehas had mostly had long association with Maoris as neighbours, school-mates, work-mates and employers. The Maoris included local elders and a contingent from Kotare, the rural community where I was currently completing my second fieldwork term. They came partly out of friendship and partly to hear 'what she is saying about us'. Facing such an audience was a daunting experience, but a most rewarding one. At the end of the first lecture, satisfied that I was talking in general terms and not betraying confidences, Maori spokesmen expressed approval in formal speeches: as one said, 'we recognize ourselves in what you say, though we would have put it differently.' From then on they threw themselves wholeheartedly into the discussion. From the comments the Pakehas made and the questions they asked it became apparent that there were many things they did not know or misunderstood, but also that they sincerely wanted to learn. As the sessions proceeded, they developed into a direct and increasingly frank dialogue between Pakeha and Maori in which grievances were aired and misunderstandings sorted out. I saw for myself how fruitful direct encounter could be, and from that time on I have directed all my work to that end.

In the following years the four lectures given at Kaitaia grew into a series of ten presented several times a year for the Department of University Extension (formerly Adult Education) in Auckland and at weekend schools in other parts of the Auckland University district; a cyclostyled version was produced as a Discussion Course posted out with a box of books to adult education groups in rural areas; and the Discussion Course in its turn provided the framework for the first edition of *The Maoris of New Zealand*. Since then the latter has also been used as a Discussion Course by the Department of University Extension at the Victoria University of Wellington. At each step in its development the text was tested on live audiences including Maoris and associated whenever possible with visits to *marae*.

I began work on a second edition in 1973, for two main reasons. The first edition, which was related closely to the early nineteen sixties, was becoming out-dated in some respects, with the publication of the 1966 and 1971 Censuses, legislative changes and significant social developments, especially in the cities. Secondly, I was painfully aware of deficiencies and omissions in the first edition. In particular I had failed to give due prominence to the underlying values of Maoritanga. *Aroha, mana* and *tapu* were discussed only briefly and in the limited contexts of kinship, leadership and health respectively, *noa* and 'Maori time' were mentioned only in passing, and *whakamā* appeared only in the Glossary. This was not because I considered such ideas unimportant, but because I felt that I had neither the competence nor the right to explore them at depth. In recent years, however, I have received much encouragement and help in developing my under-standing of Maori beliefs and values from Maori elders, especially Wiremu Parker of Ngāti Porou and Tawhao Tioke of Tūhoe. It is with their support that I have ventured to devote a chapter to 'basic concepts in Maori culture' in this edition. I am delighted that since it was written Maori statements on some of these themes have appeared in print, notably in *Te Ao Hurihuri* (King, 1975).

Two years in the writing, this second edition is a very substantial revision and amplification of the first. Only chapters 1, 2, 3, 9 and 10 remain basically the same with minor amendments. Chapters 13, 14, 15 and 16 have been partially and chapters 4, 6, 8, 11 and 18 almost entirely re-written. Chapter 12 is an expansion of four pages in chapter 7 of the first edition, and chapters 5, 7 and 17 are entirely new.

The word *Rautahi* used as a title for this second edition is a com-bination of the Maori words for 'an hundred' (*rau*) and 'one' (*tahi*). I first heard it in 1964 when Maoris of many different tribes living in the timber-mill town of Kawerau created it as the name of the Maori Community Centre they had built by concerted effort for common use. The symbolic use of numbers is a characteristic Maori literary device. The Kawerau Maoris coined the term to express their view of them-selves as 'many yet also one'; but it is easily given a wider reference. *Rautahi* can be interpreted as a succinct description of Maori social organization: many tribes, one people (see Figure 7, p. 315). At a deeper level it expresses the abstract idea that unity and diversity do not necessarily contradict and at best involve each other: unity discovered in diversity, diversity transcended in unity. In this sense, the word can be taken as a motto and charter for relations not only between Maoris but also between all New Zealanders.

The main emphasis of the book is on the contemporary scene. The first three chapters, which present a highly condensed summary of Classic Maori society and the history of Maori-Pakeha contact, should be regarded mainly as background and introduction to the other fifteen. Those who wish to explore these areas in depth are referred to sections A and B of the Bibliography. The major part of the book is devoted to the study of Maori society and culture today, that is, in the context of New Zealand society as a whole and in the first half of the nineteen seventies. For this purpose I have obtained statistical material and information from Government Departments and other organizations in published and unpublished form. The Statistics Department in particular was most helpful in supplying material from the 1971 Census both in advance of final publication and in greater detail. In other cases I have used the most up-to-date figures available at the time of writing, ranging from 1973 to 1975. Information on legislation is accurate up to the end of July 1975. I have also consulted the work of other research workers and writers, both Maori and Pakeha, wherever relevant, citing the reference both in the text and in the Bibliography. And I have drawn extensively on my own experience in a variety of Maori communities beginning in 1953 and comprising two years' full-time fieldwork in the city of Auckland (1953-4), fieldwork visits totalling over twelve months to a rural community in the Far North (referred to in the text as Kotare) in 1955, 1958 and 1960, shorter visits to most parts of the North Island, ten years' residence in Wellington and attendance at numerous Maori gatherings over more than twenty years.

As an anthropologist by training I have ordered my material largely within an anthropological framework, but I have endeavoured to keep this from being too obtrusive, limiting the use of technical words to those which actively aid understanding. My use of Maori words is much more extensive, and for this I make no apology. I have followed two simple rules, using Maori words wherever they cannot be translated without distorting their meaning and whenever Maoris commonly use them when speaking English.

As an anthropologist also I use an objective approach. To me 'being objective' means examining all the material available, favourable and unfavourable, looking at all sides of a question, and building up as balanced a picture as possible. But it does *not* mean being cold, impersonal and unfeeling. On the contrary, I believe that where human beings are involved true understanding can be achieved only through the exercise of sympathy (literally, 'feeling with'), that is, making the imaginative effort to stand where others stand and see through their eyes. As a human being I could not live with Maori friends, laugh, work, worship and most importantly weep with them for our dead without developing both a deep affection for particular individuals and an insight into Maori feelings and beliefs which is not accessible to the outside observer. What I write comes from the heart as well as the head.

Nevertheless, as a Pakeha whose contact with Maoris began in adulthood, I cannot hope to 'know' Maori culture and what being Maori means in the same way as a Maori brought up in it, experiencing and learning to understand it from the inside. I do not pretend to present a Maori view of Maori culture, only what I have learnt to understand of it. But because I have learnt what I know from scratch, slowly and painfully and by making mistakes, I know from experience what most Pakehas do not know and need to have explained, what misconceptions and misunderstandings need to be corrected, what problems overcome, before they can begin to see things from a Maori point of view.

To Pakeha readers and those who use this book for teaching purposes, I cannot emphasize too strongly that it does not, and does not pretend to, give the whole picture or the whole truth about contemporary Maori society and culture. That is entirely beyond the scope of one writer or one book. As an objective study by a Pakeha 'outsider', however sympathetic, it needs to be complemented and filled out by subjective statements from Maoris with 'inside' experience. Also, although I have stressed the importance of tribal, regional and personal variations, I have not been able to explore them in any detail. To help redress the balance in both these respects, I have included writings by Maoris and studies of particular communities in the Bibliography. But in addition I would urge readers and especially study groups using this book to establish personal ties with Maoris in their vicinity, and to seek their help in translating my objective generalizations into meaningful local and personal terms.

Finally, I should like to express my appreciation to the many people who have helped me pursue the studies on which this book is based. I acknowledge a particular debt of gratitude to: the Department of Statistics, Maori Affairs, Justice and Education, and especially to Jock McEwen (formerly Secretary of Maori Affairs), to Bill Herewini and Brownie Puriri of Maori Welfare, to Don McKenzie (Director of the Justice Department Research Unit) and his staff, and to Alan Smith, Turoa Royal and Tamati Reedy of the Maori Education Division, for help given cheerfully as friends as well as officials; to my Anthropology Professors, Ralph Piddington, Raymond Firth and Jan Pouwer, and to Stewart Morrison (formerly of University Extension) for instruction, encouragement and intellectual stimulation; to the President and Executive of the Ratana Church of N.Z.; to Pei Te Hurinui Jones of the King Movement and to colleagues in Anthropology, Sociology, Maori Studies and University Extension, especially Matiu Te Hau, Wiremu Parker, Bruce Biggs, Koro Dewes, Pat Hohepa, Rangi Walker, Bernie Kernot, John Rangihau, Bob Mahuta, Peter Sharples, Bill Willmott, David Bettison and Jean Barton, for information, comments on the draft text and help in formulating ideas; to Jeff Gamlin of the Government Research Unit; to my parents for teaching me to love learning for its own sake and for loving support of many kinds; and to my *tama whāngai* John for his photographs and what I have learnt watching him explore his Maori heritage.

To the many Maoris who have accepted me into their homes, put up with me, taught me and given me their friendship, I can only say, this book itself is my way of saying thank you, *he tohu aroha mō a koutou manaakitanga i a ahau. Nā a koutou awhina i oti ai.* Because there are so very, very many of you, I have singled out by name only those *kaumātua* particularly close to me who have left this world to go to their eternal rest. To them, as representatives of all of you, I have dedicated this book.

Nā reira, kia ora ano koutou katoa.

Wellington                                                                 Joan Metge

# chapter 1

# The Maoris before 1800-I

## Settlement and the development of Maori culture

The Maoris whom the European explorers found living in New Zealand in the late eighteenth century were easily identified, on physical and linguistic grounds, as Polynesians. Their oral traditions included accounts of an original homeland called Hawaiki and of ancient quarrels which precipitated a great migration by voyaging canoes southwards across the Pacific to New Zealand (Buck, 1949: 4–73).

All tribes told the story of how Maui, the demi-god, fished the North Island of New Zealand out of the sea. Some attributed its rediscovery to Kupe, who circumnavigated it and sailed home, having seen only birds. Others gave the credit to Toi who, leading an expedition in search of a grandson lost at sea, landed in the Bay of Plenty, settled among the people he found living there and established a ruling aristocracy. Most tribes traced their dominion and prestige not to Kupe or Toi, but to ancestors who, they claimed, set out from Hawaiki on organized expeditions in sea-going canoes, carrying cultivated plants. Making landfall mostly in the Bay of Plenty, they settled in various parts of the country, assimilated the original inhabitants by marriage and conquest, and developed in subsequent generations into many independent tribes.

Early this century, a Pakeha scholar, Stephenson Percy Smith, fitted the varying tribal versions together in a scheme that brought Kupe to New Zealand in about AD 950, Toi in about 1150, and a final, dominant wave of immigrants in a 'great fleet' in about 1350. This scheme enjoyed a long popularity but has been discarded by scholars after re-examination of the traditions (Simmons, 1969a; Roberton, 1962).

Though even Maoris make shorthand reference to 'the seven canoes of the great fleet', the traditions use the word *heke* (migration)

1

not 'fleet', and each tribe concentrates on the story of its own ancestral canoe. The names of eight canoes – Aotea, Arawa, Horouta, Kurahaupo, Mātaatua, Tainui, Tākitimu and Tokomaru – were familiar to most tribes, but there were many others of regional importance. Some canoes left together, met at points on the way, or made landfall about the same time and place, but none sailed the whole way together. Guarded use of the genealogies indicates that the captains of the famous eight canoes might have lived anywhere between 1200 and 1400. In 1956 Andrew Sharp attacked the idea of purposive two-way migration, maintaining that the canoes which reached New Zealand did so either by accident or by taking a long chance on discovering land to the south. He provoked a continuing controversy (Sharp, 1959, 1963; Golson, 1972).

In recent decades, scientific study has greatly illumined our knowledge of Maori prehistory. Linguists have demonstrated that the language of the eighteenth-century Maori belonged to the same group as those of East Polynesia. Archaeologists have established that New Zealand was inhabited well before AD 1200, that its early inhabitants lived mainly by fishing and hunting *moa* (Dinornis) and other birds now extinct, and that their culture was unmistakably of East Polynesian provenance (Duff, 1956). The problem is to determine how this early culture, which archaeologists variously describe as Moahunter, Archaic Maori and New Zealand East Polynesian, was related to the 'Classic Maori' culture of the eighteenth century. Some scholars have suggested that the latter developed from the culture imported by the 'fleet'. As yet, the archaeologists have found no evidence of the intrusion of a new cultural group (Golson, 1959; Groube, 1967).

Summarizing existing knowledge, Green (1974) suggested that the first arrivals brought an early form of East Polynesian culture and by adapting it to the New Zealand environment developed a New Zealand East Polynesian culture; that the bearers of this culture spread throughout the country, passing through at least two socio-economic phases, varying according to environment; that another distinctive culture then developed out of the earlier one in the northern part of the North Island as a result of adaptive innovations in isolation, influenced by the different environments from Polynesia and based on expandable food resources, especially of *kūmara* and fernroot; and that this 'Maori culture' also passed through several phases to a climax in Classic Maori and spread in certain of its regional aspects into southern areas, where it influenced or replaced later aspects of the New Zealand Polynesian culture.

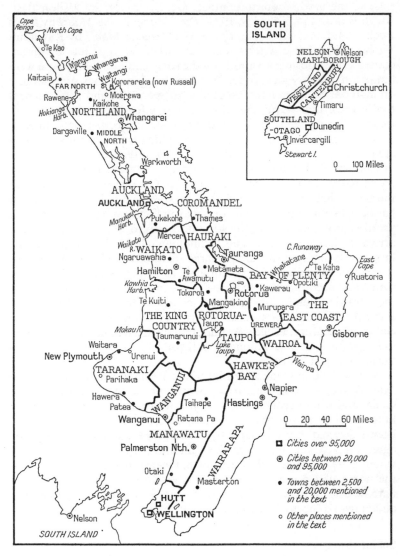

*Figure 1    New Zealand 1975*

## The Maoris in the late eighteenth century

The standard works of reference on Maori society and culture at the time of the first European contacts are *The Maori* by Elsdon Best, which was first published in 1924, *The Coming of the Maori* by Peter Buck (1949), and *Economics of the New Zealand Maori* by Raymond Firth (1959). These writers made use whenever possible of direct, contemporaneous observations by the early explorers, but these were limited in quantity and scope. To fill in the picture, they drew largely on material collected later, especially between 1814 and 1850, on oral traditions written down after 1840, and on informants' memories collected in the eighteen nineties, and even later. Projecting material back into the past in this way has problems which were not fully appreciated when these works were written. Many of the features they establish as typical of Classic Maori culture are mentioned rarely or not at all by early observers. On these grounds Groube recently advanced the thesis that 'much of the change in Maori material culture which has been assumed to be prehistoric may in fact have taken place in the protohistoric period from the stimulus given to Maori culture by the arrival of European ideas and technology' (1964: 17). In particular, he suggests that concentration in large villages, carved meeting-houses, storehouses on piles, and certain elaborated forms of carving, ornaments and decoration, were post-European developments. In this and the following chapter I have drawn mainly on the works of Buck and Firth to build up a picture of Maori society and culture in the late eighteenth century. While they undoubtedly need to be re-examined in the light of modern techniques and theory, I believe they stand up to the test remarkably well.

When Captain Cook sailed into New Zealand waters in 1769, the Maoris were a pre-literate, tribal people whose tools were mainly of stone, and whose economic and political organization was based on kinship. Cook estimated the population at 100,000. Up to 250,000 has been suggested, but estimates by archaeologists and a demographer agree on 110,000. Whatever their number, the Maoris were overwhelmingly concentrated in the north. Over four-fifths lived either to the north of the central uplands of the North Island or along the narrow coastal plains of Taranaki to the west and between Opotiki and Hawke's Bay to the east (Green, 1974: 30–2).

## Social structure

### Iwi and waka

The free men and women who made up the majority of the population were divided into some fifty tribes (*iwi*), independent political units which occupied separate territories, endeavoured to settle internal disputes peacefully, and defended their political and territorial integrity by force of arms. The tribes varied in size from a few to many thousand members. In addition to tribal members, the population of each tribe's territory included a few spouses belonging to other tribes, a number of slaves captured in war, and occasionally groups of refugees paying tribute as vassals. Each tribe was a descent-group in the broadest sense, membership being based on descent (or adoption by a descendant) from an ancestor identified as the tribe's 'founder', traced through both male and female links. Most tribes were known by their founder's name, prefixed by a word meaning 'descendants of': Ngāti, Āti-, Ngāi-, Aitanga-, Whānau- or Uri-. The rest bore names derived from an incident in their history.

The roster of tribes was not fixed: tribal histories make it clear that tribes waxed and waned. Sections of tribes (*hapū*) became tribes when large and powerful enough to enforce their right to independent action. Tribes weakened by war or famine were reabsorbed into related ones as sub-tribes. Whether a particular group was tribe or sub-tribe at any given time was often a matter for debate.

Tribes deriving from ancestors who came to New Zealand in the same canoe formed a *waka* (canoe), a loose association rather than a federation for defined ends. They recognized some obligation to help each other if asked, but frequently fought each other. The most important *waka* were: the Tainui tribes, whose territory stretched from Tamaki (where Auckland now stands) south to Mokau; the Arawa tribes of the Central Plateau; and the Mātaatua tribes of the Bay of Plenty. The tribes of the East Coast (between Cape Runaway and Wairoa) derived from Horouta and Nukutere, the Ngāti Kahungunu of Hawke's Bay and Ngāi Tahu of the South Island from Tākitimu. In Northland and Taranaki, canoe traditions were diverse and relatively unimportant.

## The hapū

The tribe was made up of a number of tribal sections called *hapū*, each of which controlled a defined stretch of tribal territory. Like the tribe, the *hapū* was a descent-group defined by descent from a founding ancestor through both male and female links and distinguished by his name. The 'founders' of all sections of a tribe and through them their members were linked by descent from the founder of the tribe. The *hapū* operated as a group on many more occasions than the tribe, especially with regard to land use, the production and use of capital assets such as large canoes and meeting-houses, and the entertaining of visitors. The large majority of a *hapū*'s members lived together on *hapū* territory, forming, with slaves and spouses from other groups, one or two local communities. In conversation and speech-making, the community was identified with the *hapū* and by its name. Thus though outside spouses never became members of the *hapū* descent-group, they were assimilated to it as an operational group and given rights of use in its resources as long as they lived on its territory. Members of a *hapū* who left its territory did not forfeit their membership. They could even pass on a claim to membership to their heirs. But they were not reckoned as part of its effective strength unless they returned.

Though the term is commonly translated as 'sub-tribe', *hapū* were often subdivisions of sub-tribes and even of sub-sub-tribes. When a *hapū* grew too large for effective functioning, some of its members broke away under the leadership of one of the chief's sons or younger brothers and established themselves independently, either on part of the original territory or on land acquired by conquest or occupation, sooner or later acquiring a new name. Remembering their origin, minor *hapū* formed in this way often joined forces under the original name for large-scale undertakings.

## The whānau

The basic social unit of Maori society was the household, which usually consisted of an extended-family: a patriarch (*kaumātua*) and his wife or wives, their unmarried children, some of their married children (usually the sons), and the latter's spouses and children. Many also included slaves.

The free members of a household were described collectively as the *whānau* of its *kaumātua*. But *whānau* seems also to have been used to describe a *kaumātua* and his descendants, a bilateral descent-group including persons who were no longer members of his household, but excluding affines. This double use has caused a lot of confusion. Writers speak of *iwi* being divided into *hapū*, and *hapū* into *whānau* – and then proceed to define *whānau* as 'the extended-family household'. We may speak of a *hapū* being divided into *whānau* only if we define the latter as a descent-group.

## Descent-group affiliation

In most societies organized on the basis of descent, descent-group membership is obtained by affiliation through one kind of parent only, either the father (patrilateral affiliation) or the mother (matrilateral), and each descent-group consists of members attached through a line of links of one sex, either males (a patrilineal group) or females (a matrilineal group). But Maoris could attach themselves to any one descent-group through either parent and to different descent-groups of the same order through both parents at once (ambilateral affiliation). As a result, Maori descent-groups were composed of persons who traced their descent back to the founding ancestor through a line of mixed male and female links (ambilineal groups), and there was some overlapping in the membership of groups of the same order. Since marriage between tribes and *hapū* was the exception rather than the rule, this was of significance mainly at the *whānau* level (Firth, 1957, 1963; Scheffler, 1964).

If a Maori's parents belonged to the same descent-group at any level, he had a double qualification for membership, though usually he stressed that through the parent of higher rank. If they belonged to different groups he had claims to membership in each one.

But a claim to membership was only a claim until it was validated by contact with the group and participation in its activities. To obtain the full benefits of membership in a descent-group, it was necessary to live on its territory in close association with other members. If this were not possible, the rights accorded the claimant diminished in proportion to the frequency and length of his visits. A Maori normally gave primary allegiance to one group by living with it, while maintaining secondary ties with one or two others. He could change priorities by changing his residence. Unvalidated claims could be passed on for three or four generations, but were eventually extinguished if not taken up.

In affiliation as in other respects, Maori society preferred the male before the female. Young married couples usually lived with the husband's parents, so that most children were brought up and identified themselves with their father's people. However, occasionally a man settled with his wife's group (if, for instance, they were short of manpower and he a younger son); a woman often sent a child home 'to keep warm' her place among her own folk; and even adults sometimes went to live with their mother's kin.

### Social status

Among the free, social status depended on seniority of descent within each descent-group. The elder always ranked above the younger, the descendants of the elder above those of the younger. Those who could trace their descent back to the ancestor of their *hapū* through older and preferably male siblings in each generation (i.e. through senior lines) were recognized as *rangatira* (aristocrats). Those who derived from junior lines or whose forebears had lost status through failure or enslavement were reckoned as *tūtūā* or *ware* (commoners). Closely related to the chief, the aristocrats had more wives, more land and more slaves than commoners and were consequently wealthier. The distinction was, however, by no means clear-cut. Commoners could always claim to be aristocrats because they were related to the chief by descent from the same ancestor and often also by marriage, since aristocrats took women of lower rank as secondary wives. Best shrewdly remarked that a Maori never admitted to being a commoner – it was always the other fellow.

The third and lowest class of Maori society was made up of slaves (*taurekareka*). Mostly war captives, they were generally well treated but regarded as property. To Maoris, enslavement was the worst fate that could befall a man, a bar sinister on a descent-line, even if the victim escaped to revenge himself. Women slaves were mostly taken as concubines by the free. The children of such unions were free, but of low rank.

Differences in rank were associated with differences in *mana* and *tapu*. *Mana* was spiritual power which possessed and was possessed by individuals, groups and things and accounted for their effectiveness. An individual inherited an initial store of *mana* varying with the seniority of his descent, but he could increase or decrease it by his own actions. In other words, there was scope for social mobility. According to their *mana*, people were more or less *tapu* or *noa* in relation to each other. The word *tapu* is best rendered 'under religious restriction': it was a state that required respectful treatment and was dangerous to the transgressor. *Noa* was a state of ordinariness and freedom from restriction. All free men were *tapu* to some extent, aristocrats more so than commoners. Women were *noa* as a category in relation to men, but individual women were *tapu* during menstruation, pregnancy and childbirth and if chiefs' daughters or mediums of the gods. Slaves were entirely *noa*.

## Settlement

The most conspicuous features of the Maori cultural landscape were fortified strongholds known as *pā*. Strategically situated on hill or headland, they were protected by palisades, ditches, earthworks and fighting platforms. Inside the fortifications, houses were crowded closely, often on artificial terraces. Some of the *pā* in the densely populated, agricultural north may have been occupied more or less permanently, but most lacked water supply and were probably used as citadels, where the people gathered when threatened, and perhaps for community ceremonies. The largest could accommodate several thousand persons (Groube, 1967: 15–19; Green, 1974: 36).

When not living in *pā*, the people lived in unfortified settlements called *kāinga*. These are usually described as villages, but the early records suggest that they were typically hamlets of five or six houses scattered over the countryside with the *pā* as focus. Larger villages may, however, have occurred in fertile lowland areas, especially in the north. Households appear to have moved several times a year between the *pā* and hamlets close to a variety of resources, while individuals and nuclear families built temporary shelters on camping excursions.

The domestic complex or homestead consisted of one to four houses (*whare*), used mainly for sleeping, a cooking-shelter (*kāuta*) over an open fire and earth-oven (*hāngi*), a rubbish dump, and possibly one or two roofed storage pits (*rua*). These were often enclosed in a courtyard by a wall of poles. The sleeping-houses consisted of one rectangular room, with a single door and window in the front wall and a stone-lined hearth. In cold situations, the floor was often sunken below ground level. Most sleeping-houses were small (not more than ten feet by six) and simply built of poles and thatch, but some were 'superior houses', twice that length, with wall posts, rafters, ridge posts and ridge poles of worked timbers, and an open front porch. All were furnished alike with piles of bracken covered with plaited flax mats. Clothes, ornaments and various items of equipment were kept in the sleeping-house, food utensils in the cooking-shelter. Community latrines were secluded on the edge of each settlement.

According to most authorities, each major settlement (whether *pā* or *kāinga*) had a *marae*, an open space used as a gathering place, a large house variously described as a *whare runanga* (council house) or *whare hui* (meeting-house), and one or two storehouses set on piles (*pātaka*). The *marae* was not a structure as in parts of Polynesia: it had no visible boundaries and was defined only by encircling dwellings. The community used the *marae* primarily for formal assembly: for receiving and entertaining visitors and for community ceremonial and discussion. Where the people lived close enough, as in *pā*, they also used it for much of the business of daily living: for eating, working at handcrafts, playing games, and talking in the sun. It was living-room, workshop, recreation ground and forum all at once. The *whare runanga*, richly ornamented with carving (*whakairo*), scroll patterns painted on the rafters (*kōwhaiwhai*) and reed panelling (*tukutuku*), served as an extension of the *marae* at night and in wet weather, while the carved *pātaka* held community stores of food and heirlooms.

Pointing out that the earliest explorers do not mention meeting-houses or *pātaka*, Groube recently put forward the hypothesis that they were post-European developments, stimulated by the acquisition of iron tools and potatoes (which increased leisure and food stores), and the building of churches by the missionaries. But though the early explorers did not mention 'meeting-houses' or storehouses on piles, they did record seeing larger than average houses ornamented with carving, which they identified as 'chiefs' houses', and ground-level buildings used as communal stores. Traditional stories suggest that the 'chief's house' was not only the chief's family sleeping-house, but was also used for community assembly and for accommodating guests. Built by communal labour, it was a focus and symbol (as the chief was) of group loyalty and pride. There is, however, no doubt that such houses increased greatly in size and elaboration after the introduction of European tools and techniques.

## Economic organization

The whole of Maori life was firmly based on an annual cycle of food-getting. Building projects, ceremonial visits, feasts and war expeditions were planned to fit into this seasonal round.

Each tribe engaged in a variety of food-getting activities, the emphasis varying with the environment: fishing (with lines, traps and nets), fowling (with snares and spears), rat-trapping, gathering (shell-fish, berries, shoots, pith and roots), the cultivation, in warmer, northern areas, of the *kūmara* and small quantities of taro, gourds and yams, and the semi-cultivation of fernroot in much the same areas by periodic harvesting and burning. Little of the food thus won kept for longer than a year, making it virtually impossible to plan further ahead (Shawcross, 1967).

The annual work pattern varied from tribe to tribe according to the dominant type of food-getting. For the agricultural tribes, the busiest times were planting in October and harvest in February and March; for the forest dwellers, the bird-snaring and rat-trapping season from June to September. Eels were trapped mainly in March, April and May, while different kinds of fish followed each other round the coast, as they do today. Even for tribes engaged in the same activities, the seasons differed with variations in soil and climate.

Whatever the pattern, the people enjoyed no great leisure. When work was slack in one pursuit, there was usually something to be done in another. Industry was widely praised and idleness rebuked. Skill and energy in procuring food added to the stature even of a chief.

Lacking metals, the Maoris made tools from wood and stone. They had only a few mechanical aids, none highly elaborated: the wedge, the skid, a simple lifting tackle, the cord-drill, and the fire plough. But they displayed great skill in adapting techniques to natural conditions, animal habits and the substances available; and they gave a highly artistic finish to all they made, even to such utilitarian objects as canoe bailers, bird snares and the steps of digging-sticks.

## Organization of labour

The work of men and women was reciprocal and complementary, while various minor employments fell to the lot of the very young and the very old. Men did the work that required strength and was arduous, exciting and/or *tapu*: clearing ground for cultivation, planting, climbing or felling trees, snaring birds, trapping rats, digging fernroot, fishing at sea, carving, building, making canoes, working stone, tattooing, and performing esoteric rites. Women engaged in the less *tapu* and/or safer, monotonous tasks: routine work in the gardens, collecting ground products and berries, carrying home fernroot, firewood and water, gathering shell-fish, preparing and preserving food, plaiting mats and kits, and weaving cloaks. The chiefs might, if they chose, avoid the more tedious of the men's tasks, but in all others they worked alongside their people, setting them an example in skill and industry. Work that was unpleasant, dull and damaging to *tapu* was done by the slaves: drawing water, carrying loads, helping the women with the cooking, paddling the canoes. The children helped by fetching and carrying, learning in the process. The aged busied themselves on tasks requiring patience and skill. The old men made tools and ornaments, the old women plaited and wove, and both made twine and cordage.

Every free man and woman mastered at least the rudiments of the principal crafts of his or her sex. Individual work patterns were highly varied, for when workers finished or grew tired of one occupation, they turned to another.

Persons of rank and exceptional aptitude received special training and devoted most (though not all) their time to a particular craft, usually a non-seasonal one. Such specialists were called *tohunga* (expert), the different types being distinguished by qualifying terms; e.g. *tohunga whakairo* (carver), *tohunga whaihanga* (master builder), *tohunga ahurewa* (specialist in religious knowledge, i.e. priest). They frequently executed commissions for the less skilled, who recompensed them with gifts of food, garments and ornaments. Their fame travelled abroad, and they received invitations even from other tribes.

Despite their knowledge of and skill in exploiting the natural environment, the tribes periodically suffered unpredictable disasters – migration of birds and fish from their usual haunts, droughts, frosts, and insect plagues. Attributing these to offended gods or spirits, they used religious measures to avert them. Rites accompanied and regu-

11

lated every stage of productive effort. To protect the life principle (*mauri*) of forest, gardens or fishing-grounds from inadvertent or enemy interference, a priest localized it in some material object (also called *mauri*), recited incantations over it, and hid it away. Sometimes he set up a ritual post (*rāhui*), sharpening its teeth with spells to kill meddlers. The people themselves observed many religious regulations, never taking cooked food (for instance) into the forest, gardens, canoes or meeting-house, carefully disposing of the evidence of a kill, and making offerings of first-fruits. At signs of depletion or after a death in the vicinity, the chief often reserved a particular resource from use by imposing a *tapu* on it, setting up a *rāhui* as a symbol.

Whenever possible, Maoris worked together. Even in tasks that could be done alone, they preferred to work side by side, enlivening their labour with gossip and rhythmic working songs. Most everyday tasks were carried out by members of the same household in varying combinations. When a larger and more diversified labour force was required, the villagers worked in a group (*ohu*) under the direction of the chief or a *tohunga*. Communal working-bees of this kind prepared the ground for planting, took the large nets fishing, built large eel-weirs and the better sleeping-houses, and did much of the planting and harvesting.

For a major enterprise such as building a war canoe or meeting-house, the chief frequently invited experts and workers from other villages to help. Under his direction, the visitors were given both their daily food and periodic feasts, and sent home loaded with gifts.

## Land

Despite the comparatively small population, the tribes between them laid claim to most of the country. Even if they did not live permanently in an area, the owners visited it at least periodically to substantiate their claim. Boundaries were carefully delimited, using natural features and, where necessary, boundary stones.

Ownership of land could be claimed by right of discovery, conquest, ancestral inheritance, cession, and occupation (*take-ahi-kā*, literally 'burning fire'). Occupation was necessary to validate claims made on other grounds, while even defeat did not completely extinguish a group's title if members kept their fires alight on the territory, as vassals paying tribute to their conquerors or fugitives in the forests and hills. In the final analysis, whether a tribe could hold its land depended on its military strength.

Under the Maori system of land tenure, rights of occupation and usufruct were divided among sub-groups and individuals, but the right of alienation was reserved to the group. Each *hapū* of the tribe controlled a defined stretch of the tribal territory, which it guarded jealously. Trespassers and poachers were punished severely, and persistent border violations led to fighting even between *hapū* of the same tribe. Within the *hapū*, *whānau*, nuclear families and individuals held rights of occupation and use over specific resources: garden plots, fishing-stands, rat-run sections, trees attractive to birds, clumps of flax, and shell-fish beds. These they could bequeath to their children. But they could *not* hand them over to outsiders – even to a spouse – until the *hapū* as a whole had discussed and approved the transfer; and they had to surrender their claim to particular pieces (though never without recompense) whenever the *hapū* (or its chief as trustee) required it for other purposes. Similarly, the *hapū* could alienate no part of its territory without the consent of the rest of the tribe. To put it another way, the rights of individuals and lesser groups were always subject to the over-right of the greater group. In a real sense, the land was owned ultimately by the tribe. For this reason, an attack on any part of the tribal territory rallied the whole tribe to its defence.

The Maoris valued the land not only as a source of food and raw materials, but also because of its permanence and connection with their ancestors. A well-known proverb stated: 'Man perishes, but the land remains.' The *mana* of the tribe as a whole was bound up with its land. Tribal history and songs abounded in references to its natural features, all of which were named, and tribesmen gladly fought and died to protect its sacred burial grounds, shrines and *marae*.

## Other property

Goods used in common and most of those produced by communal effort were held in common by the group that used or produced them. Each household owned its sleeping-houses and cook-house, a stock of food, and one or more small eel-weirs and canoes. The local community owned the larger canoes and eel-weirs, the great fishing-nets, and the meeting-house. Some of the food produced by group co-operation went into communal storehouses, but the rest was shared among all households according to need, with a bonus to those who contributed most in equipment, skill and energy. Heirloom weapons and ornaments were held by the chiefly families, but could not be given away without general consent. As with land, the rights of the greater group incorporated those of the lesser. Property held by the *whānau* belonged *ipso facto* to its *hapū* and ultimately to the tribe. In practice, the larger groups rarely laid claim to the property of their sub-groups, and always with recompense.

13

While most property was held by groups, individual ownership was by no means unknown. As we have seen, individuals held rights of use in specific pieces of land. Maoris also recognized individual ownership of goods which could be used by only one person at a time, particularly those he had made himself: tools, weapons, ornaments, clothing, and materials for manufacture. True, an individual was obliged to hand over any article admired or asked for by a superior; but he always received a counter-gift of at least equal value.

Borrowing was prevalent, but governed by strict rules. An article could be borrowed only when the owner was not using it; it had to be returned when finished with or on demand; and it should be acknowledged with a gift or counter-loan. Goods belonging to the aristocracy or associated with certain parts of the body (such as hair combs) were protected from borrowing by *tapu*. Borrowing that broke the rules was regarded as theft and severely punished, by physical violence, sorcery, or 'legal plundering' (*muru*, p. 26).

A person about to die made a public statement (*ohāki*) disposing of his (or her) personal property and land interests. Special items (such as greenstone heirlooms and feather cloaks) went to the eldest son or occasionally daughter. The rest of the estate was divided fairly equally, except that daughters living away from the parental home usually received a lesser share of the land. Certain types of property passed only to offspring of the same sex: birding trees, hunting and fishing equipment, and weapons from father to sons, flax-bushes, weaving-sticks and calabashes from mother to daughters. The details of all gifts and divisions were made public, and disputes over inheritance were judged by the community as a whole.

### Distribution of wealth

While none was very rich and none very poor, chiefs and aristocrats were generally wealthier than commoners. Since they usually had more than one wife and many slaves, their households produced more food and craft goods. The chiefs received a portion of the first-fruits of every crop and of the first hunting and fishing expeditions of the season, tribute from vassals, and a stream of gifts from their followers in acknowledgment and anticipation of favours; they had exclusive rights to stranded sea animals and rare birds; and they controlled the use of most communal property. They did not, however, use this wealth for their own indulgence. They were expected to feed all needy tribesmen; except in the case of tribute, they had to repay all gifts with counter-gifts of greater value; they provided the greater part of the hospitality offered to visitors; and they underwrote the cost of calling in allies to help with war expeditions or building projects. Their prestige depended on liberality rather than wealth.

## Gift exchange

The Maoris had no money, nor did they engage in trade. Goods and services that were lacking or scarce were obtained by gift exchange, i.e. by giving gifts in expectation of a return. Gift-giving was an essential part of all formal meetings between groups, from intervillage marriage to the making of peace between tribes. Counter-gifts might be made immediately or delayed for months or even years. Gifts were also given in return for services: to a specialist or to workers who helped build a meeting-house or war canoe. The main items in gift exchange were foodstuffs, flax cloaks, ornaments, stone for implements, obsidian and greenstone. Coastal tribes exchanged crops and sea-foods against the products of inland forests, lakes and rivers, and there was a well-developed north–south movement of crops and craft-goods exchanged for greenstone, the major source of which was on the west coast of the South Island.

No article had a set value. The givers never specified what or how much they wanted in return – but they were adept at dropping hints. The return had to be at least equivalent in value. The Maoris were not concerned to secure a bargain. On the contrary, they gave as generously as they could, for, besides securing a better counter-gift, generosity increased the giver's *mana*, always a primary concern with the status-conscious Maoris.

## Utu

Gift exchange was one manifestation of *utu*, a principle which 'pervaded the whole of Maori life . . . [and] was found in varying social context as one of the fundamental drives to action' (Firth, 1959: 412–17). *Utu* can most usefully be translated as the principle of reciprocity, of compensation in the widest sense. It was the rule that whatever one party gave to, did to or did for another must be reciprocated with a return of equivalent or higher value, either immediately or at later date. This rule applied equally to positively valued gifts such as compliments, goods and services, and to negatively valued ones, such as insults, injury and homicide. Exchange of good gifts both defined and maintained the relation as a friendly and on-going one, since at any given time one party was under obligation to the other. Similarly even enemies were bound to each other by the obligation to repay insults and injuries, though in this case the obligation was rather to themselves, since their *mana* was diminished by non-retaliation. (It is significant that the Maori term for 'enemy' was *hoa-riri*, 'angry friend'.) Because *utu* united both positive and negative cases in this way, the giving of gifts could be used to transmute a hostile relation into a friendly one, as at a peace-making feast, or to prevent a friendly one being disrupted, as when a member of one *hapū* injured a member of another in the same tribe. To fail to give or receive *utu* diminished the *mana* of both parties and placed the relation in jeopardy. So too did giving to excess, since it made it difficult for the receiver to make a worthy return. The moral principle of *utu* was thus reinforced by both social and religious sanctions.

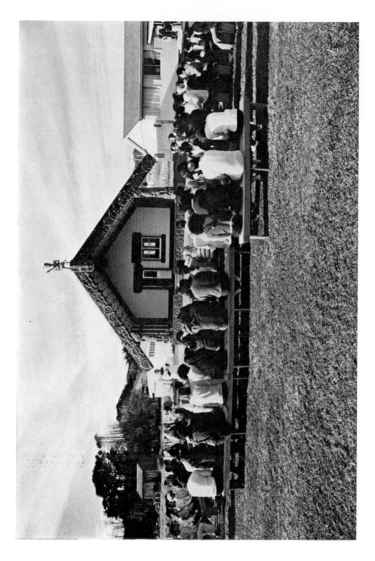

1 The spiritual dimension of reality: beginning the day with prayer at the Maori Artists and Writers Conference, Te Kaha *marae*, June 1973

2 Living and working in the country

# chapter 2

# The Maoris
# before 1800-II

## Kinship, marriage and family

As children and adults, free Maoris lived always encircled by kinsfolk, whom they reckoned in hundreds and even thousands. Each free individual was related to all members of his local community, except slaves, by descent or marriage (and often both), and to all fellow tribesmen by descent. Strangers were not accepted as permanent residents in a village unless they could demonstrate descent from a common ancestor or were attached to a local family by marriage or adoption.

### Kinship terminology and behaviour

To find out how Maoris ordered relations between kinsfolk we cannot do better than study their use of kinship terms, for each term was associated with a particular pattern of sentiment and behaviour. Maori kinship terminology was 'Classificatory' in type. Each individual (EGO) classified his kinsmen into a limited number of classes by extending the names for parents, siblings, children, parents' parents and children's children to all relatives of the same sex and generation. In this context, 'the same generation' means, not 'the same age', but 'the same number of steps from a common ancestor'.

In the first ascending generation, EGO used *matua tāne* (father) for his own father and both parents' brothers and also for their male cousins as far as he could trace them, and *whaea* (mother) for his own mother and both parents' sisters and female cousins. In the first descending generation he used *tama* (son) and *tamāhine* (daughter) not only for his own children but also for those of his siblings and both his male and female cousins. (His siblings' children, however, he could also call *irāmutu*.) Similarly, he used *tupuna* (grandparent) and

17

*mokopuna* (grandchild) for all relatives of the second ascending and descending generations respectively, indicating sex when necessary by adding *tāne* (man) and *wahine* (woman). Great-grandparent and great-grandchild were described as *tupuna tuarua* and *mokopuna tuarua* – grandparent and grandchild 'of the second grade'. (Beyond that limit, *tupuna* and *mokopuna* were used without qualification to mean *ancestor* and *descendant*.) In EGO's own generation, the rule was the same for kin of the opposite sex: a man used *tuahine* for both sisters and female cousins, a woman *tungāne* for both brothers and male cousins. But both men and women made a distinction between older and younger siblings of the same sex, calling the former *tuakana* and the latter *teina*. (These terms had no sex connotations: a man used them for his brothers, a woman for her sisters.) They extended these terms to their cousins of the same sex also – but on the basis of seniority of descent, not of age. Thus to a male EGO *all* the sons of his father's older brothers were *tuakana* and *all* the sons of his father's younger brothers were *teina*. The relationship between particular *whānau* or *hapū* was often described as '*tuakana* and *teina*', because they stemmed from ancestors standing in that relationship to each other. The importance of seniority was also indicated by use of the terms *mātāmua* for the firstborn among siblings and *pōtiki* for the youngest.

For affines there was another set of terms: *hunarei* (father- or mother-in-law), *hunaonga* (son- or daughter-in-law), *taokete* (brother-in-law of a male and sister-in-law of a female), *autāne* (brother-in-law of a female) and *auwahine* (sister-in-law of a male). The extension of these to less immediate affines was possible but rare, for in most cases they were already related to EGO by descent, and the blood tie took precedence over the affinal.

The use of the same kinship terms for close and distant kin reflected a similarity of attitudes and behaviour. For instance, EGO gave respect, obedience and service to his classificatory 'mothers' and 'fathers' as to his parents, was protective to his 'sisters', and fondled and if necessary chastised his 'sons' and 'daughters'. The frequency and intimacy of the relationship diminished as genealogical distance increased, varying in degree though similar in kind. When necessary, EGO could distinguish classificatory from immediate kin by adding *kēkē* ('other') to the term involved.

As the terminology indicates, the Maori kinship system placed major emphasis on generation level and seniority of descent, minimized the importance of genealogical distance, and made no distinction at all between father's kin and mother's. Like all 'Classificatory systems', it had three advantages. First, it enabled the individual to establish and handle relations with a very large range of kin. Secondly,

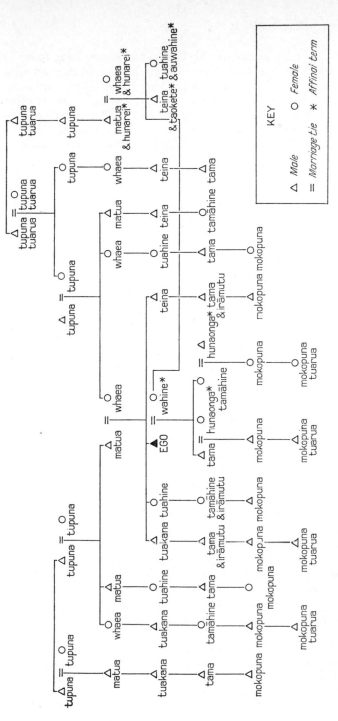

*Figure 2   Classic Maori kinship terminology*

NOTE   When EGO was a woman there were several differences in the terms used for relatives of her own generation. See p. 18.

19

it supplied a ready guide to the behaviour appropriate to most strangers met socially. Buck wrote: 'When I was told than an aged visitor whom I had never seen before was *tipuna* to me, my heart warmed towards him. I placed him in the same category as my other *tipuna* who resided in the same village and had lavished affection upon me' (Buck, 1949: 342). Finally, it ensured that there was always someone to step into the breach if a person lacked or lost a close relative.

### Marriage and divorce

Before marriage, most young people were allowed – indeed expected – to enjoy a series of love-affairs, provided that they managed them discreetly and did not get too deeply involved. Only girls who were already betrothed and chiefs' daughters set apart under *tapu* (*puhi*) were expected to remain virgins. The latter, specially trained in the social arts and constantly guarded, attracted many suitors and were destined to contract marriages advantageous to their people.

When it came to the choice of marriage partners, the young were expected to accept spouses chosen for them by the senior members of their *whānau* or (if of high rank) their *hapū*. Marriage was too important an issue to be left to individual preference, for it was the means of establishing new or closer relationships with other groups, as well as ensuring recruitment. Aristocrats usually betrothed (*taumau*) their children while still in infancy. Commoners more often waited till they were of marriageable age. When the time came to fulfil the contract, the bride's kinsfolk escorted her to her husband's home where they were welcomed with a feast and exchanged wedding gifts of approximately equal value with their hosts. Religious ritual was carried out only when the couple were of high rank and was directed mainly to ensuring the fertility of the union. But though arranged marriages were the ideal, commoners at least frequently secured the mates of their own choice. They could always initiate arrangements themselves, either by dropping a hint to their parents or by declaring their preference at a public gathering for general debate. If they doubted family approval, they either eloped or slept late together where they were sure to be discovered. The family that considered itself injured as a result (usually the girl's) descended upon the offender's kin and plundered them of goods (*muru*, p. 26). Such action actually established the marriage, by publicizing it and compensating the losers (Biggs, 1960: 40–53).

Most marriages were not only between members of the same tribe but between members of the same *hapū*. Inter-tribal marriages were distrusted because they gave outsiders access to family land, created divided loyalties, and could involve the groups in war if they failed.

Those that did occur were usually arranged to establish or strengthen alliances. Within the *hapū*, there were strong sanctions against marriage between first and second cousins and between a high-ranking woman and a commoner. A male aristocrat could always take a commoner as a second wife.

Commoners usually had only one wife, but chiefs took up to about four. The wife of highest rank – usually the first – took precedence over other wives, and her children over theirs, regardless of age. If they lived in one household, she superintended their work and guarded their virtue. Many chiefs, however, maintained their wives in the latter's home communities. Polygamy added to a chief's prestige and multiplied his wealth, bringing him land and slaves as dower, and increasing the workers under his direction.

Once married, women in particular were expected to be completely faithful. A husband who caught his wife with a lover was entitled to kill them both, unless they were of high rank. Adultery involving a married woman was a sin that brought supernatural punishment on the whole group.

Divorce was simple and not uncommon. There was neither ritual to be revoked nor marriage-payment to be returned. Husband and wife could simply agree to part, or adultery or desertion could cause the kin of the injured party to take compensation from those of the guilty in a *muru* raid. This effectively dissolved the union, leaving both free to make other matches.

The widowed and divorced were expected to remarry. A widow could excuse herself from marrying again only until her husband's second burial (p. 28). After that she was given the choice of accepting one of her husband's brothers or returning home for her own folk to find her a husband. A widower had a claim on his dead wife's family to replace her with another woman.

## Family life

After marriage, a couple lived in the household of an older male, usually the husband's father. Few men became head of their own household until well in their prime. While members of the *whānau* carried out most daily activities in groups based on sex and age, the nuclear family was not entirely lost in the larger group. Husband and wife had certain exclusive rights and duties to each other (especially sexual ones). With their children they occupied a separate sleeping-house or a defined section of the family one, held rights to specific pieces of land and other property, and occasionally camped independently in the forest or by the sea.

Children were greatly desired, especially sons. Barrenness was considered grounds for divorce or taking a second wife. On the evidence of the genealogies, families usually comprised less than six children, including those that died in infancy. Various methods of limitation were practised, including abortion and (rarely) infanticide, but the major factor was a *tapu* on sexual intercourse during suckling, which lasted up to two years.

Birth, being surrounded with *tapu*, took place outside the village, in the open or in a temporary shelter which was later destroyed. When a child was about a week old, a priest performed the *tohi* rite, in which he ritually cleansed him by sprinkling, dedicated him to the god either of peace or war, and asked the gods to endow him fitly. The home-coming of an aristocratic child was marked by feasting and the performance of a rite (*pure*) to fix his *mana*.

Adopting children was common practice. It was, however, limited to relatives, being used to revive relationships weakened by distance and to keep warm rights of inheritance. Adopted children lost all rights to land belonging to their original parents.

### Education

Children received their early education within the family circle. In particular, they were often in the company of their grandparents, who taught them good speech and behaviour, genealogies, relationships, and tribal history, by singing and telling them endless stories. Children's games often imitated parents' activities or were of a competitive nature. Children regularly attended public gatherings and ceremonies. Fear of *tapu* was inculcated early. On the other hand, no great effort was made to check aggressiveness, since it was considered desirable that they grow up proud and fierce.

As they grew older, children spent more and more time assisting their parents, developing skill in the crafts of their sex, and learning the associated rites. Those who showed special aptitude in carving, building or weaving were apprenticed to an expert, after an initiation ceremony which placed them under the craft's tutelary god. Aristocratic boys who had been dedicated to Tū, the god of war, received a final polishing under a noted warrior, while those dedicated to Rongo, the god of peaceful arts, worked with the food-getting experts. A selected few whom tests proved to have retentive memories were sent to a *whare wānanga* ('school of learning') for instruction from the tribe's leading priests. *Whare wānanga* were held in only a few centres in each tribe in the winter (between April and September), in houses temporarily set aside under *tapu* or (more rarely) built for the purpose. Student numbers were small, only six to ten at a time. The primary object of the teaching was to pass on traditional knowledge unchanged. To alter or question it was to affront Tāne, the god who obtained it for man. The curriculum comprised three 'baskets' of esoteric knowledge, that pertaining to the gods (reported to include belief in a Supreme Being), human and tribal history, and ritual concerned with man's welfare.

Instruction of a less sacred character seems to have been given to larger audiences in subjects such as astronomy and agriculture. Sorcery (*mākutu*) was taught in a separate school, generally out-of-doors, or by direct apprenticeship to a practising sorcerer.

## Religion

The values and sanctions of Maori society were derived from a spiritual conception of the universe. All human activities and relationships had their charter in an elaborate mythology and were governed by an elaborate system of ritual (Buck, 1949: 431–536; Johansen, 1954, 1958).

The Maori believed in a pantheon of spiritual beings (*atua*) with supernatural powers. The existence of a supreme god, Io-matua-kore, was revealed to those who reached the upper grades of the school of learning (Buck, 1949: 526–36). All tribes shared belief in eight major gods, offspring of the primeval parents Rangi and Papa: Tāne, god of the forests and father of man; Tū-matauenga, god of war and inventor of snares, nets and digging sticks; Rongo, god of peace and agriculture; Tangaroa, god of the sea; Tawhirimātea, the weather god; Haumia, god of uncultivated food; Ruaumoko, the earthquake god; and Whiro, the god of darkness and evil. Each tribe also had its own exclusive tribal gods, mostly of war. Finally, there were family gods and familiar spirits, which originated from abortions, miscarriages and the ghosts of the dead.

*Atua* were invisible spirits of uncertain form. The Maori associated them with visible symbols (*ariā*), which might be natural phenomenon (rainbows, comets, trees, stones), living creatures (lizards, birds, fish), carved god-sticks, or rough stone images.

Men sought to influence the gods, to procure benefits or avert disaster, by acts of homage, offerings and incantations (*karakia*). The gods always received a token share of the first-fruits of any project – the first *kūmara* dug, the first bird or fish taken, a girl's first piece of weaving, the first man slain in battle. Stones, leaves, and locks of hair were also offered, and a slave might be sacrificed to secure success in war or building. *Karakia* were chanted formulae of ancient words. Their efficacy was held to lie in faultless repetition, though the *mana* and delivery of the chanter were also important. A mistake was an ill omen and brought supernatural punishment. All men made minor offerings and had a store of lesser *karakia* for everyday use, but the more important rites were left to ritual specialists. The *tohunga ahurewa*, graduates of the school of learning, dealt only with the superior gods. Those who served the family gods were shamans rather than priests; they achieved office by spirit-possession and were largely self-taught. Women could become mediums of the family gods, but of none higher. Those who used their command over familiar spirits to work evil (*tohunga mākutu*) were feared rather than respected.

The most important rites were conducted privately by the *tohunga ahurewa* at the community altar (*tūāahu*), a sacred pool or stream (*wai tapu*) or in the latrines, which were also highly *tapu*. The altar consisted of one or a pile of unworked stones. It was out of doors and often hidden away from public view.

Anything associated with the supernatural was invested, temporarily or permanently, with *tapu* (p. 8). Transmitted by mere contact, *tapu* was highly dangerous if not handled according to prescribed rules. Infringement brought automatic punishment, usually in the form of sickness or death, according to the intensity of the *tapu* violated. Natural resources were *tapu* and could not be tapped till the guardian spirits had been placated and the *tapu* nullified. Conversely, any particular resource could be conserved by placing it under a *tapu*. All free men were endued with *tapu*, its degree increasing with rank, and so were all objects and activities of social value. A *tapu* that became restrictive or had served its purpose could be removed by special rites (*whakanoa* – to make common), involving cooked food, a woman, or cleansing with water.

## Leadership

Leadership in Maori society was provided by hereditary chiefs, assisted and to some degree limited by a few highly trained priests (*tohunga ahurewa*) and the heads of households (*kaumātua*).

Each *hapū* had one chief (*rangatira*), the most senior in the tribe (by descent) being recognized as paramount (*ariki*). The double use of *rangatira* to mean both 'aristocrat' and 'chief' is confusing, but it points up the chief's role as trustee and representative of his group: he was as it were the *rangatira* of his *hapū*. In most tribes the chieftainship passed down the senior line of descent to the first son in each generation. If the chief's first-born was a daughter, she occupied a special position with the title of *kahurangi* or *tapairu*, but her brother inherited the chieftainship. Among Ngāti Porou, however, women could and did become chiefs in their own right. If, through physical or mental incapacity, the hereditary chief was not equal to his position, the people might choose a younger brother, uncle or cousin as their effective leader, but the chief remained the ceremonial figure-head to his death. *Rangatira* and *ariki* were educated in the *whare wānanga*, and were often fully trained priests.

By virtue of their rank and wealth, the chiefs exercised great influence, but their power was far from absolute. Lacking coercive force, they depended on the voluntary support and service of their kinsfolk, which they had to hold by good leadership and liberality. Matters of community importance were discussed publicly in assemblies at which the heads of households and under certain circumstances all free men had the right to speak. A wise chief was guided by public opinion.

For tribe and *hapū* respectively, *ariki* and *rangatira* determined the over-all pattern and initiated each phase of economic activity, underwrote and directed all communal projects from feasts to war, took the lead in all *marae* ceremonial, and conducted negotiations with other groups. They acted as trustees of their group's land, property and *marae*, and their views usually – though not invariably – carried the day in discussions about their distribution. Both had important ritual functions, notably the imposition of *tapu* (p. 24). The *ariki*, taking precedence over the other *rangatira*, acted as director of joint projects, chairman of discussions, and conciliator of disputes between *hapū*. He alone could perform the exhumation rites, and it was his prerogative formally to declare peace or war with other tribes. Because of his high *mana*, he was greatly sought after to grace all sorts of occasions. But the *rangatira*, less hindered by personal and social *tapu*, were closer to their people. They brooked no interference from the *ariki* in their control of their warriors, and could, by the power of their oratory, win the support of the people away from him on particular issues.

The *tohunga ahurewa* were either chiefs themselves or closely related to the chief. Full graduates of the *whare wānanga*, they were masters of all esoteric ritual, experts in tribal history and genealogies, and reputedly able to control the elements. They alone performed the rites associated with the life crises and death of the chief and all important group enterprises, especially the making of war. They could avert or confirm supernatural punishment for wrongdoing. Their knowledge gave them power almost equal to the chief's.

Also important were the household heads, older, wiser men with grown-up children and grandchildren. Each planned and directed the daily activities of his household, taught, guided and disciplined its members, carried out certain limited rituals on its behalf, and spoke for it in public assembly. As a group, the *kaumātua* formed a community council (*runanga*) which advised and could influence the chief.

In most tribes leadership was the monopoly of older well-born men. But in practice women of character and ability often exerted a powerful influence from behind the scenes, and tribal histories contain plentiful accounts of able commoners and younger sons rising in the social scale as a result of outstanding services.

### Social control

The Maoris had neither courts, justices nor police. Members of different tribes obtained redress for injury by recourse to sorcery or war. Within the tribe, social control was exercised directly by the chiefs and elders, reinforced by public opinion, the institution of *muru* (legal plundering), and use of religious sanctions. In so war-like a society, the individual found that his physical and emotional security depended largely on retaining the approval of his community by conforming to its norms. When offences *were* committed against kinsfolk, the victim's *whānau* or *hapū* formed a *taua muru* (plunder party) and made a raid on the offender's group. The latter offered no resistance while the raiders helped themselves to goods in compensation (*utu*). The size of the groups involved and the value of goods taken varied with the rank of the protagonists as well as the magnitude of the offence. Paradoxically, the taking of heavy compensation increased the *mana* of the plundered group, because 'the clouds only settle round the highest peaks'. Finally, *tapu* and the threat of sorcery (which was most effective when the victim had sinned) operated to protect the persons, property and authority of chiefs and elders. Together, they rendered the fierce and turbulent Maoris obedient, orderly and law-abiding in their own communities.

### War

War was waged to obtain *utu* (compensation), for insults and slights as well as material injury, by shedding blood. To leave insults unavenged diminished the *mana* both of individual and group. War also provided an outlet for the frustrations and limitations of village life, and was often used by astute leaders to counter internal dissension. Ostensibly, the acquisition of land was of secondary importance. The victors withdrew to their own territory between engagements, and moved in permanently only after a series of successes. War always had to have a legitimate cause (*take*). This was never hard to find, for each group kept a detailed reckoning of past insults and injuries. Most northern tribes were in a state of hostility with several others at once and so lived under constant threat of attack. Fighting itself was intermittent, a series of short engagements occurring mainly between November and April, when cultivation could be left to the women and war-parties could live off the land (Vayda, 1960).

Each *hapū* maintained its own war-party, described as a *hokowhitu-a-Tū* literally 'the god of war's twenty times seven' but varying in fact from one hundred to several hundred warriors. Combined armies were hard to mobilize and harder to keep together, because each *hokowhitu* acknowledged the authority only of its own chief. War-parties moved to the attack in single file over bush tracks, sending scouts ahead to survey enemy numbers and defences. Their main weapons were designed for hand-to-hand fighting: clubs of bone, stone and greenstone, and staffs with blades for striking at one end and stabbing points at the other. They rarely met in battle formation in the open but preferred to make rapid raids and then withdraw, relying heavily on surprise, and frequently resorting to ambuscades, stratagems such as mock retreats, and treachery. The success of an engagement was measured by the rank of the slain. Younger women and children might be taken as slaves, but most of the defeated were killed and eaten. Apart from providing much needed protein, cannibalism completed the victors' revenge, by reducing the defeated to food.

## Peaceful gatherings (hui)

As a means of enhancing *mana*, lavish hospitality and gift-giving were as important as success in war. Celebration of the life crises of chiefs, completion of a meeting-house, the opening of a war campaign, or the making of peace – all these attracted many parties of visitors (*manuhiri*). Against their coming, the hosts prepared gift displays of food, mats and garments, sometimes on special stages. The visitors came in *hapū* groups, each of which established its own encampment. (Even related *hapū* were very wary of treachery and sorcery.) The day after their arrival, they were ceremonially welcomed on the *marae* and feasted there with food cooked in family *hāngi* and brought in procession with appropriate chants. Later the host chief allotted a section of the gift-stack to each visiting chief, who divided it among his followers. The visitors stayed for weeks, attending periodic feasts given by their hosts, discussing common issues, and competing with them in sport and dancing. Only when the food was exhausted did they leave (Firth, 1959).

## Sickness and death

Any departure from normal health the Maoris ascribed to attacks by spirits due to sorcery or a breach of *tapu*. To treat it they called in the appropriate *tohunga*. Having questioned the patient till he discovered his offence, the *tohunga* exorcized the spirit, purified the patient and,

27

if he diagnosed sorcery, employed counter spells that turned the attack back on its originator. The *tohunga* had some knowledge of the therapeutic value of plants, but the accepted theory of disease limited experimentation.

Death was surrounded with extremely powerful *tapu*. The dying and the dead were removed to a shelter on the *marae* large enough to accommodate close relatives. This was afterwards burnt. The body was laid on fine mats and covered with a fine cloak, with family heirlooms on the chest. The deceased's closest female relatives sat on either side of the body, keeping up an almost continuous wailing. They cut their hair short, gashed their bodies with obsidian knives, and fasted during the day. Mourners came in *hapū* and tribal groups, wearing chaplets of greenery and bearing valuable death-gifts (*kōpaki*). (These were always returned on a similar occasion.) The corpse remained unburied as long as mourners kept arriving, often for two or three weeks. After the first few days the wailing and dirges ceased to be continuous, the speech-making ranged more widely, and hosts and guests engaged in competitive displays of singing, dancing and, athletics. Finally the corpse was hidden away in a cave, a tree, or in the earth, wrapped in mats and protected by *tapu*.

The ethnographers state that after a year or two the body was exhumed, along with others, by the *ariki*; the bones were scraped and painted with red ochre, exposed on the *marae* and sometimes carried from settlement to settlement for the people to weep over, then tied together, placed in a wooden coffin or flax mat, and finally deposited in a secret burial place. According to the archaeologists, however, secondary burials are much less numerous than primary ones. Perhaps secondary burial was reserved for the highborn, or frequently interrupted by war.

The spirits of the dead, it was believed, travelled north along spirit paths to Te Reinga, a cape in the far north, where two oceans meet. There, having drunk forgetfulness from the waters of a small stream, they slid down the exposed root of a *pōhutukawa* root into a cave that gave entrance to Te Pō, the underworld realm of Hine-nui-te-Pō, Goddess of Death and Childbirth, where they joined their ancestors in their homeland Hawaiki.

# chapter 3

# The years between

## 1769–1840: The coming of the Pakeha

The first encounter between Maori and European took place in 1642, when Abel Tasman's two ships anchored in Golden Bay, Nelson. It was brief and hardly auspicious: Maori canoes rammed a cockboat, killing four Dutchmen. Captain James Cook, who first arrived in 1769, established friendly relations only after several Maoris were killed in skirmishes. From Cook and the explorers who followed him, the Maoris obtained cloth, iron tools, pigs and potatoes, in exchange for food and craft goods.

The 1790s brought sealers and deep-sea whalers to New Zealand waters. The former set up temporary shore-camps in the South Island, nearly exterminated the mainland herds, and departed within twenty years; the latter put into the northern harbours periodically for refitting. The coastal tribes helped them cut timber for spars and exchanged potatoes, pork and labour for blankets, tools and guns. But the visitors frequently infringed Maori custom and ill-treated the Maoris they took aboard as crew. Relations deteriorated as the Maoris took their revenge whenever they could. In 1809, for instance, they killed and ate nearly everyone aboard the *Boyd* at Whangaroa. For many years shipping avoided New Zealand.

Undeterred, the Reverend Samuel Marsden, senior chaplain in New South Wales, landed in the Bay of Islands in 1814. Welcomed by a Maori chief he had befriended in Sydney, he preached the Christian Gospel there on Christmas Day and founded a mission for the Church Missionary Society, with stations at Rangihoua (1815), and later Kerikeri (1819) and Paihia (1823). In 1822 the Wesleyans settled at Whangaroa, moving to Hokianga in 1827. Traders established depots and built up flourishing trades in general provisions in the Bay of Islands, timber in Hokianga, and dressed flax further south along the coast. The Maoris protected the missionaries, studied their skills. and sent many children to the mission schools, but for many years showed little interest in Christianity. The first convert was not baptized till 1825, the second in 1828. As soon as they had earned enough, many tribes stopped work, bought guns, and set out in pursuit of the traditional goals of revenge and glory.

Until well into the 1830s both islands were rent by ferocious inter-tribal wars. The Ngāpuhi chief, Hongi Hika, returning from a visit to England in 1820, sold the presents given him and bought muskets. For ten years he led two thousand warriors in campaigns against ancient enemies as far south as Kawhia and Rotorua, taking their *pā* with great slaughter and carrying numerous slaves back to Northland. Led by Te Rauparaha, Ngāti Toa of Kawhia and sections of Te Ati Awa migrated southwards; joined by Ngāti Raukawa from the southern Waikato, they established themselves on the Manawatu plains, displacing the tribes in occupation; and later invaded and occupied parts of the South Island. The Waikato tribes attacked the people to their south and east in Taranaki, Hauraki and Rotorua.

Introduced diseases and muskets took heavy toll. Weakened and disheartened, the Maoris turned increasingly to the missionaries for help in making peace. The northern chiefs accepted Christianity, and their people followed as groups. The missions opened new stations inland in the north and then, with the help of returned slaves, in Waikato, Rotorua and the Bay of Plenty. There also peace-making was associated with mass conversion (Wright, 1959; Owens, 1974).

Between 1830 and 1838, the number of Europeans living permanently in New Zealand jumped from 150 to over 2,000. Each summer more ships called at the northern harbours, especially in the Bay of Islands. European middlemen settled there, bringing prosperity to the local tribes, from whom they bought provisions for revictualling ships and exporting to Sydney. At the same time, periodic influxes of sailors and other lawless types created serious problems of law and order in Kororareka, the main settlement. The British Resident, James Busby (appointed in 1833) was 'a man-of-war without guns', lacking effective authority. European settlers, missionaries and a confederation of northern chiefs pressed for annexation.

In 1838 Australian settlers and land speculators began buying large blocks of land from the Maoris. A New Zealand Land Company was formed in England, made extensive purchases in the Cook Strait area, and dispatched settlers who reached Port Nicholson (later Wellington) in January 1840. Shortly afterwards Captain William Hobson of the Royal Navy landed at the Bay of Islands to treat with the Maoris for the cession of New Zealand to the British Crown.

Already important changes had been effected in Maori life and culture. Many traditional artefacts and garments had been replaced. To gather flax, *hapū* lived for months in temporary shelters near the swamps. Periodically they were overwhelmed by diseases against which they had no immunity, such as influenza and measles. Acquisition of guns altered the location and defence works of *pā* and greatly increased casualties in war. Conversion to Christianity undermined the power of the *tohunga* and led to the abandonment of polygamy, slavery, warfare and cannibalism.

Until contact with Europeans, Maoris had no name for themselves as a people, only a multiplicity of tribal names. Now they began to use the term *tāngata maori* to distinguish themselves from Europeans, adding the adjective *maori*, which means 'usual, ordinary', to the word for 'man'. Europeans treated *maori* as a noun, and the Maoris ultimately accepted the name. The use of the term *Pakeha* for Europeans was fairly widespread among the Maoris as early as 1820. Many origins have been suggested for the word, but none established (Wilson, 1963).

### 1840: The Treaty of Waitangi

Hobson invited the chiefs to gather at Waitangi, where he presented them with a Treaty. After a day's debate, some fifty signed it on 6 February 1840. Another five hundred signatures were collected in a tour of the country, but the chiefs of a number of important tribes (notably those of Waikato-Maniapoto, Taupo and Rotorua) refused or were not asked to sign. In May Hobson proclaimed British sovereignty over the whole country.

Under the Treaty of Waitangi, the Maori chiefs ceded 'all the rights and powers of sovereignty which they possessed over their respective territories' to the Queen of England. The Queen 'confirmed and guaranteed to the chiefs and tribes of New Zealand the full, exclusive and undisputed possession of their lands and estates, forests, fisheries and other properties, which they might collectively or individually possess, so long as it was their wish and desire to retain the same in their possession', reserving (however) the right of pre-emption to the Crown. In the final article, the Queen 'extended to the Natives of New Zealand her protection and imparted to them all the rights and privileges of British subjects'. The Treaty had no standing in international law, but successive Secretaries of State undertook to see it honoured (Wards, 1968).

### 1840–1860: Acculturation and conflict

The Maoris now entered on a period of rapid and enthusiastic adoption of Pakeha goods and ways. Flax garments and blankets alike were superseded by clothes, stone tools by iron and steel. Encouraged by the Government, Maori tribes put down thousands of acres of wheat, maize and potatoes, with ploughs and bullock teams. They acquired horses, pigs, and cattle, which, however, they mostly left to run wild. In 1853 the Waikato Maoris had ten flour mills in operation and others under construction. In 1855 there were forty-nine Maori-owned cutters and schooners employed in the coastal trade. For many years the Maoris supplied provisions to the infant Pakeha settlements and later the Australian goldfields. They also entered paid employment, as carpenters, sawyers, blacksmiths and wheelwrights, as well as labourers. In 1852 the Surveyor-General wrote that 'the natives seem to have started with an energy quite surprising in the pursuit of gain . . . all other pursuits seem merged in habits of thrift' (Firth, 1959: 450).

But closer contact between Maori and Pakeha brought problems as well as progress. The Crown, investigating pre-Waitangi land deals, angered the settlers by disallowing many of their claims and the Maoris by retaining possession of the disputed areas, known thereafter as 'surplus lands'. Within a few years there was trouble over land at each of the New Zealand Company settlements. In Nelson, twenty-three Pakehas were killed trying to arrest Te Rauparaha and Te Rangi-haeata for resisting the survey of land they denied having sold (the 'Wairau Incident'). In the north, Maori discontent at being stopped from selling land privately was compounded by loss of income through transfer of the capital to Auckland and imposition of custom dues. In 1844 a Ngāpuhi chief, Hone Heke, cut down the flagstaff (symbol of British sovereignty) at Kororareka and sacked the township. A thousand warriors rallied to his support, but other northern Maoris remained neutral or actively aided the Government. After a year's turmoil, the revolt was put down by the new Governor George Grey, who also arrested Te Rauparaha and made peace with Te Rangi-haeata.

The settlers gave the Maoris little help in adapting themselves to their new situation. When self-government was granted in 1852, imposition of a property qualification for voting in effect disenfranchised the Maoris, who owned land collectively. Though Maoris paid nearly half the customs dues, less than five per cent of the national revenue was set aside for Maori purposes. The Constitution Act provided for the establishment of 'native districts' where Maori custom would have the force of law, but none was ever proclaimed; and little was done to provide judicial and other governmental institutions in Maori areas. Schools for Maoris were provided by the missions, under Government subsidy. The Native Department was active mainly where land was wanted, and in 1856 was combined with the Land

Purchase Department. Matters were not improved when the bottom dropped out of the market for agricultural products in 1856 (Ward, 1973).

As the Pakeha population grew, overtaking the Maori in 1858, the Maoris became increasingly disturbed. Their grievances crystallized around the loss of their land. By 1850 Pakehas had acquired large areas of the North Island and nearly all the South Island, and still more arrived seeking land. During the fifties, the North Island tribes held a series of great intertribal gatherings to discuss the prevention of further sales. In 1858, after much discussion, the people of the Waikato, Taupo and parts of Hawke's Bay decided to elect a Maori King, to preserve the land and provide leadership and government. The Waikato chief Te Wherowhero was chosen, crowned as Potatau I, and provided with a flag, council of state, code of laws and police force. The next year the people of South Taranaki joined the King Movement. The other tribes declined to do the King fealty, but supported his stand on the land issue.

## 1860–1865: War

After five years' skirmishing between land-sellers and landholders in Taranaki, war finally broke out there in 1860, when Governor Gore Brown authorized purchase of the Waitara block, rejecting the veto of the chief Wiremu Kingi. Reinforced by war-parties from the Waikato and south Taranaki, Kingi declared for the Maori King and challenged government troops in the rugged hill-country for a year. A truce was declared and Kingi retreated into the Waikato.

At this point, Grey, returning for a second term as Governor, attempted to meet Maori grievances by introducing governmental institutions into Maori districts. But the Maoris no longer trusted the Government. Hostilities were resumed in May 1863. Grey swiftly defeated the Taranaki 'rebels' and then invaded the Waikato from Auckland. The Ngāi Terangi of Tauranga rallied to the support of the Maori King, but war-parties from other east coast tribes were halted in battle near Matata by 'friendly' Arawa tribes, who refused to allow 'rebels' to cross their territory. In the Waikato, the Kingites used guerilla tactics with some success, but they could not withstand the superior artillery and gunboats of the Pakehas. They retreated from one *pā* to another, making a final desperate stand under Rewi Maniapoto at Orakau Pā. The Kingmaker Wiremu Tamehana and his people made peace. Tāwhiao, who had succeeded his father as King in 1860, retired into Maniapoto territory, fixing a boundary (*aukati*) closing it to Pakehas. This area has been known as the King Country ever since.

The Government immediately confiscated nearly three million acres of Maori land, as punishment for 'rebellion' and in order to break up the heartland of Maori sovereignty. It was plainly most interested in land for settlement. Large areas were taken from groups which had taken little or no part in the fighting, while the aggressive Maniapoto, who occupied steep, forested hill-country, escaped lightly. Just over half the land confiscated was later paid for or returned in Crown grants, reducing the final total to about 1,400,000 acres.

### 1865–1900: Protest and adjustment

The rest of the nineteenth century is commonly described as a period of withdrawal, despondency and decline, but the pattern varied widely from one part of the country to another (Sorrenson, 1956).

Violence broke out again in 1865 in Taranaki in a nativistic cult called Hau Hau, which quickly spread across the centre of the island. Fighting became bitter and unrelenting. Titokowaru, who assumed leadership in Taranaki in 1868, was suppressed within a year, but Te Kooti, escaping from probably unjust imprisonment on the Chatham Islands, raised the standard of resistance in Poverty Bay and the Urewera mountains. A gifted guerilla leader, he evaded Government troops for four years, finally retreating undefeated into the King Country in 1872. In these campaigns, Arawa again fought for the Government, and so did men from Wanganui, Ngāti Porou and Ngāti Kahungunu.

The defeated Waikato and Maniapoto isolated themselves in the King Country, resentfully rejecting Pakeha law and political organization. They continued, however, to borrow Pakeha tools and techniques, adopting them into the framework of a communal way of life. Thus preserving the integrity of their land and social order, they declined comparatively little and in parts increased. In Taranaki, the prophets Te Whiti and Tohu established a flourishing community at Parihaka. Te Whiti and Tohu were twice arrested for non-violent opposition to the Government, and in 1881 the community was forcibly dispersed. The settlement was later re-built, but declined after the prophets' deaths.

Most of the neutral and 'friendly' tribes, especially those of Northland, Hawke's Bay, Manawatu and the South Island, actively sought contact with Pakehas. For at least two decades, they lost land faster than ever, suffered much social disorganization, and declined significantly in numbers.

In 1865 the Government set up a Native Land Court, which first determined title to land on a *hapū* basis, and then allotted individual

shares in each block to the members of the owning *hapū* (individualization). This meant that land could be bought from individual owners.
Besides Te Whiti's people and the King Movement tribes, Ngāti
Tūwharetoa, Tūhoe, and Ngāti Porou refused to submit their lands to
the Court. But elsewhere, owners were persuaded or forced to sell in
large numbers, often by the most doubtful expedients. Once a part-
owner took a block to Court, the others had to attend or lose recognition of their interests. Even if they won their case, objectors often had
to sell to pay expenses. To attend Court sittings, Maoris left homes
and cultivations to live in unsatisfactory conditions in the towns,
squandering their money and contracting diseases. Between 1865 and
1892 Maoris sold seven million acres and leased another two and a
half million to Pakehas.

In 1867 the Maoris were given manhood suffrage and four Maori
seats in Parliament. This was intended as a temporary expedient until
they were more fully assimilated to Pakeha ways. Maoris obtained
full adult suffrage along with the rest of the population in 1893, but
the separate Maori electorates remained.

Beginning in 1867, the Government set up 'Native Schools' in
Maori settlements, first under the Department of Native Affairs and
after 1879 under the new Department of Education. A Code for
Native Schools drawn up in 1881 laid down a policy of assimilation
which remained in force for fifty years. The syllabus was the same as
for the primary schools administered by regional Education Boards;
English was the language of instruction; and the children cleaned
school buildings and grounds as part of their training in the Pakeha
way of life. (The regional Boards also established schools in Maori
areas, so that Maori children were never limited exclusively to the
Native Schools.)

In the early eighties, the Waikato and Maniapoto began warily to
emerge from isolation. Tawhiao made peace with the Government in
1881, and later returned to the Waikato with his people. Te Kooti
was pardoned. The Maniapoto chiefs opened up the King Country
for the main trunk railway. The tribes which had withheld their lands
from the Native Land Court gradually submitted them. For a while
they too suffered land losses and disorganization and declined in
numbers.

By 1890 Maoris everywhere were entering paid employment, mainly
of an unskilled and seasonal kind: bush-work, scrub-cutting, building
roads and railways, sheep-shearing, digging kauri-gum. In several
areas Maori landowners developed commercial farming on a group
basis, growing grain in Hawke's Bay and the Bay of Plenty, sheep-
farming on the East Coast, and dairying in Wairoa, Taranaki and the
King Country. But without sole title, would-be farmers could not

35

raise development loans nor prevent others taking a share of the profits.

Throughout this period the Maori chiefs and elders were active in protesting, on behalf of their people, at the loss of their land and of control over their own affairs. Sir James Carroll, Member of Parliament for Eastern Maori (1887–93) and Gisborne (1893–1919) and Cabinet Minister in the Liberal Government, helped check alienation but could not stop it. During the eighties, representatives of the tribes outside the King Movement, meeting annually in inter-tribal conference at Waitangi, pressed for the establishment of separate Maori civil institutions. Ignored, they set up numerous local committees and in 1892 an extra-legal Maori Parliament (Kotahitanga). In 1894, after several unsuccessful bids to bring the other tribes under its leadership, the King Movement set up its own Great Council, which made laws and imposed taxes and fines. The Kotahitanga met for eleven years, providing a forum for inter-tribal discussion and modifying Government policy by frequent petitions. It disbanded in 1902, after the Government passed legislation establishing local Maori Councils (Williams, 1963).

In 1897 several young Maoris completing professional training founded the Te Aute College Students' Association, primarily as a social reform movement. Though commonly referred to as the Young Maori Party, they were only briefly constituted as such and never a political party. With the support and encouragement of the elders, they travelled widely during the next two decades speaking to the people on their *marae* in Maori. One of this group, the lawyer Apirana Ngata, attended and played a decisive role in the later meetings of the Kotahitanga.

## 1900–1935: Recovery

Towards the end of the century, the Maori population as a whole began to increase again. Dr Maui Pomare (appointed Officer for Maori Health in 1901) and his assistant Dr Peter Buck launched a campaign to improve Maori health, housing and sanitation, with the active support of the elders, the Young Maori Party and local Maori sanitary inspectors. The Maori population regained the level of the 1850s in 1921, and in 1928 its rate of natural increase rose above that of the Pakehas.

For a while, the annual conference of Maori Councils replaced the Kotahitanga in bringing the tribes together to discuss Maori problems. But the Councils were not generally successful: within ten years most were at a standstill.

Meanwhile, Maori land continued to be sold: six million acres between 1896 and 1921. In 1905 the Government set up Native Land Boards with power to make advances to Maori farmers, but both funds and terms were limited, and the Native Minister had the right to vest land in them without the owners' consent.

The first practical attack on the problem was made by the Maoris themselves. Under Ngata's leadership, the Ngāti Porou of the East Coast developed incorporation, a scheme whereby owners formed themselves into an incorporated body which could negotiate loans, develop and work their land as a unit, and later consolidation, a complicated system of exchange which concentrated each owner's shares in one block. On these bases, they began dairying in the rich Waiapu valley, and in 1924 founded the first co-operative Maori dairy factory at Ruatoria.

In the 1920s, the Government gave the Native Land Boards and the new Native Trust Office authority to advance loans from accumulated Maori funds. On the recommendation of several Royal Commissions, it also paid (or undertook to pay annually) substantial compensation for unfulfilled promises and unjust confiscations. Finally, in 1929, the Government passed the Native Land Development Act, authorizing the application of public funds to the development of Maori land. Groups of holdings were gazetted as 'development schemes' and gangs of owners employed to clear, fence and sow them in grass. Unless obviously unsuitable, these schemes were later divided into fully equipped one-man holdings and settled by occupiers chosen from and by the owners.

Unfortunately, the beginning of land development coincided with the great depression of the thirties, which curtailed expenditure for for some years. Where established, development schemes helped mitigate the effects of the depression, but elsewhere many Maoris were forced back to subsistence agriculture and bartering produce for clothes.

During this period, two great leaders emerged in the western central districts. The Wanganui prophet and seer, Wiremu Ratana, attracted a large following as a healer and in 1925 founded a new Maori church with a strong political wing. In the Waikato, Te Puea Herangi of the Maori Royal Family organized her people to undertake such projects as building a capital for the King at Ngaruawahia and developing farming, restoring their confidence in themselves.

About 1930, the Department of Education made fundamental changes in its policy for Maori schools. The curriculum was broadened to include aspects of Maori culture, and more emphasis was placed on practical education, in model cottages and workshops, to equip the children to live and work in a mixed community (Holst, 1958: 56).

## 1935–1961: Accelerated change

Returning prosperity and the election of a Labour Government in 1935 opened a new era for the Maoris. Land development schemes were pushed ahead: by March 1939 253,000 acres had been developed to grass and nearly two thousand Maori families settled on the land. Maoris were granted the same social security payments as Pakehas, and the amount spent on Maori schools, housing and welfare was substantially increased.

During the Second World War most of the young men served in the Armed Forces. Exempt under law from compulsory service outside New Zealand, Maoris maintained the Maori Battalion at full strength overseas throughout the war, despite heavy casualties, and served in other companies and services as well. At home Maoris set up a large and efficient War Effort Organization, and moved in large numbers to work in essential industries. As a result, the proportion of Maoris living in cities and boroughs increased from 9 per cent in 1936 to fifteen per cent in 1945, and Maoris entered many occupations new to them. During this period, the word 'Native' was officially dropped in favour of 'Maori'.

After the war social and economic change continued at an accelerating pace. Returned servicemen took advantage of rehabilitation schemes to train as tradesmen, acquire farms and businesses, and attend university. In 1945 the Government added Welfare Officers to the staff of the Department of Maori Affairs. Between 1945 and 1961, the number of Maoris in urban areas increased at an average rate of 16 per cent a year. There was also a steady increase in the percentage of children going to secondary school, in the range of Maori occupations and incomes, and in the proportion of Maoris in the trades and professions. Many laws that discriminated between Maori and Pakeha (e.g. regarding access to liquor, registration of births, deaths and marriages, and jury service) were eliminated. Several important Maori organizations were established on a national basis, notably a hierarchy of Maori Committees and Councils, and the Maori Women's Welfare League. After the stocktaking Hunn Report on Maori Affairs was published in 1961, the Government intensified its efforts to solve Maori land and housing problems, established a Maori Education Foundation and a Maori Arts and Crafts Institute, and adopted 'integration' as its official policy.

# chapter 4

# Maoris and Maori culture today

In the 1970s the Maoris are New Zealand's largest and most distinctive minority. The 1971 Census recorded a Maori population of 227,414, making up 7·9 per cent of the New Zealand population. With their brown skins and Polynesian features, Maoris have high visibility in a population mainly of British stock. (They are not so readily distinguished from the Polynesian immigrants popularly known as 'Islanders', but the latter are much less numerous: 45,413 in 1971, or 1·6 per cent of the total population.) While Maoris have the same basic rights, the laws include some provisions which distinguish them from other citizens. As a group they have a distinctive demographic character, and they differ from the non-Maori population in their patterns of employment, income, housing, health, family life, education, crime and delinquency. While they share a large area of common culture with other New Zealanders, they also cherish patterns of behaviour, organization and values that are distinctively Maori. Above all, they are intensely proud of their ethnic and cultural identity.

## Who is a Maori?

New Zealanders make a basic twofold distinction between 'Maori' and 'Pakeha' (or 'European'). Though terms indicating mixed ancestry such as 'half-caste' and 'part-Maori' are sometimes used, they do not identify a separate, third category. Thus the 'Maori' group includes not only Maoris with only Maori ancestry but many with mixed ancestry as well. There is no clear-cut, generally agreed-upon formula for deciding whether a particular person is Maori or Pakeha. Individuals make decisions on the information available to them in particular situations. Certain general tendencies however do emerge.

39

Both Maoris and Pakehas invariably identify as 'Maori' all those who 'look Maori', that is have brown skins and/or Polynesian features. Those whose Maori ancestry is not apparent in their appearance are left to make their own choice. They usually identify themselves as Maori when they are half Maori or more ,were brought up by Maoris, and/or find Maori company and ways congenial. Maoris sometimes attempt to define 'Maori' in cultural terms, distinguishing between the 'real Maoris' who speak Maori and are 'steeped in Maoritanga' and those who are 'just brown-skinned Pakehas', but in my experience they do not sustain this position for long. In practice, they usually accept as a Maori anyone with a Maori ancestor, if he or she desires acceptance. Pakehas also sometimes attach cultural connotations to the category Maori, not in terms of Maori culture but rather of 'lower-class' socio-economic status and life-style.

Maoris who accept identification as Maoris do not thereby automatically deny their 'Pakeha side'. On the contrary, most recognize it by describing themselves as 'part Maori and part Pakeha' or 'both Maori and Pakeha' or even 'Pakeha too' in appropriate situations. Some do so regularly. Individuals who regard themselves as Pakehas also sometimes acknowledge the Maori in their ancestry, usually for particular purposes rather than regularly. With the high rate of inter-marriage of recent years, increasing numbers of individuals of mixed parentage face the question, 'who are you, Maori or Pakeha?' From my own experience, supported by a recent study (McDonald, 1975b), I would suggest that more and more are refusing to make a clear-cut choice and insisting that they are both, not just on occasion but as a general rule. They express their position by using such terms as 'half-caste' (especially on the East Coast), 'half-and-half', 'Maori and Pakeha', 'a bit of both'. McDonald suggests, cogently I believe, that for the Maoris who use them these terms 'do not represent an arithmetic measure of genetic material nor a description of descent but are instead claims to affiliation in two cultures . . . a claim to being bi-cultural.' She found that Maoris with Pakeha spouses preferred to use such terms for their children, keeping their options open as it were. The Maori father who insisted on registering his daughter as 'part-European' was making the same point as well as protesting against imposed terminology.

There is no single legal definition of a Maori: each Act of Parliament lays down a definition which applies in the case of its own provisions only. The Maori Social and Economic Advancement, Maori Housing, Maori Purposes Fund, Maori Soldiers' Trust, Maori Trust Boards and Ngarimu Scholarships Acts all accept 'anyone descended from a Maori as otherwise defined' as a Maori for their purposes. The Maori Affairs Act 1953, one of the most extensive pieces of legislation relating to Maori matters, especially land, defined a Maori as 'a person belonging to the aboriginal race of New Zealand, including a half-caste and a person intermediate between half-caste and a person of pure descent from that race', though it extended certain provisions to 'any descendant of a Maori so defined'. However, in 1974 the Government passed a Maori Affairs Amendment Act which altered the definition of a Maori to read: ' "Maori" means a person of the Maori race of New Zealand and includes any descendant of such a person.' The Adoption Act 1955 defines a Maori as 'a person who is a Maori within the meaning of the Maori Affairs Act 1953': whether or not this definition is altered by the amendment of the latter is however immaterial, because the Adoption Act mentions Maoris only to emphasize that its provisions apply to all, whether Maori or not. The Electoral Act 1956 made a threefold distinction between those who were 'more than half Maori', whom it directed to enrol on the Maori electoral roll, those who were 'less than half Maori', whom it directed to enrol on the general roll, and 'half-castes', who might choose to enrol on either. This distinction was however abolished by the Electoral Amendment Act 1975 which adopted the definition of a Maori enacted in the Maori Affairs Amendment Act 1974 and provided that all adult Maoris so defined be given the right to choose whether they wished to vote on the Maori or general electoral roll on electoral enrolment forms distributed at the time of the Census. In summary then: in mid-1975 all laws which distinguish Maoris at all use the same, very wide definition. None, however, requires that persons who qualify under this definition *must* declare themselves as Maori; in effect, it is left to the individual to take advantage of the right to do so if and for whatever purposes he wishes. He may do so for some purposes and not for others: his choice is not absolute and may be reversed. And whatever decisions he makes, he is free to change his mind without question or penalty.

Up to 1966, Census schedules asked citizens to declare their 'degree of Maori blood, if any'. In 1971 this wording was changed: now they are asked to declare whether they are 'of full European descent', full New Zealand Maori, Cook Island Maori, Indian etc., or to give particulars, as '¾ European – ¼ New Zealand Maori, or ½ New Zealand Maori – ½ Samoan'. The New Zealand Census includes statistics on 'the Maori population' in volumes on *The Increase and Location of Population* and *Maori Population and Dwellings*. It counts in 'the Maori population' all those who declare themselves as half Maori or more and of mixed Maori and other Polynesian descent.

The 1966 Census included a Table entitled 'Population Wholly or Partly Maori' which distinguished the categories of full-Maori, three-quarter-Maori, half-Maori, Maori-other-Polynesian and Maori-other races as counted in 'the Maori population', and quarter-Maori as counted in the non-Maori population. These fractions are obtained by calculating the proportion of Maori to Pakeha forebears in a person's ancestry. A 'three-quarter-Maori', for instance, is a person who has three Maori and one Pakeha grandparents or six Maori and two Pakeha great-grandparents, while a half-Maori is either the child of parents who are full Maori and full Pakeha, or the grandchild of two Maoris and two Pakehas. Many Maoris claim such complicated fractions as five-eights, eleven-sixteenths, and twenty-five thirty-seconds.

Birth and death registration forms include questions relating to 'degrees of Maori blood, if any' and 'Maori tribes, if any'. The replies are used for statistical purposes only and not recorded on the Register. Other Government Departments officially use the same classification as the Statistics Department, but identification tends to be made by a recording officer rather than the subject. There is some doubt as to how well statistics compiled on these bases match those based on Census schedules.

Census declarations of Maori descent are generally accepted by officials at face value. Proof is rarely required and there is no legal penalty for mis-statement. According to the 1966 Census, 60 per cent of the Maori population declared themselves to be full-blooded. This was a marked increase from 51·5 per cent in 1961. Yet a medical team seeking full-blooded Maoris for blood-group research found that even in a remote community only 25 per cent could be proved to have no Pakeha ancestor. I personally know Maoris with one or two Pakeha grandparents who invariably declare themselves as 'full Maori'. The Maori electoral roll undoubtedly includes persons who are technically less than half Maori, the ordinary roll some who are more. Inaccurate declarations are sometimes due to mistakes in calculation or lack of knowledge, but most are an expression of subjective feelings. It is a matter of identification. Part-Maoris who identify themselves as Maoris tend to overstate their degree of Maori ancestry: 'I always put myself down as full Maori because I feel full Maori.' Those who identify themselves as Pakehas understate it: for instance as 'quarter-', rather than 'half Maori' if they are actually 'three-eighths'.

The Census does *not* give an objective count of the number of persons who are half-Maori or more. Instead it gives us something of far greater significance, the number of those who identify themselves as Maoris: in other words, a reliable measure of the Maori social group.

**Legal status**

Legally, Maoris have the same basic rights as all New Zealand citizens: they can vote and stand for Parliament, they have equal access to all State social services, including education and social security, they can enter any trade or profession if appropriately qualified, they earn the same wages and pay the same taxes, and (subject to the same regulations) they can marry and move freely around and in and out of New Zealand.

At the same time, however, the statute books include several Acts and clauses which deal with Maoris only or make a difference between Maoris and Pakehas. The most important are concerned with the ownership and administration of Maori land, the constitution of bodies dealing with Maori affairs (e.g. the Department of Maori Affairs and tribal trust boards), parliamentary representation, and Maori community government. About half these provisions involve no more than separate organization or procedures; the other half give Maoris special protection or privileges (Hunn, 1961: 77).

These differentiating clauses were passed in fulfilment of the Treaty of Waitangi and other agreements, to protect Maoris from allegedly detrimental practices such as drinking, or to offset handicaps, such as language difficulties. For many years now the Government has been gradually removing them from the statute books. (Thus restrictions on the sale of liquor to Maoris were abolished in 1948, separate registration of births and deaths in 1961; and Maoris became eligible for jury service in 1961.) In several cases, however, Maori representatives have successfully applied to the Government to delay or modify proposed changes. In 1952, for instance, they persuaded the Department of Education not to abolish the Maori Schools all at once but to transfer them to Board control gradually, with community consent. The provisions that remain are justified, under attack, on the grounds that they involve not privilege but compensation for special difficulties.

*The Department of Maori Affairs*

Legal distinction of the Maoris as a minority group is reinforced by the existence of a special Government Department of Maori Affairs. While the Departments of Health, Education, Employment and Justice accept the chief responsibility for Maoris in those fields, the Department of Maori Affairs keeps in close touch with them and acts when necessary to protect Maori interests. In addition, the Department attends directly to the determination and improvement of Maori land titles, the development and settlement of Maori land, some provision of houses for Maoris, and Maori welfare work. It also handles Maori applications for subsidies, provides services for the Maori Land Court, and publishes a quarterly magazine partly in Maori (*Te Ao Hou* – 'The New World'). The Maori Affairs Amendment Act 1974 provides that

> in the exercise of its functions the Department shall always, to the extent possible, have regard to . . . the retention of Maori land in the hands of its owners, and its use or administration by them or for their benefit; . . . the preservation, encouragement, and transmission of the Maori language, Maori customs and traditions, Maori arts and handicrafts, and other aspects of Maori culture essential to the identity of the Maori race: . . . the qualifications of Maoris for and their entry into all trades, professions and occupations: . . . the promotion of the health, education, and general social well-being of all members of the Maori race.

For administrative purposes, the Department of Maori Affairs is divided into nine districts: Tokerau (Northland), Waikato-Maniapoto (Waikato, King Country, Thames, Tauranga), Waiariki (Rotorua, Taupo, Bay of Plenty), Tairawhiti (East Coast, Wairoa), Aotea (Taumarunui, Taupo, Taranaki, Wanganui), Ikaroa (Palmerston North, Wairarapa, Hawke's Bay), Te Waipounamu (South Island, including Chatham Islands), Auckland and Wellington. The first seven districts were originally identical with the seven Maori Land Court Districts but adjustments were made when Auckland and Wellington Districts were created to accommodate changes in Maori population distribution. The names and boundaries of these districts are frequently used for ordering Maori affairs for other purposes as well, for instance in the organization of competitions to select the cultural clubs' for the biennial Polynesian Festivals (p. 183).

## Maori culture

New Zealanders generally agree in recognizing the continuing existence of something called 'Maori culture', but the meaning they give it varies quite widely, especially between Pakehas and Maoris.

If asked what Maori culture means to them, most Pakehas begin by mentioning the Maori language and the distinctive Maori arts and crafts – action songs, wood carving, painted scroll-work (*kōwhai-whai*), reed panels (*tukutuku*) and weaving. Then, after some thought, they add certain 'customs' that are demonstrably derived from pre-European ('Classic') Maori culture: the making of earth ovens (*hāngi*), the use of carved meeting-houses, mourning wakes (*tangihanga*), and the observing of *tapu*. This view of Maori culture sees it as belonging to the past rather than the present, and to the private, leisure-time sector rather than the whole of life: in short as a collection of bits and pieces surviving from what was once but is no longer an integrated system. Setting Classic Maori culture up as the standard in this way means that change is interpreted as decline, loss and Europeanization, and 'Maori culture' is seen as inevitably 'dying' or being 'watered down'.

Most Maoris intuitively reject this view of Maori culture with its emphasis on the past and a few 'occasional' activities. For them Maori culture is a matter of present experience, a living and lived-in reality either for themselves or for others well known to them. It encompasses a wide range of behaviour, including everyday practices as well as ceremonial. Most importantly, it includes not only outward visible forms but also deep inward feelings and values, which are relevant to and expressed in all they do.

The misunderstandings that occur between Maoris and Pakehas on this subject can be attributed at least in part to the fact that Pakehas tend to use a restricted definition of 'culture' in the general context as well as the Maori one. They associate 'culture' primarily with the artistic, intellectual and ceremonial aspects of social life, in contrast with everyday life, especially at home and at work. They also tend to interpret it in terms of readily observable objects and activities, underestimating if not ignoring the importance of beliefs and values.

Anthropologists, whose field of study is the whole of mankind, prefer to give 'culture' a wider definition, covering the whole of life not just selected aspects, and inward ideas as well as outward forms. In the light of this understanding, I offer my own definition of culture as 'a system of symbols and meanings in terms of which a particular group of people make sense of their world, communicate with each other, and plan and live their lives'. Expressing the same idea in an extended metaphor, I also find it useful to describe a culture as a 'language' consisting of 'words' (which unite a particular form with a primary meaning and also with associated meanings or connotations) and rules for putting these 'words' together in patterns which 'say something', that is convey meaning between 'speakers' and 'hearers'.

This approach contains several important insights. It stresses that a culture is an abstraction, not a thing-in-itself with an independent objective existence, but a complex 'idea' in the minds of people. It is essentially a group possession, produced and maintained by interaction between members over many generations. Individuals learn and use it largely unconsciously and with varying degrees of mastery. Like the group itself, a culture never attains a fixed or perfect form but is always in the process of change and development, as it is inherited, employed, re-worked, amplified and transmitted, individually and collectively. The elements of a culture are of many different kinds, ranging from the material and directly observable to the abstract and invisible: objects large and small, language, behaviour patterns, and ideas, including beliefs, attitudes and values. These varied parts do not simply co-exist, but are related to each other in a complex and more or less coherent system. Moreover, the meaning of each part lies not in itself but in its relation to the other parts in the mind of the people. Thus the more tangible elements derive their meaning from the underlying beliefs and values, of which they are at once expressions and symbols; while beliefs and values that really matter are expressed in and give meaning to particular forms of behaviour. Finally, the elements of a given culture are not necessarily peculiar to it. They may appear in a similar form in another. But because meaning derives from context, similar forms may have different meanings when they appear in different contexts. What is distinctive about a culture is not its elements taken separately but the way they are related to each other – their arrangement in a unique configuration.

Applying this anthropological understanding to the Maori case, I would define Maori culture as 'the system of symbols and meaning shared by those who identify themselves as Maoris at any given time'. This approach defines Maori culture in terms of living people instead of its imagined content at a period in the past, and provides for changes over time. Everything Maoris do often or enjoy doing is surely part of their culture, no matter where it came from originally. As one Maori put it: 'All the things I see in the Pakeha way of life that I like, they are all part of my Maori culture too.' Seen in these terms, present-day Maori culture includes: not only observable objects and ways of behaving such as meeting-houses and mourning wakes, but also invisible ideas and values such as the *aroha* (love) that unites the descendants living *and* dead of a common ancestor in a solidary group, and the obligation of *utu* (reciprocity); not only those features that can be traced back to pre-European times, but also others that have been borrowed, invented and creatively developed during nearly two hundred years of interaction with Pakehas, such as the voluntary associations called *komiti* (p. 171), and ceremonies such as 'unveilings' (p. 259) and the 'flower ceremony' (p. 141); not only the practices and beliefs that are obviously and strikingly different from those of the surrounding society, but also those which are shared with it, such as rugby football, school, money, Christianity, the mass media, parliamentary representation and the English language. Whatever their origin, these varied elements are interrelated in a single system, each deriving its meaning for Maoris from its place in that system. Instead of a static entity rooted in the past which is becoming increasingly out-of-date and out-of-place in the modern world, Maori culture should be seen as a dynamic on-going affair always in the process of creative adaptation to a changing environment – as it has been ever since the Polynesian forebears of modern Maoris settled these islands.

As already indicated, defining Maori culture in this way means that it includes many elements that are also part of Pakeha culture (similarly defined). These are usually identified as belonging *only* to Pakeha culture and Maori adoption of them is widely interpreted as assimilation to the latter. This is I believe a fundamental error. For while these shared elements may look alike to the casual observer, closer examination reveals that they do *not* mean the same thing to Maoris and Pakehas. Maoris have not simply taken these elements over unchanged: instead they have taken them *into* their own on-going system of symbols and meanings, re-working and re-interpreting them in the light of their own goals and values, and making them very much their own. Thus, most Maoris handle a football, a wage-packet or a social get-together in a subtly different way from Pakehas, in (as it were) a Maori idiom. When they speak English, they often use distinctive grammatical constructions, speech rhythms and imagery, and they give many words a different range of meanings.

Most Pakehas fail to appreciate these differences or their origin in a different view of the world. They normally assume that in the areas of common experience there is only one cultural code, the dominant Pakeha one. They overlook the possibility that Maoris may give other meanings to shared words, objects and actions, and may have other priorities and goals. So, judging Maori behaviour by their own standards, they all too frequently interpret it as a variant – sometimes admired but more often seen as inferior – from the 'proper' way, attributing the differences to the Maori personality or social environment, instead of their own lack of understanding. For their part, many Maoris are also unaware how often common words and actions are interpreted differently by Pakehas. So, giving their own meanings to familiar words and actions without checking what the other party understands them to mean, Maoris and Pakehas often talk past each other and misinterpret the message actually being sent.

The range of experience shared by Maori and Pakeha expands year by year. Nevertheless there are still sectors of Pakeha life and culture with which comparatively few Maoris are familiar. And there are also quite extensive sectors of Maori life to which relatively few (though increasing) numbers of Pakehas have access, where things are done and judged the Maori way, within an entirely Maori frame of reference.

## Maoritanga

Maoris themselves talk about 'Maoritanga' rather than 'Maori culture'. Formed by adding the noun ending '-tanga' to 'Maori', Maoritanga is readily translatable into English as 'Maoriness', but the Maori form is generally used by Maoris when speaking English as well as Maori. Its coining is usually attributed to Sir James Carroll, who constantly exhorted his people to 'hold fast to your Maoritanga'. He would not define what he meant precisely, saying it was for others 'to give it hands and give it feet'. Sir Apirana Ngata, who played an active part in doing so, has described Maoritanga as

> an emphasis on such Maori characteristics and such features of traditional Maori culture as present-day circumstances will permit, the inculcation of pride in Maori history and traditions, the retention so far as possible of old ceremonial, the continuous attempt to interpret the Maori point of view to the *Pakeha* in power (Sutherland, 1940: 176–7)

In my experience, Maoris use Maoritanga in two distinct but closely related ways. They use it first to stand for a general attitude of pride in being Maori and of identification with Maoris and Maori ways: an attitude that is often described as '*te ngākau Maori*' ('the Maori heart') or '*te wairua Maori*' ('the Maori spirit'). Thus a person is said to have 'kept' his Maoritanga or to have 'lost' it. Secondly, 'Maoritanga' is used to refer collectively to '*ngā tikanga Maori*' ('Maori ways'), those ways of looking at and doing things which Maoris hold to be distinctively and/or characteristically Maori. Maoritanga in this latter sense covers considerably less ground than the anthropological definition of Maori culture given above, but it emphatically includes those Maori ideas and values which underlie and find expression in all kinds of behaviour, including those shared with Pakehas (National Council of Churches, 1964).

When asked to identify Maori ways in detail, Maoris usually focus on a few of central importance, notably language, land, tribe, *marae* and *tangihanga*, providing a sample rather than comprehensive coverage. For them, Maori ways are so closely interwoven that mention of these few calls up a host of associated ideas, as playing a note on the piano calls forth both over- and undertones. I have come to the conclusion that without working it out consciously Maoris use these key 'ways' as symbols for Maoritanga as a whole. This is a perfectly legitimate way of proceeding, known in literary terms as synecdoche – using the part to stand for the whole. The problem is that Pakehas too often take the symbols at face value as constituting the whole and fail to appreciate their full ramifications. (For discussion of Maoritanga

3   Living and working in the city: Maori and Pakeha workmates make a Christmas *hāngi* on a construction site, Wellington, 1974

**4**  The sacredness of the land: *tangata whenua* elder Te Puru ō Tamaki Downs carries sacred soil from the old *marae* site at Orakei to the new in a casket specially carved for the purpose, escorted by Harry Dansey of Te Arawa, Member of the Orakei Marae Trust Board, Auckland, 1973

by Maoris see: Rangiihu in National Council of Churches, 1964: 11–16; and Walker in Bray and Hill, 1974: 45–54.)

As a Pakeha who learnt and is still learning the 'language' of Maoritanga as an adult, I shall endeavour to summarize here what I have come to appreciate as significant aspects of Maoritanga. I cannot stress too strongly that this presentation is neither complete nor definitive. It is a model constructed by an 'outsider', albeit a sympathetic outsider aided by an anthropological training and generous help from insiders, and as such it requires to be checked and completed by the insiders' view that Maoris alone can supply.

Though presented in the form of a list, these Maori ways do not exist as a collection of separate items: logically and in social life they form a configuration, a whole which is more than the sum of its parts, and whose parts are therefore to be understood only in relation to each other and in the context of the total system. There is nothing necessary or fixed about the order of presentation, each entry being related to all the others as well as those on either side. I have however begun with the five that Maoris generally name first, and I have ordered them in two main groups.

First, those which involve a union of outward and visible forms with inward, invisible ideas:

the Maori language, as used both for everyday and ceremonial purposes;
attachment to the land of one's ancestors as a social and economic asset and as a symbol of group identity;
emphasis on kinship as an important basis for ordering social relations and on descent as a determinant of relative rank and membership in tribes and sub-tribes;
the institution of the *marae*, comprising both the physical complex of land and buildings and the ideas and practices centred on it;
the marking of significant events and group encounters by large-scale gatherings (*hui*), of which the most important is the *tangihanga* (mourning wake):
distinctively Maori methods of group organization and decision-making, including the public expression of assent and striving towards unanimity;
respect for and practice of traditional knowledge and skills, where 'traditional' means 'inherited from Maori forebears' but not necessarily of pre-European derivation: oral history and literature, the study of *whakapapa* (descent-lines), various ceremonial forms, a variety of crafts, and the arts of story-telling and speech-making;
preparation and enjoyment of foods regarded as *kai Maori* ('Maori food').

49

Second, those abstract concepts and values which underlie and inform the whole Maori experience of life:

an essentially 'religious' view of the world and man's place in it, expressed in a series of complementary oppositions: between spiritual and earthly realms and beings, *tapu* and *noa*, *ora* and *aituā*, *tika* and *hē*;
a view of the man–woman relation that stresses complementarity; the concept of *mana*, used to express and explain differential status and achievement;
the concept of *aroha* (love) and the associated virtues of *awhina* (helping) and *manaaki* (caring for);
the concept of *utu* (reciprocity);
a conception of time that stresses relativity and the continuity of past, present and future;
a conception of unity (*kotahitanga*) which involves the explicit recognition, even exaggeration, of differences, followed by their mediation.

## *Variations in knowledge and practice*

The cultural 'language' of Maoritanga, like any language, is an ideal system. Individual Maoris vary widely in the extent to which they are consciously aware of, act out and live up to its ideal patterns. While some speak Maori fluently and often, others speak it rarely or inadequately. Some faithfully observe their obligations, for instance to kin and *marae*, others evade them when they can. Some observe traditional taboos meticulously, while others overlook them except in the presence of elders. Some are interested in acquiring traditional knowledge and skills, while the interests of others lie elsewhere, with modern technology for instance.

In part, this variation is the variation to be found in all societies, arising from differences in personal temperament and experience, social status, wealth and power. To revert to the language analogy, when it comes to actually using a language in everyday life, most people draw on something less than its full vocabulary, produce sentences that fall short of grammatical perfection, and develop their own personal style.

In the case of Maoritanga, however, the normal range of variation both in understanding and in practice has been greatly increased by contact with Pakehas and Pakeha culture. In school, in personal interaction and in the mass media, Maoris are continually and subtly made aware that Pakehas place relatively little value on 'Maori ways' and require at least outward conformity to 'Pakeha standards' as the basis of acceptance and upward mobility. Increasing numbers of Maoris are growing up and living in situations where opportunities to experience Maori ways in depth are restricted and sometimes lacking, especially in the cities.

Nevertheless, while the proportion of Maoris who are truly knowledgeable of Maori ways is decreasing it does not necessarily follow, as Pakehas commonly assume, that Maoritanga itself is diminishing in content and importance nor that it will die out in a generation or two. Pakehas have been predicting the demise of Maoritanga for at least a hundred years in much the same words as they use today. As these predictions have proved wrong in the past, so I believe they will prove wrong in the future, for three main reasons.

In the first place, though it is obvious that younger Maoris speak Maori less frequently, know less and are openly critical and impatient of many aspects of Maoritanga, differences between the generations are themselves part of the Maori cultural design. In Maori society, young people have always been expected to concentrate on active pursuits such as sport, courting, acquiring work skills and generally enjoying themselves. They are neither expected nor encouraged to take an interest in the more traditional, ceremonial and political concerns of their elders. As they grow older, however, their interests and attitudes undergo a marked change. Round about the age of forty, many turn their attention to those aspects of Maoritanga they were impatient of when young and deliberately set about improving their knowledge and practice.

Secondly, while some of those who grow up in a predominantly Pakeha environment consciously prefer Pakeha ways, by far the greater proportion profess pride in being Maori regardless of how much they know of Maori ways. In fact it is often those who know least who are most self-conscious and assertive of their Maoritanga, because of their need to find an identity of their own. Realizing the emptiness of mere assertion of Maoritanga, increasing numbers of young people are now making a conscious effort to learn about Maori ways long before middle age. They join Maori associations, increase their participation in Maori gatherings, and seek instruction both from the elders available to them and from educational institutions like the universities.

Thirdly, most young Maoris know more about Maori ways than they – or most observers – know that they know. Even if they do not speak Maori themselves, they have usually heard it spoken around them sufficiently to have absorbed its sounds and rhythms and a basic vocabulary. What is more, they have learnt, in homes and peer groups, to use many English words and phrases with Maori meanings and to respond to visual imagery. And though they may be quite

51

unable to explain the meaning of concepts such as *aroha, utu, mana* and *whakamā*, yet they typically act in ways that make sense in those terms.

## Tribal variations

Recently a leading Maori elder, John Rangihau, suggested in that half-joking way Maori speech-makers use to make their audience think seriously, that

> there is no such thing as Maoritanga. . . . Each tribe has its own way of doing its own things. Each tribe has its own history. And it's not a history that can be shared among others. . . . I can't go around saying because I'm a Maori that Maoritanga means this and all Maoris have to follow me. That's a lot of hooey. You can only talk about your Tuhoetanga, your Arawatanga, your Waikatotanga. Not your Maoritanga. I have a faint suspicion that this is a term coined by Pakeha to bring the tribes together. Because if you cannot divide and rule, then for tribal people all you can do is bring them together and rule . . . because then they lose everything by losing their own tribal identity and histories and traditions. (Rangihau in King, 1975: 232–3.)

At a time when Maoritanga is widely used as a word but much less widely understood as a concept, this is a timely warning. Maoritanga is not a homogeneous product; on the contrary, it is an idea, or rather a system of things and ideas, in which differentiation and variation are of key importance. As modern communications and increasing awareness of what they have in common bring Maoris together in country and city, there undoubtedly is a trend towards standardization and compromise in some regards, but it is balanced by a counter trend which emphasizes distinctive features and differences. Maoritanga and its tribal forms are neither rivals nor alternatives: rather the former is made manifest in and through the latter. Membership in a particular tribe and pride in its particular history and *kawa* are themselves key features of Maoritanga. Whether they are Tūhoe, Arawa, Waikato, Ngāti Porou, Ngāpuhi or members of other tribes, Maoris mostly agree on and act in terms of the same basic principles. The differences are in general differences of particularity and detail. Nevertheless, their importance should not be underrated. Anyone wishing to understand Maoritanga must approach it through one of its tribal forms. From that vantage point it becomes possible to recognize and appreciate the interplay between varying forms, especially at *hui*.

## Conclusion

Like languages, cultures do not stand still but are continually renewed and transformed by the collectivity of 'speakers' in interaction
with each other and their environment, including members of other
groups. The Maori culture of today, like the Maori language, is not
identical with that of a hundred nor fifty nor even twenty years ago,
but is a modern transformation, maintaining continuity with the past
while continually incorporating change. It is no longer possible to see
Maori culture as a discrete and separate entity: it exists in the context
of a multi-racial society continually open to outside influences. In
fact it could be cogently argued that present-day Maori culture owes
nearly as much to the Pakehas as it does to Maori forebears, for
much of its definition and development takes place in relation to and
reaction against the unavoidable and dominating pressure of the
Pakeha majority. As they have come out of cultural isolation into the
mainstream of New Zealand life, the Maori people have become not
less but more aware of their identity as a group. When we are totally
immersed in our own culture we live in it like a fish in water: it is only
when confronted with possible alternatives that we become aware of
ourselves and of the cultural milieu we formerly took for granted.
This growth in self-awareness has been largely thrust upon the
Maoris. Pakehas who, lacking this sort of pressure, honestly attempt
to learn about the Maori point of view should find a bonus in
increased understanding of themselves.

In defining Maori culture as I have done in this chapter, I have
stressed its ideal quality and distinguished it analytically from what
Maoris actually do in practice. In social life, however, ideal and
practice are inextricably linked and it is both impracticable and misleading to concentrate on one or the other. In the following chapters I
shall attempt to explore both together, sometimes beginning with
Maori cultural ideas and then examining how these affect and are
realized in behaviour, and sometimes beginning with patterns of
behaviour (inferred from statistics, reported in research studies or
encountered personally) and seeking to understand and explain them
by reference to cultural factors.

# chapter 5

# Basic concepts in Maori culture

Before concentrating on particular aspects of Maori life such as employment, kinship or the *marae*, it is necessary to explore more fully the basic concepts referred to in the previous chapter, for they pervade and underlie all aspects of Maori life, manifesting themselves under many different headings.

These concepts are in many cases identified by Maori words which were in use in Classic Maori times as part of a thoroughly religious system of thought. But while the words have remained in use the concepts for which they stand have been developed and re-worked over 150 years in interaction with both Christianity and science. Their present use can be fully understood only in the contemporary setting, though reference to past meanings is helpful. As with all beliefs of key importance, these concepts do not lend themselves to neat, clear-cut definition but have a range of connotations and in-built ambiguities which individuals play upon and exploit.

## The physical and spiritual dimensions of reality

Maoris are fond of asserting that they are 'a religious people'. This is a statement not about church membership or attendance but about their understanding of the nature of the universe and of life itself. In the midst of a society where such views are often misunderstood and devalued, Maoris continue to believe in a spiritual reality that transcends limitations of time, space and the human senses, and at the same time pervades and operates in the world of human experience. Few Maoris are prepared to adopt atheism, rationalism or even agnosticism as a creed (National Council of Churches, 1964: 13–14, 18–19; Marsden in King, 1975).

While agreeing on the existence of this spiritual reality, Maoris vary considerably in the ways they formulate their beliefs in detail and how they translate them into action. Nevertheless, the majority would accept certain propositions as basic.

First, most Maoris acknowledge the existence of One Supreme God and lesser spiritual beings of varying degrees of power and beneficence. Following the missionary translators of the Bible, many use the term *atua* for both the supreme and lesser beings, distinguishing God by capitals and an accompanying description, as for instance *Te Atua Kaha Rawa* (Almighty God) or *Te Atua o Nga Mano* (God of Hosts). Others avoid *atua* with its pre-Christian connotations in favour of personal names and other titles. God's personal name is most often rendered as Ihowa or Ihoa, transliterations of Jehovah, but the name of Io, the Supreme Being of Classic Maori cosmology, is also used at times. The three Persons of the Trinity (*Te Tokotoru*) are identified by the titles *Matua, Tama* and *Wairua Tapu*. The name and major title of the son, Jesus Christ, is transliterated into Maori as Ihu or Hehu Karaiti, and he is also identified by the title *Ariki* (Lord). The lesser spiritual beings are angels (*anahera*) associated with God as messengers and servants, guardian spirits (*atua kai-tiaki, tipua*) associated with particular families and places, and ghosts of the dead (*kēhua*) who have not been properly dismissed to the spiritual realms. God and the spirits associated with him are well-disposed to men, giving blessing and protection to those who approach them with respect and sincerity, but because their goodness is fraught with power, they can be dangerous to those who ignore them, scoff at them or do wrong. The same is true of guardian spirits, except that they are mainly concerned with family members and hostile to strangers. *Kēhua* are generally ill-disposed to men, resenting their hold on life. Many Maoris believe that persons with the right qualities can harness certain of the lesser spiritual powers to work good or ill to others. The biblical translators rendered 'devil' into Maori as *rewera*, but in my experience Maoris make little use of the term or of the concept of wholly evil spirits.

Secondly, Maoris do not accept the idea that the universe is limited to the world in which men live and die. Instead they see the World of Men as existing in relation to two other realms, Te Pō and Te Rangi. (These are sometimes given a plural form as Nga Pō and Nga Rangi to indicate they have many parts or aspects.)

Te Pō, literally Night, is associated with ideas of darkness and death. In Classic Maori cosmology, Te Pō was presided over by Hine-nui-te-Pō, the Great-Lady-of-the-Night, who received and wept over the spirits of the dead. Pakeha translators have variously rendered Te Pō as Hades and Sheol, but it was closer to the latter, lacking the elements of judgment and punishment. The dead joined their ancestors in the spiritual homeland of Hawaiki, where they lived much as on earth in a rather shadowy way. But Te Pō was not the complete negation of light and life. Hine-nui-te-Pō was not only the Goddess of Death, she was also the Goddess of Conception and Childbirth. Te Pō was a womb in which new life was generated out of death, the realm not only of endings but also of new beginnings. Integrating the idea of Te Pō into the framework of Christian beliefs, modern Maoris have retained much of this traditional understanding of it as a place where the dead are reunited with their ancestors and death contains the seeds of life. Significantly, they fail to identify it with Hell as a place of eternal punishment, an idea which in general they leave to one side.

In contrast with Te Pō, Te Rangi (Sky or Heaven) is the realm of Day and associated with the ideas of light and life. It is the abode of God Himself, who is conceived as dwelling in its highest reaches, while his spiritual servants occupy the lower heavens. In pre-Christian belief, the spirits of notable chiefs were drawn up into Te Rangi to become stars. Today speakers farewelling the dead of all ranks often bid them go to join the Lord and those who have gone before in Te Rangi. Its life is very much the eternal life of Christian belief, not simply everlasting but infinitely rich in quality (see the discussion of *ora*, pp. 60–1.) But although light and life are generated in the heavens, they are not confined there. From Te Rangi they are diffused into the World of Men, and they are potentially present even in Te Pō.

The relation of Te Rangi and Te Pō is not one of conflict and negation, as it is between Heaven and Hell, but one of complementarity. As light cannot be comprehended except in relation to darkness, as life cannot be appreciated except in relation to death, so Te Rangi and Te Pō define and complete each other. Together they are united as spiritual realms in contrast with the World of Men, alternatives that are equally possible and even interchangeable, not mutually exclusive. Speakers farewelling the dead may dispatch them to Te Pō or Te Rangi, not infrequently in the same speech.

The World of Men is Te Ao-Tū-Roa, the World Standing Long. In contrast with the spiritual realms, it is a place where things are measured and so finite and limited, a world of time, space and mortality. It is sometimes described in speeches as Te Ao-Matemate, stressing its tendency to loss of power, to de-generation. Yet human experience in this world includes opposite tendencies, the incursion from the spiritual realms of spiritual power and beings which are not subject to limitations. In Te Ao-Tū-Roa, light and darkness, life and death come together, sometimes in conflict but also in rhythmic alternation, manifest in the cycles of night and day, the seasons of the year, and the fluctuating fortunes of human beings. While Maoris give due weight and mourning to death and loss, they also stress continuity and renewal as equally part of man's experience. In particular, they see the individual as part of the group, his life and death as part of an on-going life that outlasts his.

Maoris typically express their understanding of the relations between Te Rangi, Te Pō and Te Ao-Tū-Roa in spatial terms. Te Rangi is 'above' (*kei runga*) to the other two, Te Pō is 'below' (*kei raro*). The dead seek Hawaiki by spirit paths leading northwest from Cape Reinga in Northland. Funeral speeches bid them 'go away' ('*Haere, haere, haere atu*') and offer comfort to the living 'left behind' ('*te hunga i mahue ake nei*'). However, while some Maoris undoubtedly take them literally (as some Pakehas take Christian imagery), these spatial expressions are essentially metaphors, used to express the otherwise inexpressible. Instead of seeing the three realms as three tiers or decks in a single structure, Maoris relate the World of Men on the one hand and the spiritual realms on the other as different but interlocking dimensions. When they speak of God, the ancestors or the recent dead, they perceive them as at once 'far off elsewhere' and 'very close', especially at *tapu* times and places, where the two dimensions meet. God and the lesser spiritual beings from the spiritual realms are perceived as penetrating and acting in this world of ours, as immanent in it as well as transcendent.

A term which is also used in this context but is particularly difficult to grasp is Te Ao-Marama. Sometimes it is used in contrast with Te Pō, when it seems to be a synonym for Te Ao-Tū-Roa, or perhaps refers to Te Ao-Tū-Roa and Te Rangi together. But at other times it is clearly contrasted with the World of Men and Mortality. The dead are often farewelled with the words: '*Waihotia ake te Ao-Matemate, tomokia te Ao-Marama*' ('Leave the world where all things tend to death and enter the World of Light'). It has been suggested to me by an elder that Te Ao-Marama is a completely abstract concept, applicable to any situation where knowledge, enlightenment and understanding are ruling principles. As such, it can be experienced in this world by the wise and single-hearted, but in general it is achieved in all its fullness only after death.

Finally, Maoris see most things in the World of Men as having a physical and a spiritual aspect. Above all, man himself is a union of body (*tinana*) and *wairua* (spirit or soul). Many older Maoris also maintain belief in the *mauri*, the essence which gives a thing its specific natural character, but this concept no longer has general currency, probably because it was not reinforced by Christian beliefs as *tinana* and *wairua* were. During man's earthly life, *tinana* and *wairua* are the complementary halves of his identity, and whatever happens to one for good or ill affects the other. In sleep the *wairua* is believed to leave the body and move in the purely spiritual dimension, bringing back messages encoded in dreams. Particularly vivid dreams are held to foretell future happenings to those who interpret them aright. When a man dies, his body returns to *te kōpū o Papa-tūā-nuku*, the bosom of Mother Earth, but his spirit, after lingering a few days to be farewelled, travels by spirit paths to join God and his ancestors in the spiritual realms.

Thus in the Maori view, physical and spiritual reality, Man and God, the World of Men and the spiritual realms of Te Rangi and Te Pō are irrevocably linked in a web of reciprocal relationships in a single cosmic system. Everything that happens in this World of Men is seen as having a spiritual as well as a physical explanation, cosmic as well as earthly significance. And this is true not only of happenings that are strange and inexplicable, but equally of those with obvious physical causes and achievements due to ability and effort. (For Maori statements on this subject see: Cameron in National Council of Churches, 1964: 18–19; and Marsden in King, 1975: 191–219.)

Closely associated with this emphasis on the interrelatedness of physical and spiritual reality are three pairs of contrasting ideas or 'oppositions': *tapu* and *noa, ora* and *aituā, tika* and *hē*.

## Tapu and noa

*Tapu* is one of the Maori words that crops up most frequently in conversation between Maoris, whether in Maori or English, and one of the most widely known though only partly understood by Pakehas. Mention of *noa* is rare by comparison. Yet the two concepts go together as a set and cannot be properly understood except in relation to each other.

Since the missionaries used the word *tapu* to translate 'holy' into Maori where it occurred in the English Bible, it has become usual to define the meaning of *tapu* as 'holy' in English. But careful listening reveals that Maoris often used *tapu* (which they rarely translate even when speaking English) in contexts where 'sacred' does not fit. Williams's *Dictionary of the Maori Language* defines *tapu* as an adjective as 'under religious restriction' and as a noun as 'ceremonial restriction, quality or condition of being subject to such restrictions'.

People, places, objects and actions may all be described as *tapu*, their degree of *tapu*-ness varying however from mild to intense. Some things are permanently *tapu*, for example churches and burial grounds, but many are *tapu* only in certain contexts and for limited periods. Intense tapus may be 'lifted', either partially, as when the *tapu* on a newly built meeting-house is modified so that it can be used, or entirely, as when the *tapu* on the place where a dead body has lain is removed after burial. There are four main ways of lifting a *tapu*: by chanting traditional formulae, by washing or sprinkling with water, by the ritual action of a woman, or by ritual consumption of cooked food. Tapus may also be 'imposed' for a term by decree of the elders, for example on fishing grounds after a drowning. In some cases the state of *tapu* is readily explained as stemming from close contact with God, and hence as a state of sanctity; but in others it is rather a matter of pollution, through contact with death, blood or hostile spirits. *Tapu* is a good example of the way that Maori thought sometimes puts together in one category ideas that Pakehas see as different. (Of course, the reverse also happens.)

Everything designated as *tapu* must be either avoided or handled with care according to prescribed rules. Breach of these rules is believed to result in sickness, trouble or even death, through the action of an offended God or spirit or as an automatic reflex. Consequently when things go wrong, even when the immediate cause is obvious, Maoris commonly review their behaviour to see if they have wittingly or unwittingly breached a *tapu*.

In comparison with *tapu*, Maoris rarely use *noa* when speaking English, translating it, when they refer to it at all, as 'common'. There is a tendency to think of *noa* as an empty, colourless background to *tapu*. This is a mistake. *Noa* has positive as well as negative aspects, as *tapu* also has. In fact, Williams's *Dictionary of the Maori Language* gives *noa* a much wider range of meanings than *tapu*, defining it as:

1. free from *tapu* or any other restriction; 2. of no moment, ordinary; 3. indefinite; 4. within one's power; 5. denoting absence of limitations or conditions, to be translated according to context, e.g. without restraint, spontaneously, of oneself, gratuitously, without consideration or agreement, at random, without object, fruitlessly . . . quite, just, merely.

*Tapu* and *noa* together form an exhaustive classification: what is not *tapu* is *noa* and vice versa. However, the content of the two categories is not invariable. Things *tapu* and things *noa* always stand in the same relation to each other, but one and the same thing may be *tapu* in one context and *noa* in another. Except for a few closely associated with God or death, people, places, objects and actions are *tapu* and *noa* not in absolute terms in and of themselves, but in relation to other people, places, objects and actions. Thus, although men as a group are *tapu* in relation to women who as a group are *noa*, men who are young or of junior descent are *noa* in relation to men who are old or of senior descent, while women of high rank are *tapu* in relation to some men and other women, and all women are *tapu* during menstruation, pregnancy and childbirth. Similarly the meeting-house and open space in front of it (the *marae* proper) are *tapu* in relation to the dining-hall and kitchen of a *marae* complex which are *noa*, but the whole of the *marae* complex is *tapu* in relation to the ordinary land around it (see p. 232).

Though opposites, *tapu* and *noa* are not negations of each other: they are complementary opposites, pre-supposing and completing each other, incomplete and meaningless on their own. Each has both positive and negative aspects, being positive where the other is negative and vice versa. Where *tapu* implies the presence of super-natural power (whether good or evil) and attracts attention and respect, *noa* implies the absence of such power and attracts neither attention nor respect. On these counts *noa* has negative value while *tapu* is positive. But *tapu* also stands for danger, restrictions on freedom of action, and anxious introspection to detect slips. *Noa* on the other hand is safety, freedom from restriction, and relaxed, out-going warmth. On these counts it is *tapu* that has negative value and *noa* that is positive. A Maori elder expressed appreciation of the positive aspects of *noa* when he described *noa* as 'the antidote for *tapu*'. Life would be impossibly burdensome if everything were *tapu*. and dispiritedly dull if everything were *noa*. It is the contrast that makes life worth living.

The *tapu-noa* relation is often used by Maoris as a pattern or model to describe the relation between other contrasted categories, for instance between 'man' and 'woman', traditional knowledge and non-traditional knowledge, formal social relations (e.g. in a welcome ceremony) and informal social relations (e.g. at the meal that follows the welcome), Maoritanga and 'Pakehatanga' – the Pakeha way of life. This is *not* to say that one category (e.g. man) 'is' *tapu* and that the other (e.g. woman) 'is' *noa*, but that the relation between them is like the relation between *tapu* and *noa*. By seeing Maori ways (including the concept of *noa* itself) as *tapu* in relation to non-Maori ways, Maoris are not rejecting the latter, but on the contrary recogniz-ing them as a necessary and significant part of their life experience.

### Ora and aituā

The concepts of *ora* and *aituā* also form a pair of complementary opposites, though not, like *tapu* and *noa*, an exhaustive classification.

*Ora* contains the ideas of 'life' and 'well-being'. Sometimes it is interpreted in terms of physical life as compared to death, as when a speech-maker, having paid his respects to the dead, says: '*Te hunga mate ki te hunga mate, te hunga ora ki te hunga ora*' ('Leave the dead to the dead; let the living now speak to the living'). But its full meaning is much wider, including the idea of spiritual as well as physical life and health, and life after death as well as before. This was implicit in the original pre-European meaning, which thus accorded well with the Christian concept of 'eternal life', the creative power of God that sustains and enriches the life of this world and transcends death. *Ora* was extensively used by the biblical translators in this sense, and is now closely though not exclusively associated with the person of Christ, who is *Te Kai-whaka-ora*, the *Life-giver* (cf. John 10.10, 11.25 in the Maori Bible). During a funeral wake the dead are often told: '*Kua whiti atu koe i te mate ki te ora*' ('You have passed from death into life').

Maoris set the idea of *ora* in opposition to both *mate* and *aituā*, but especially to the latter which has the wider and more abstract meaning.

*Mate* is an adjective which can mean both 'sick' and 'dead': its basic meaning would seem to involve weakening of physical being. It is used in phrases to render 'hungry', 'thirsty' and 'in love'. *Mate* is also used as a noun but as such signifies 'a death' or 'a dead person' rather than 'death' in the abstract.

*Aituā* means 'misfortune, calamity' in both the specific and general senses. It can be used for misfortunes of many kinds, but it is applied particularly to death, the ultimate *aituā*, foreshadowed by all lesser ones. (In Classic Maori mythology, Te Pō is the realm and Hine-nui-te-Pō the Goddess not of *mate* but of *aituā*.) Death threatens *ora* on a cosmic scale. As well as ending man's physical existence it presents the greatest possible challenge to his belief in a reality that transcends the physical. Maori thinking meets this challenge by seeing death not as the negation of life but as its necessary contrast and complement. In the first place, death makes men, who normally take it for granted, think seriously about the meaning of life, and greatly enhances their appreciation of its value. Secondly, death is never final but is always succeeded by new life. As one of many Maori proverbs on the subject has it: 'One fernfrond dies, another pushes up in its place.' Those who die physically live on both in the spiritual world and in their descendants.

These ideas come through most clearly in the Maori handling of death in the *tangihanga*. Instead of hiding death behind a screen of privacy, they take the *tūpāpaku* (corpse) to a *marae* to lie in state and gather there in large numbers, expressing their grief in stylized wailing, speeches and tears. Having brought the conflict between life and death out into the open, they resolve it by the public expression of love (*aroha*) for the dead and for each other, and of faith in God's care (*manaakitanga*) for both. Every *tangihanga* is both a lament for the fact of death and a re-affirmation of belief in the creativity and continuity of life (see especially Witi Ihimaera's novel, *Tangi*).

*Tika and hē*

Maoris contrast the right (*tika*) way of doing things with the wrong (*hē*) way.

Literally, *tika* means 'straight, direct; keeping a straight course'. Being *tika* involves keeping to the prescribed path. For Maoris the *tika* ways are those laid down by God and by the group, especially the ways of one's ancestors. The associated noun *tikanga* can mean 'rule, plan, custom, or reason'. 'Maori ways' are '*ngā tikanga Maori*'.

Being *hē*, on the other hand, involves departing from the prescribed path, just as to err in English means 'to go astray'. Departure from the right way either results from or causes confusion and perplexity, so that *hē* also means 'perplexed, at a loss'. The individual who insists on going his own way or is not properly instructed by those responsible for him, in fact loses his way and 'doesn't know who or where he is'.

## Man and woman

It is often said that in Maori thinking 'man is *tapu* and superior, and woman is *noa* and inferior'. This is a rather misleading formulation, because as we have seen, men can lose their *tapu* for various reasons, and women become *tapu* under various circumstances. Maori attitudes are more accurately represented by saying that Maoris see the relation between men and women as homologous with (or having the same form as) the relation between *tapu* and *noa*. In other words, Maoris see the categories 'man' and 'woman' as complementary opposites, whose characteristics and functions differ from but complete each other, and which could not exist without each other.

Most tribes reserve the position of chief of a tribe or sub-tribe and the right to 'speak on the *marae*' (i.e. during welcomes and public debate) to men only, though some make exceptions for women holding national office such as an MP. The Northland tribes neither specifically forbid nor encourage women to aspire to such roles, but the East Coast tribes pride themselves on giving their women equal opportunities and on the capacity they display. Nevertheless in Maoridom in general, men undoubtedly have higher status and value than women in the field of public leadership.

This is not, however, the whole story. Women are recognized as having positive value on other important counts, especially as providers of food, without which the orators' expression of welcome would be meaningless; as bearers and rearers of children, to Maoris 'the true wealth of the people'; and as sources of warmth, security and affection. Certain ceremonial roles are also reserved to women: the 'calling' of visitors on to the *marae*, wailing (*tangi*) for the dead, and the lifting of certain *tapus*. These may be less prominent than those performed by men but they are no less vital. A *rangatira* of the Arawa tribe, among the strictest in forbidding women to speak on the *marae*, explained to me that

> it is not a matter of thinking men superior, but a division of labour. The men do the speaking in the public eye, the women work behind the scenes. A man relies on his wife to support him when he rises to speak by providing food for the kitchens, weaving a cloak for him to wear, and joining him in the song with which he embellishes his speech. If she refused to do any of these things he would be too ashamed to speak. So she really has the greater power. Often women know as much about *whakapapa* and tribal lore as their husbands if not more, and many men talk over what they plan to say with their wives the night before.

This view of man and woman as equally valuable in different ways is beautifully expressed in a Whānau-ā-Apanui proverb: '*Te mate ki te tāne, he whare pakaru; te mate ki te wahine, he tākere haea*' ('When death comes to a man, a house is destroyed; when death comes to a woman, a canoe hull is shattered'). The choice of symbols for man and woman needs explanation, being the opposite of what Pakehas expect. For Maoris the word 'house' calls to mind not the family dwelling but the meeting-house which is named for and symbolically represents a male ancestor and his descendants, while 'canoe' is a common image for a woman in Maori oral literature, referring both to her sexual role and her function as carrier of that most precious freight, a child. To Whānau-ā-Apanui, whose territory is a narrow coastal strip between mountains and sea coast, meeting-house and sea-going vessel are assets equally necessary and valued for a satisfying life.

### Mana and related concepts

*Mana* is another of the words that Pakehas use frequently but with very partial understanding, largely missing its significance in contemporary Maori life.

As we have seen, in Classic Maori times, *mana* signified power of supernatural origin which possessed rather than was possessed by both men and things. It was possession by *mana* which made both *tapu*, and *mana* itself that punished breaches of *tapu*.

Maoris continue to use the word *mana* extensively, whether speaking Maori or English. It is not easy to discover exactly what they

63

mean by it. If asked they almost invariably render it into English as 'prestige' or 'standing', words which to English speakers imply power in a purely social and political sense. On the whole I am inclined to believe that the social referent of *mana*, formerly its secondary meaning, has become the primary one for most Maoris most of the time. Nevertheless the older meaning remains present for them as an overtone and under certain circumstances returns to prominence. But for elders steeped in Maoritanga, *mana* still retains its full force, signifying power beyond the ordinary possessing and possessed by extra-ordinary individuals (Schwimmer, 1963). In my experience, when Maoris use the word *mana* in English it can almost always bear both interpretations and is in fact interpreted differently by different hearers.

Whether its social or supernatural aspect is emphasized, however, the concept of *mana* is widely used, as in former times, to express and to explain the differential achievement and status of both individuals and groups. Those who achieve success and high positions in a particular field or in community life in general are said both to 'have *mana*' by virtue of their achievement and status, and to have achieved success and status by virtue of their *mana*.

Individuals build up their *mana* from several sources. Every Maori inherits some *mana* from his ancestors; whether it is more or less depends on seniority of descent, sex and birth order in the family. This basic inheritance can be amplified by direct contact with the supernatural, as Christian priest or minister, *tohunga* in the Ringatū Church, or charismatic prophet or healer, and/or by achievement in a variety of fields both traditional and modern. Nowadays, when Maoris move round the country a great deal outside their tribal territory, there is a general tendency to place less emphasis than formerly on *mana* obtained by descent and more on *mana* obtained by personal achievement. Achievement in non-traditional spheres, for example as doctor, artist, MP or scholar, is respected, but those who aspire to truly high *mana* must back it up with achievement in traditional ones as well, as orators, carvers and experts in tribal history.

How much *mana* a person has at any given time depends not on any precise or objective measure but on the subjective assessments of the individual himself and of those around him. These are usually interrelated, for only a rarely self-possessed Maori does not care about other people's opinions. Thus far from being fixed, a person's *mana* fluctuates according to his performance and the state of his relations with others. A Maori maintains or increases his (or her) *mana* when he acts in accordance with the expectations of other Maoris, succeeds in some enterprise and wins recognition and approval from others (including Pakehas), or when he 'puts down' someone else. (The word often used in this context is *whaka-iti* – to 'make small', literally to 'belittle'.) He (or she) loses *mana* when he disappoints expectations or fails in an enterprise, when he does wrong, or when he is criticized or 'put down' by others. To a considerable extent, *mana* varies with context. A man may have high *mana* in his home-place but substantially less in a town where he is not known. He can, however, build up his *mana* there too, in time, by achievement.

Not only individuals but also groups have *mana*, especially tribes and sub-tribes, and all that has been said about an individual's *mana* applies to that of groups. Commonly the *mana* of a group and that of its leading members (*rangatira*) are closely related, so that they increase and decrease together. Exceptional success on the part of even youthful members can reflect glory on the whole group, as, for instance, Moana-nui-a-Kiwa Ngarimu did on Ngāti Porou when he won a Victoria Cross during the Second World War. Equally, wrong-doing on the part of members 'drags down' their people with them.

When a man's *mana* is threatened or diminished, whether by his own doing or another's, he can fight to rebuild it either by doing well at some task or by belittling his belittlers. However, to adopt either of these strategies, a man must be reasonably confident of carrying them off. If a Maori is unsure of his *mana* or conscious of wrong-doing, he will not assert himself. Instead he becomes *whakamā*.

*Whakamā*

*Whakamā* is translated in Williams's *Dictionary of the Maori Language* as 'shy, ashamed', but once again the Maori word has a range of meanings that can be conveyed only by several English words. *Whakamā* covers not only shyness and shame but also feelings of inferiority, inadequacy, self-doubt and (but not necessarily) guilt. Its root meaning could be rendered as 'conscious of being at a disadvantage'.

Whatever its cause, *whakamā* manifests itself in behaviour that is recognizably of the same order but ranges in intensity from limited responsiveness and monosyllabic answers, through withdrawal into the self while physically present, to actual running away from the threatening situation. When Maoris become *whakamā* in a Maori context, other Maoris recognize the phenomenon, understand its likely causes and know how to handle it. If it stems from criticism, failure or undue humility, the elders in particular will set out to build the person up. When *whakamā* is due to consciousness of wrong-doing, it can be overcome by confession and acceptance of the punishment or expiation required by the group or its representative elder or *tohunga*. In some cases, the withdrawal from social interaction itself would seem to be a form of self-punishment, offered to the group by the offender and terminated by a forgiving gesture in return. An old proverb advises: '*Waiho mā te whakamā e patu!*' ('Leave him alone; he is punished by shame'). But when a Maori becomes *whakamā* in relation to Pakehas, whether in particular situations (as in the classroom or at work) or in general, the problem is compounded because Pakehas do not understand what is happening and frequently misread the manifestations of a sense of inferiority as guilt for wrong-doing.

## *Whakaiti and whakahīhī*

A person who does not push himself forward is described as *whakaiti* 'self-belittling'. Humility is a quality that is expected of the ordinary person and admired in those whose *mana* would justify self-assertion.

In contrast, the strongest reproach Maoris can level at a person is to accuse him of being *whakahīhī*, that is, arrogant, setting himself above others. Most Maoris prefer to limit achievement to the general level rather than risk such an accusation. It is however used to test the calibre of would-be leaders: if they are of the right stuff, they will not be discouraged, but persist in proving they have the *mana* to sustain their aspirations. The truly *whakahīhī* rush in where angels fear to tread, over-estimate their ability and other people's admiration, throw their weight around, and collapse quickly under stress or rebuke.

## Aroha

In a world where human beings are divided on many counts, especially in terms of sex, age, descent and status, Maoris see *aroha* operating as a principle of mediation and reconciliation.

The word *aroha* is usually translated into English as 'love', but the correspondence between the two concepts is far from perfect. The root meaning of *aroha* is 'love for kin', and it implies not only affectionate feelings but also the issue of those feelings in action. In pre-European times kin were friends (*hoa*) and friends were kin: when peace was made enemies were turned into friends by marriage. Nowadays, when the two categories are no longer synonymous, *aroha* is used in the context of friendship as well as kinship, but in the event of conflict the sense of obligation to kin is likely to prove the stronger. Since the missionaries used *aroha* to translate the concept of self-sacrificing love (Greek *agape*) in the Bible, *aroha* is now widely used in that sense also. A meeting-house in Wellington bears the name Arohanui-ki-te-tangata ('Goodwill towards all men'). On the other hand, *aroha* does *not* properly apply to erotic love, despite its occasional use to translate 'love' in that sense in popular songs.

However, *aroha* also retains a number of meanings that are not covered by 'love'. It is appropriately used to express both sympathy and sorrow in the context of bereavement, gratitude on receipt of a gift or service, yearning for an absent kinsman or friend, pity and compassion towards someone in trouble and approval for a person or action.

In Maori imagery, *aroha* is closely associated with the heart (*ngākau*), and is appropriately used whenever one's heart goes out to, is stirred by, or warms to another. *Aroha* thus stands for all those feelings of empathy that link men together and men with God, and provides the basis for and impetus towards social interaction and positive reciprocity.

*Aroha* issues in action as *awhina* and *manaaki*, two closely related concepts which overlap but are not quite identical. *Awhina* refers mainly to the provision of tangible help and support in the form of goods, money, personal attendance and labour. *Manaaki* means 'caring' in the fullest possible sense, giving not only practical help but also moral support, comfort and protection from harm. It is the word that is used most often when saying 'God bless you': '*Mā te Atua koe e manaaki*'.

## Reciprocity

The principle of reciprocity, so highly significant in Classic Maori society, continues to play an important part in inter-personal and inter-group relations in Maori society, though the word *utu* is not greatly used. This is possibly because Pakehas commonly translate it as 'revenge', giving it a purely negative meaning.

Overtly at least, the emphasis today is on the obligation to reciprocate good gifts. Maoris who grow a good crop, make a good haul of fish, or have a win at the races give a substantial proportion away to friends and relatives, knowing full well that the bread thus cast upon the waters will return to them in their time of need. Gifts of money and labour and the 'gift' of attendance and moral support at *hui* are remembered, often through the records of receipts and work lists, in order that they may be reciprocated on an appropriate occasion in the future.

In my experience Maoris no longer explicitly justify the repayment of insults and injuries in terms of the need to protect their *mana* from diminishment: since the adoption of Christianity such retaliation is seen as a moral evil rather than an obligation owed to the self. However, when misfortune strikes, some older Maoris will still attribute it to failure to counter 'ill-speaking' by another (among other things). And it is a hypothesis at least worth exploring that some of the physical assaults which get Maori children into trouble at school and on city streets occur when they are faced with a choice between reacting immediately to provocation or accepting further erosion of their self-image.

Maoris have adopted the use of money into their system of reciprocity with some reservations. Visitors to *hui* regularly present gifts in the form of cash. However, where both personal and group relations are concerned, there is a feeling that the actual sum should not be specified beforehand nor paid back exactly. To do so is to change the transaction from a social to a commercial one. Hence Maori parents prefer not to 'charge' children living at home a fixed amount of 'board' but rely on them to 'give what they feel like'. Services such as help with hay-making or laying concrete paths should be repaid in kind not in cash (for an example of a clash of cultural values on this point, see Noel Hilliard's novella, *Night at Green River*, 1969: 15–17).

## Time

Maoris are well known among Pakehas for being 'happy-go-lucky about time': they are often said to 'have no sense of time'. The expression 'Maori time' is widely used by Pakehas to mean 'well past the time appointed', in other words late. In contrast, 'Pakeha time' means 'punctually, up to time'. Like many other Pakeha judgments of Maori behaviour, this is both ethnocentric and superficial. Behind differences in punctuality lie deeper differences in the conceptualization of time itself.

In the first place, Maoris and Pakehas emphasize different ways of measuring and indicating time. Pakehas place the primary emphasis on clock and calendar, which divide time into units of fixed value and number them, while Maoris in general prefer to order time in terms of sequences of events, both natural and man-made. The difference is relative, not absolute. Pakehas enjoy those situations, mainly private ones, where they can 'forget about time' and activities do *not* start 'on the dot', while Maoris are by no means blind to the usefulness of clock and calendar in organizing public life in a modern complex society. Nevertheless, Pakehas tend by and large to regard clocks and calendars as *the* way of ordering time, not merely a convenient device for bringing people and services together but an independent objective standard virtually identical with time itself.

This attitude comes out in various idiomatic phrases which use 'time' where the proper referent is 'hour' or 'o'clock': for instance, 'what is the time?', 'name a time', 'on time', 'behind time'. To Pakehas who equate time and the clock in this way, 'Maori time' has connotations of failure, of falling short of a standard. Maoris, on the other hand, take clock and calendar much less seriously and order time whenever possible by other means, especially by reference to the task in hand or an expected sequence of events. Ask a Maori to 'name a time' and he will usually indicate not an hour but 'before or after such-and-such an event' or 'when such-and-such is finished'. 'For the village Maori . . . the nature of the task and progress towards a goal give pattern to time. It starts and stops, goes quickly or slowly, is noticed or not noticed: but it does not grind regularly on' (Ritchie in Schwimmer, 1968: 390).

The Maori attitude to and way of ordering time are particularly well exemplified at formal Maori gatherings (*hui*). Every *hui* follows a basic pattern made up of events which should occur in a certain relationship to each other. Each of these events begins not at a pre-arranged hour but after the preceding one has ended, and takes, or more accurately is given, whatever length of time is necessary to complete it in accordance with Maori ideals, especially those of honouring the dead and caring for visitors. Guests must be welcomed with due ceremony before they can be involved in any other activity. If a party arrives just as a meal or a service is to begin, the latter are delayed until their welcome is properly carried out, even if it takes hours. The ruling principle is the fulfilment of customary obligations. This is what Maoris mean by 'Maori time' – not lateness, a failure to meet a standard, but a way of ordering time which gives priority to Maori values. With growing numbers of Pakehas attending *hui*, the elders often spell it out explicitly by announcing: '*Tahia te taima a te Pakeha ki te taha, waiho tonu ki tā te taima a te Maori*' ('Let Pakeha time be set aside and from now on let us act according to Maori time'). At a *hui*, time is no object, and there is all the time in the world for the things that really matter.

Maoris and Pakehas both know from their own experience that time goes fast or slow according to interest, that in certain circumstances, absorbed in good company, a book, music or worship, it is possible to transcend the constraints of time and space and communicate with people of other times and places. Pakehas in general however assume that this experience, being subjective, is illusory and that 'real time' proceeds objectively, outside their consciousness, a framework or constraining force to which they must conform. But though this is the dominant view, at least some Pakehas would reject it, and the language itself contains evidence for an alternative one. Phrases such as 'take your time', 'doing something in your or its own time' and 'making time' suggest that time may also be viewed as relative to particular people and things, a dependent rather than an independent variable. Maoris in general take up this second option, stressing the relativity and subjective aspects of time. As a result, they do not regard the passage of time as a divisive force, as Pakehas tend to do, but stress instead continuity and connections through the years, especially by means of descent.

Significant differences also occur in the way Maoris and Pakehas view the relation between past, present and future. Pakehas take it for granted that human beings stand in the present with their backs to the past and faces to the future. What lies behind is dead and gone by. In deciding how to act in the present, they base their behaviour partly on what they have learnt in the past, but even more on what they see in the future. Perhaps because of their own immigrant history, most explicitly reject interest in 'past history'.

Maoris on the other hand describe the past as *'nga rā o mua'*, 'the days in front', and the future as *'kei muri'*, 'behind'. They move into the future with their eyes on the past. In deciding how to act in the present, they examine the panorama of history spread before their eyes, and select the model that is most appropriate and helpful from the many presented there. This is not living in the past; it is drawing on the past for guidance, bringing the past into the present and the future. Recently, I watched two prominent Maoris of different tribes and generations meet in a public situation for the first time. Exchanging formal greetings, each in turn recalled that the ancestors of their respective tribes were related as older and younger brothers, reviewed episodes of co-operation between their tribes based on this relationship, and then proceeded to use the older-brother-younger-brother model to order their behaviour to each other for the rest of the gathering. Where rapid change is involved this procedure has its drawbacks, but it provides a sense of identity and a firm basis for governing social interaction, especially between Maoris.

For Maoris then the past is not dead and gone but very much alive and relevant to them where they stand in the present. Their ancestors, far from being remote and shadowy figures as they are to Pakehas, are entirely real and supportive in present crises, especially those who founded their tribe or sub-tribe or gave them their personal name. Significantly, they talk of them in the present tense. The same is true of significant events. Inter-tribal relations are still affected by battles and alliances that took place generations ago, while Maori attitudes to Pakehas as a group are influenced for good or ill by issues such as the Treaty of Waitangi, the Land Wars, confiscations and shared comradeship in two World Wars.

### Kotahitanga – unity

Maoris place a high value on unity in social life, whether in family, descent-group, local community or voluntary association, expecting and bringing strong pressures to bear on individuals to place the good of the group above personal wishes and convenience. The word used for the ideal of unity is formed by adding the noun ending *-tanga* to the numeral 'one': *kotahitanga* or 'one-ness'. This word is also used with more specific meaning to refer to small family clubs (p. 00) and as the title of a political movement (p. 195).

One-ness does not however come naturally to Maoris any more than to others. Far from being 'just one big happy family with never a cross word spoken', the image they like to project to the outside world, Maori groups have their share of internal differences, rivalries and conflicts. And when groups of similar or different kinds come together at *hui*, conference or sports tournament, the possibility of conflict is always present. In working towards unity Maoris usually begin by recognizing differences and conflicts where they exist, even highlighting them, then having brought them out into the open, they proceed to overcome them by the use of various strategies of mediation. For instance, if a decision is to be made at a Maori gathering, those present begin by presenting as many differing views as possible; these are debated and reduced to the two or three most likely; and finally the supporters of the less favoured courses give up their preference to support the most popular, so that the decision may be unanimous. In the ceremonial welcome accorded to visitors to a *marae*, hosts and visitors begin by confronting each other as two distinct parties, first across the full width of the *marae*, then more closely as the visitors move halfway across it; speeches of greeting are exchanged across the gap, then the visitors approach the reception line of the hosts, physical contact is made by handshake and *hongi* (pressing noses), and finally the two groups break ranks and inter-mingle, symbolically becoming one.

The Maori conception of unity then does not involve the elimination of difference, the achievement of a bland sameness; rather it provides for the integration of parts with different and even conflicting features into a greater whole. Maoris have a familiar model for this conception of unity in their traditional socio-political order, in which competing *whānau* united in one *hapū* vis-à-vis other *hapū*, and competing *hapū* in one tribe vis-à-vis other tribes. Both Winiata and Kernot have suggested that disputes and factionalism are not breaches but the very stuff of Maori community life (Winiata, 1967; Kernot, 1972).

71

Closely related to this conception of one-ness, with its emphasis on the interrelatedness of all sectors of social life, is a dislike of compartmentalization and over-strict differentiation of roles. Maoris commonly carry the concerns and personal relations of one sector of life over into others. Workmates often spend their leisure time together, while relations at work are affected by relations in the outside community, especially between senior and junior kinsmen. A person is one, they say, whether at work or play; in particular, a Maori is a Maori all the time. This attitude is often a point of contention with Pakehas, who make more clear-cut distinctions, for instance between work and private life, and expect Maoris to confine their Maoriness to the latter.

## Concrete and abstract

I should like to conclude this chapter with a reference to the way Maoris use the concrete (words, objects, actions) to signify and express abstract ideas. I have not included this under the heading of Maoritanga because all human groups use this procedure extensively, including Pakehas. Whether Maoris use it with greater frequency and skill is a matter of debate and beyond objective proof.

From early in the history of contact, Pakehas have been given to comment that Maoris express themselves in physical and concrete ways rather than abstractly. In confirmation, it is alleged that the Maori language lacks abstract words. These judgments are based on misunderstandings on the Pakeha side. In the first place, the Maori language may lack words to translate certain abstract concepts of importance in English, but it does have a considerable store of abstract words, for many of which English has no equivalent, as we have seen in this chapter. Secondly, Maoris make frequent and effective use of concrete forms of expression to signify and convey abstract ideas, often of great richness and complexity. Now this is a practice, as already indicated, with which Pakehas are perfectly familiar. Yet they frequently fail to appreciate what Maoris are doing.

The reason lies partly in unfamiliarity with the Maori system of meanings, and partly in the fact that Pakehas take the symbolic use of the concrete so much for granted in their own language and culture that they do not realize its importance. Outside their own set of symbolic connections Pakehas often presume that the meaning a word, object or action has for them is all the meaning it has. This is a great pity, because when Pakehas take what Maoris say and do at face value, they are missing half the meaning – and the fun.

In proverbs and in everyday conversation, Maoris make apparently factual observations about natural and man-made phenomena which are really shrewd and illuminating comments about human affairs: examples occur on pp. 267–8. They simply cannot see the meeting-house purely as a concrete object. For them it is symbolically the body of an ancestor which also stands for and calls to mind the descent-group that bears his name, its members living and dead, the *aroha* that binds them together and insures against need and loneliness, the territory that they once owned, of which the *marae* is the symbol and perhaps all that remains, the events that happened on that territory, the warmth and bustle of gatherings at the *marae*, the group's present doings and future hopes, its *mana* in Maori and in Pakeha eyes. . . . When Maoris say that their *marae* is a 'standing-place for our feet' (*tūrangawaewae*), they do *not* mean it literally, or not *only* literally. In the Maori welcome ceremonial referred to above, the gradual physical *rapprochement* of the two groups serves both to achieve and to express a gradual reduction of tension and defensiveness and increase in friendliness. For Maoris, physical contact – whether by handshake and *hongi,* by the comforting arm around the shoulders or in the football scrum – underlines the Maori commitment to unity and togetherness, and expresses belief in the brotherhood of man as well as, if not better than, abstract verbalizing.

As final illustration of the way Maoris see the concrete and the abstract as going together and completing each other, here is a poem from the pen of the young Maori writer, Arapera Hineira, in which she states her personal and essentially Maori philosophy of life by using the image of the *kūmara* (sweet potato) vine, which extends itself by putting down suckers that turn into roots.

*Expression of an inward self
with a lino cut*

I build something up,
complicated and complex,
I hope,
but alas!
nothing so deep emerges.
Only simple lines –
hacked out of a piece
of worn out lino –
that curve and dip
to a traditional line
almost moronic
in their upward
outward bend to the left
to the right.

What the hell!
Why should I lie
to myself?
I am what I am
carved out of a long line
of heavy-footed deep-rooted
simplicity,
wanting to love well,
eat well, die with the thought of
kumara vine stretched out
reproducing an image –
many images of itself,
its hope
drenched in warmth
with roots forever seeking
the sun.

# chapter 6

# The bases of daily living

This chapter deals with certain basic issues that lend themselves to statistical measurement and analysis: population size, increase and distribution, employment, income, living conditions and health standards. It will make use of census data on these topics. Now statistics are an invaluable aid in charting the general features of a subject and identifying issues for further investigation and explanation. But it should always be remembered that their message is *not* self-evident and requires careful interpretation; and even when handled well, they can tell no more than part of the story. In this and other chapters statistics are used to provide a basis for discussion, never the last word. There are many dimensions to human life that are not amenable to measurement.

## The demographic background

For nearly fifty years, the Maori population has been increasing faster than the rest of the New Zealand population, despite the fact that it gains no members and actually loses some (319 in 1971) by migration. The Maori rate of natural increase was 30·3 per 1,000 in 1971, that of the rest of the population 12·0. As a result, Maoris have also increased as a proportion of the total population, from 4·5 per cent in 1926 to 7·9 per cent in 1971 (Table 1).

This rate of increase is due to a high birth-rate combined with a low death-rate. From 1940 to 1964 the Maori birth-rate stood at over 40 per 1,000. Since then it has declined slightly, but at 36·5 per 1,000 in 1971 is still well above the non-Maori rate (21·3 per 1,000). The main reasons for this high birth-rate are a high proportion of women of child-bearing age, especially between sixteen and twenty-nine, a pattern of early marriage, and only recent development of interest in family planning. The overall Maori death-rate, which was formerly very high, has also declined steadily since 1940, until it is actually lower than the non-Maori rate (6·2 compared with 8·5 per 1,000). However, when calculated by age-groups the Maori rate is consistently above the non-Maori rate. In 1965–67 the life expectancy at birth was 61·4 years for Maori males and 64·5 for Maori females, compared with 68·7 and 74·8 years for non-Maori males and females respectively (Statistics, New Zealand Department of, 1974: 84–100).

Table 1    Changes in Maori Population 1857–1971 (selected Censuses only)

| Census | Maori population | % of total population | Average annual increase since previous Census |
|---|---|---|---|
| 1857–8 | 56,049 | 48·6 | — |
| 1874 | 47,330 | 13·7 | — |
| 1881 | 46,141 | 8·6 | — |
| 1896 | 42,113 | 5·7 | — |
| 1901 | 45,549 | 5·6 | 1·6 |
| 1921 | 56,987 | 4·5 | 1·6 |
| 1926 | 63,670 | 4·5 | 2·2 |
| 1936 | 82,326 | 5·2 | 2·6 |
| 1945 | 98,744 | 5·8 | 1·9 |
| 1951 | 115,676 | 6·0 | 2·9 |
| 1956 | 137,151 | 6·3 | 3·5 |
| 1961 | 167,086 | 6·9 | 4·0 |
| 1966 | 201,159 | 7·5 | 3·8 |
| 1971 | 227,414 | 7·9 | 2·5 |

Table 2    Age Distribution 1971

| | Maoris % | Non-Maoris % |
|---|---|---|
| Under 15 years | 49·1 | 30·3 |
| 15–19 | 10·5 | 9·0 |
| 20–24 | 8·1 | 8·2 |
| 25–34 | 12·3 | 12·4 |
| 35–44 | 9·2 | 11·1 |
| 45–54 | 5·6 | 10·9 |
| 55–64 | 3·3 | 9·0 |
| Over 65 | 1·9 | 9·1 |
| Total: | 100·0 | 100·0 |
| Total population: | 227,414 | 2,635,217 |

Mainly because of the high rate of natural increase, the Maori population is heavily weighted in the younger age-groups. In 1971 59·6 per cent were under twenty, but only 5·2 per cent were over fifty-five, compared with 39·3 and 18·1 per cent for the rest of the population (Table 2).

The youthfulness of the Maori population makes it likely that its rate of increase will remain high for a long time. It has been officially estimated that Maoris will number 450,000 in 1990 and make up 11 to 12 per cent of the population (*New Zealand Maori Population and Labour Force Projections 1970–1990*: 6–9). The rate of Maori increase could fall, however, if there is any increase in the average age of marriage, family limitation or intermarriage with Pakehas.

*Distribution and migration*

The distribution of the Maori population differs from that of the non-Maori population in several ways. Firstly, Maoris are overwhelmingly concentrated in the northern half of the North Island: 70 per cent north of Taumarunui, Taupo and Wairoa in 1971, compared with 42 per cent of the non-Maoris. Secondly, comparatively large numbers of Maoris live in areas where there are not many Pakehas, notably in the Far North, the eastern Bay of Plenty and the East Coast. Thirdly, they are less extensively urbanized, nearly a third living in rural areas compared with a fifth of the rest of the population. Finally, the Maori urban population[1] shows a high degree of concentration in a few centres: nearly half in the Urban Areas of Auckland (45,777 Maoris in 1971) and Wellington (25,558), and another quarter in Rotorua (8,755), Hamilton (6,686), Gisborne (5,780), Hastings (5,167), Tauranga (4,463), Christchurch (4,440) and Whangarei (4,427) (*New Zealand Census of Population and Dwellings 1971*; Tables 3 and 4; Figure 3).

Over the last thirty years, the Maori pattern of distribution has been radically altered by migration. Until about 1945, the most important regions of Maori settlement were Northland, the East Coast, the Bay of Plenty, the Waikato-King Country and Rotorua-Taupo, in that order; and over 80 per cent of the Maori population lived in the country. Since then, however, Maoris have moved in increasing numbers out of the remote predominantly Maori areas into those that offer better economic opportunities. As a result, Northland and the East Coast have long since become reservoir areas: both currently lose all their natural increase by emigration. Between 1966 and 1971 the Maori population of the eastern Bay of Plenty also decreased, while that of the Waikato-King Country barely maintained itself. In contrast the number of Maoris living in the Auckland region increased at a phenomenal rate, displacing Northland as the premier

[1] In this book the term 'urban areas' is reserved for centres of over 2,000 inhabitants identified in the Census as either Urban Areas or Boroughs. 'Urban Area' is a technical term used in the Census for particularly large urban areas usually comprising more than one administrative unit. 'Urban population' refers to persons living in 'urban areas' so defined.

Table 3    Population Distribution by Regions 1966 and 1971

| Regions | 1966 Maoris % | 1971 Maoris Nos | 1971 Maoris % | 1971 Non-Maoris % |
|---|---|---|---|---|
| Northland | 10·86 | 21,065 | 9·26 | 3·18 |
| Auckland | 19·29 | 50,265 | 22·10 | 24·18 |
| Waikato – King Country | 11·30 | 23,074 | 10·15 | 5·66 |
| Coromandel – Hauraki | 3·79 | 8,632 | 3·80 | 2·95 |
| Bay of Plenty | 10·65 | 21,075 | 9·27 | 2·86 |
| Rotorua – Taupo | 7·47 | 17,725 | 7·80 | 2·10 |
| East Coast – Wairoa | 9·12 | 17,814 | 7·83 | 1·45 |
| Hawke's Bay – Wairarapa | 6·76 | 16,261 | 7·15 | 5·80 |
| Taranaki – Wanganui | 5·54 | 11,674 | 5·13 | 5·06 |
| Manawatu | 4·41 | 9,827 | 4·32 | 4·79 |
| Wellington | 5·48 | 16,060 | 7·06 | 11·57 |
| South Island | 5·29 | 13,837 | 6·08 | 30·26 |
| Other | 0·04 | 105 | 0·05 | 0·14 |
| | 100·0 | 227,414 | 100·0 | 100·0 |

Table 4    Urban-Rural Distribution 1966 and 1971

| | 1966 Maoris % | 1971 Maoris Nos | 1971 Maoris % | 1971 Non-Maoris % |
|---|---|---|---|---|
| Urban Areas | 43·6 | 125,216 | 55·1 | 68·5 |
| Boroughs over 2,000 not included in Urban Areas | 12·2 | 29,891 | 13·1 | 10·4 |
| Total urban areas | 55·8 | 155,107 | 68·2 | 78·9 |
| Rural areas | 44·2 | 72,307 | 31·8 | 21·1 |
| Grand total | 100·0 | 227,414 | 100·0 | 100·0 |

area of Maori concentration in 1956 and almost doubling itself between 1961 and 1971. The Maori population in the Wellington region also increased significantly in these ten years, and the proportion of Maoris living in the South Island rose from 3·8 per cent in 1956 to 6·1 per cent in 1971.

Above all, both within and between regions, Maoris have been moving from the country to the city. In 1961 barely 40 per cent of the Maori population lived in urban areas: in the space of ten years the proportion rose to 68 per cent. Moreover, almost half of the Maori urban population is concentrated in the two largest cities in New Zealand, neither of them particularly close to traditional areas of Maori settlement. In any discussion of contemporary Maori life, this recent, rapid urban movement must always be taken into account.

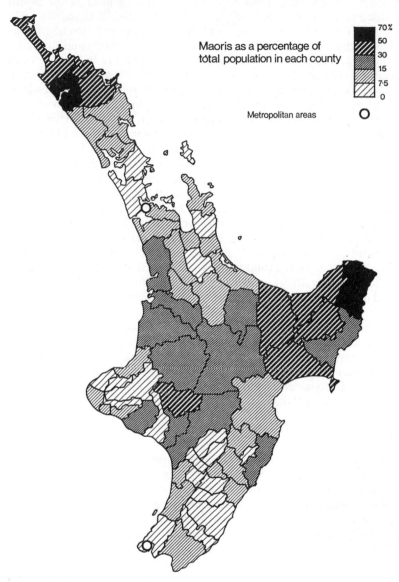

Maoris as a percentage of
total population in each county

70%
50
30
15
7·5
0

Metropolitan areas    O

*Figure 3    Maoris and Pakehas: relative distribution in rural areas 1971*

Because of the differences in their distribution, the ratio of Maoris to non-Maoris varies from less than 1:100 over most of the South Island to more than 100:100 in parts of the North Island. In 1971 Maoris made up at least one-third of the rural population of the Far North, the East Coast-Wairoa, the eastern Bay of Plenty and Rotorua-Taupo, actually outnumbering non-Maoris by 2:1 in Waiapu County (East Coast) and by 11:10 in the counties of Hokianga (Far North), Opotiki (Bay of Plenty) and Wairoa. In urban areas Maori representation rises well above its average for the total population in towns close to areas of Maori rural concentration. In 1971 Maoris made up 22 per cent of the population in Rotorua, 19 per cent in Gisborne, 13 per cent in Whangarei and 11 per cent in Hastings and Tauranga. In the timber milling town of Murupara (Bay of Plenty) they constituted 60 per cent of the population of 2,760. They also made up between 25 and 40 per cent of the population of Ngaruawahia, Kawerau, Opotiki and Wairoa Boroughs, and between 15 and 25 per cent in seven others. In contrast, Maori representation is less than 3 per cent in all South Island centres and less than 7 per cent in a third of all North Island ones. In Auckland, despite their numbers Maoris form only 7 per cent of the total population, and in Wellington 9 per cent. Predominantly Maori communities occasionally occur in both country and urban areas which otherwise have comparatively few Maoris.

In rural areas the pattern of Maori settlement is mainly dispersed. Most families live on their land, even when not farming. Fully nucleated Maori villages (commonly called *pā*) occur occasionally where there is employment within commuting distance, mainly in Rotorua and Hawke's Bay. A few have been swallowed up in the spread of urban settlement. In general, however, urban Maoris live scattered among Pakehas.

**Earning a living**

Maoris over fifteen years are directly employed in the New Zealand labour force to an extent entirely comparable with the rest of the population (85·7 per cent of Maori males compared with 81·2 per cent of non-Maori males in 1971, and 36·2 per cent of Maori females compared with 33·8 per cent of non-Maori females). The slightly higher percentages are probably due to a smaller proportion of Maoris over sixty-five and retired and a tendency to leave school earlier. Because of the high proportion of Maoris under fifteen, however, workers make up a much smaller proportion of the Maori population (31·2 per cent) than of the non-Maori one (39·8 per cent), with obvious implications for per capita income.

Employers and persons working on their own account figure less

**5** Learning from the *kaumātua*: Paora Kingi Delamere, president of the Ringatū Church, passes on his knowledge to the younger generation at the Maori Artists and Writers Conference, Te Kaha *marae*, June 1973

**6** Members of Ngā Tamatoa by the tent 'embassy' they set up in Parliament grounds before the 1972 elections

prominently in the Maori labour force than in the non-Maori one, while the proportion of wage and salary earners is substantially higher for Maori males and lower for Maori females. In recent years, as family farms and businesses have given way to larger concerns, the proportion of employers and self-employed persons has fallen for both Maoris and non-Maoris, though rather faster for Maoris. The proportion of Maoris who are unemployed is also high in comparison with non-Maori workers (Table 5).

Table 5   Occupational Status 1971

|  | Maoris % | | Non-Maoris % | |
|---|---|---|---|---|
|  | male | female | male | female |
| Persons actively engaged in the labour force as: | | | | |
| Employer | 1·8 | 0·6 | 8·0 | 2·5 |
| Working on own account | 3·0 | 0·7 | 8·3 | 3·2 |
| Wages or salary earner | 91·0 | 88·7 | 82·4 | 92·2 |
| Unemployed | 3·5 | 9·2 | 1·0 | 1·8 |
| Relative assisting without payment | 0·1 | 0·2 | 0·0 | 0·1 |
| Not specified | 0·6 | 0·6 | 0·3 | 0·2 |
|  | 100·0 | 100·0 | 100·0 | 100·0 |
| Total persons actively engaged in the labour force | 50,105 | 20,793 | 734,868 | 313,073 |

The participation of Maori workers in primary production, once their mainstay, has been declining for many years. In 1971 such employment accounted for 13·3 per cent of all Maori workers, only slightly above the non-Maori rate (11·5 per cent). An exceptionally high proportion of Maori workers (44·9 per cent compared with 30·8 per cent of non-Maori workers in 1971) were employed in secondary production as craftsmen, production process and related workers. Maoris were also over-represented in comparison with non-Maoris in transport and communications, and to a lesser extent in service occupations and the Armed Forces. But they were dramatically under-represented in professional and technical occupations, in management and administration, and in clerical and sales work (Table 6).

Maoris are to be found in almost every occupation available in New Zealand, including some highly specialized ones as jurists, physical scientists, and ship's officers, and some requiring abilities Maoris are popularly supposed to lack, as for instance accountants and commercial travellers. A number of Maoris have reached positions of

The bases of daily living

Table 6    Occupations 1971

| | Persons actively engaged in labour force | |
| | Maoris % | Non-Maoris % |
| --- | --- | --- |
| Workers in: | | |
| Primary production (farming, fishing, hunting, forestry) | 13·3 | 11·5 |
| Secondary production | 44·9 | 30·8 |
| Transport | 7·7 | 3·5 |
| Labourers not elsewhere classified | 7·4 | 2·1 |
| Service, sport and recreation | 8·1 | 6·8 |
| Sales | 2·1 | 10·9 |
| Clerical work | 6·4 | 16·8 |
| Administration and management | 0·2 | 2·7 |
| Professions and technical work | 3·8 | 13·0 |
| Armed Forces | 1·5 | 1·0 |
| New workers seeking employment | 2·1 | 0·2 |
| Occupations inadequately described or not reported | 2·6 | 0·7 |
| | 100·0 | 100·0 |
| Total persons actively engaged in force | 70,898 | 1,047,937 |

national prominence in the very occupations in which they are under-represented: for instance, three Maoris hold the rank of full Professor in New Zealand universities, in Anthropology, Maori Language and Business Administration, and others occupy positions as Moderator of the Methodist Church of New Zealand, diocesan Bishop and Archdeacon in the Anglican Church, Superintendent of a major psychiatric hospital, and Assistant-Director General (Social Work) of the Department of Social Welfare.

It is often asserted that Maoris are concentrated to a much greater extent than non-Maoris in unskilled and semi-skilled jobs. The statistical evidence which could check and give precision to this general impression is unfortunately incomplete and out-of-date. There would seem little doubt that Maoris are over-represented as labourers and drivers: they comprised 16 per cent of all general labourers and 11·4 per cent of all drivers in 1971, though only 6·3 per cent of the labour force. The position is less clear with regard to other occupations because the Census gives only total figures for each trade grouping, without distinguishing between fully qualified tradesmen and less skilled workers. Evidence from other sources suggests substantial increase in the proportion of Maoris becoming qualified tradesmen in (for instance) the building trades, partly through assistance provided by the Government.

82

Since 1959 the Department of Maori Affairs and the Technical Institutes in four cities (Auckland, Wellington, Christchurch and Hamilton) have co-operated in the provision of trade-training and other employment courses for young Maoris. In the trade training schemes trainees receive intensive instruction as a group for one or two years and are then placed with employers for another three or four years to complete their apprenticeships. In 1973 eighteen courses were provided in twelve trades: carpentry, plumbing, electrical wiring, painting and decorating, plastering, bricklaying, motor mechanics, diesel mechanics, panel beating, automotive electrical work, sheet metal work, and fitting and turning. Up to 1972 2,143 boys had been taken into training in these schemes, and of these 802 had completed their apprenticeships, 683 were in the process of doing so, and 380 were taking the training courses. There was a drop-out rate of 7 per cent during apprenticeship training with private employers. These training schemes have been notably successful, with trainees obtaining above average results in trade examinations and several winning national awards. In 1973 trainees had an overall pass rate of 80 per cent compared with 70 per cent for all apprentices, while the pass rate was 90 to 100 per cent for trainees in particular courses.

With the help of these trade training schemes, Maori representation in the apprenticeship trades has been greatly increased and distributed over a wider range. In 1972 Maoris enrolled in the initial courses (380) and registered as apprentices with private employers (1,489) together accounted for 7 per cent of the total number of apprentices. Maoris were represented to some extent in over thirty different trades and at well above their average proportion in eight, making up 11 per cent of all apprentices in carpentry and plumbing, 13 per cent in panel beating and sheet metal work, 20 per cent in bricklaying, 21 per cent in painting and decorating and 38 per cent in plastering.

Besides trade training, the Government also sponsors vocational training courses in shorthand-typing (twelve girls in 1973), farming (five boys annually since 1965) and carving (eight boys in 1970 and 1971 and twelve since 1972), and pre-employment courses run in conjunction with the Technical Institutes. The latter are mainly residential courses for young Maoris from the country, who are given an intensive introduction to city life and helped to settle into jobs with good prospects. By 1973 1,380 boys and girls had passed through these courses, the annual intake rising from 60 in 1966 to over 200. In 1972 a rather different course was designed for young urban Polynesians, which aims to help recent school-leavers improve their qualifications in order to obtain better jobs. By the end of 1973, 130 young people had entered eleven courses of this type in Wellington.

The over-representation of Maoris in 'blue-collar' occupations and in the unskilled and semi-skilled sectors of industry have a number of interacting causes. Maoris living in rural areas have limited opportunities to acquire qualifications for or knowledge of the range of occupations available in the cities. When they migrate they tend to find jobs through friends and relatives and so mainly in the same or similar sectors. Even in the cities an unduly high proportion of Maoris leave school without the qualifications for entry into skilled trades and 'white-collar' occupations. High starting wages and overtime make unskilled and semi-skilled jobs attractive to wage-earners with many dependants.

Maori workers sometimes have to contend with discrimination on the part of employers. This varies from one occupation, employer and area to another. It is usually not openly acknowledged but emerges indirectly in hiring, firing and promotion practice. When pressed, employers deny colour prejudice or racism as such and justify reluctance to employ or promote Maoris on the grounds that they are unpunctual, prone to absenteeism and do not stay long in one job. A valuable piece of research on work patterns among bus drivers has shown that these widespread views about Maoris as workers are impressionistic and do not hold when Maoris are matched with other workers of comparable status (Pierce, 1967). Since 1945 Vocational Guidance and Maori Welfare Officers have successfully opened up fields of employment once closed to Maoris, including banks and insurance firms, by persuading employers to try selected Maoris with good qualifications. Discrimination sometimes operates to the advantage of the Maoris. Many employers prefer them for jobs requiring dexterity or ability to relax under stress, especially as drivers and telephone operators. Such jobs are however mostly semi-skilled.

Maoris generally have certain attitudes and preferences regarding work that stem partly from tribal, partly from rural experience, and beyond these from deeper values of Maoritanga. Most have a strong preference for active, physical work, especially while young, plenty of variation in tasks, and alternation between intense effort and relaxation (Firth, 1959: 176–203). They also like work with human interest, especially that involving group work and/or service to the public. They appreciate freedom to plan the details of work organization and help recruit colleagues. Maori men in particular enjoy a challenge and a spice of danger. And they commonly value opportunities for individual advancement less than opportunities to be part of a group on the job and to contribute handsomely to kin and community causes (see Ritchie's essay 'Workers', in Schwimmer, 1968; also Ritchie, 1963, chapter 6).

Maori-speaking Maoris give the word *mahi* as the translation of the English 'work', but investigation of how they use *mahi* suggests that the correspondence is far from exact. Pakehas tend to define 'work' primarily as work done for payment, contrasting it with 'play'. Thus housewives and students are explicitly excluded from the labour force, and building or painting your own house at weekends is 'relaxation'. Maoris contrast *mahi* on the one hand with *kōrero* ('talking', especially formal speech-making), and on the other with *māngere* (lazy). The primary meaning of *mahi* is thus not paid employment but 'activity', expenditure of energy in bodily movement. It does not however mean *only* this – *mahi* often involves a high degree of planning, decision-making and skill, as in fishing or wool grading. *Mahi* is expected of and valued in those who are young and in the prime of life; inactivity is frowned upon as laziness. Sitting around talking is appropriate behaviour for the elderly, whose physical strength is waning. A much used proverb to this effect is quoted on p. 268. This valuing of *mahi* by all age groups is undoubtedly a factor in job preferences and also in the tendency to leave school early. A Maori university student told me that when he meets old schoolmates round town they invariably say: 'What, still at school? When are you going to work?' The emphasis, however is on being active and useful, not on being in paid employment nor in a steady job. For most Maoris there is no social stigma attached to frequent job changes or short spells of unemployment, especially if they are spent helping relatives on farms, hunting or working at the *marae*. By such changes many Maori workers build up an impressive range of skills in both rural and urban employment.

*Ngā kai-mahi* can be rendered literally into English as 'the workers', but it does not have quite the same connotations. In the first place, it is used primarily in a *marae* situation, for those who undertake the practical tasks, like making the *hāngi* and peeling vegetables, in contrast to the *kai-kōrero*, the formal speech-makers. Secondly, in their own setting Maoris do not make any clear-cut distinction between the main body of workers and those who direct their activities. As in the past, they expect their leaders to emerge from within the group, sharing the same training and experience as those they direct, knowing how to do all the tasks required, and able to do them better. Those 'in charge' are *kai-mahi-rangatira*, leading workers, not an entirely different category. This goes a long way to explain Maori attitudes to foremen and managers: hostile to those who stress their special training and superior status, co-operative to those who can demonstrate practical knowledge of the job.

Maoris often hesitate to move into a new occupation, firm or work situation where they would be isolated among Pakehas. They sometimes turn down the opportunities for special training or promotion if it would lead to being set above or in authority over Maori relatives and friends. This is particularly true in country areas, where relations at work are often carried over into community life and vice versa.

Although many of the Maori values regarding work are at odds with older forms of industrial management, they stress features that are being increasingly recognized as significant in industrial relations. Having chosen jobs in the first place because they give room for manoeuvre, Maoris (and other Polynesians) typically modify their working set-up whenever and as much as possible in order to maximize attractive features, such as opportunity for social interaction and interdependence on the job or during breaks. Where management and supervisory staff are sympathetic to these adjustments they find that work performance does not slip but is enhanced. Despite Pakeha belief that Maori values are an obstacle to business success, there are several highly successful enterprises which are primarily Maori in orientation as well as staffing, not merely tolerating but actively incorporating Maori values and principles of organization. Owned or managed by Maoris or by Pakehas with a deep understanding of Maoris, these enterprises are located mainly in the clothing industry and in the smaller urban centres. Typically work units are small enough for the development of close personal interaction: expansion is handled by the budding-off of new units. Workers are frequently kinsmen not only of each other but also of executives and supervisors, and they may also be shareholders themselves. The organization of working hours is governed by agreement rather than order or the time clock, and workers share the responsibility of recruitment, discipline and counselling, so that staff advertisements and personnel officers are unnecessary. The barriers between the work situation and the outside world are relaxed. Workers carry on their association outside working hours in social clubs and sports teams, and the factory is open to visits from relatives and elders. The keynote in these enterprises is flexibility, reflected in continuing adaptation, innovation and development in the work handled, forms of organization and goals. They have not merely survived but have moved forward in many ways.

## Incomes

In view of the changing value of money, trying to interpret census data on incomes is fraught with problems: only the most general outlines can be discerned. According to the 1971 Census, Maoris in the labour force were concentrated in the lower- and lower-middle income brackets in higher proportions than non-Maoris and substantially under-represented in the rest of the range. This pattern showed little change from 1966. It could be accounted for partly by the higher proportion of Maoris in the younger age-groups and in rural areas, and partly by concentration in unskilled and semi-skilled occupations, especially those with seasonal patterns of employment and a higher rate of unemployment.

In the country, most Maori families supplement their cash income with a non-cash increment from the land. Many live rent-free on land in which they have shares, keeping hens, pigs and perhaps a cow, and cultivating *kūmara* and other vegetables. Firewood, wild pig and fowl may be obtained from unutilized land. Wherever they live, in town or country, Maoris make expeditions to gather sow thistle and watercress and to sea, lake or river to fish, catch eels and crayfish, and gather shellfish and sea-eggs.

On the other hand, the real family income is frequently reduced by large families and lack of budgeting experience. Like their forebears, modern Maoris place a high value on generosity and sharing. They pride themselves on 'not counting the cost' nor 'making a god of money' and distrust the thrifty as 'mean' and 'selfish'. Consequently they do not find it easy to resist pressures to spend cash on immediate consumption.

Because of their special difficulties, the Government has for many years provided special access to finance for housing and land development for Maori families. In the late fifties and sixties, acting largely

Table 7    Incomes 1971

| $ NZ | Persons actively engaged in the labour force (specified incomes only) | |
|---|---|---|
| | Maoris % | Non-Maoris % |
| 0– 599 | 11·5 | 5·7 |
| 600–1,399 | 13·9 | 11·7 |
| 1,400–2,199 | 22·0 | 17·9 |
| 2,200–2,999 | 28·5 | 23·0 |
| 3,000–3,999 | 16·5 | 20·6 |
| 4,000–5,999 | 6·4 | 14·6 |
| 6,000–7,999 | 0·7 | 3·4 |
| 8,000–9,999 | 0·3 | 1·4 |
| 10,000 and over | 0·2 | 1·1 |
| | 100·0 | 100·0 |
| Total persons actively engaged in the labour force (specified incomes) | 67,174 | 1,031,315 |

on their own initiative, Maoris established small local Investment Societies and Credit Unions which have quietly played their part in improving the financial situation of many families. A budgetary advisory scheme begun by a Maori doctor in Kaikohe in 1956 with the support of local citizens has developed into a national movement serviced by the Department of Maori Affairs.

## Housing

Like other New Zealanders, Maoris live mainly in single-storied homes of wood, brick or concrete situated on 'sections' of a fifth of an acre (more or less). Until the middle sixties, the supply and standard of Maori housing gave cause for serious concern, with a much higher proportion of temporary and sub-standard dwellings, more occupants in fewer rooms, and limited amenities. The Government has provided special housing assistance for Maoris from 1936 by the allocation of State rental houses and by granting housing loans through the Department of Maori Affairs, which also arranges the building, but for a long time the Maori housing situation seemed to be getting worse rather than better. The Hunn Report estimated that in 1960 there was a backlog of 6,400 houses and an accruing annual demand of 800 to 1,000. The Government intensified its housing campaign, providing another 12,000 houses by 1969 through the Department of Maori Affairs and the State Advances Corporation. At the same time increasing numbers of Maoris were able to tap other sources of finance. The Census shows that by 1971 the gap between Maori and non-Maori housing standards had been reduced to almost minor proportions (Tables 8, 9 and 10). Between 1961 and 1971, the proportion of Maori-occupied dwellings classed as temporary fell to the same level as for non-Maoris, and 'huts, whares and baches' dropped from 7 per cent of Maori-occupied dwellings to 1·3 per cent. The number of Maoris per house dropped from 6·8 to 5·5, though remaining higher than the non-Maori figure of 3·4 persons per dwelling. Though the proportion of Maori dwellings equipped with various amenities consistently fell below that for non-Maoris in 1971, in most cases the discrepancy was less than 10 per cent. The major difference lies in the realm of home ownership. Between 1961 and 1971 the proportion of Maori-occupied dwellings being bought on mortgage increased to within 7 per cent of the corresponding non-Maori rate, but the proportion of houses owned without mortgage fell, while the proportion rented increased to over 40 per cent. This pattern clearly reflected the urban migration and the recency of most home loans, and might be expected to continue for some time.

The majority of new houses built for Maoris are in urban areas.

Table 8    Types of Dwellings 1971

|  | Dwellings occupied by | |
|  | Maoris<br>% | Non-Maoris<br>% |
| --- | --- | --- |
| Private house and private house partly sublet | 86·5 | 84·8 |
| Flat | 11·9 | 13·1 |
| Combined shop and dwelling | 0·2 | 0·6 |
| Huts, whares, baches etc. | 1·3 | 0·5 |
| Permanent private dwellings | 99·9 | 98·9 |
| Temporary private dwellings | 0·1 | 0·1 |
| Non-private dwellings* | — | 0·9 |
|  | 100·0 | 100·0 |
| Total inhabited dwellings | 41,720 | 768,117 |

* Non-private dwellings were not classified as occupied by Maoris or non-Maoris and are all included under the latter.

Table 9    Tenure of Dwellings 1971

|  | Dwellings occupied by | |
|  | Maoris<br>% | Non-Maoris<br>% |
| --- | --- | --- |
| Renting | 42·8 | 25·0 |
| Free dwelling with job | 7·1 | 4·2 |
| Loaned without payment | 3·5 | 1·6 |
| Buying with table mortgage | 30·5 | 31·1 |
| Buying with flat mortgage | 3·9 | 10·7 |
| Owned without mortgage | 12·3 | 27·5 |
|  | 100·0 | 100·0 |
| Total permanent private dwellings tenure specified | 42,210 | 755,216 |

Building in the country has been restricted by the Town and Country Planning Act which limits the size of subdivisions and by Government policy which in the past authorized loans only for houses where permanent employment was available. In recent years, however, several county councils have been persuaded to relax building restrictions or re-zone land to permit residential subdivision around *marae* and in established Maori settlements. Taking account of the wish of elderly Maoris to live on their own land, the Department of Maori Affairs has either built or financed flat units for the elderly in several semi-rural areas, and the eligibility of Maori Trust Boards to receive subsidies has been officially extended for that purpose. The Department introduced a new loan scheme for up-grading houses in rural areas in 1968 and is now prepared to approve loans for family houses in such areas in special cases.

In urban areas the Government favours interspersing Maori homes among Pakeha ones, a policy known as 'pepper-potting'. In some cases a fairly high local density of Maori-occupied houses has been approved either for historical reasons (as at Okahu Bay in Auckland and Waiwhetu in Wellington) or because of the shortage and high cost of sections. Urban Maoris debate the relative merits of 'pepper-potting' and concentration, and individuals have varying preferences.

Table 10   Household Amenities 1971

| Amenities not shared* | Permanent private dwellings occupied by | |
| --- | --- | --- |
| | Maoris % | Non-Maoris % |
| Hot water service | 96·6 | 99·5 |
| Flush toilet | 88·8 | 97·6 |
| Refrigerator | 91·3 | 96·7 |
| Electric washing machine | 83·1 | 92·0 |
| Telephone | 59·4 | 87·2 |
| Television | 82·0 | 84·9 |

* The number of shared amenities is very small in each case.

## Health

In health standards the discrepancies between the Maori and non-Maori populations have been materially reduced over the last twenty years but not entirely eliminated. Concern for this problem prompted the Health Department to undertake a special study, *Maori-European Standards of Health* (Rose, 1960), based on analysis of mortality statistics for 1954–8 and to follow it up with a second report, *Maori-European Comparisons of Mortality* (Rose, 1972), using in addition statistics for 1964–8 and 1969–70. Because age is an important variable in mortality and Maori and non-Maori age structures are markedly different, comparison of Maori and non-Maori mortality rates is no simple matter: they must either be 'adjusted for age' (by calculating what the Maori rate would be if the Maori population had the same sex and age composition as the non-Maori) and/or reckoned by age-groups.

The overall improvement in Maori health is indicated by the fact that the age-adjusted Maori mortality rate for all diseases fell from being 1·98 times higher than the non-Maori rate for 1954–8 to 1·68 times higher for 1964–8. When mortality rates were reckoned by age-groups, the Maori rates showed marked reductions for ages up to thirty-five years, with greatest progress in the youngest groups, from birth to a year, and from one to four years. Maori infant mortality, long a matter of particular concern, was halved between the two quinquennia, dropping from 59·4 per 1,000 live births in 1954–8 to 29·0 for 1964–8 and still further to 24·8 for 1969–70. This was still however higher than the non-Maori rate of 15·6 per 1,000 live births for 1969–70. Above the age of thirty-five years there was little significant change in the mortality rates of Maori males, but female rates fell slightly for every age-group from thirty-five to seventy-five.

Advances in communicable disease control had almost or entirely eliminated some diseases, for instance, diphtheria, typhoid and poliomyelitis, for both Maori and non-Maori by 1968. For nearly all other causes of death, Maori mortality rates were higher than non-Maori rates in 1964–8 and 1969–70. However, they have dropped dramatically from much higher levels in 1954–8 in the case of respiratory tuberculosis, influenza and pneumonia, infectious intestinal diseases, and deaths associated with maternity, and they have decreased to a lesser extent in most other cases also. Rheumatic fever, a prime cause of heart disease in Maoris over twenty-four, was largely controlled under that age. Maori deaths from various forms of cancer were small in numbers but reckoned as age-specific rates they were consistently slightly higher for Maori males and markedly higher for Maori females than for non-Maoris, mainly because of delays in seeking treatment. Accidents and homicide figured as the cause of death twice as often for Maoris as for non-Maoris, but Maoris were much less prone to suicide.

A study of *Maori Patients in Mental Hospitals* published in 1962 by the Department of Health (Foster, 1962) indicated that the number of Maoris entering psychiatric hospitals was increasing, especially under forty years. Of those in hospital, a higher proportion of Maoris than non-Maoris were diagnosed as schizophrenic, manic or mentally deficient, but few were admitted for psychoneurosis or alcoholism. Later statistics, though less detailed, confirm a continuing increase in the proportion of Maori psychiatric patients. How much this increase is due to increase in the actual incidence of mental illness among Maoris and how much to increased willingness to seek professional help or decreased community tolerance, and why such changes have occurred, are questions which require detailed investigation. With regard to diagnosis, there is also the possibility of misunderstanding due to cultural differences. Behaviour diagnosed as fitting certain clinical syndromes could possibly have another meaning in a Maori context. The doctors and staff of psychiatric hospitals are predominantly Pakeha though there are several outstanding Maori psychiatrists and in some areas a significant proportion of Maori nurses.

Since the early sixties the Wellington Medical Research Unit has carried out intensive health surveys in selected Maori communities. The reports highlight the contribution of obesity to Maori health problems and indicate significant differences between rural and urban areas (Prior in Schwimmer, 1968: 270–87).

While research workers recognize that Maoris may inherit pre-dispositions to some diseases, such as diabetes and gout, higher Maori mortality rates are attributed mainly to environmental factors such as poor housing and sanitation, overcrowding, and residence in areas where medical services are thinly spread. Maori distrust of 'Pakeha' medical services has almost disappeared. There is every reason to expect that Maori health standards have gone on improving since 1970 and will continue to do so in the future.

### 'Maori sickness'

When the cause of an illness is not readily understood or medical treatment unsuccessful, Maoris frequently diagnose mate Maori ('Maori sickness') due to mystical causes and curable only by 'Maori' methods. The main causes of 'Maori sickness' are hara (wrong-doing, especially breach of tapu) and sorcery (mākutu). Often it involves both, a wrongdoer falling an easier prey to sorcery than the innocent.

Maoris are generally reluctant to talk about sorcery in detail, especially to Pakehas or strangers. They feel (on the one hand) that belief in it does not 'fit' either with Christian faith or a 'modern' approach to life and (on the other) that even talking about it can be dangerous.

In my experience, most Maoris hesitate to disavow belief in sorcery entirely: few cannot relate, among friends, some direct or indirect experience of it. But fear of sorcery is dormant most of the time, becoming dominant only under stress and in the face of the unaccountable. A diagnosis of sorcery usually involves attributing responsibility to some particular person, usually an elder or tohunga known to envy or have been offended by the victim. While they stress its power and the dangers of offending the powerful, stories of sorcery relieve as well as create fear, because they usually end in recovery. Once originator and cause are known, sorcery can be dealt with. If the victim has high mana, that alone will repulse the sorcery. Otherwise he may remove himself to a safe distance from the suspected sorceror, or consult either a Christian minister or a tohunga. Countered, sorcery recoils on the originator, whose illness or death is interpreted as proof of guilt. Belief in sorcery undoubtedly plays a part in mental illness among Maoris, particularly as a culturally phrased explanation.

*Tohunga*

The word *tohunga* is widely used by both Maoris and Pakehas to refer to a Maori who uses extra-ordinary knowledge and powers to diagnose, heal or inflict illness. However, Maoris, especially if Maori-speaking, also give the word wider meanings, using it to refer to an expert in esoteric knowledge, in which case it may be applied to a carver, a university professor or a theologian, and as a title for ministers of the Ringatū Church, only some of whom, the *tohunga takuta*, are healers.

The number of recognized *tohunga* (in the limited, popular sense of the word) is comparatively small, not more than two or three in most tribal areas, but their reputation travels the length of the land. Calling as a *tohunga* depends in the first place on possession of manifest prophetic and healing gifts. These may appear in anyone, but tend to run in families. Men and women so gifted usually receive some instruction from older practitioners, and then develop their own variations. Their doctrines and methods are partly of traditional origin, partly borrowed from Pakeha healers, and partly idiosyncratic. Most *tohunga* claim to heal by faith in a supreme God, though some employ spirits. Many are ministers of the Ringatū church (p. 186). While they use herbal and folk remedies (often of post-European development), *tohunga* are chiefly concerned with curing 'Maori sickness'. They are often accused of, but mostly deny, practising sorcery. In dealing with psychosomatic illnesses, *tohunga* are often highly effective, and doctors with experience of Maori patients send such cases to a *tohunga*. On their side, today's *tohunga* usually advise patients to see a doctor for purely medical conditions.

To Pakehas the word *tohunga* has connotations of paganism and/or charlatanry, and the *tohunga* is seen as opposed to the Christian minister. Maoris on the other hand see the two as closely related and by no means mutually exclusive. Both are experts in sacred knowledge and specialists in communication with the spiritual world. Maoris who suspect *mate Maori* from whatever cause will call in either a minister or a *tohunga* according to their preferences and contacts, and sometimes both. Most Maori ministers have been quietly handling these problems for years using methods common to both Christianity and Classic Maori religion: prayer, confession, exorcism, sprinkling with water, blessing and expiation. Such ministers regard the *tohunga* as colleagues and allies and may consult or pass cases on to them.

In the late nineteenth and early twentieth century, when the Maori population was at low ebb, *tohunga* were so numerous and, in the opinion of many, played upon the misery and fears of the Maori people so much that Maui Pomare as Officer for Maori Health persuaded Parliament to pass the Tohunga Suppression Act 1907. Few successful prosecutions were made under it, and in 1963 it was repealed on the grounds that it distinguished unnecessarily between Maori and Pakeha faith-healers. In the twenties Ratana regarded it as part of his God-directed mission to turn the Maori people away from belief in *tapu* and reliance on *tohunga*. Now that Maori health is so greatly improved and *tohunga* no longer keep Maoris away from medical care, it can be appreciated that they have a contribution to make. For the *tohunga* are not only the counterpart of Pakeha faith-healers and practitioners of folk-medicine, they are skilled psychologists and religious counsellors, with the advantage for Maoris that they speak Maori and share Maori beliefs and values.

# chapter 7

# Language

Language is both a part of culture and a vital expression of it. For Maoris the Maori language is one of the pillars (*pou*) of Maoritanga, but only a minority speak it as a mother tongue. Except for a few of the very old, virtually all Maoris speak English. Far from being an alien language, English has long since become an integral part of contemporary Maori culture, and considerably modified in the process. 'It is probably true to say that most Maoris today are bilingual, somewhere along the line between complete competence in both languages and total ignorance of one or the other' (Biggs in Schwimmer, 1968: 82).

## Maori

How many Maoris know Maori and how well? How often do they use it? Any definitive answer to these questions must await the outcome of the socio-linguistic survey of language use in Maori communities at present being conducted by the Maori Research Unit of the New Zealand Council for Educational Research. In the meantime, certain general points can be made.

First, it must be stressed that the situation is a very complex one, involving marked variations between rural areas and urban areas, between rural areas which have a substantial Maori population and those which do not, between urban areas close to Maori-speaking rural areas and those at a distance, and most of all between the generations.

There are many Maori communities where Maori is the primary language in most homes and the main means of communication among adults, notably the Ureweras, the eastern Bay of Plenty and the East Coast, the Waikato and King Country, northern Northland,

Taranaki and Wanganui. Even here however the children increasingly use English among themselves and Maori mainly to adults.

The proportion of Maoris who speak Maori decreases with age. 'Most (almost all) of the older Maoris I know speak Maori; more than half of the Maoris I know aged between thirty and forty speak Maori; less than half of the people under thirty with whom I am acquainted do so, and the proportion continues to drop with age' (ibid.: 767). Whereas in 1913 90 per cent of the Maori children attending Maori schools were reported to speak Maori, a survey of 277 Maoris entering secondary schools between 1953 and 1958 revealed that only 26 per cent spoke Maori.

Most Maoris know some Maori, if only a vocabulary of key words, and have heard it spoken around them often enough to have a feeling for its sounds and rhythms. Of the 277 secondary school entrants just referred to 62 per cent showed in tests that they had some understanding of spoken Maori. Given opportunity and motivation, Maoris with this past experience have a headstart in learning to speak it.

Even in urban areas, most Maori homes include some Maori-speaking members, often one or two for whom it is the mother-tongue.

I can best illustrate the complexity of the situation by reference to Kotare as I knew it between 1955 and 1958. I would estimate that Maori was used almost exclusively in 5 per cent of the Maori homes there, and English almost exclusively in 10 per cent; while in the remaining 85 per cent the language used and the standard of its use varied with the age of the speaker and person addressed. Those over fifty-five spoke Maori habitually to each other and most of the time to their middle-aged children, but mainly English to their grand-children. Those in the middle, parental generations, between about twenty-five and fifty-five, spoke mainly Maori to their parents, used Maori or English with spouses and peers according to subject, mood and fluency, and addressed their children mainly in English. Young adults and adolescents spoke mainly English among themselves and to younger siblings, but used Maori sometimes to parents and grand-parents. Pre-school and school children spoke mainly English. About half understood enough Maori to obey commands or answer intelligently in English, and another quarter could reply in simple Maori.

Whether they speak Maori themselves or not, most Maoris feel strongly that it is the right and proper language for all distinctively Maori formal occasions. At large-scale gatherings on the *marae* and in the home during *tomo* (marriage discussions) and welcomes to special visitors, the ceremonial greetings, speeches and songs are invariably in Maori. If Pakeha visitors are numerous or important, speakers may repeat their speeches in English or have them translated by an interpreter, but normally no allowance is made either for Maoris who do not speak Maori or for Pakeha spouses and friends. Maoris for whom Maori is their mother tongue also prefer to attend church services in Maori.

When Maoris meet together on less ceremonial occasions, the language used depends on the subject discussed and the fluency in Maori of those present. Meetings of family, *hapū* and *marae* committees, and the Maori Women's Welfare League are conducted mainly in Maori, especially in the country; sports and youth club meetings and large-scale conferences mainly in English. But usually some speakers use the other language, and some use both.

This decline in the use of Maori is closely associated with the history of the Maoris as a minority group. Working on the assumption that assimilation was in the best interests both of the Maoris and of New Zealand society, the educational authorities required English to be the language of instruction in schools for over a hundred years. Teachers were discouraged from learning Maori lest it interfere with their effectiveness in teaching English, and generations of Maori children were punished for speaking their mother-tongue in the school-room or grounds. Maori parents themselves generally supported this emphasis on English in the schools as the key to advancement for their children, especially where Maori flourished as the language of home and community (Barrington and Beaglehole, 1974). In some areas (e.g. Hawke's Bay and Manawatu), Maoris favoured English even in the home, the better to help the next generation deal with Pakehas on an equal footing. The effects of the devaluing of Maori in the schools were muted as long as the majority of Maoris lived in Maori-speaking communities, but when they moved out into close contact with Pakehas as neighbours and workmates especially in the cities, even highly motivated families found it difficult to maintain their use of Maori against majority pressures. The Department of Education officially stopped the punishing of children for speaking Maori at school in the early sixties, after strong representations from university lecturers in anthropology and education, but it continued for some time in practice.

Moves to give Maori a place in the education system began in the twenties, but they emphasized academic study at the higher levels. Maori was introduced as a subject at university level in 1925 and in the university entrance examination in 1929, made a compulsory subject in church secondary schools in the thirties and later in Maori district high schools, and made a school certificate subject in 1945. Until the late sixties however it was available only at secondary school level and in most schools, if at all, as one option among many.

Secondary school principals were generally reluctant to admit Maori to their timetables, the main arguments being a lack of qualified teachers, an (alleged) lack of Maori literature, and the greater usefulness of languages spoken overseas.

Other factors contributing to decreasing use of the Maori language have been the attraction of Maoris to new areas of experience, such as modern industry, for which the language did not have the vocabulary or the time to develop one, intermarriage (usually resulting in the use of English in the home), and the influence of the news media, which are overwhelmingly in English. In 1974 regular radio programmes in Maori were given a total of thirteen and a half hours a week all on the stations of the YA non-commercial network. This included three and a half hours of re-broadcasts of the Maori News (ten minutes weekly) and constitutes 0·4 per cent of the total broadcast time *on those stations*. There are no Maori programmes on the commercial network. On television no time is regularly devoted to Maori programmes, though snippets of Maori may be heard from time to time, mostly without warning. Radio and television in particular reach into the most remote country homes. The Director of the Maori Research Unit reports that in the Northland communities surveyed in 1973 a line can be drawn in Maori families between the children who speak Maori and those who speak only English, a line which coincides with the date of the coming of television in the area.

### The future of the Maori language

With such a drastic falling off in the proportion of children speaking Maori and diminishing use even among adults, can the Maori language survive?

As already pointed out with regard to Maoritanga generally, it is unwise to assume that the young will carry their attitudes and practice into the future unchanged. Maori children, adolescents and young adults speak mainly English, even when they hear Maori spoken in the home, because it is the language of their current occupations and interests: school, sport, films, radio and television. It seems more 'modern' and practical. Some children even deny understanding or speaking Maori, lest doing so brand them as 'hayseeds'. Often they have not had the opportunity to learn Maori because of living in a predominantly Pakeha environment with busy parents and restricted access to grandparents, traditionally the language teachers of Maori society. But as they grow older most Maoris become increasingly interested in Maori ways. First they develop an interest in *haka* and action-songs. Then as they marry and have children they spend more time with their parents and older kin and become involved in the running of family clubs and *hui*. Some seek to serve their people as welfare officers, teachers, wardens and ministers. Finding themselves shut out of full participation in Maori community life if they cannot speak Maori, they start learning or pick it up again. Visiting friends who spoke little Maori fifteen to twenty years ago, I now find them seizing opportunities to do so, and several have become proficient speech-makers in Maori.

Paradoxically, while marked by continuing decline in the proportion of children speaking Maori, the last ten years have also seen a remarkable upsurge of interest in Maori on the part of young Maori adults. This interest was dramatically expressed from the floor during the Young Maori Leadership Conference in Auckland in 1970, especially by members of the urban 'gangs' then in the limelight (p. 174). In 1971 the Maori youth movement, Ngā Tamatoa, obtained 30,000 signatures to a petition to Parliament seeking:

> That courses in Maori language and aspects of Maori culture be offered in ALL those schools with large Maori rolls and that these same courses be offered, as a gift to the Pakeha from the Maori, in ALL other New Zealand schools as a positive effort to promote a more meaningful concept of Integration.

Supported by Maori bodies and university staff, the petition received a favourable recommendation from the Select Committee which considered it and a promise of implementation from the Minister. In 1971 also Maori students at Victoria University of Wellington formed Te Reo Maori Society specifically to foster knowledge and teaching of the Maori language. Besides conducting weekly language sessions on the campus, members of Te Reo Maori have helped schools in the area with visits and advice, and at the end of 1974 presented the National Film Library forty tapes of Maori language and literature materials prepared with the help of the Department of Anthropology and Maori and financed from the Government Education Department. Maori youth groups acting in concert initiated a National Maori Language Day on 14 September 1972 and within two years had extended it to National Maori Language Week. Each year they mount a massive publicity campaign for the Maori language, enlisting the co-operation of newspapers, radio and television. In January 1974 Te Huinga Rangatahi o Aotearoa (an expanded form of the N.Z. Maori Students' Federation) published the first issue of a newspaper, *Rongo*, in Maori and several other Polynesian languages. In content and presentation this was of a commendably but impractically high standard for a group with little financial backing, and the second issue had not appeared by the end of the year.

Pressure from Maori youth groups for the wider teaching of Maori is by no means a new development. The Young Maori Leadership Conferences of the fifties and sixties regularly passed strong recommendations on these lines, as did many other Maori organizations. But in the seventies the young have found the means to make their voices heard more widely, mainly by effective use of the news media. Moreover, instead of waiting for official moves, they have recruited teachers and organized classes themselves. Seeing their enthusiasm, tribal elders have responded by arranging *whare wānanga* schools where teaching is mainly in Maori to meet their needs.

Official attitudes to the Maori language have undergone a marked change in recent years. The process began back in the fifties when a small band of advocates led by John Waititi, Assistant Officer for Maori Education, and Beth Ranapia of the Correspondence School and later School Publications worked to convince administrators of the value of extending its teaching in the schools. A major step forward was taken with the publication of John Waititi's Maori language texts, *Te Rangatahi* I (1962) and II (1964), based on modern language teaching principles and the language and life of his own tribal community. In the sixties advances in the study of language learning and bilingualism began to reach New Zealand. Two specially commissioned reports by linguists made recommendations based on the new insights that children are most receptive to language learning at a young age and can cope with a second language better if their first is developed instead of repressed (Benton, 1965; Bender, 1971). As a result of advice from such sources, reinforced by pressures from the community, the Department of Education has adopted a policy of encouraging the teaching of Maori at all levels of the school system. To this end it has approved the introduction of Maori into the primary school syllabus and greatly increased facilities for training teachers of Maori (p. 159). Though the establishment of a fully bilingual school is not yet in sight, Maori is in use as the medium of instruction in several pre-school and infant classrooms. Between 1969 and 1974 the number of pupils studying Maori in state and private secondary schools rose from 2,249 (1,926 Maoris and 323 Pakehas) to 5,576 Maoris and 3,500 Pakehas. In addition, Maori is increasingly being taught in primary and intermediate schools.

Expansion has also occurred at the tertiary level, funded indirectly by the State. Courses in Maori language are now offered at five universities and eight teachers' colleges. Maori may be taken as a major subject for the B.A. degree at the universities in Auckland and Wellington, but in 1974 must be combined with anthropology for a postgraduate degree, though an M.A. in Maori is in the planning stage at Auckland. Waikato, Massey and Canterbury Universities are still building their Maori courses up to B.A. level. Maori is also widely taught in evening courses at universities, schools and technical institutes.

The Government has also borne the major responsibility for increasing the amount of Maori reading material on general sale and the outlets for writing in Maori. First in the field was *Te Ao Hou*, a quarterly magazine dealing with Maori affairs published by the Department of Maori Affairs since 1952. Though the greater part of the text is usually in English, *Te Ao Hou* has stimulated interest in Maori by re-publishing old texts difficult of access with commentary and translations, and by running literary competitions in Maori as well as English. The Department of Education publishes two series of School Bulletins in Maori, *Te Whare Kura* (twenty-three numbers between 1962 and 1974) and *Te Tautoko* (four numbers). Between them these series cover the range from beginners to advanced reading level. Sold in Government and educational bookshops they are widely sought by speakers and learners of Maori from outside the schools. The New Zealand Maori Council has also included Maori material in its publications, *Te Kaunihera Maori* (1963–9) and *Te Maori* (1970 to the present).

In the Maori Affairs Amendment Act 1974, the Government gave 'official recognition' . . . to the Maori language of New Zealand as 'the ancestral tongue of that portion of the population of New Zealand of Maori descent' and authorized steps to encourage its learning and use within and without the Department of Maori Affairs and in particular to extend to Government Departments and other institutions information concerning and translations from or into the Maori language.

Increasing recognition of Maori in official quarters both reflects and encourages greatly increased interest on the part of New Zealanders in general. Up to and sometimes over half the students enrolled in Maori language classes at secondary and tertiary institutions are Pakehas, and it is becoming common for parties composed largely of Pakehas to visit *marae* and for Pakeha spokesmen to reply to welcome speeches in carefully prepared Maori. Newspapers in areas with a substantial Maori population print occasional articles and advertisements in Maori. New Zealand Broadcasting Corporation announcers have followed a policy of correct pronunciation of Maori words and place-names since the early sixties, and introduced the use of Maori greetings in 1973. In 1973 and 1974 there has been a small but significant increase in news items and features in which Maori is spoken, sometimes but not always with translation. Two major landmarks on television have been the drama series, *Pukemanu*, in which Maori characters figured quite prominently and spoke Maori in appropriate situations, and the documentary series, *Tangata Whenua*, which

101

showed Maoris speaking Maori formally and informally in Maori situations, and replying to questions in Maori or English as they chose. Reorganization of the NZBC in 1975 includes plans for a Polynesian Radio station, which would greatly extend the amount of Maori on the air.

## The Maori language in the modern world

The view that Maori is a primitive language inherently inferior to English has been demolished by linguists who insist that every language constitutes a fully developed system adjusted to the needs of its speakers. However it is still often argued that however admirably adapted to a tribal life-style, the Maori language cannot cope with the complexities of life in the modern world. Such an argument betrays a curiously fixed and inflexible idea of language. In fact Maori has changed and developed greatly over the last 150 years to meet the challenge of new cultural experience. It has done this in three main ways, by borrowing words, modifying the meaning of existing words, and creatively developing new ones.

In borrowing extensively from English, Maori speakers have been following the example of speakers of English, which owes much of its richness and flexibility to the assimilation of words from other languages. Whatever their source, words borrowed into Maori become Maori words, modified in form so that they sound Maori and often modified in meaning as well. Transliterations are often hardly recognizable because of changes to avoid un-Maori sounds: e.g. *pirihimana* (policeman), *hoia* (soldier), *wini* (window), *paraikete* (blanket), *tarau* (trousers), *taraiwa* (driver), *kaunihera* (council). The word 'flour', transliterated into Maori as *parāoa*, is used to mean 'bread' as well as 'flour', as in the different kinds of bread, *parāoa koroua* (baking-powder bread), *parāoa rewena* (leavened bread) and *parāoa parai* ('fried bread', dough cooked in boiling fat). As is explained elsewhere (p. 171), a *komiti* is not always a committee in the strict sense of the English word. Besides filling cultural gaps, borrowed words have also widened the range of synonyms and words with subtle shades of meaning. For instance, Maoris can now use either *matua* or *papa* for a classificatory father, *papa* conveying more warmth; *kakano* or *kara* can be used to signify 'colour', *kakano* indicating differences in colour and/or texture, *kara* referring more specifically to colours. Sometimes the new word tends to replace the old, but wherever stress is laid on the value of Maori the displaced words are revived. Finally it should be emphasized that these borrowed words are used in the context of Maori grammatical forms which differ significantly from English ones. This means they may be used in ways that would be 'wrong' in

English, and they are modified in accordance with the Maori rules. For instance, *puruma* (broom) is used as a verb as well as a noun, and so is *tuari* (steward); nouns remain the same in singular and plural; and new Maori words are created by addition of the prefixes *kai-* (one who does something) and *whaka-* (to make something be done) and the suffix *-tanga* (-ness), as in *kai-ruri* (surveyor, *ruri* deriving from 'rule'), *kai-rehita* (registrar), *whaka-kororia* (to glorify), and *Kingitanga*.

As in all languages, subtle and sometimes dramatic changes in word meaning are always in progress. These may be largely unconscious or the result of deliberate re-application of a word to new purposes. We have already explored important examples of such changes in chapter 5, e.g. in the meaning and use of *atua, ariki, mana* and *aroha*. The term for the Maori 'school of learning', *whare wānanga*, is nowadays used to signify both the university and Maori schools of instruction which depart from the older model in significant ways. *Rangatahi*, the technical name of a particular kind of fishing net, has come to mean 'young people acting or with the capacity to act as leaders' (p. 204). The word *inoi*, which once meant simply to beg or entreat, is now used alongside *karakia* to mean 'prayer' in a specifically Christian sense.

Finally, new words have also been created by derivation from or combination of existing ones, to avoid a clumsy transliteration, out of pride in the resources of the language, or simply a sense of aptness. A cat is a *ngēru*, derived from *ngerungeru*, meaning 'soft, smooth, sleek'. The term *papakāinga* was coined to describe communal residential land on a *marae* reserve (p. 229), *waka-rere-rangi* for aeroplane, *kai-tiaki-moni* for treasurer, and *kai-whakahaere* for manager or boss.

Because Maori was not used as a teaching medium in the schools, it remains largely undeveloped in subject areas for which the schools are the main preparation, for instance advanced technology, commerce, the natural and the social sciences. In certain other fields where it has developed an extensive and sophisticated vocabulary, interest has waned among the younger generation, for instance in land legislation, farming and other rural occupations, theology and political administration. However these are all relatively specialized areas, in which the majority of English speakers are not particularly knowledgeable either. Despite the lack of reinforcement from the schools, Maori has retained and developed its resources for the important task of inter-personal communication in home and community. To many Maoris Maori is the 'language of the heart' to which they turn to express their deepest thoughts and feelings, in which they can say things which would sound either sentimental or crude in English. It is also pre-eminently the language of the *marae* and of ceremonial occasions. And if the majority no longer command and use its full repertoire as a matter of course, there are enough experts left to consult when need arises.

For New Zealanders, Maori and Pakeha, whose first language is English, Maori has a value that is only just beginning to be appreciated. Quite apart from the access it gives to Maori culture, learning Maori with its very different structure and its emphasis on figurative modes of expression reveals how much our view of the world is affected by our language, and makes us aware of alternative possibilities.

### Standard Maori and tribal variations

Maoris recognize at least seven major variants of the Maori language associated with certain canoes (Arawa, Tainui, Mātaatua) and regions (Northland, East Coast, Taranaki-Wanganui and the South Island). Though not dialects as defined by the linguists, the differences between these variants are marked enough for Maori speakers to be able to place each other by their speech. In some cases a particular pronunciation feature is seized upon as the major marker, e.g. Maoris from Taranaki and Wanganui are identified by their habit of 'dropping their aitches', Tūhoe by their use of plain 'n' where other tribes use nasalized 'n' (ng). But there are also many other subtle and important differences in delivery and in vocabulary. The latter can cause misunderstanding when words which are inoffensive in one area have different connotations in another, e.g. *tahae*, which is used to refer to a young boy by Tūhoe and Ngāti Porou but means 'thief' to others.

Over the last 150 years these tribal variations have been modified through the influence of the Bible, migration and inter-tribal mixing, especially in the towns. At present a counter tendency is arising for some groups to stress the distinctive speech characteristics of their tribe in order to strengthen their tribal identity.

### English

Outside their homes Maoris find it practically impossible to manage without learning English. It is the language of instruction in all educational institutions, the language of nearly all identifying signs, official forms and notices, and advertisements. Maori translations are sometimes provided in predominantly Maori areas, and birth, death and marriage certificates, census schedules and electoral registration forms are available in Maori on request. A few shopkeepers, farmers, ministers, teachers and university lecturers speak fair to fluent Maori, but the overwhelming majority of Pakehas with whom Maoris have to do speak only English. Newspapers, radio and television are almost entirely in English.

Virtually all Maoris speak enough English for practical purposes, but the English they speak frequently differs from standard New Zealand English in significant ways. Linguists in fact recognize the existence of a Maori–English dialect, which far from being – as it is usually judged – a 'poor' form of English is a complete and effective language system in its own right incorporating certain distinguishing features of sound, syntax and meaning resulting from the interaction of English and Maori. These include a tendency to conclude sentences on a rising inflexion, the use of Maori words of key importance without translation, the use of English words with the meaning associated with the corresponding Maori word (e.g. 'granny' not only for own grandparents but also for their siblings and cousins) or in grammatical positions they can occupy in Maori but not in English (e.g. 'key' and 'broom' as verbs as well as nouns), and the use of words and phrases which are direct translations of Maori idioms (e.g. 'you-fellas' from *koutou* which indicates 'you-others' as distinguished from *tatou*, 'you and us together', and 'Thing' from 'Ko-Mea' instead of 'So-and-So'). For many Maoris this is their only form of English, but increasing numbers speak it in addition to standard English, switching codes according to company.

In the past, teachers concentrated on 'correcting' the 'poor' English of Maori children. The constant experience of correction, with its implicit devaluing of the language of home and community, is now recognized as a factor in discouraging Maori children from staying at school and from mastering standard English. Nowadays following the advice of linguists at least some teachers begin with the language Maori children use naturally and try not to eradicate but to add the standard form to it.

### Bilingualism

Most Maoris today are bilingual to some degree where the majority of Pakehas are monolingual. Some in every generation demonstrate particular mastery in both languages. In the tradition of Ngata, Buck and Kohere, many leading elders have a reputation as orators and writers in English and Maori, for instance Pei Te Hurinui Jones of Waikato and Hohepa Taepa of Arawa, whose recent death was a sore loss in this as in other respects. Several young Maoris are currently writing prose and poetry in both languages (see p. 272). Most Maoris, however, probably use one language more than the other, often for different and complementary purposes.

While linguists and teachers are beginning to recognize that bilingualism may have advantages as well as disadvantages, there is a dearth of research on bilingualism in New Zealand. From my own experience, I am convinced that many Maoris, far from being confused by access to two languages, use them to play sophisticated intellectual games. They make jokes or hidden allusions by playing upon the resemblance in sound between Maori and English words which have very different meanings, and by exploiting the double meaning of words usually regarded as translations of each other. For instance, '*Ko te heru*', which means 'It is a comb' in Maori, is used to convey the sentiment 'Go to hell', while young Maoris refer to *marijuana* not as might be expected by transliterations of its colloquial English names but as *kōhatu* which means 'a stone'.

It is to be hoped that the teaching of Maori language in schools and other settings will increase the number of New Zealanders who can enjoy and exploit the resources of the two languages in this and other ways.

# chapter 8

# Land

Like their forefathers, modern Maoris feel strongly about the land (*whenua*). What they value is not, however, land in the abstract, but the land they have inherited from their forebears; and they value it mainly for its sentimental and social significance. It is the 'land of our ancestors', a legacy bequeathed by a long line of forebears who loved and fought and died for it, and a tangible link with the heroes and happenings of a storied past. Often, it is associated with their own early life, kinsfolk and friends. Even more important, inherited rights in Maori land are bound up with rights of precedence in Maori community life and on the *marae*. The older generation, in particular, recognize an almost mystical connection between land and personal standing.

## Tāngata whenua and 'immigrants'

In each local district, Maoris give a special status to those they call *tāngata whenua* (literally 'people of the land'). To qualify for this title and the privileges attached to it, a Maori must first of all be descended from a line of forebears who lived and owned 'Maori land' in the district continuously over many generations. ('Maori land' is a technical term for land held by Maoris under special laws.) Many older Maoris hold that he should also own (or be heir to) shares inherited from these forebears in land in the district. They recognize those who have descent *and* land as *tāngata whenua* under any circumstances, but express doubts about the status of those who have local descent without local land shares, though in practice I have never heard them deny the title to a claimant. The younger generations place much less emphasis on land ownership as a qualification (University of Auckland (k): 29–30). In most cases, members of local descent-groups share in the ownership of a *marae*, and this is increasingly accepted as sufficient. Those who are *tāngata whenua* in a place do not necessarily live there: many in fact do not. But they can fully enjoy the benefits of their status only in the district itself, while living there or on visits, and their standing in the community depends at least partly on active participation in its affairs. Those who are *tāngata whenua* in a place are said to 'belong' there.

Maoris who have no ancestral connection with and hence own no 'Maori land' in the district where they live are identified as 'immigrants', even when locally born. The Maori term differs from area to area, including *tāngata haere mai* ('people who have come in'), *rawaho* ('outsiders'), *konene* or *manene* (strangers), and even *tauiwi* (foreigners). 'Immigrants' are more or less permanent residents in the district, and should be distinguished from *manuhiri*, temporary 'visitors' or 'guests', usually from beyond its limits. (However, when a gathering at the *marae* is sponsored by a limited section of the community – for instance, a family or a club – not only 'immigrants' but even *tāngata whenua* who are not members of the sponsoring group become *manuhiri* for its duration.)

The ratio of *tāngata whenua* to 'immigrants' varies with local conditions. In Kotare, within commuting distance of a town, 70 per cent of the Maori residents in 1955 were *tāngata whenua*, 13 per cent were 'immigrants' married to or adopted by *tāngata whenua*, and 17 per cent were independent 'immigrants'. In more isolated districts independent 'immigrants' rarely exceed 5 per cent. In market-gardening and timber-milling settlements, on the other hand, and in towns and cities, they often form the main element in the population.

According to Maori tradition, *tāngata whenua* should always take precedence in the social life of the community, and are the only proper source of leadership. This view is still held strongly in most country areas. Normally it is the *tāngata whenua* elders who perform the ceremonial at public gatherings and initiate and lead group discussion. Local organizations frequently bar 'immigrants', openly or in fact, from holding office. When a decision has to be made, the voices of the *tāngata whenua* carry most weight. Nevertheless, it is becoming increasingly common for 'immigrants' to be accepted as leaders in sectional associations and even as elders (*kaumātua*) of the community as a whole, if they have been in the district a long time and are particularly well-qualified, if the *tāngata whenua* are short of suitable leaders, or if they are liberally minded. In urban areas where 'immigrants' outnumber the *tāngata whenua*, the former usually ask the latter to take the lead on ceremonial occasions, but in other respects they maintain their independence.

Being a *tangata whenua* means most in relation to the *marae*.

Descendants of the original owners of a *marae* inherit special 'rights on the *marae*', of which the most important is the right to speak there in public as host (p. 236). In most places, all *tāngata whenua* have rights in the main *marae*, and some (if not all) in each lesser one. In the country, where virtually all Maori gatherings are held at a *marae*, this gives the *tāngata whenua* a decided advantage. 'Immigrants', who by definition lack rights in the local *marae*, speak there – whether at local or large, public gatherings – at the courtesy of the *tāngata whenua*. In theory, the latter could 'tell them to sit down' at any time and for any reason. In practice this rarely happens, largely because 'immigrants' are careful not to give offence by pushing themselves forward.

Maoris describe a *marae* on which they have rights as their *tūrangawaewae*, literally 'a standing-place for the feet'. I have heard elders on occasion use the same word for their inherited land holdings. 'If we lose our land', they say, 'we lose our *tūrangawaewae*', and 'the land is a *tūrangawaewae* for us'.

Many Maoris are *tāngata whenua* in more than one district, and have rights in more than one *marae*, by virtue of land rights inherited in different places from different forebears. Most of those so placed claim the privileges of their status regularly only in one place – but they like to feel they can do so in others when occasion arises.

When formally welcoming visitors from outside the community at *hui*, speakers use *tāngata whenua* to mean 'the hosts' in contrast to 'the guests' (*manuhiri*), temporarily including 'immigrants' helping with the work. The term may also be used in a tribal context: within the limits of the tribal territory every member of the tribe is a *tangata whenua* in relation to members of other tribes.

## Land tenure

Land owned by Maoris falls into two distinct categories: 'Maori land', a technical term for land governed by special Maori land legislation, and land owned by Maoris on ordinary freehold title, sometimes but erroneously called 'European land'.

'Maori land' is land held on special Maori freehold title determined by the Maori Land Court in accordance with the Native Land Act 1862 and successive Acts up to the Maori Affairs Act 1953 and its Amendments. Most 'Maori land' has remained continuously in Maori hands, handed down from generation to generation; a comparatively small proportion, though alienated, has become 'Maori land' again by Crown grant or by application to the Maori Land Court.

With a few minor exceptions, transactions involving 'Maori land'

109

must be dealt with in the Maori Land Court and 'Maori land' cannot be alienated from Maori title without the Court's approval. The Maori Land Court, whose jurisdiction and powers are set out in the Maori Affairs Act 1953, currently consists of seven Maori Land Court Districts presided over by a Chief Judge and five other Judges, some of whom operate in more than one District. These Judges are appointed by the Governor-General and are paid out of monies appropriated for that purpose by Parliament. The position of Registrar of each Court District is occupied by the District Officer of the corresponding District of the Department of Maori Affairs (p. 44), and the administrative side of the Court's work is carried out by public servants working in the Court Section of the Department of Maori Affairs, under the direction of a departmental officer with the status of Deputy Registrar, who works in close association with the Judge. Court sittings are held in some cases in rooms designed for the purpose on Departmental premises and when these are not available in the Magistrate's Court and other places, especially when the Court goes on circuit.

The Hunn Report estimated that in 1960 'Maori land' amounted to roughly four million acres and was decreasing by about 14,000 acres a year as a result of alienation from Maori title. There is no precise information on the amount of 'Maori land' left at the end of 1974, but the figure of three and a half million acres (approx. 1,410 hectares) is widely quoted. Most of it is located in the central sector of the North Island: in the King Country, the Central Plateau, the central and eastern Bay of Plenty, and the northern East Coast. Northern Northland also has a considerable amount but holdings are small and discontinuous. Little is found in the rich farming areas of the Waikato, where land was lost by confiscation, Hauraki Plains and southern Northland. Much 'Maori land' is inferior in quality and located in heavily dissected areas difficult of access; the Hunn Report estimated a sixth as 'undevelopable' in 1960. However, advances in development methods and afforestation have since greatly extended its potential for production.

Land acquired by Maoris on ordinary freehold title, whether by inheritance or purchase, is not 'Maori land' in the technical sense, but it may be transferred to Maori title on application to the Maori Land Court.

How much land Maoris own on ordinary freehold title is impossible to discover because Maori owners are not separately identified in Land Department records. It is quite clear however that the amount is increasing at a significant rate and constitutes a growing proportion of the land owned by Maoris. The greatest number of such holdings is in urban areas, where 90 per cent of the houses owned by Maoris are built on purchased land, but over the last five years Maoris have also bought a number of fair-sized farms on good quality land, especially in the Bay of Plenty and Taranaki.

*Alternative policy approaches to 'Maori land'*

Up until 1967 Maori land legislation made it possible, but not easy, for a Maori owner to have a holding of 'Maori land' transferred from Maori title to ordinary freehold title. After presentation of the Pritchard-Waetford Report reviewing the 'Maori land' issue, the (National Party) Government passed a Maori Affairs Amendment Act 1967 which provided (among other things) that 'Maori land' holdings with less than four joint owners should be transferred to the ordinary Land Transfer Register and exempted from the jurisdiction of the Maori Land Court. Both the Report and the Act aroused much opposition from Maoris, including the New Zealand Maori Council, on the grounds that it removed existing safeguards against individuals selling the land to non-Maoris. On the other hand they also received support, especially from younger Maoris who found the 'Maori land' legislation limiting. When a Labour Government came to power committed to retaining Maori land in Maori ownership it passed another Maori Affairs Amendment Act in 1974 repealing this provision and making it possible for transfers already made to be reversed on application to the Court. The Government also took steps in this Act to involve the Maori people more closely in administrative discussions of land matters by replacing the existing Board of Maori Affairs with a Maori Land Board with a higher proportion of Maori members (at least five out of nine) and authorizing the establishment of Maori Land Advisory Committees with a balance of four Maoris to three Government officials. Appointments to the Maori Land Board and to Maori Land Advisory Committees in the seven Maori Land Court Districts were announced in June 1975.

The Maori Affairs Amendment Acts of 1967 and 1974 represent two opposing approaches to Maori land ownership, especially the question of Maori title. They are often characterized as a Pakeha and a Maori approach, but this is an over-simplification. Rather they represent different ideas on the nature of land ownership and the best way to give Maoris control over their land, ideas which both have their Maori supporters. The 1967 Amendment Act stresses individual rights and responsibilities and is based on the premise that Maoris should be allowed to handle their affairs like everyone else without special supervision or interference. The pre-1967 and the 1974 legislation is based on the view that the land is an asset which belongs to the Maori people, not individuals, and must be protected from

111

alienation, exploitation and the selfish or irresponsible actions of individuals by special measures.

## The alienation of 'Maori land'

The continuing alienation of 'Maori land' is a matter of long-standing concern to the Maori people, concern expressed repeatedly at Maori gatherings and by Maori organizations of many kinds in representations to Parliament (pp. 166, 210). While some of the land alienated from Maori title remains in Maori hands on ordinary freehold title, most of it does not. In recent years, increasingly significant amounts have been lost by being taken over by local bodies and sold or leased to meet rating arrears (3,376 acres valued at nearly $ 100,000 between 1964 and 1974) or for public purposes such as roading, education and conservation (9,253 acres valued at over a million dollars over the same period). In 1975 losses from these causes have become a major focus of concern for many Maoris, leading to requests for increased protection for 'Maori land' on these counts. A protest group formed in Auckland in March 1975 under the name *Te Roopu o te Matakite* (those who see) brought the issue to national attention and debate by organizing a 'Maori Land March' starting from Te Hapua in the far north on Maori Language Day (14 September) and ending with a reception in the forecourt of Parliament on 13 October. There the march leaders presented the Prime Minister with a 'memorial' signed by Maori elders calling for an immediate halt to alienation of what is left of 'Maori land' and its return to Maori control. The marchers included members from many different tribes, all political parties and age-groups, and Pakehas as well as Maoris. While Maoris generally varied in their views on the appropriateness of the march as a method of action, they expressed themselves strongly in support of the *take* (subject or cause).

In September and October 1975 also, in response to representations by the Maoris of the Waikato and Taranaki, the Government arranged the return to Maori ownership of the sacred mountains of Taupiri (in the Waikato) and Taranaki (Mt Egmont in Taranaki). The land is being vested in the Tainui and Taranaki Tribal Trust Boards respectively on behalf of the tribes involved, without individualization. Because Taranaki has long been part of the Egmont National Park and is much used by the New Zealand public for recreation, the Taranaki Trust Board plans to vest the area in the Crown in perpetuity for its current use, in consideration of which two places on the National Park Board will be reserved for Maori representatives.

7  The Maori Women's Welfare League meets in annual conference in the Wellington Town Hall, transformed for the occasion by quilts provided by the Cook Island Independent Branch in Porirua (Wellington); June 1975

8 The New Zealand Maori Council takes a break from a meeting in the Maori Committee Room in Parliament Buildings to talk to visiting college students, July 1975. Note the enlarged copy of the Treaty of Waitangi on the side wall and the photographs of Te Rangi Hiroa (Sir Peter Buck) and Sir James Carroll

## 'Maori land' titles

When titles to 'Maori land' were first determined by the Maori Land Court, it was on a *hapū* basis. Land was identified as belonging to a *hapū* consisting of so many named adult members. Most *marae* and trust properties are owned in this way, by a group of specified owners who have vested their undivided individual rights in trustees elected from their number. In the majority of 'Maori land' blocks, however, titles have been individualized, that is, the Court has determined what proportion of the whole belongs to each of the named owners without giving him (or her) sole title. This proportion is an *interest* or *share*. When a block is held jointly by a number of owners (*multiple owner-ship*), all of them must be consulted before anything is done with it, and part-owners have claims on income from it in proportion to their shares. If a part-owner wants sole control over his share, he applies to the Court for a *partition* order, which divides the block into two or more new ones. When an owner dies, his 'Maori land' holdings remain in his name until his heirs apply to the Maori Land Court for a *succession* order. If the deceased held a block as a sole owner, his heirs succeed to it as part-owners with equal shares. If he was only a part-owner, they are awarded shares of his shares.

As long as they have not been individualized, shares in 'Maori land' are protected from being taken in execution for debts or as assets in bankruptcy; but shares held in severalty or jointly with others are not so protected.

The legislators who framed the 'Maori land' law directed that titles be determined 'in accordance with ancient custom and usage'. This was interpreted by the Court to mean that when an owner died his or her land holdings should be divided equally among all his or her children. This overlooked the fact that in pre-European times rights lapsed if not validated by occupation (see p. 12). It also overlooked the claims of spouses, especially widows, who were formerly given rights of usufruct for life in land they had used during marriage. When the Maori population began to increase contrary to expecta-tions, the practice of the Court established by precedent compounded the difficulties inherent in any attempt to reconcile customary with freehold title.

Over many generations, division of shares among many heirs and constant partitioning have produced many blocks of 'Maori land' with hundreds and even thousands of owners, many blocks too small for economic use and many Maoris with shares in many blocks but control over few or none. Because individuals can inherit shares in the same block from different sources, shares often outnumber owners. Shares become progressively smaller and unequal with each passing generation. Sometimes it costs more to succeed to a share than it is worth. Though a block may earn high rent or timber royalties, few of the shareholders receive much when the income is divided among many.

Multiple ownership and fragmentation were long regarded as serious obstacles to the development and use of Maori land. Without sole title, owners cannot obtain development loans from the ordinary agencies. Even when this difficulty is overcome by State aid or incorporation, many blocks can support only one or two owners. Others may derive some benefit from their land by leasing it or by living rent-free, cultivating gardens and cutting firewood on it, but this is rarely worth much in money terms, and rates must still be paid in cash.

The obvious solution to most Pakehas would be for the small shareholders to sell out to the large or to the occupiers of the land. But the Maoris holding the land at present – mostly older folk – are reluctant to do this. For their shares, no matter how small, are part of their ancestral heritage and visible evidence of their descent. At least some feel them to be the basis of their 'belonging'. Younger Maoris see belonging as a matter of feeling and action rather than land ownership, but even those who have settled in urban areas still sometimes hesitate to dispose of such a tangible link with their origins.

The Government has tried many measures to improve the title situation. Consolidation, which concentrated each owner's scattered shares in one block, proved slow and laborious and is now officially abandoned. During the fifties and sixties Government policy emphasized conversion, which involves the Maori Trustee buying shares from some owners in a block for sale to others. Under the Maori Affairs Act 1953 such purchases could be effected without the owner's consent when the shares were below $50, a provision which was much criticized and finally abolished by the Maori Affairs Amendment Act 1974. For many years the Maori Land Court has encouraged heirs to an estate to make family arrangements about succession, for instance, allotting each of the deceased's interests to one successor instead of dividing it among all. The 1967 and 1974 Amendment Acts both made provision for widows, the latter, effective, one by means of a life interest in worth-while shares owned by a deceased husband. The Department of Maori Affairs helps farmers to obtain sole title with loans and encourages them to preserve it by making wills. The 1967 Amendment Act offered transfer to ordinary freehold title as a partial solution, but this was repealed.

Despite all these measures, the title situation remains a difficult and complicated one. For the last ten years, the Department of Maori Affairs has increasingly concentrated its resources on making 'Maori land' available for use in spite of title complications by means of land development schemes and incorporations.

### The use of 'Maori land'

The Hunn Report estimated that in 1960 not quite half the total area of 'Maori land' was administered by or on behalf of the Maori owners, nearly one fifth was leased to Pakehas, and the remaining third was lying idle. While up-to-date figures are not available, the Department of Maori Affairs claims that there has been a marked increase in the area administered directly by the Maori owners and a decrease in both the area leased to Pakehas and lying idle. Because so little is known about land owned by Maoris on ordinary freehold title, it must be left out of account in the following discussion.

### *The Leased Lands*

Most of the blocks of 'Maori land' leased by Pakehas are leased directly from the owners, with the approval of the Maori Land Court. The rest are mostly Maori Reserved Lands, consisting of 'Maori Reserves' set aside from land purchases and confiscation by the Crown for the benefit of Maoris and all leased in perpetuity. Extending over 75,000 acres (30,351 hectares), these Reserved Lands are vested in and administered by the Maori Trustee. Some 3,000 leases and many thousands of beneficial owners are involved. Following representations to the Government, a Commission of Inquiry into Maori Reserved Land was appointed in December 1973 and after a year's study presented a comprehensive Report (published in 1975) recommending sweeping changes in the administration of Maori Reserved Lands. These recommendations are currently under consideration by the Government.

Until recently there was also a substantial number of holdings amounting to 193,000 acres known as the 'Vested Lands'. These were vested in the Maori Trustee who leased them out for varying terms. Since 1970, however, as a matter of policy, the Maori Trustee has handed these holdings back to the owners to manage, as the leases have run out and sometimes before, when the owners have been able to pay extra compensation to the lessors. In this way a large area of Vested Lands became part of the Te Ati Hau Incorporation in 1973.

In terms of area the greater part of the leased lands is used for grazing or forestry, but some 27,000 titles are located in urban areas and leased for residential purposes.

*Development schemes and stations*

The Department of Maori Affairs has been and still is the main agency in bringing 'Maori land' into production. It does this by developing large tracts, often comprising many blocks, as 'land development schemes' and running them as undivided units ('stations') until the development debt is substantially reduced. If suitable, they are then subdivided into farms on which selected owners or owners' nominees are established as 'settlers' (formerly 'assisted units'). If not, the Department may continue to run the station on behalf of the owners but increasingly returns them to the latter for management as incorporations.

When this form of land development was introduced in the 1930s the aim was to settle as many Maori families on their own farms as possible, and schemes were divided into units which proved far too small for profitable operation, especially after the Second World War when farming became increasingly a business proposition. In the seventies, the Department settles comparatively few new settlers on individual farms each year (nine in 1973), always making sure they have enough land, equipment and finance to ensure success. The main trend at present is towards establishing effective productive units by incorporation rather than subdivision.

In mid 1973 the Department of Maori Affairs controlled seventy-six schemes in various stages of development involving 110,113 hectares (approximately 260,000 acres). These are distributed all over the North Island, with nearly half the total area in the Waiariki (Rotorua-Taupo-Bay of Plenty) and Tairawhiti (East Coast) Maori Land Districts. Together they produce about 1 per cent of the wool and 1 per cent of the meat produced in New Zealand each year. The number and area of the schemes is always changing, however: between mid 1972 and mid 1974 ten schemes were returned to their owners for management and ten new ones were established.

In 1973 there were five other stations on 'Maori land' administered by the Maori Trustee, fifteen by the Department of Lands and Survey on behalf of the Maori Land Board, and several by the Tribal Trust Boards (see p. 133). Profits from the latter go into trust board funds but those of the rest are distributed among owners.

*Owner control*

The use and control of their land by Maoris themselves takes two main forms, the one-man or rather one-family farm, and the Maori land incorporation.

Maori land incorporations are a particular form of corporation developed as far back as the 1890s in an effort to get 'Maori land' into production despite multiple ownership. Under legislation consolidated in the Maori Affairs Act by its 1967 amendment, the owners of any block of 'Maori land' owned by three or more persons may, if at least half agree, form themselves into a Maori incorporation. This halts alienation, since shares in an incorporation can be sold only to other owners or the Maori Trustee, and makes possible the negotiation of loans and so development and production. The owners elect a management committee to negotiate loans and decide overall policy and appoint a manager to supervise farm operations. Where possible owners are employed on wages. All receive dividends in proportion to their shares in the land.

Up until the middle sixties, Maori farming did not present a very encouraging picture. The general level of production was well below the national average: in 1961 less than one fifth of the dairy farmers under supervision by the Department of Maori Affairs produced the level of butterfat currently considered the minimum for economic operation. Especially in Northland and the East Coast, the area of the earliest land development schemes, falling production, reversion of pastures and abandonment of Maori farms were urgent problems, highlighted by periodic newspaper reports. Out of 298 registered incorporations, over half were inactive. There was a widespread Pakeha stereotype of a Maori farm as readily identifiable by sagging fences, rush- and weed-infested pasture and neglected stock. There were however good reasons for this state of affairs, reasons not appreciated by the self-appointed critics, and therefore worth stressing, First, only one Maori in three had sole title to his land, the rest leasing part or all of their farms from other owners, with limitations on security of tenure and compensation for improvements. Most of the farms, subdivided in earlier years, were far too small for economic operation even on good land and burdened with loan repayments. The land was in general not good and access difficulties increased freight and other costs. Farmers often had to take other jobs to raise cash. Sons of labourers, bushmen, road-builders and pioneer farmers, many Maori farmers had had little opportunity to learn good farming methods. Though most were dairy farmers, they did not generally find dairying congenial, because of loneliness. As for incorporations, management committees often lacked business experience, and they found it difficult to resist pressure from shareholders who were also kin to distribute profits instead of spending them on the property.

Nevertheless, there were hopeful signs to set against the problems. Year by year the Ahuwhenua Trophy Competition founded by Lord Bledisloe for Maori farmers attracted increasing numbers of good entrants in both dairy and sheep and cattle sections. Many of the functioning incorporations, such as Puketapu IIIA in the King

117

Country and Mangatu on the East Coast, were well established and expanding steadily.

Over the last ten years these hopeful signs have multiplied and the situation has shown marked, even radical, improvement. With the cities offering a better and more congenial living than subsistence farming, many with insufficient land have moved out, especially those who were not committed to farming as a way of life. Steady progress has been made in the amalgamation and incorporation of small holdings in viable units. Having chosen farming as an occupation rather than being forced into it, young Maoris are increasingly preparing themselves through special farm training and apprenticeship schemes, employment on development stations and incorporations where promotion prospects are good, and such standard New Zealand practices as share-milking. Although the total number of Maori farmers has probably continued to decline, this is at least partly offset by an increase in the number of farm managers: over a third of such positions on development stations and incorporations are held by Maoris. And the overall standard of competence and productivity has improved dramatically, in spite of the difficulties that have beset all New Zealand farmers since about 1973.

In particular, the incorporation has come into its own as a form of land use. In 1964 the Department of Maori Affairs attached conditions to some of its loans to incorporations which enabled it to insist on a reduction of dividends if necessary. With the Department to blame for their heartlessness, the management committees of a number of marginal incorporations were able to get them back on to a sound financial basis. In 1967 the Department of Maori Affairs reviewed the register of incorporations kept by the Maori Land Court and removed those which had not fulfilled the terms of their establishment, promising re-instatement if improvements were made. Stricter accounting procedures were introduced but dropped after spectacular improvement in practice and a sharp drop in complaints from shareholders. Since then, the Department has withdrawn from its watchdog role, as the incorporations have shown themselves fully capable of efficient management. In 1974 there were 170 functioning incorporations, farming 755,000 acres (approximately 315,000 hectares) and carrying 97,270 head of cattle and 647,700 sheep. Many incorporations have greatly diversified their activities. Puketapu incorporation successfully operated as a timber-milling company from 1946 to 1961, engaged in house-building in a small way for a period, then sold its sawmill assets and has since developed its agricultural potential for both meat and wool. Increasing numbers of incorporations, especially in Rotorua and on the East Coast, are involved in afforestation schemes and selective milling. In November 1974 the Minister of

Maori Affairs called an 'inaugural conference' of Maori Land Incorporations to review progress and plan future development. One
hundred and twenty six incorporations were represented at the conference, and 68 remits were filed in advance. A report of deliberations
and recommendations was sent to the Government for consideration,
and a committee set up to investigate the formation of a federation of
Maori land incorporations.

Among incorporations, Mangatu on the East Coast occupies a
rather special place as one of the earliest and largest, and an inspiring
example of what can be achieved under Maori management. Mangatu
covers 104,000 acres of heavily dissected hill country inland to the
north west of Gisborne. Established by Act of Parliament in 1893, it
consists of 2,400 members of Te Aitanga-a-Mahaki tribe. Mangatu is
farmed as eighteen separate sheep and cattle stations which function
independently under an overall management committee. Increasingly
economies are made by combined purchasing and planning. When
delegates to the incorporation conference visited Mangatu in November, they were told that the incorporation had: a permanent
workforce of up to 130 men, boosted to 200 by seasonal workers;
113,448 sheep including 78,633 breeding ewes; 17,817 cattle of which
nearly 7,000 were breeding cows; a fat lamb kill of 39,000 for the year
to June 1974; more than 2,200 fat bullocks killed in the same period;
a wool clip of 3,328 bales; Angus and Hereford studs, plus newly
established breeding programmes for Romney, Perendale and Coop-
worth rams; a station truck fleet and permanently employed building
gang; and an administrative office in Gisborne 35 miles away with a
secretary and a staff of 8. About 25,000 acres are still in native bush,
and small quantities are being milled.

Impressive as this record is, Mangatu is no special, isolated case.
At least two other incorporations are of comparable proportions in
area and/or assets, Te Ati Hau Incorporation in the Wanganui River
valley and the Ngāti Whakaue Incorporation of Rotorua, and others
are heading in the same direction. There is a general trend towards
bringing scattered holdings belonging to the members of the same
tribe together under central management by incorporation. Tūhoe,
for instance, have brought all their lands at Ruatoki, Ruatahuna,
Waiohau, Te Whaiti and Waimana into the Tūhoe Incorporation.
What was originally devised as a means of overcoming a special
'Maori problem' has in this case brought Maoris into the forefront of
new developments in farming and business management.

Finally, in recent years, Maori owners have become involved in
afforestation on a large scale. Using a variety of measures such as
trusts and holding companies to overcome title problems, they have
made available extensive tracts of land, which are being utilized, often

119

in conjunction with adjacent private and Crown holdings under joint arrangements with the NZ Forest Service or private companies. In this way, they are literally partners in such major enterprises as the Aupōuri Forest in Northland and the Tūwharetoa, south-east Taupo, Tarawera and Rotoaira Forests in the centre of the North Island.

# chapter 9

# Kinship

Maoris are very interested in how people are related and how kinsfolk (*whanaunga*) ought to behave to each other. They themselves regard this interest in kinship (*whanaungatanga*) as one of the things that distinguish them from Pakehas. A Maori once said to me: 'The Pakeha lives only for his own immediate family, but a Maori never turns a relative down.' Maoris are always pleased when they can establish kinship with a stranger. They know at once how to treat him, and constraint vanishes. A mother told me that she had been most upset when her daughter wrote home from the city that she wanted to marry a boy from another tribe, but she quickly withdrew her objections when it came out at the *tomo* (p. 140) that an ancestor of his had married the sister of one of hers. That made him one of her 'bones', a favourite word for relatives of common descent.

Most Maoris can identify upwards of two hundred relatives either by name or as offspring of named relatives. In other words, they have a large kinship universe. (This term is used by anthropologists to describe a circle of cognatic and affinal kin centred on and differing with each individual EGO.) In addition to having many children, they like to trace kinship 'a long way out', recognizing their own and their parents' cousins up to the fourth degree and further, and accepting as kin anyone who can demonstrate relationship to one of their known kinsmen. While they see some of their known kin rarely or not at all, they keep in touch with many, gaining and losing effective kin, as time passes, by birth, death, marriage, migration and quarrels.

Many Maoris live in rural communities where their forebears lived for generations, with the result that they are related to most other residents. Relatives living in the same or adjoining districts naturally see a lot of each other, visiting each other's homes and helping each other from day to day in many ways. In general, of course, they see most of, and do most for, their closest kin, but, as in any society, close relatives do not always get on well, and distant relatives sometimes become close friends.

But these days few Maoris remain in one place all their lives. They migrate to other country districts, towns and cities, and they marry people from other places and tribes. As a result, most Maoris have relatives scattered all over New Zealand. Close relatives living in different places keep in touch with each other by letter, telephone and visits. More distant ones do not usually correspond, but news passes along the grapevine from one related family to another. Before and after visiting their home community, Maoris living in the city commonly call on each other to collect news and parcels for kin at home and to deliver those sent in return. From time to time, scattered relatives gather for family weddings, twenty-first birthday parties, *tangihanga* and unveilings, and they often meet at other gatherings.

When Maoris travel, they visit and often stay with kinsmen wherever they go, seeking out even those they have never met. They are most offended if they discover relatives have visited their area without calling. Those who leave their home community permanently usually go somewhere where they have kinsmen who (they know) will take them into their home, help them find jobs and accommodation, and save them from being lonely.

## Kinship terminology

The full range of traditional kinship terms is still used in Maori in formal speech and by those who pride themselves on speaking the language properly (pp. 17–19). But in ordinary colloquial usage significant changes have taken place. First, certain terms of English origin, *pāpā*, *māmā*, *akara* (uncle), *āti* (auntie), *karanipā* and *karanimā*, have come into common use, side by side with, and sometimes replacing, *matua*, *papa* and *tupuna*. However they are applied the Maori not the English way. *Papa*, *mama*, *karanipā* and *karanimā* are used not only for own father, mother and grandparents respectively but also for all kin of the same sex and generation, and *akara* and *āti* for all the relatives formerly described as *matua kēkē* and *whaea kēkē*. Secondly the old terms for siblings-in-law of the opposite sex have disappeared and *taokete* is used for siblings-in-law of both sexes. Thirdly, wide variations occur in the usage of terms for relatives of EGO's own generation. At least some Maoris continue to use *tuakana* and *teina* in the traditional way (p. 18). But many have widened their use, applying them to senior and junior relatives of the opposite as well as the same sex. (Ngāti Porou, I am informed, have always favoured this usage.) Some use *tungāne* and *tuahine* for all relatives of the same generation, including those of the same sex. Others favour the transliterations *parata* and *hīta* for own brothers and sisters and refer to cousins as *kaihana*.

These additions and changes both express and foster an increasing emphasis on the distinction between own and other parents and children and a decreasing emphasis on seniority of descent and cross sex differences.

Maoris continue to use *karanga rua* (double calling) for a situation where two people are related in two ways, e.g. when one is *tuakana* to the other when the relationship is traced through one link and *teina* when through another. Sometimes there are so many ties they talk of *karanga maha* (many callings).

When speaking English, Maoris commonly use English kinship terms, not according to standard usage, but as equivalent to Maori ones. Even those who do not speak Maori do this, having learnt it in childhood from their elders. Thus Maoris typically use *aunt* and *uncle* for their *mātua kēkē* and *whaea kēkē* (classificatory 'mothers' and 'fathers'), including many who strictly speaking are cousins at various removes. They use *grandfather* and *grandmother* for all whom they call *tupuna* in Maori, *niece* and *nephew* for the children of cousins of the same generation as well as siblings, and *grandson* and *granddaughter* for the children of *nieces* and *nephews* as well as of own children. Sometimes they even use *brother* and *sister* to describe cousins of the same generation. This can lead to misunderstanding. Pakehas not unnaturally assume that a Maori is either teasing or deliberately misleading them when he talks of his grandchildren though his eldest child is still at school, or of nephews when he has no siblings.

In English, Maoris often use the term 'Maori cousin'. Amongst themselves they usually reserve it for relatives so distant they cannot trace every step in the relationship, but in speaking to Pakehas they use it for anyone beyond second cousin, in the firm belief that Pakehas never trace kinship further.

Modern Maoris frequently use kinship terms metaphorically, to describe how they feel about a person. Thus kinsmen often call an older man 'our *matua*' though he is *tuakana* to some, because he fills a fatherly role for the group as a whole, protecting, guiding and sometimes disciplining younger members. In the same way, a motherly woman may be called *whaea* by others than her classificatory 'children'. Occasionally a very elderly and respected person is referred to as 'our *tupuna*' by a whole community, and older folk frequently refer to the children of the community as '*ā matou tamariki*' ('our children'). 'Auntie' and 'Granny' or 'Nanny' are also widely used in this way.

### Rights and duties

Maoris recognize certain obligations towards kinsfolk outside their own immediate family, and expect the latter to do the same for them in return. These mutual rights and duties are phrased in very general terms, and it is left to the individual to decide the extent to which he observes them. But most Maoris are brought up to think their fulfilment important, and they feel both ashamed and guilty if they do not carry them out properly.

Maoris agree that kinsfolk ought, first of all, to keep in touch and take a personal interest in each other's fortunes. Their homes should be open to each other at all times: in theory, at least, they are entitled to enter without knocking and to make themselves at home even in the owner's absence. They should cheerfully share the use of their possessions. They should give or lend money on request, though a refusal may be justified if the giver is short himself, or the borrower already borrowed heavily without repayment. In particular, kinsmen should help each other with the expenses and the work involved in staging weddings, twenty-first birthday parties, *tangihanga* and unveilings. (The obligation to attend a kinsman's *tangihanga* is the most binding of all kinship obligations. If possible, kin should 'pay their respects' on the first day.) Kinsfolk should be loyal and 'stick by each other', right or wrong. Finally, there should be no strict accounting of obligation, moral or pecuniary, between kinsfolk. Their relations should be based on 'Maori *aroha*' (love), which 'does not count the cost' (see p. 66).

On certain occasions, especially at family-sponsored gatherings, specific duties are allotted on a kinship basis. The older kinsmen close to the person or persons honoured assume responsibility for various aspects of the work as 'chief helpers', the most senior male often being identified as 'general director' (p. 249). At a *tangihanga*, the women closest to the deceased act as chief mourners, keeping vigil by the coffin and leading the wailing. Close male kinsmen dig the grave or act as pall-bearers. At weddings, the bridesmaids, groomsmen, flowergirls, waiters and waitresses are often selected so that an office is assigned to each of the related lines on both sides. At unveilings the ties attaching the cover of the gravestone are loosed by someone close to the deceased.

Apart from these specialized roles, kin of varying degrees differ not so much in what they do for each other, as in how much time, money and energy they spend in doing it. Kin who are close, not only genealogically but in residence and friendship, drop in and out of each other's houses and perform small services for each other all the time, while more remote kin help each other mainly on special occasions.

Most Maoris live up to their ideals about how kin should behave to each other. They pride themselves on always providing meals and beds for kinsmen who drop in without notice. Whenever a Maori goes to the beach for shellfish, digs his *kūmara* or catches a trap full of eels, he gives some away to kin. Maoris turn up in force at gatherings sponsored by kinsmen and give freely of both money and labour. At the same time they do not hesitate to ask kinsfolk for labour, transport, produce, money or company when they need them, or even to help themselves. Kinship loyalties are very strong. If a Maori commits so serious a breach of law or social convention that his kin feel they cannot actively defend him, at least they will not give him away. For a Maori to 'get a relation into trouble' is completely reprehensible. This attitude is one of the limiting factors in recruiting Maoris for the police force.

Viewed from outside, Maori kinship obligations seem burdensome. But their fulfilment is not a matter of giving all the time: sooner or later it brings an ample return. It is, among other things, a form of insurance against future troubles. The Maori who cheerfully helps kinsmen in trouble and at weddings and *tangihanga* knows they will rally round when he needs help in his turn. A wedding or even a *tangihanga* costs a Maori nuclear family only a fraction of what it costs a Pakeha one, because kin give so much in food and money and provide so many workers. Maoris never need to hire caterers on such occasions. When they travel, Maoris rarely bother with hotels: they stay with relatives. Sooner or later those same relatives or others will come to stay with them. It all evens out in the long run. Anyway, from the Maori point of view, the cost in terms of time and money is a small consideration besides the intangible rewards. Maoris like to have lots of kin around them on important occasions in their life. When they have lost someone near and dear to them, the presence of numerous relatives is a great consolation. To be abandoned by one's kin is the ultimate disaster.

Maoris grumble a good deal about the demands made on them by relatives in general and in particular. They complain that they are always walking off with small treasures like family photographs; they borrow things and keep them 'for years', sometimes literally; they always know one's private business; and they 'expect you to drop everything and neglect your family to work flat out at their *hui*'. But they admit that all this is a small price to pay for the unfailing love and support received in return.

Modern conditions have undoubtedly increased both the opportunities for abusing this system of mutual rights and duties, and the extent to which abuse occurs. Migration scatters kin brought up together, and brings into contact others who hardly know each other. In the city, in particular, it is easy for the less scrupulous to trade on the dutiful feelings of kin, staying indefinitely in their homes, and demanding assistance they have neither means nor intention of repaying. Maoris are becoming more wary in their dealings with kin they do not know very well, but close kin can also be very demanding.

Brought up to feel it morally wrong to refuse kinsfolk, Maoris find it difficult to recognize and resist immoderate demands. This helps explain why Maori tenants and owners often do not limit overcrowding and parties in their homes. Also they know that if they antagonize kin, whatever the justification, the latter will tell the 'folk back home', who may then withhold help in their time of need. It is extremely difficult for a Maori to say no to relatives.

# chapter 10

# Descent and descent-groups

No longer all-important as in pre-European times, descent yet remains significant in a number of ways: as the basis of inheritance of shares in 'Maori land' (whose social value was discussed in chapter 8); in the study and use of *whakapapa* (descent-lines), especially in speech-making at *hui*; as one factor in determining social status and the choice of leaders, especially in a ceremonial context; and as the basis of membership in groups of varying corporateness (tribe, sub-tribe and large-family) and of claims on their resources.

## Whakapapa

In form a list of names, sometimes but not invariably linked by words indicating begetting or marriage, a *whakapapa* traces descent from a particular ancestor to a particular descendant. (*Tātai ingoa*, a recital of names, is a synonym.) Most often attention is limited to a single link in each generation, giving 'a single line coming straight down', as an elder described it; but the names of spouses and siblings are sometimes included and collateral lines explored. Every Maori has not one but many *whakapapa*, which vary with the ancestor taken as starting point and the links chosen in each generation. The study of *whakapapa* is almost inseparable from that of traditional history, which recounts the doings of the ancestors named in the *whakapapa* (Metge, 1964a: 53).

Today this twin study has become the special province of experts, usually men over fifty-five and prominent in community and tribal affairs (*kaumātua*). Most own handwritten '*whakapapa* books' inherited from family predecessors, but they also know a large number of *whakapapa* by heart. A typical *whakapapa* book contains several dozen *whakapapa*, giving the ancestry of the owner's family and other sections of his tribe, and the main descent-lines of related tribes. Usually only the names are recorded, without explanation: links, cross-references and accounts of ancestral doings are carried in the owner's head.

The experts use *whakapapa* mainly when speaking in public: to establish their right to speak on that particular occasion and that particular *marae*, to demonstrate a connection between themselves and/or the members of the local community and the person or persons being honoured, and to settle matters of precedence. They are also consulted for advice on land matters and applications for assistance from tribal trust funds.

Though less strict than their forebears, the experts regard the study of *whakapapa* and traditional history as *tapu*. Most will not discuss the subject nor consult their books where there is food or smoking, or where food is habitually served. *Whakapapa* books are carefully stored away from contaminating influences, often in secret hiding places. Their very existence may be concealed from strangers.

While some knowledge of *whakapapa* may be acquired at *hui*, mastery requires concentrated study. Some experts hold periodic '*whakapapa* classes', preferably at the *marae*, for interested members of their descent-group, or select one or two descendants for private tuition. They prefer to instruct their senior male heir, but if he is uninterested or absent, they accept other kinsmen, including women. Many experts, however, make little effort to pass on their knowledge, because (they claim) young people today neither value nor know how to use it.

### Rank and leadership

Once the key to social rank, descent in a senior line is today only one of several factors determining social status in Maori eyes (p. 211). In most tribes, so much intermarriage has taken place between *rangatira* and commoner families over the last hundred years that even the experts find it difficult to separate or rank them in order. Since rank based on seniority of descent is largely relative within the tribe, making inter-tribal comparison difficult, it loses importance in cities and places where members of different tribes gather. Young Maoris value senior descent far less than their elders. As we have seen, they often fail to distinguish between older and younger siblings of the same sex when speaking Maori (p. 123), and they pay no attention when older kinsmen object to their chosen spouse on the grounds of rank (p. 140).

In descent-group and local community, the most senior males are still respected as the 'proper' leaders, but if they lack personality and drive, others may assume the effective leadership, leaving them to act only in a ceremonial capacity.

## Descent-groups

To a Maori it is axiomatic that he belongs to a tribe and at least one *hapū* within it. Many are also active members of family groups formed primarily on the basis of descent.

As in pre-European times, both tribe and *hapū* are descent-groups, membership being based on descent traced ambilineally (through mixed male and female links) from an ancestor regarded as founder (pp. 4–5). The number and names of the recognized tribes and *hapū* have changed little over the past hundred and twenty years. Once lists and maps were made they came to be accepted as definitive and 'right', and the fluidity of the traditional system was frozen. Tribes and *hapū* continue to grow larger in size and genealogical depth without segmenting, and changes in classification are rare.

Key to map of tribal areas

| *Regional grouping* | *Tribe* | *Canoe* |
|---|---|---|
| The Northern Tribes (Tai-Tokerau) | 1. Aupōuri<br>2. Rarawa<br>3. Ngāti Kahu<br>4. Ngāpuhi<br>5. Ngāti Whātua | Kurahaupo<br>Ngātokimātāwhaorua<br>Mamari<br>Mahuhu<br>and others |
| The Tainui Tribes | 6. Ngāti Tai<br>7. Ngāti Paoa<br>8. Ngāti Maru<br>9. Ngāti Tamaterā<br>10. Ngāti Whanaunga<br>11. Waikato<br>12. Maniapoto | Tainui |
| The Taranaki Tribes | 13. Ngāti Tama<br>14. Ngāti Mutunga<br>15. Ngāti Maru<br>16. Te Ati Awa<br>17. Taranaki<br>18. Ngā Ruahine<br>19. Ngāti Ruanui<br>20. Ngā Rauru | Tokomaru<br><br><br>Kurahaupo<br><br>Aotea |
| The Wanganui Tribes | 21. Ngāti Haua<br>22. Te Ati Hau | Tainui and Arawa<br>Aotea and Kurahaupo |

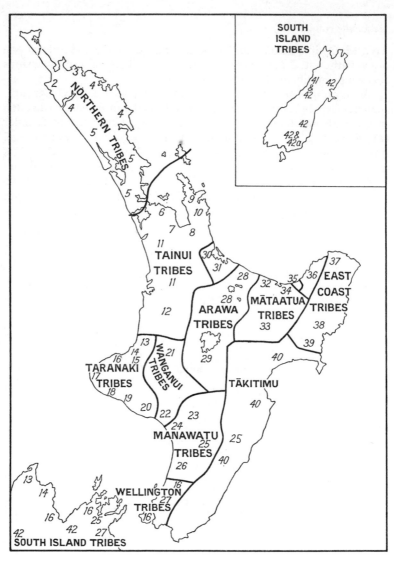

*Figure 4    Maori tribal areas 1975*

| Regional grouping | Tribe | Canoe |
|---|---|---|
| The Manawatu Tribes | 23. Ngāti Raukawa | Tainui |
| | 24. Ngāti Apa | |
| | 25. Rangitāne | Kurahaupo |
| | 26. Muaupoko | |
| The Wellington Tribes | 16. Te Ati Awa | Tokomaru |
| | 27. Ngāti Toa | Tainui |
| The Arawa Tribes | 28. Arawa | Arawa |
| | 29. Ngāti Tūwharetoa | |
| The Bay of Plenty Tribes | 30. Ngāi Terangi | Mātaatua and Tainui |
| | 31. Ngāti Ranginui | |
| | 32. Ngāti Awa | Mātaatua |
| | 33. Tūhoe | |
| | 34. Whakatōhea | |
| | 35. Ngāi Tai | Tainui |
| | 36. Whānau-ā-Apanui | Mātaatua and Horouta |
| The East Coast Tribes (Tai-Rāwhiti) | 37. Ngāti Porou | Horouta and Nukutere |
| | 38. Rongowhakaata | |
| | 39. Te Aitanga-ā-Māhaki | Takitmu |
| Takitimu | 40. Ngāti Kahungunu | |
| | 25. Rangitāne | Kurahaupo |
| The South Island Tribes | 13. Ngāti Tama | Tokomaru |
| | 14. Ngāti Mutunga | |
| | 16. Te Ati Awa | |
| | 25. Rangitāne | Kurahaupo |
| | 27. Ngāti Toa | Tainui |
| | 41. Poutini | Tākitimu and others |
| | 42. Ngāi Tahu | |
| | 42a. Ngāti Mamoe* | |

* The Ngāti Mamoe of the southern part of the Southern Island were completely assimilated by the invading Ngāi Tahu in the eighteenth and nineteenth centuries. Today Ngāti Mamoe and the southern Ngāi Tahu are virtually one people, though the former are sometimes distinguished by name for ceremonial purposes.

## The tribe

Forty-two groups claim and are widely accorded the title of *iwi*. Of these, Waikato and Arawa are really federations of tribes, whose members refer to their subdivisions as *iwi* rather than *hapū*. The Waikato became welded into a single political unit during the inter-tribal wars of the early nineteenth century (p. 30). The eight tribes of the Rotorua-Maketu area first adopted the canoe name as a unifying symbol in the 1860s when they formed the loyalist Arawa Flying

Squadron, but recognition of Arawa as one *iwi* did not become complete until the Arawa Trust Board was established in 1923. (Ngāti Tūwharetoa, who also stem from the Arawa canoe, remain a separate tribe.) Two of the modern tribes do not appear on any of the nineteenth-century maps. According to its elders, Ngāti Kahu of Whangaroa won recognition from representatives of many tribes assembled at Rotorua in 1920 for the visit of the Prince of Wales, when their spokesmen successfully argued a case based on independence in pre-European times. Ngāti Ranginui of Judea (Tauranga) asserted and gradually re-established a separate identity during the 1950s, under the leadership of Maharaia Winiata. On the other hand, Uri-o-Hau, formerly a tribe in its own right, is usually classified today as a *hapū* of Ngāti Whātua.

Maoris associate each tribe with the territory over which it exercised sovereignty at the Treaty of Waitangi. But the tribe no longer owns all the land involved. What has not been alienated to Pakehas has been partitioned into many blocks and is held mainly in individualized shares. At most a few blocks and a tribal *marae* are still held by the tribe as a unit.

The tribes are unequal in size. Their membership varies from one to ten thousand or so, their territory from a county to a major region. Their members do not all live on the tribal territory, but those who do usually outnumber other Maoris, except in the cities.

Membership in a tribe depends on birth, though it can be conferred by legal adoption. No official ratification is required or provided, either by the law or the tribe itself. A Maori simply 'follows' the tribal membership of his parents. He is required to furnish a *whakapapa* to prove it only when applying for assistance from a tribal trust fund or when speaking on behalf of the tribe in public. (In the latter case, he is concerned to demonstrate not membership so much as seniority of descent within the tribe.) In country areas the Maori community knows the ancestry and connections of every *tangata whenua* as well and often better than he does himself. Elsewhere people accept a man's assertion until given cause to question it. Pakehas and Maoris of other tribes may be referred to and treated 'as if' they belonged to a tribe, especially if married to a member; and occasionally Maoris announce the 'adoption' of a distinguished visitor 'into the tribe' during speech-making on the *marae*. But in the final analysis such persons do not become 'real' members of the tribe, and they are not expected to exercise the rights of membership – especially in the field of leadership – unless invited. (The conferring of quasi membership is nevertheless a compliment of no mean order.)

Because their parents belong to different tribes, many Maoris can claim to belong to two or more. Usually they stress membership in one most of the time, especially if living in its territory, but recall membership in the others occasionally, when meeting their members, visiting their territory, or attending gatherings where they are specially honoured. As one elder explained: 'I am Rarawa here among my mother's people where I farm family land, but Ngāti Kahu when I visit my father's people at Mangonui.' In urban areas, where most Maoris are living outside their tribal territory, it is becoming increasingly common to hear them say, 'I am both Ngāti P' or 'I am half Ngāti T and half Ngāti K'.

Only Waikato and Ngāti Tūwharetoa acknowledge a paramount chief: most tribes recognize several leaders of senior descent as the *rangatira* (chiefs) or *kaumātua* (elders) of the tribe. These are chosen formally or gradually accorded the status as they prove their wisdom and ability as orators. Such men act as spokesmen for the tribe in its formal relations with other tribes, within or without its territory. Through their speeches at *hui* they influence, though they cannot dictate, the thinking and the decisions of tribal members (pp. 200–3).

Twenty tribes own land and capital. All such tribal holdings are vested by law in Trust Boards of tribal representatives. Five Trust Boards deal with the assets of one tribe only: Aupōuri, Arawa, Tūwharetoa, Whakatōhea and Ngāi Tahu. Three control assets for several tribes jointly: Tai-Tokerau for the five northern tribes, Tainui for Waikato and Maniapoto, and Taranaki for the eight Taranaki tribes (Figure 4). The tribes involved in these three and in Arawa are represented on their Boards in proportion to their strength. By law, Trust Boards must submit their list of officers, annual budget and land transactions to the Minister for approval.

Apart from the Aupōuri Trust Board, which was set up in 1947 to control a communal farming enterprise in Te Kao, the Boards were created originally to administer compensation moneys paid by the Crown in settlement of land claims: to Tai-Tokerau for unreturned 'surplus lands'; to Tainui, Taranaki and Whakatōhea in compensation for unjust land confiscations; to Arawa for rights to the Rotorua lakes; to Tūwharetoa for rights to Lake Taupo; to Ngāi Tahu in purchase of South Island lands. Paid as fixed annual sums in perpetuity, income from these sources has been badly affected by inflation in recent years. The trust boards also receive varying incomes from investments in farming and other enterprises such as the Arawa Trust Board Building, while the Tūwharetoa Trust Board receives a proportion of fishing licence fees in the Taupo area. All the trust boards disburse substantial amounts for educational purposes. Grants are also made to *marae* committees, to sponsors of tribal *hui*, and to *kaumātua* to present at *hui* in other areas in the name of the tribe.

The tribes differ to varying degrees in dialect, custom and cere-monial. Some differences have already emerged, and others will be noted in succeeding chapters. For this reason, and because fellow-tribesmen are kin 'if you go back far enough', a Maori always feels friendly towards a stranger belonging to his own tribe and wary of one from another. Stories of past alliances and hostilities still live in the memories of the older folk and affect their attitudes. From them, the young acquire many prejudices about other tribes. Knowing less about historical causes, however, they discard or modify them more easily. Wherever members of different tribes are thrown together, as in urban areas, tribal antagonisms upset the smooth working of non-tribal organizations, yet friendship and marriage between members of once hostile tribes are so common as to be almost the rule. Tribal differences undoubtedly lend a spice to both.

Within the last twenty-five years several apparently tribal names have been coined by attaching the prefix 'Ngāti' to a transliteration of a city name, e.g. Ngāti Pōneke (from Port Nicholson, Wellington), Ngāti Akarana (Auckland), and Ngāti Hamutana (Hamilton). These are used to refer to Maoris living in the city named, including *tāngata whenua* and 'immigrants' of different tribes 'under the one umbrella'. Apart from casual conversation, such quasi-tribal names are sometimes used at public gatherings by orators speaking to or on behalf of a group of tribally heterogeneous urban residents. They are purely descriptive, convenient labels for the Maoris of a particular city, indicating neither organizational nor sentimental unity. Several appeared first as club names, but in each case have been given a wider application. The older generation dislike them intensely. An elderly Ngāpuhi living in Auckland told me that she hated being called Ngāti Akarana – if she had to go under any tribe but her own, she would prefer it to be Ngāti Whātua, the *tāngata whenua* tribe of the area. But her son and daughter, like most of the city born and bred, defended the title as extremely useful.

Tribal membership today carries few material advantages and no specific obligations. Land and wealth are inherited directly from parents or acquired by one's own efforts. From tribal resources a member receives at most a small grant towards education or *tangi-hanga* expenses. He does not expect the tribe to protect him or to redress his wrongs, and he fights in its defence only (if selected) on the football field. Yet tribal membership remains important to a Maori, because it gives him a defined place in the Maori social world. No Maori has not got a tribe. His membership connects him with exciting figures and events in the past, in which he can feel pride, and with a social grouping recognized and honoured by outsiders.

*The hapū*

*Hapū* stem from ancestors who lived in pre-European times, at least six generations ago and often more, and comprise anything from a few hundred to several thousand members. Each *hapū* is associated with the territory it formerly owned as part of the tribe, though today it rarely owns more than a *marae* reserve. Usually this territory coincides with that of a local community; occasionally two small *hapū* occupy a single district. A *hapū* whose founder is particularly remote is often divided into several minor *hapū* which occupy adjacent districts and join forces under the name of the major *hapū* on important occasions. Where *hapū* members predominate in the *hapū* territory, as in most country areas, *hapū* and community are identified for ceremonial purposes. Thus at *hui* the host speakers welcome and are greeted in return in the *hapū* name.

Membership in *hapū* as in tribe is derived from parents. Since inter-*hapū* marriage has been common for over a hundred years, most Maoris belong to at least two. As with the tribe, they normally give allegiance to one, but recall their connection with others when convenient.

Members of the smaller *hapū* frequently form themselves into *hapū* clubs, generally described in Maori as *komiti hapū*, but also known as *kotahitanga* (unity) or *kaporeihana* (corporation). Unlike the tribal trust boards, these are not usually legally constituted. In theory open to all *hapū* members, in practice they are firmly attached to the home district and *marae*, and consist mainly of those resident there. Some include, some exclude, members' spouses. In function, they vary considerably. Some manage the *hapū*'s *marae*. Others, existing in addition to a *marae* committee, maintain *marae* equipment, provide hospitality for visitors between *hui*, or administer a fund to help members with *tangihanga* expenses. With or without a club, *hapū* members as a group may also run gatherings of *hapū* importance, such as the *tangihanga* for a leading elder or the opening of a new meeting-house.

Membership in a *hapū* has most meaning in its home district, for there *hapū* members are *tāngata whenua* with special rights and privileges, especially on the *marae*. It has significance anywhere in the tribal territory and for fellow tribesmen, establishing the existence and nature of kinship links. But outside their tribal territory Maoris 'go under' not their *hapū* but their tribe, for only the experts know and are interested in the internal divisions of other tribes. In country districts, even the children can name their *hapū* without hesitation, because they continually hear and share in activities undertaken in its name; but young people brought up in urban areas, among members

135

of other tribes, are often unsure of the name of their *hapū*, because it has no social reality for them.

## The large-family

In any Maori rural community, the local people distinguish anything from two to a dozen kin-groups which they describe in English as 'families' and identify by a surname: 'the Rewis', 'the Browns', 'the Hohaias'. These 'families' consist of a nucleus of persons descended through both males and females from a common ancestor (recognized as 'real' members), plus spouses and foster children ('attached' members). Including children, they usually number between thirty and fifty and are distributed among several households. The family ancestor is usually deceased, a grandfather or great-grandfather of the eldest members. In most cases he was a *tangata whenua* in the district and bequeathed the title to his descendants along with local land. Only occasionally have 'immigrants' lived in a district long enough to form a 'family'.

In Maori, a 'family' of this type is sometimes called *whānau*, sometimes *hapū*, and in some areas *whaamere* (Hohepa, 1964: 65–9). Because Maoris use 'family' in Maori and English as often if not more than other terms, I shall use it too. But to avoid confusion with the nuclear family of parents and children I shall use the form *large-family*.

The large-family is basically a descent-group like *hapū* and *iwi*, though for practical purposes it includes persons attached to its 'real' members by marriage and adoption. Unlike *hapū* and *iwi*, however, it remains strictly limited in size and depth. As the family ancestor recedes in time, family members group themselves into 'branches' stemming from key personalities among the elders. These 'branches' act with increasing independence, until eventually, when all who remember the ancestor personally have died, they separate and become large-families in their own right. Large-families that have segmented in this way recognize a special bond, and turn to each other for assistance when they cannot handle a crisis on their own. In most Maori communities, the large-families of *tāngata whenua* stock stem from related ancestors and are linked within the framework of the local *hapū*.

The name used to identify a large-family usually derives from that of its ancestor. Not all family members actually bear it as their own surname. For one thing, female members and their descendants take their surnames from their husbands and fathers. For another, until quite recently Maoris often took their father's first name as a surname instead of his last, so that surnames changed with each generation. Even today, in communities where there are only two or three surnames, confusion is avoided by identifying wives and children by a man's first name in common speech, though they are registered under his last name.

In each generation, some family members leave the home district to settle elsewhere. Emigrants and their offspring are reckoned as members as long as they keep in touch with those who remain and return at least occasionally to take part in family activities. Those who do not are eventually forgotten.

Husbands and wives who have married into the family and children fostered from outside the group by family members are accepted as 'just like members of the family' for practical purposes, but cannot become 'real' members. They take part in family discussions, subscribe to family clubs, and share the work involved in family *hui*. But except under special circumstances they cannot act as spokesmen for the group nor inherit land outright from the family ancestors.

Since affiliation can be made through either or both parents and they can also attach themselves to their spouse's group, many Maoris are active members in two or even three large-families. This is possible because family activities are essentially 'occasional', taking place from time to time and on special occasions. Usually, however, they give one their first loyalty and most time, money and labour. Which one they prefer depends on where they live and how well they know and like its members.

Most large-families acknowledge one man as 'head of the family'. This ought to be the most senior male in the most senior branch, but seniority is waived if necessary in favour of personality, age and traditional knowledge. Women are not usually eligible for the title, but often wield the effective power. Sometimes the head of the family is referred to as its *mātāmua* (literally eldest sibling), but most often he is simply its leading *kaumātua*.

Besides dealing with each other as effective kin in everyday life, members of a large-family also act together as a group for two main purposes: staging *hui* to celebrate crises in members' lives (notably weddings, twenty-first birthday parties, *tangihanga* and unveilings) and managing a family *marae*. When two or more central figures are involved in a *hui* (as at weddings and unveilings), their large-families work together. If the person or persons honoured are of high rank, the other large-families of the *hapū* proffer assistance, putting the *hui* on a *hapū* basis.

Particularly active and closely knit large-families often form permanent 'family clubs' or *komiti*. The main purpose of such clubs is to build up a fund to finance family *tangihanga*, but they also provide a framework for running other family *hui* and family *marae*. Family clubs usually comprise all the married members of the large-family, real and attached, living in the home district. Occasionally they are limited to women only or divided into men's and women's clubs. In Northland they are commonly called *komiti wāhine* (literally women's clubs) and presumably began as such but the description is no longer accurate, for the men subscribe in their own name, attend club meetings, and do most of the talking.

Family clubs build up funds by monthly subscription, donations and levies. Those with a *marae* may derive income from hiring it to outsiders and running card evenings and dances, but must set up a second fund for *marae* maintenance and improvements. The main fund is reserved for *tangihanga*: to pay bills incurred in catering for those in the family and to provide donations to be presented at other people's. Other *hui*, which can be set for a particular date, are normally financed by special collection.

The effectiveness of family clubs fluctuates widely. When there are no deaths in the family for a long period, even flourishing clubs 'fall asleep'. But an emergency soon brings them back to life.

So far we have been talking about large-families in rural communities. Groups of relatives which are identified as 'families', sponsor family *hui*, and form family clubs, are also found in towns and cities. Investigating the membership of such 'families' in Auckland, I found that some were basically descent-groups like the rural large-families, but others comprised several distinct groups of cognates linked by tenuous affinal and foster ties (Metge, 1964a: 164–70). Lonely and insecure, urban immigrants lacking accessible cognates join forces with any relatives they can find, forming *kin-clusters* rather than large-families.

Large-families and kin-clusters in urban areas are mostly composed of 'immigrants', and so rarely have *marae*. The former are usually shallower in depth than rural ones, deriving from a living *kaumātua* whose home serves as centre for family activities. Members of kin-clusters usually come from the same or neighbouring districts in the country.

Like rural ones, urban family clubs exist mainly to build up a fund for use in the event of death. Especially when they take their dead home for burial, urban residents have the additional costs of a hearse or rental van and transport for mourners. As a result, their subscriptions are often higher than in the country. In addition to *tangihanga*, urban clubs organize other *hui* both on the home *marae* and in town, and arrange trips to rural *hui* on a group basis.

Whether in country or city, the large-family means social security to its members. It makes demands on their money, time and labour, but it also assures them of financial and moral support at their life crises. Above all, it relieves them of anxiety over their responsibility as Maoris to honour their dead with a *tangihanga*.

# chapter 11

# Marriage and family

## Marriage

For Maoris, getting married and having children is one of the most important aims in life, especially for women. They regard those who remain single as not merely foolish but neglecting a duty. Reckoned by age-groups, the proportion of Maori adults who are or have been married is consistently higher than that of the Pakehas, the proportion of the never-married consistently lower. (The never-married make up a larger proportion of the *total* adult Maori population, because of the high percentage under 25.) Maoris also tend to marry younger.

Modern Maoris accept legal registration, by authorized persons in the presence of witnesses, as the normal and proper way to establish a marriage. At the same time, they neither condemn nor ostracize couples who are not legally married. In the everyday life of a Maori community, the latter are treated the same as everyone else, though their status may be thrown up at them in a quarrel. Maoris argue that if Pakehas had not introduced registration, *de facto* unions would be valid by Maori standards.

In law, the term 'Maori marriage' is reserved for *de facto* unions established by mutual consent between persons not already married. Today these are valid only for purposes of succession and if contracted before 1952. But Maoris also apply the term to unions involving at least one partner who is legally married to someone else. 'Maori marriages' of the former kind are most common among the older generations in predominantly Maori areas, and decrease year by year. Those of the latter are much more numerous.

While they value marriage highly as an institution, Maoris are less concerned about its stability. They are sorry when a marriage breaks down, but not surprised. Like their forefathers, they regard marriage as a practical arrangement, which should be ended when it ceases to work.

Broken marriages are reputed to be common among Maoris, but exact figures are difficult to obtain. In 1971 the percentage of adults who were divorced and legally separated was slightly lower than for Pakehas (2·4 per cent compared with 2·8 per cent), but this left 'Maori marriages' out of account. In Kotare and Auckland, I found that between 10 per cent and 15 per cent of my married informants were partners to a *de facto* union.

The elderly sometimes try to arrange matches for young kinsfolk, but they rarely succeed: young Maoris choose their own spouses. Having done so, however, they usually seek the formal approval of their kin. First, the boy tells his parents. If they approve, they take a party of kinsmen to call on the girl's family. This meeting of the two kin-groups is known as a *tomo* in Northland but as *tono* and *taumau* elsewhere. It is usually held in a home and attended only by close kin on invitation; but if the couple are of high rank or different tribes, it may be held publicly on a *marae*.

At a *tomo*, the two 'sides' discuss the match in a series of formal speeches. If they agree, they proceed immediately to plan the wedding *hui*. But sometimes approval is withheld, most commonly because of different religious affiliation, unequal rank, or past hostility between the groups. This rarely prevents the marriage. If they are over twenty-one, the couple marry anyway with or without the support of some kin. If minors, they frequently live together until the birth or promise of a child wins parental consent.

Maoris like to surround weddings with elaborate ceremonial. Most of this was borrowed originally from the Pakehas, but it has been extensively modified. Whenever possible, the ceremony is performed in a church and associated with a *hui* involving speech-making, feasting, dancing and the overnight accommodation of guests at the *marae*. In many cases, the *hui* is held at the groom's *marae*, recalling the reception accorded the bride's kin in pre-European times when they escorted the bride to her new home (p. 20). Bridal attendants are often chosen from the two sides equally in a way that gives representation to the main family lines in each. As a result, bridal parties may comprise as many as six bridesmaids, six groomsmen and two flowergirls. In Northland, the hosts frequently allocate tasks such as waiting at table on the same basis. When bride and groom arrive at the *marae* after the ceremony, they are accorded a formal welcome, including a formal 'calling' on to the *marae*, a challenge, action-songs and speeches of welcome, and greetings from a long line of well-wishers (p. 250). Because the elders disapprove of mixing serious talk with food (p. 59), toasts are reduced to a minimum or held after the tables have been cleared. Many guests give money instead of presents, laying it on the cake or giving it to the directing elder (p. 249). When the wedding cake has been cut, pieces are distributed to guests and equal parts are given to the parents on each side for absent kin.

In Northland, the bottom tier is reserved for the delightful 'flower ceremony'. From a central position on the *marae*, an elder 'calls' the names of the tribes and *hapū* represented among the guests, and at each call a member comes forward to claim, on behalf of the group named, a piece of cake wrapped in a paper napkin and adorned with a wedding favour (usually an artificial flower). Formerly, it is said, each claimant had to prove his right to represent his group by reciting his genealogy, and sometimes several contested the honour; but nowadays most claimants 'sing for their flower', anything from an ancient chant to the latest popular hit song.

This ceremony, like the welcome ceremony at *hui* (pp. 250–5), is a ceremony of unification. It stresses the fact that those present belong to different descent-groups and gives them the opportunity to take pride in that membership. At the same time, because Maoris 'have' tribes and *hapū* and Pakehas do not, it stresses their unity as Maoris. (To make sure Pakehas do not feel left out, however, flowers are often 'called' for particular Pakeha guests or for 'Ngāti Pakeha'.) In singing for their flower, the claimants contribute actively to the entertainment of their hosts and co-guests and to the general atmosphere of friendly give-and-take. Very often singers and audience collapse together in laughter. It is a very happy little ceremony.

Afterwards the guests disappear to sports fields or hotel or to the meeting-house for a quiet sleep or chat while the hosts clean up and prepare for the evening. The festivities commonly conclude with an evening dance. In Northland in the fifties this was opened by the bridal couple leading their families in a Grand March round the floor, making sure they drew in all the 'workers' who had worked so hard to make their 'day' a success.

## Family

The English word 'family' has a number of meanings, as any dictionary makes clear. It can be applied to the small-family of parents and children, whether living together or not; to a set of siblings, excluding their parents; to a household; to the descendants of a common ancestor, that is, a lineage; and to a set of people including both the descendants of a founding couple and their spouses. Both Pakehas and Maoris use the word in all these senses, but they tend in general to place the primary emphasis in different places. When Pakehas talk of 'the family' and 'family life' without qualification, they almost invariably mean the small-family of parents and children. This is for them the primary unit, and other kinds of family are seen as secondary, built up of small-family units by addition. To Maoris on the other hand, 'the family' normally means the large-family, and the small-family is seen as a subdivision within it, not a separate planting but a new shoot budding-off from the parent stock. Where Pakehas emphasize the uniqueness and independence of each small-family, Maoris emphasize its continuity and interdependence with others. This comes out clearly in Arapera Hineira's poem quoted on pp. 73–4.

Family life is at once one of the most fascinating and most difficult areas of study in every society. In the Maori case, anthropologists and psychologists have explored different aspects of the subject, to a large degree independently of each other. Anthropologists have virtually ignored the internal relations and life of small-family and household to concentrate on relations between their members and kin outside, with particular reference to the form and functioning of corporate kin-groups such as the large-family, *hapū* and tribe. Only Pat Hohepa, drawing on personal experience as well as controlled fieldwork, has given us a few valuable pages on sibling relations in Waima (Hohepa, 1964: 53–8). The area thus neglected by anthropologists has been explored in depth by psychologists in an impressive array of publications: first the Beagleholes' study of Kowhai, *Some Modern Maoris* (1946), then the Rakau Studies (James Ritchie, 1956a and 1963; Jane Ritchie, 1957; Earle, 1958; Mulligan, 1957), Jane Ritchie's work on *Maori Families* in the city (1964) and Jane and James Ritchie's on *Child-rearing Patterns in New Zealand* (1970). These psychological studies are built on theories which were developed in the study of Western societies and assume the primacy of the small-family unit and of parent-child relations as the main determinants of personality formation. They have produced much valuable information and stimulating insights, but I believe that their theoretical framework, with its Pakeha assumptions and goals, has led them to ignore or misinterpret certain features and to miss the full richness and flavour of Maori family life. Recently, the appearance of short stories and novels by Maori writers re-creating Maori family life from their own experience has provided an invaluable complement and corrective to the research studies. With their depiction of a rich diversity of personal and family relations, these creative works point up both the achievements and the limitations of the objective scientific approach, emphasizing in particular the fallacy of drawing a line around the small-family and the need to view it in its wider setting.

Much of the writing on the subject, both in research studies and in fiction, relates primarily to small rural communities with limited employment opportunities in the fifties and sixties. Those set in the city (Metge, 1964a; Jane Ritchie, 1964) deal only with certain sectors of the population, mostly excluding for instance those of professional status. Urbanization and changes in education and employment patterns have greatly widened the range of family patterns and personal and family goals.

For all these reasons, I shall not attempt to summarize research findings but will venture general observations based mainly on my own experience. To readers who are particularly interested in this field, I would strongly recommend, first the book *Maori* with text by James Ritchie and photographs by Ans Westra, which presents the fruit of the Ritchies' research warmed by personal sympathy and understanding, the short stories in *Contemporary Maori Writing* (Orbell, 1970), *Pounamu Pounamu* (Ihimaera, 1972), *A Piece of Land* (Hilliard, 1963), and *Waiariki* (Grace, 1975), and Witi Ihimaera's novels, *Tangi* (1973) and *Whanau* (1974).

## Small-family and household

The majority of Maori small-families occupy a house of their own and function as an independent domestic unit, in line with the New Zealand norm. Nevertheless, between 20 and 30 per cent of Maori households involve kin and sometimes non-kin from outside the small-family, especially grandparents and parents' siblings. Households accommodating more than a small-family represent a stage in the development of the domestic cycle rather than a separate type of household arrangement. They are formed when adult offspring marry or other kin seek temporary accommodation, to dissolve in most cases within a few years as the elderly die and junior couples move out into homes of their own.

Even when they form a separate household, Maori small-families are usually less self-contained than Pakeha families. Almost invariably in rural and frequently in urban areas they are embedded in one or more large-families and/or an extensive kinship network. Often several related households regularly co-operate in activities such as bulk-buying, outings and family festivities, and both adults and children move between households with a fair degree of freedom, to eat, sleep and participate in daily life.

## Having children

Maoris place a high value on having children, which they consider one of the main purposes of life and marriage. For them 'a home is not a home without children'. Not so long ago, families of ten to fifteen children were by no means exceptional. Out of thirty-five married women past child-bearing age in Kotare in 1955, eight had raised more than ten children, and fourteen had raised between five and ten. Four out of five children in Kotare at that time had more than four siblings. In 1961, according to the Census, 25 per cent of Maori household heads had five or more children currently dependent upon them. During the sixties, discussions at Maori Women's Welfare League and Young Maori Leaders' Conferences revealed an increasing interest in family planning, especially among the younger generations (University of Auckland, 1962 m: 24–5), and the League has continued to support this cause on the grounds that the spacing of children is better for the mother's health and ensures that each child receives adequate attention. For this and other reasons, the average size of Maori families has decreased somewhat over the last ten years, but it is still well above that of Pakeha families. In 1971 21.4 per cent of Maori household heads had five or more unmarried children, compared with only 5.5 per cent of non-Maori household heads. (These percentages are not quite comparable with that for 1961 given above, the wording on the census schedule having been changed from 'dependent children' to 'unmarried children'.)

While they much prefer that children should be born to parents who are married Maoris rarely reject a daughter, own or classificatory, who has a baby while unmarried. Their love for their *mokopuna* normally outweighs all other considerations. Often the two sets of grandparents race each other to collect the child. Sometimes, however, a girl living in the city may conceal the birth of a child from her relatives because of *whakamā*.

### Adoption

Many Maori adults bring up children who are not their biological offspring. Sometimes they adopt these children under the terms of the Adoption Act 1955, but often they do not. Pakehas typically reserve the word 'adoption' for cases legitimated by the Courts and identify the others as 'fostering', but for Maoris this distinction is not particularly valid or important. In English they use the term 'adoption' but it is important to realize that their understanding of 'adoption' differs significantly from that embodied in New Zealand law and official welfare practice.

In Maori a child adopted according to Maori custom is described as a *tamaiti whāngai* and the adoptive parents as *mātua whāngai*. The basic meaning of *whāngai* is to feed, and in this context it means to feed not only with food but with affection and instruction, to nurture in the full sense of the word. Synonyms also sometimes used are *tiaki* (look after), *whakatipu* (to make grow), and *taruima* (to treat with

**9** The crowded city: at close quarters with the law; Auckland 1972

**10** The courtyard of Tūmatauenga: hosts (in the foreground) and guests encircle the *marae* proper listening to the speeches at the opening of the small meeting-house on the Orakei *marae*, May 1973

care). In the *whāngai* relationship, whether legalized or not, the adoptive parents usually take a child who is known to be a relative, the identity of the child's biological parents is not concealed either from the child or the community, and the tie between the child and its adoptive parents is seen as taking precedence over but not negating that with the biological parents. It is a matter of addition, not substitution. A *whāngai* usually reserves the terms 'Mum' and 'Dad' for his adoptive parents, and his or her primary affection and service is to them at least while under their care. He interacts with his biological parents mainly on the basis of their kin relationship with his adoptive parents, calling them sometimes 'auntie' and 'uncle', sometimes 'brother' and 'sister'. If the adoptive parents become old or sick or live too far from schooling, they may send the child back to his biological parents to care for. However, if the latter are not their own offspring, they are just as likely to hand the responsibility on to one of their own sons or daughters or even grandchildren. Usually a special and lifelong tie of affection is established between a *whāngai* and his adoptive parents and their other children, even if he is nurtured for only part of his childhood. Even more than biological children, a *whāngai* is consciously chosen as an object of affection.

Maoris take *whāngai* for many reasons, among which the needs and wishes of adults are considered as important as the child's. Many *whāngai* relationships result from the birth of a child outside marriage, but relatives also lay claim to children born to a married couple, sometimes the first or second, sometimes the youngest in a large family. Sometimes Maori elders arrange an adoption to bring together lines that have diverged over the generations. Perhaps most often married couples who cannot have or have ceased producing children will claim a newly born child from their kin to fill what is felt to be a lack in the home. Some Maori families act as 'foster parents' in the official sense to unrelated children placed with them by the Department of Social Welfare. This is perceived initially as different from the *whāngai* relationship but frequently develops into one if the children remain any length of time. Legal adoption of unrelated children, including Pakehas, also occurs but not so frequently.

'Maori adoption' is often criticized by Pakehas, especially welfare workers. It undoubtedly presents problems in some cases. Adoptive parents who are elderly can be over-indulgent or lack the vitality and adaptability to manage lively children and adolescents. The biological parents, taking advantage of the law, may claim the children back when old enough, to make use of their labour in house or cowshed. Some *whāngai* develop behaviour problems because they feel insecure and unsure of their identity. Criticism is however based on experience of the problem cases only, and on a Pakeha view of the family which stresses the parent-child relation. We badly need a properly controlled study to investigate whether such difficulties arise more frequently in the case of *whāngai* than of other children and what proportion of all *whāngai* relationships run into trouble. In my experience, this relationship can be highly successful, enriching the lives of both parents and children. Many Maoris I know who have good jobs and well-balanced personalities were raised during at least part of their childhood by classificatory parents or grandparents, for whom they express particular affection and gratitude, especially for instruction in Maori.

### Parent-child relations

Differences between Maori and Pakeha attitudes to the small-family are correlated with different ideas about the relation between parents and children. While Maoris emphasize this relationship as an important one, I am convinced they do not conceive it in quite such exclusive terms as most Pakehas. Children are thought of as belonging not only to their parents but also to the wider group of kin. Parents' relatives – not only parents' parents but collateral relatives like grandparents' and parents' siblings and cousins – exercise rights and responsibilities that Pakehas see as belonging to the parents alone: rights to scold and chastise, praise and reward, responsibilities to help in difficulties and to provide refuge and encouragement, not only in support of and in the absence of the parents but also in opposition to them. While young Maori couples often refuse relatives who ask for their child as a *whāngai*, they admit their right to make the claim and feel *whakamā* about refusing it. Parents for their part look to other relatives for help and advice with handling their children, and wise and forceful *kaumātua* are in frequent demand to 'talk to' their young relatives. Perhaps because they are used to sharing child care with older relatives, Maori parents also frequently entrust their younger children to the care of the latter's older siblings and cousins. Such delegation includes the right to scold and discipline but also carries the responsibility to protect and champion the younger siblings.

This approach to the parent-child relation, like the Pakeha one with its more exclusive emphasis, has its strengths and weaknesses. It is particularly well adapted to a rural way of life, where mother as well as father are often engaged for long hours in work away from the house, and where there are other adults and many children in the household. Participation in child-rearing by other kin helps greatly to ease the strains and diminish the damage that can occur when parent and child differ radically in temperament, where the parents and/or the marital relation are under stress, or where re-marriage follows death or marital breakdown. It widens the range of models available to children, their sources of affection and instruction, and their social experience, increasing social ease and self-reliance. On the other hand, diffusion of parental care can mean that physical and emotional problems go unresolved because no one is close enough to the child to recognize and attend to them. Some children, failing to identify deeply with any one adult, also fail to develop the capacity for lasting attachments in later life. Under urban conditions, when relatives are either absent or otherwise engaged, parents used to having advisers and mediators to turn to often feel uncertain of their own judgment and either fail to assert their authority or overdo the disciplining. Children released from adult supervision and interest become increasingly dependent on and involved in peer group 'gangs'. These problems arise mainly when this particular approach to child-rearing breaks down because of human failure and/or unfavourable or unfamiliar circumstances. They should be set against the failures of the Pakeha approach, not its successes.

*Relations between siblings*

Within the small-family, relations between brothers and sisters are ordered largely in terms of birth order and sex, though particular circumstances and personalities may alter this. The first-born son in the family is often referred to and addressed as 'Tama' or 'Boy', the first born daughter as 'Hine', 'Girl' or 'Girlie', and the youngest of either sex as 'Baby', 'Bubs' or 'Bubba'. Used by other relatives as well as parents, these terms frequently become personal nicknames which are continued into adulthood. A child named after a grandparent or other senior relative is often addressed by his siblings by the appropriate kinship term, for instance as 'Koro' (a respectful term for an elder), 'Kui' (short for *kuia*) or 'Uncle', and this too may be taken up by others to become a personal name.

In general the older siblings in a family assert – and are expected to assert – superiority over the younger, and brothers have higher status than sisters, not absolutely but in the context of birth order (Hohepa, 1964: 58 65). Parents generally delegate tasks and authority to the eldest who pass it down the line, especially to siblings of the same sex. According to Hohepa, boys offer more resistance to orders from their older sisters than from their brothers, forcing the girls to call on extra sanctions such as threats of punishment or withdrawal of services. Older brothers on the other hand can usually count on their sisters carrying out their requests with comparatively little fuss, even those near their own age. Up to about twelve years, the younger siblings are very much at the beck and call of the older ones, delegated a variety of tasks by a variety of taskmasters outside school hours. However, they escape this delegation whenever possible to go playing and exploring in peer groups. Once they reach their teens, parents and elder siblings insist more firmly on their help in house and garden, on the farm and at the *marae*. By this time they are sufficiently skilled after several years participation under supervision to be able to do most of the tasks expected of them on their own and soon become delegaters in their turn. Since the tasks involved are rarely formally organized or rostered, the children have a fair degree of choice and variety open to them and opportunity to develop a range of skills, especially in country areas.

Parents reserve the right to punish for serious misdemeanours but allow older siblings to deal with minor ones on the spot. Hohepa observes that they do so mainly by scolding with or without a slap, kick, jolt or earpull, and the chastisement is not prolonged because the offender usually bursts into tears or moves out of reach at the first blow. Overzealous or unwarranted punishment results in the chastiser being chastised by an adult.

Within the sibling group a special bond of attachment often develops between an older sibling and a younger one of the same or opposite sex. In such cases the younger sibling fetches and carries for the older without complaint, while the latter treats him or her kindly, comforts him in distress and champions him against others.

The pattern of sibling relations developed during childhood usually continues to a large extent in adulthood. Orders are replaced by requests and matters of common concern worked out by discussion, but younger siblings are still expected to behave circumspectly in the presence of their elders, special deference is given to the *mātāmua* (eldest of either or both sexes), and all things being equal the opinions of the older siblings generally carry more weight. A younger sibling who has acquired special qualifications and/or proved to be particularly able may become a leader in family and community affairs, but within the family circle he continues to give his seniors due respect. The pair bond between particular siblings is also usually maintained even through separation. It is often extended to each other's children, who may be taken as *whāngai* and/or supported financially both in crises and on a long-term basis.

## Grandparents and grandchildren

The relationship between grandparents and grandchildren is a particularly important one in the Maori family, involving affection and a greater degree of equality and intimacy than that between parents and children. In up to a third of Maori homes grandparents are part of the household. If they do not live there permanently they come to stay on long visits and/or ask for one or more grandchildren to stay with them as *whāngai*. It is well known that grandparents 'spoil' their grandchildren; they caress and give them frequent presents, give in easily to their requests, reprove them mildly rarely using physical punishment, and protect them from parental and sibling wrath. The grandparents' home is always a sure refuge to grandchildren, especially when in difficulties at home, an accepting environment where they are valued regardless of performance. For their part, the grandchildren return the 'old folks'' affection, though they do not always know how much until they lose it. As grandparents become older they often choose the most promising of the grandchildren, one with the *ngākau Maori* ('Maori heart'), to teach their traditional knowledge and skills. And when they become really old and their health fails, it is a grandchild or great-grandchild who usually assumes the role of guide and protector.

Even when speaking English, older Maoris use '*mokopuna*' (grandchild) without translating it, a sure sign of the emotional freight it carries. The word is not restricted to own grandchildren but is often applied to the grandchildren of siblings and cousins, as is the associated behaviour. The traditional Maori word for grandparent '*tupuna*' has largely given way in family life to the transliteration '*karani*' and the English forms 'Granny' and 'Nanny', used for both sexes: in old age and in relation to *mokopuna* the sexes become increasingly identified. These terms too are applied not only to own grandparents but to relatives of the same generation. The warmth of the relationship between 'Grannies' and their *mokopuna*, and its formative influence on children fortunate enough to know it, emerges particularly clearly from the work of Maori writers, for whom it is a significantly favourite theme (see also Powell, 1963).

Nanny Miro . . . among all my nannies, she was the one I loved most. Everybody used to say I was her favourite mokopuna, and that she loved me more than her own children who'd grown up and had kids of their own. She lived down the road from us, right next to the meeting house in the big old homestead which everybody in the village called 'The Museum' because it housed the prized possessions of the whanau, the village family . . .

Nanny didn't really care about money though. 'Who needs it?', she used to say. 'What do you think I had all these kids for, ay? to look after me, I'm not dumb!'

Then she would cackle to herself. But it wasn't true really, because her family would send all their kids to her place when they were broke and she looked after them! She liked her mokopunas, but not for too long. She'd ring up their parents and say: 'Hey!

149

When you coming to pick up your hoha kids! They're wrecking the place!' Yet always, when they left, she would have a little weep, and give them some money (Witi Ihimaera, *Pounamu Pounamu*, 1972: 1–2).

# chapter 12

# Education

E tipu, e rea, mō nga rā ō tōu ao.
Ko tō ringa ki ngā rākau ā te Pakeha hei ora mō tō tinana,
Ko tō ngākau ki ngā taonga ā ō tīpuna hei tikitiki mō tō māhunga,
Ko tō wairua ki te Atua, nānā nei ngā mea katoa.

Grow up, O tender plant, for the days of your world.
Your hand to the tools of the Pakeha for the welfare of your
    body,
Your heart to the treasured possessions of your ancestors as a
    crown for your head,
Your spirit to God, the creator of all things.

       (Sir Apirana Ngata, in a Maori school-girl's autograph book)

Education in the full sense of the word takes place over a broad front, covering the whole process of learning, by children and adults all through their lives. In contemporary New Zealand, formal education in primary, secondary and tertiary institutions has come to be of such central importance that it is commonly referred to as 'education' as if it constituted the whole. All children are required by law to attend school between the ages of six and fifteen, and their relative success or failure in the school system has important implications for their future, because of the way it affects others' valuation and their own self-image. Nevertheless, a great deal of essential learning takes place outside the school situation, in home and community, in childhood and in adulthood. For Maoris this extra-school learning is not always complementary to what is learnt at school: sometimes, and to varying degrees, there is contradiction and conflict.

## Schooling

Going to school is as much part of normal experience for Maori

151

children as it is for Pakehas. Like other New Zealand children, almost all Maori children begin school on their fifth birthday, and the large majority attend state rather than private schools: 96·4 per cent of those at primary school and 91·1 per cent of those at secondary school in 1973.

Up until 1969 a small proportion of State primary and secondary schools were officially identified as 'Maori Schools' and administered directly by the national Department of Education instead of by the regional Education Boards (Holst, 1958; Barrington and Beaglehole, 1974). The distinction between Maori and Board Schools was largely administrative. The syllabus was basically the same and teachers moved freely between the two services, but the Maori Schools received special assistance with staffing and equipment. The Maori Schools were nearly all rural schools with small rolls situated in remote, predominantly Maori, communities on land given by Maori parents. Despite their name their intake was not limited to Maori children, and Pakeha children made up about 8 per cent of their total roll. After 1945, as a result of population movements, the proportion of Maori children attending Maori Schools fell steadily, till in 1963 they accounted for only 20 per cent of the Maori children in primary school and 6 per cent of those at secondary school. When the Department of Education proposed to transfer the Maori Schools to the control of the regional Education Boards, Maori spokesmen strongly opposed the change, arguing that the local communities regarded the Maori Schools as their schools in a particularly affectionate way and that the Department had more understanding of their needs and of Maori ways generally than the Boards. The Department agreed to wait on community approval in each case and the transfer took place gradually. It was finally completed by the Maori Schools Act 1969. Many of the communities concerned, however, feel that they were pressured into agreement and continue to express regret at the change, especially where it has led to the local school being closed and the children transported to a larger school outside the community (Ritchie, 1956b).

Most of the Maori children at private secondary schools attend one of eight boarding schools catering specially for them: for girls, Queen Victoria in Auckland, Hukarere in Napier and Te Wai Pounamu in Christchurch, all Anglican, Turakina (Presbyterian) near Palmerston North and St Joseph's (Catholic) near Napier; for boys, St Stephen's and Te Aute, both Anglican, near Auckland and Hastings respectively, and two Catholic schools, Hato Petera in Auckland and Hato Paora near Fielding. These schools occupy a very special position in Maori education and in the hearts of the Maori people. Over the years they have produced a high proportion of Maori leaders from local to national levels, and their pupils have a significantly better record of passes in national examinations than Maori students at State schools. They are well known and valued for the stress they place on the teaching of Maori language and culture – not simply the surface features of arts and crafts but the deeper inward values. Where pressure on places permits they have always taken some Pakeha pupils. For many years these schools struggled with serious financial difficulties, since Maori parents cannot generally afford high fees and pupils are mainly on grants and bursaries. As a result, Hukarere and Te Wai Pounamu have been converted to hostel communities from which the girls attend local secondary schools. Queen Victoria and Turakina teach classes to fifth form level and send senior boarders to state schools in the sixth and seventh forms. In 1970 past and present pupils of Queen Victoria mounted a nation-wide fund-raising campaign which made it possible substantially to improve buildings and equipment. The Government stepped up its financial aid to five of these boarding schools in 1972. In particular, it has assumed full responsibility for the teaching side of St Stephen's and Te Aute leaving the boarding side to the church trust board.

*Achievement in the school system*

Over the last twenty years or so, educational authorities, Maori leaders and the Press have expressed growing concern that Maori children as a group do not seem to do as well in nor get as much out of their schooling as Pakeha children. What is commonly described as the 'under-achievement' of Maori children has been identified as a problem area in education and become the subject of research and special investigation in educational reports, not in isolation but in the context of continuing evaluation of the educational system as a whole. (See especially Ausubel, 1961a, b; Education in New Zealand, New Zealand Commission on, 1962; Maxwell, 1962; Schwimmer and Ritchie, 1964; Barham, 1965; Benton, 1965; Barrington, 1966; Lovegrove, 1966; New Zealand Educational Institute, 1967; Ewing and Shallcrass, 1970; New Zealand Post Primary Teachers' Association, 1970; Harker, 1971a, b; Bender, 1971; Education, New Zealand Department of, 1971; Bray and Hill, 1973, 1974; New Zealand Educational Development Conference, 1974.)

While they enter school at the same age as other New Zealand children, records indicate that Maori children on average take longer to pass out of the primers, are subsequently several months older than their classmates and fall increasingly behind the average level of attainment, especially in English language skills, as they move through primary school. With 'social promotion' the rule above the primers in primary schools, almost all Maori children now proceed to secondary school (in the 1940s the proportion was only one in three). How ever, they typically leave secondary school at an earlier age and with fewer qualifications than non-Maoris (Education, New Zealand Department of, 1974). Thirty-eight per cent of the Maori pupils who left school in 1972 were in their first or second year at secondary school, compared with only 13 per cent of the non-Maori leavers. In 1973 Maori pupils made up 13·3 per cent of all pupils in third forms, 11·0 per cent of the fourth forms, 10·1 per cent of the fifth forms and only 3·5 per cent of the sixth and seventh forms. Where pupils are 'streamed' according to past achievement as in most New Zealand secondary schools, Maori pupils are generally over-represented in the lower, 'vocational' forms and under-represented in the higher, 'academic' forms. Because of early leaving and under-representation in the 'academic' stream, proportionately fewer Maori pupils proceed to national examinations. In 1972 only 16·1 per cent of Maori school-leavers left with School Certificate in one or more subjects, 4·7 per cent with the Sixth Form Certificate, and 4·5 per cent with University Entrance or higher qualifications. The corresponding percentages for non-Maori leavers were 26·2 per cent, 11·6 per cent, and 28·3 per cent. What is as important as the quantitative evidence, Maori children themselves express dissatisfaction with their school experience both verbally and by leaving.

Various explanations have been advanced for the fact that Maori children are failing to realize their full potential at school. In the 1950s and 1960s there was a general tendency to locate the causes in the personality and home experience of the Maori children, but more recent reports have widened the scope of enquiry to include the school system and the relations between the two. It is taken for granted that Maori children as a group have the same intellectual potential as Pakeha children.

In the past much of the blame for the under-achievement of Maori children was laid on rural residence. Maori children living in rural areas often had to travel long distances to school over poor roads, and to help with farm chores. Their homes were small and over-crowded, and their schools suffered from staff shortages and changes. While these conditions still apply in some areas, urban migration has greatly reduced the proportion affected, rural roading is much im-proved, and hostel accommodation and boarding allowances are now fairly readily available.

Under-achievement at school is frequently identified as a con-comitant of lower socio-economic status. It is pointed out that a high percentage of Maori parents are engaged in un- and semi-skilled occupations with fluctuating incomes and long working hours; and the percentage with large families is also high. Under such circumstances, mothers and older children commonly go to work to help support the family, and parents rarely have the time or background to supervise homework. Several research studies suggest that the discrepancy is greatly reduced if not eliminated when Maori and Pakeha children are matched on the basis of parents' occupation.

From time to time, especially in the Press, Maori parents are taken to task for lack of interest in their children's progress at school. Education officers and research workers insist that Maori parents as a group are no less interested in their children's school experience than Pakeha parents, but because they usually left school early themselves they do not know how best to help and are extremely diffident about approaching teachers, whom they regard as vastly superior in knowledge and status. Many have difficulty understanding the ramifications of the school system as a whole, and so feel inferior and confused (*whakamā*) in dealing with any part of it.

Currently a popular explanation for the learning difficulties of Maori children is the idea of 'cultural deprivation' or 'intellectual impoverishment' in the home environment. These conditions are diagnosed on the basis of a reputed lack of books, parents' failure to read, tell stories and talk at length to their children, and an allegedly impoverished English vocabulary. Such features are assumed, following overseas studies, to be associated with rural and lower-class status, compounded in the Maori case by the problems of acculturation. While widely accepted by teachers and embodied in a handbook issued by the Department of Education (1971), this view is at present under attack from linguistic and educational experts, on the grounds that it ignores the range of variation in Maori homes and uses a narrow and ethnocentric definition of intellectual stimulation. There is a growing proportion of Maori homes in which books are both numerous and valued and parent-child interaction close and frequent. In those cases where Maori children do not have close contact with their parents, they commonly interact intensively with grandparents and peers. In place of books, they are exposed to aural and visual stimulation of kinds not recognized by teachers trained in a culture that stresses the written word. Works like Sylvia Ashton-Warner's *Teacher* (1963) and Elwyn Richardson's *In the Early World* (1964) show what skilful teaching can elicit from Maori children from allegedly deprived backgrounds. In doing so they cast serious doubt on those early research projects which found Maori children limited and unimaginative in their cognitive functioning. It would seem now that the limitation was in the tests rather than the tested.

Until quite recently the teaching of Maori children was based on the assumption that bilingualism was a major handicap and so firmly to be discouraged. Most Maori adults recall being punished for speaking Maori at school. Knowledge of Maori was considered to lead to confusion of word-idea relations, mispronunciation, grammatical errors, and impoverished vocabulary. In addition, the children's English, learnt and spoken in the home, was seen as a 'poor' version of accepted English, to be corrected at every opportunity. Recent developments in the study of language and language acquisition have led to a re-evaluation of this position. Experts in the teaching of language skills now advocate beginning where the child is, recognizing the value and richness of his own language experience and building on it, even if it is a hitherto devalued 'dialect'. Such insights are slow to percolate through to many classroom teachers.

Recent reports have shown growing appreciation of the fact that the New Zealand school system as it has existed up to the present is almost entirely monocultural, based on a set of assumptions and principles about child development and the aims of education that have been developed in, and to serve the needs of, Western societies. Methods of measuring intelligence and achievement place heavy stress on verbal skills, especially in English and in writing, favouring not merely Pakeha children but Pakeha children from certain kinds of homes. The reading and resource material provided has been largely on subjects outside the experience of Maori children. While aspects of 'Maori culture' have been introduced into the curriculum, it has been as an optional extra and mainly in the field of art and the study of the remote past.

Above all the school system, as mediated through curricula and teachers, emphasizes the values of individuality, competition, self-discipline, restraint, striving for distant goals, and abstract expression. Yet before they start school and throughout their years there Maori children are socialized in homes, communities and peer-groups which value sociability and solidarity with family and peers above individuality, co-operation above competition, and physical and social achievements above the purely intellectual. Such values are widely identified as typical of the 'working class' and are shared to a large extent by Pakehas in similar occupations. It does not necessarily follow, however, that they can be explained entirely in terms of socio-economic status. They should be seen rather in the context of the whole Maori value system and experience, with its insistence on the wholeness of life and the complementarity of concrete and abstract. It is probably truer to suggest that Maoris choose certain occupations because they have these values than it is to suggest that they have these values because they work in certain occupations.

At school many Maori children find that what they have already learnt in home and community is either unaccepted, misinterpreted or unrecognized, while they are expected to have mastered quite different skills, such as the ability to sit quietly for long periods and to enter into intimate yet respectful interaction with adults. What this means from the child's point of view is movingly portrayed by Arapera Blank in 'One Two Three Four Five' (in Schwimmer, 1968). As Ritchie comments, the problem is not cultural poverty so much as cultural musical chairs. It is hardly surprising that the children's response to the school situation so often involves feelings of frustration, inadequacy and failure. While at primary school, many Maori children cope with the contradictory values of school and community by code-switching as they move between them, but in adolescence, as they grow rapidly towards adulthood, the conflict grows more direct. Sensing that their parents, whatever they say, are afraid that schooling will 'take our children away from us', most Maori adolescents choose to identify with community rather than school.

While the proportion of Maori teachers in the schools has increased considerably, the majority of teachers teaching Maori children have been socialized and trained in settings dominated by Pakeha cultural concepts. In general, their knowledge of Maori language, culture and values is learnt at second-hand and limited largely to 'surface' features like the arts. Even when living in Maori communities, they are constrained by the structure of the situation, especially their high status, from establishing direct and frank relations with the local community. Judging the behaviour of their Maori pupils by their own standards and experience, they commonly fail to appreciate either the degree of independence and resourcefulness developed by Maori children in their own setting, or their responsiveness to peer-group guidance. Instead they perceive Maori children as shy, inarticulate, lacking in drive and self-discipline, and often disobedient 'for no good reason'. These more or less stereotyped views of Maoris and Maori children cause them to concentrate on the difficulties and overlook the strengths arising from the children's experience. Unwittingly they set up self-fulfilling prophecies which help to determine both the way the children see themselves and the way they are presented as they proceed to the next level.

### The Campaign for Improvement

#### (a) The Department of Education

Since the Native Schools Act 1867, the State Department of Education has held special responsibility for the education of Maori children. Up until the Second World War this was exercised through direct administration of the Maori Schools, but in 1956 the Department appointed a Senior Officer for Maori Education with responsibility for Maori children in schools of all types. The staff involved were all Pakehas until John Waititi was seconded to the Department to write a series of Maori language texts in 1959. Proving invaluable as a consultant on Maori education in general, he was appointed Assistant Officer for Maori Education in 1963. In this capacity, until his premature death late in 1965, he made a major contribution to the development of departmental policy on Maori education and aroused and focused a great enthusiasm for education among the Maori people as a whole. In particular he was a prime mover in campaigns to raise support for the Maori Education Foundation and to encourage Maori adults to study for higher educational qualifications.

In 1968 the Department established a special Division of Maori and Island Education with two sections dealing respectively with the education of Maoris and Islanders in New Zealand and education in New Zealand's Island territories. The New Zealand section is staffed in 1975 by an Officer in Charge, three Inspectors, six Advisers to Rural Schools (Maori), six Advisers on Maori and Polynesian Education and a Specialist Adviser on Language. The three Inspectors and five of the Advisers are Maoris. The section is supported by two advisory committees. The National Advisory Committee on Maori Education was originally set up in 1955 but reconstituted in 1969 so that at least 50 per cent of its membership must be Maori. It meets once a year and in 1971 produced a far-ranging Report on Maori Education in which forty-six detailed recommendations were presented to the Minister of Education. The Advisory Committee on the Teaching of the Maori Language was established in 1958 on the recommendation of Maori language teachers. Primarily concerned with the development of teaching material, it meets four times a year, and nine of its ten members are Maoris.

Incorporating the recommendations of the National Advisory Committee on Maori Education, the Department's policy for the seventies emphasizes the taking of special measures where needed to give Maori children equality of educational opportunity, modification of curricula to give fuller recognition of Maori language, and increased involvement of the Maori people in working, thinking and decision-making in the educational system. Already a number of significant advances have been made. Provision has been made for schools with a high proportion of Maori and Polynesian students to receive additional staffing. (In 1972 this amounted to 234 extra full-time teachers, 112 part-time teachers, and 937 teachers' aides in 156 schools.) The number of visiting teachers and guidance counsellors has been increased and sessions on the needs of Maori children introduced into their training courses. By 1973 25 Form One to Six schools have been set up in predominantly Maori areas and a five-day hostel attached to a high school as a pilot-scheme. Particular stress is being laid on teacher training both in teachers' colleges and during service. Lecture-ships in Maori Language and Maori Studies have been established at all teachers' colleges, there being thirteen such positions in 1973, all occupied by Maoris. A special three-year course in Maori Studies began at Wellington Teachers College in 1973, and a scheme for full-time one-year courses to train native-speakers of Maori to teach the language in the schools was launched in 1974, at colleges in Auckland, Hamilton, Wellington and Christchurch with an intake of forty-three increased to forty-six in 1975. During 1972 and 1973 the Department of Education staff organized thirty-four in-service courses on teaching English to Maori children, fifteen on teaching Maori language, seven on Maori arts, and two six-week courses on teaching Maori children. The syllabuses for the School Certificate, University Entrance, Burs-ary and Scholarship examinations in Maori language have all been recently revised to emphasize oral skills. Since 1958 the Department of Education has co-operated with the Technical Institutes and the Department of Maori Affairs in the provision of special trade training schemes, and in short pre-employment and city life courses. The Department has also established pre-school groups at ten schools with predominantly Maori rolls since 1969. It plans to sponsor more advisers and provide more finance for buildings in this field.

(b) *The Maori Education Foundation*
Acting on a suggestion made in the Hunn Report, the Government established the Maori Education Foundation as an independent statutory body 'to help existing authorities identify and meet the problems involved in Maori education'. After an intensive fund-raising campaign, the Foundation commenced operations in 1962. The Foundation operates under the control of a Trust Board of eight members, of whom at least four must by law be Maoris. It has an administrative staff of four directly responsible to the Trust Board. They occupy offices adjoining those of the Division of Maori and Island Education in the Education Department in Wellington. At the end of 1971 the Foundation controlled a trust fund of $2·3 million built up by grants from the Government and the Maori Purposes Fund Board and by donations from Maori incorporations and trusts (and private individuals) which also carry a Government subsidy. The Government also meets administrative costs. Permitted by a 1972 amendment to the original Act to reduce the accretion of capital and expend new receipts as well as interest, the Foundation was (in the early seventies) disbursing about $350,000 a year, mainly in direct grants to students from primary to tertiary level, but also by paying honoraria to liaison officers and counsellors at secondary schools and universities and by supporting the developments of pre-

school education for Maoris. By the end of 1972, the Foundation had made a total of 904 grants to secondary boarding school students, 125 to university students and 37 to trade trainees. While no detailed evaluation has been made of the effect of such support, the Foundation has undoubtedly assisted many Maori students to proceed further with formal education than they could otherwise have done, so raising the overall level of achievement.

The Foundation entered the pre-school field in 1963 when it employed a pre-school specialist, Alex Gray, for a limited term to encourage Maori participation in the pre-school movement. The results proved so worthwhile that the Foundation first persuaded Mr Gray to extend his term and then appointed its own Pre-School Officer, who was for some years assisted by an officer on secondment from the Department of Education.

(c) *The Pre-School Movement*
State schools in New Zealand do not normally admit children under five years. Younger children are catered for by voluntary pre-school groups mainly of two kinds, 'free kindergartens' which are affiliated to the New Zealand Free Kindergarten Union and run by full-time teachers trained at a kindergarten teachers' college, and 'playcentres' which are affiliated to the New Zealand Federation of Playcentres and are run by the mothers themselves, a significant proportion of whom have taken part-time training courses at different levels. In both cases, programmes for the children are based on the concept of supervised 'free play' and do not aim directly at developing cognition or school skills.

Before 1960 few Maori children attended pre-school groups, but in the early sixties interest in pre-school education developed rapidly among Maori organizations and communities and led, with the assistance of the Pre-School Officer appointed by the Maori Education Foundation, to the establishment of pre-school groups throughout the country in areas with substantial Maori populations. Most of these are based on the playcentre model: one or more of the mothers with children attending undergo special training to become supervisors and run the play sessions with the help of the other mothers who attend in turns, two to a session. A playcentre has one or two supervisors according to the number of children enrolled, and many of the mothers take shorter training courses as 'mother-helpers'. Some Maori communities have developed their own variation on this pattern, the 'family play-groups', in which all mothers participate in the running of each session, with or without the leadership of one with special training. Some groups of this kind, mainly in the Waikato-Maniapoto area, formed themselves into the Maori Family Education

Association. Pakehas have copied this Maori-originated form of organization and 'family play-groups' are now widespread outside Maori communities.

It is difficult to obtain an accurate account of the number of Maori children attending pre-school groups. The figure of one in four Maori children between three and five years is widely quoted but probably overstates the case, due to a tendency in this context to identify all children of Maori ancestry as Maori. Maori children attend pre-school groups with varying proportions of Maori to Pakeha. Even those which identify themselves as 'Maori pre-schools' do not exclude Pakeha children, the name signifying orientation rather than membership.

Enthusiastically supported by educational authorities and many Maori organizations, the development of pre-school education for Maori children has been criticized by some as assimilative and based on Pakeha aims and values. Illuminating insights on this question are provided by Geraldine McDonald reporting on research commissioned by New Zealand Council for Educational Research in *Maori Mothers and Pre-School Education* (1973) and other articles (1970 and in Bray and Hill, 1974: II, 58–78). McDonald found that Maori recruitment to pre-school centres was effected mainly on a personal basis through kinswomen and friends; in short, the Maoris themselves are the most effective champions of the movement. Most of the mothers she interviewed rejected the idea prevalent among Pakehas that their children had deficiencies due to home background that pre-school experience was needed to overcome, but looked to the pre-school mainly to prepare them for school, so that they would not be lost or shamed in an alien environment. They perceived the main gains to their children as being in social development. Those interviewed expressed little criticism of existing pre-school aims and practices in general, and none mentioned favouring the use of the Maori language with the children, though some centres outside the sample were known to be doing so. The mothers valued their own involvement, especially in playcentres and family play-groups, as a means of meeting others and learning for themselves, both through participation in sessions and through taking parent education courses leading to the award of certificates of attainment at successive levels. In addition to the benefit to the children, participation in the pre-school movement has raised the educational status of many Maori women, provided them with extensive opportunities (because many leaders are required to make such centres work) for developing leadership skills, and given them confidence in their ability to get things done, to the great profit of the wider society.

While the different types of pre-school centres are perceived as having somewhat different aims and results, McDonald found that the degree of Maori participation in, and benefit derived from, pre-school education varied with the type of community in which the centre was set rather than with the type of organization. In kin-based Maori communities separate from Pakeha settlement, pre-school centres were firmly established as an integral and stable part of the community. Nearly, if not all, the mothers and often the grandmothers were involved, and Maoriness was expressed without undue emphasis in such features as flexible criteria for membership, opening with prayer, the use of Maori between adults if not with the children, communal meals, hospitality to visitors, and Maori methods of debate and decision-making. At the other end of the scale, in migrant areas where Maoris made up less than 10 per cent of the population, Maori participation in pre-school groups was small but also stable, those involved accepting a completely Pakeha orientation. But in kin-based Maori communities engulfed in Pakeha settlement, and in migrant areas where Maori representation was over 10 per cent, there was a tendency for Maori membership to fluctuate and for difficulties to arise between Maori and Pakeha adult participants. Broadly speaking, increasing Pakeha presence in community and pre-school resulted in the elimination of Maori practices and orientation in favour of Pakeha ones and decreasing participation by Maoris especially as leaders. The Maori response was either to withdraw altogether or to form a separate group under Maori leadership. While a clash of values undoubtedly underlies the difficulties that arise in mixed pre-school centres, McDonald suggests that the values that are most at fault are not the Maori ones as Pakehas tend to assume, but the Pakehas' negative stereotyping and devaluation of Maoris and Maoritanga. A small proportion of Pakehas, in a pre-school group, say less than a third, would seem to put Maori mothers on their mettle, but greater numbers cause them to withdraw because the pressure from the dominant group and culture becomes too great.

Though Pakeha in origin, pre-school groups are not necessarily nor inevitably Pakeha institutions imposed on the Maoris. Whenever circumstances permit, Maori mothers and communities have adapted their organizational forms and principles to their own needs and in doing so developed a new and important avenue to self-realization. However, there is a real and continuing danger that the Pakeha majority, by overlooking or misunderstanding Maori needs for involvement in leadership and decision-making, may initiate changes in policy – such as raising the entry requirements for training for senior positions or increasing the emphasis on the role of experts – that will adversely affect Maori participation.

(d) *Innovation in the Schools*
Although most New Zealand schools may justly be characterized as monocultural in orientation, there are a few where teachers are endeavouring to develop a school environment and teaching programme that recognizes not only the needs but also the rich cultural heritage of local minority groups. The best known and best documented of these, Hillary College, was founded in the Auckland suburb of Otara in 1966 with Maori and other Polynesian students making up 57 per cent of the roll (Johnson, 1973, 1974). Taking Ngata's advice to Maori youth (printed at the head of this chapter) as guideline, the Principal set out to create a truly multi-cultural school, in which Maori and other Polynesian pupils develop a sense of identity and self-respect by having access to their own cultures as an integral part of the curriculum, and by being successful in academic terms as well. At present, the teaching of Maori language and culture is available at all academic levels, and is taken by some 200 students, a fifth of the total roll. The multi-cultural nature of the school finds particular expression in the Polynesian Club, the strongest extra-curricular activity in the school, which teachers see as complementing classroom work. Besides learning songs, dances and arts from all over Polynesia, the Club's activities include exchanging visits with other schools and Maori communities, associating with the local Maori Women's Welfare League and Maori Committee in the provision of hospitality to visitors, and seminar study of relevant social problems. Importantly, the Club plays a central role in the public life of the school, in assembly and the welcoming of visitors. The Club is administered by a student committee, and staff, students and parents are all involved in the teaching.

The College aims to complement not supersede the home. To meet difficulties with homework, volunteer school staff man a homework centre in the school library four nights a week and conduct a week's study camp in the vacation. Parents are invited to discussion sessions before and after student field-trips. As a result, Polynesian parents identify closely with school activities. They are as well represented as Pakeha parents on the Parent-Teacher Association committee. The local Maori Women's Welfare League (of which the school has a junior branch) does the catering for school functions, while the Maori Wardens supervise them. Parents teach various skills at the Polynesian Club, while Maori writers have provided original material for English classes.

Evidence of the effectiveness of this approach is provided by the fact Polynesian students are equally represented at all academic levels, slightly outnumbering Pakeha students from the third right through to the sixth and seventh forms (cf. p. 154).

Unfortunately the situation is less happy in many of the urban schools with a high proportion of Polynesian pupils. In the early seventies, a sense of grievance built up among Maori and other Polynesian parents in the Auckland area over the high incidence of suspension and expulsion of their children from secondary school, until it found an outlet in the news media. In response the Minister of Education set up an appeal system and a Committee of Enquiry into Communication between Parents and Schools early in 1973. In a Report released in August 1973, the Committee came to the conclusion that in view of the 'delicate diffidence' of Polynesian parents, teachers must assume the greater responsibility for improving parent-school communication. It asked the schools to give high priority to caring about the values and cultures of minority groups and the welfare of the maladjusted and to involve themselves more in the community. The Report's detailed recommendations mainly reinforced those of earlier reports, but included some imaginative extensions, such as a proposal for a short-stay 'new-opportunity school', preferably residential. Consultation between the Auckland District Maori Council and the Secondary School Principals' Association produced a plan, and a class along these lines was established at one of Auckland's major technical colleges in 1974 with an initial intake of twelve.

In September 1973 the Maori lecturers at Auckland University's Centre for Continuing Education (formerly University Extension) organized a Seminar for Maori Teachers including teachers of Maori language and of Maori students as well as teachers of Maori ethnic origin. Those attending strongly recommended recognition of Maori language and culture as an integral not peripheral part of the school curriculum. They also formed a Maori Teachers' Association. Since then the Maori University Extension lecturers have played a leading part in involving Maoris and other Polynesians in discussions associated with the Government-sponsored, nation-wide Education Development Conference in 1974, many of which were held at *marae*. These too came out strongly in favour of introducing a multicultural philosophy into the education system. In February 1975 the Department of Education brought teachers of Maori from all over the country together for a week long in-service meeting on a *marae* in Ruatahuna in the Urewera's.

### Tertiary education

Information on the number of Maoris attending and graduating from universities, teachers' colleges and technical institutes is practically impossible to assemble as most tertiary institutions do not keep separate records for Maori students. The Hunn Report estimated that the number attending university in 1956 was one eighth what it ought to have been on a population basis. On the basis of estimates for 1968 on admittedly inadequate data Harker (1970) suggested that while the proportional representation of Maoris at university had improved since 1958, their numbers still needed to be increased sevenfold to achieve parity for the 18–24 years age-group. Increase in the number of Maoris gaining University Entrance, the availability of additional assistance from the Maori Education Foundation, Government sponsorship of trade training schemes and increasing use of special admission provisions at the universities, have undoubtedly combined to improve the proportion of Maoris in tertiary institutions substantially over the last decade, but almost certainly not enough to make up the leeway. The intake into trade training schemes has climbed steadily since their inception (p. 83), but in 1974 the number of Maoris accepted for teachers' college (other than those in the special Maori language teachers' course) actually decreased when an over-supply of applicants resulted in entry qualifications being raised. However, this decrease was immediately reversed for 1975 by a special recruitment campaign among Maoris with the necessary qualifications.

What little information is available suggests that the proportion of Maoris at the universities has continued to increase comparatively slowly since 1968. Staff with an interest in Maori students however are convinced that there has been a significant improvement in their achievement in terms of pass rates, grades and participation in class discussion and university life generally. Apart from the normal strains of student life, Maori students have to contend with a variety of strong and sometimes contradictory pressures, expected to do well and so lift the *mana* of their family, tribe and people, but constantly under suspicion of 'forgetting their Maori side and going Pakeha'. Not infrequently the need to meet obligations to kin and Maori causes interferes with concentration on their studies, though contributing to their development in other ways. The large proportion of Maoris at university take degrees that equip them for occupations in the 'service to people' category. After graduation many choose to work in areas where they can serve their own people, as teachers, social workers, doctors, dentists, clergymen, civil servants, lawyers, accountants and architects. Very few take degrees in science or business administration, though some have achieved high status in both fields, one for instance as a Doctor of Science working in the Department of Scientific and Industrial Research and another as the newly appointed Professor of Business Administration at Victoria University of Wellington (Fitzgerald, 1968).

Wherever they are studying in any numbers, Maori students have formed formal groups, linking up as the New Zealand Maori Students' Federation in 1958 and changing their name to Te Huinga Rangatahi

165

o Aotearoa with the inclusion of other youth groups in 1973. Especially in the seventies they show a lively interest in the problems of their people, playing a prominent part in the campaign to extend the teaching of Maori in schools and providing many of the foundation members of Ngā Tamatoa (p. 177).

A Maori Graduates' Association was founded in 1965 and currently has a mailing list of 220-300 members. Scattered all over New Zealand and involved in a variety of professional associations, they nevertheless manage to gather once or twice a year for a weekend with each other and the local people on different *marae* round the country and have lent their corporate as well as individual support to many Maori causes. Besides continuing support for the cause of Maori language teaching, they have made numerous representations to Parliament on legislation affecting Maoris, especially with regard to Maori land, education, the Race Relations Act and currently the Treaty of Waitangi Bill, actively supported campaigns to assist Maori boarding schools like Te Aute, opposed the closing of small country schools on the East Coast in favour of centralization, and suggested that the tribal Trust Boards should finance tribal *whare wānanga*.

**Educational research**

Over the years Maori education has stimulated probably more research than any other sector of Maori life, mostly in one-man projects sponsored either by the universities or the New Zealand Council for Educational Research, an independent research foundation established in 1933. In 1971 after a long battle to raise the finance, the NZCER set up a Maori Research Unit. In 1972 the Government convened an Advisory Committee on Research into Maori Schooling to advise the Director-General of Education and the Director of the NZCER on research policy and priorities.

At present, in 1975, the Maori Research Unit is engaged in two major types of work: first, collecting and disseminating information and ideas to persons and institutions involved in Maori education, and secondly basic research in certain language-related topics. It hopes in the future to undertake action research in selected schools. The unit's major research concern is a survey of language use among Maoris throughout the North Island, involving structural studies of the English and Maori spoken by Maori children and adults and a sociolinguistic study of language attitudes and language use. It was begun in 1973 and will take several years to complete.

## Adult education

While they had access to the same adult educational facilities as
Pakehas in theory, Maoris were for a long time slow to patronize
them, because they were located in the towns and met neither Maori
needs nor interests. Formal classes especially designed for Maori
adults were first provided in Auckland in 1945 at a camp for 'man-
powered' workers. When New Zealand universities accepted responsibility for adult education in 1949, the universities in Auckland and
Wellington each appointed a Tutor-Organizer especially for Maori
work, Auckland making a second appointment in 1952. Through the
fifties the three Tutors, who were all Maoris, travelled widely in their
university districts speaking at *hui*, organizing classes and weekend
schools in Maori communities, and themselves doing much of the
teaching on topics requested by the people: mainly traditional Maori
history and culture, contemporary social problems, race relations,
religion, politics, committee procedure, local administration and investment societies. The universities also assisted in the building or
renovation of several *maraes* (e.g. at Judea and Bulls) by providing
specialist tutors in arts and crafts.

In 1959 the University of Auckland, in conjunction with various
Maori organizations, convened a national Young Maori Leaders'
Conference patterned on that organized in 1939 by Sir Apirana
Ngata and Professor Horace Belshaw. Over the next five years
another twenty Maori Leadership Conferences were held on a regional
basis jointly sponsored by the University Departments of University
Extension (as they had been re-named) and specially formed Maori
committees. In a variety of ways these conferences involved a combination of, or compromise between, Maori and Pakeha ways of
doing things. Special invitations were issued to young people nominated by local Maori committees and organizations, a more general
open one to the older generations. Those attending received a cyclostyled Agenda of data papers and questions prepared by local discussion groups which met for months beforehand and/or by specialists.
Beds and meals were provided at a *marae* for the two- to three-day
meetings, while working sessions were held at a near-by school. Each
conference began and ended with ceremonial speeches and prayers in
Maori, but discussions were mainly in English. Participants were
divided into a series of Round Tables for discussion of the Agenda,
the elders having their own, but came together in plenary sessions to
hear addresses and consider recommendations.

While the conferences concluded with the passing of numerous
recommendations, their main aims and value lay in the areas of
education and communication. In their own Round Tables, away
from the inhibiting presence of their elders, the young people learnt

167

from and with each other, developing their ability to think issues through and to express themselves in public. Above all they gained confidence. In plenary sessions, where the generations met on a more equal footing than was possible in a wholly Maori setting, elders and young people listened to and learnt to respect each other, discovering common aims and interests under their apparent differences. If they produced few direct results, the recommendations directed at official bodies helped reinforce representations from other quarters. The conference agendas and reports provided a mine of information on Maori views and aspirations (University of Auckland, Department of University Extension, 1939–70). In several cases, the discussions aroused such interest that they were continued in local discussion groups for another year or more.

In the latter half of the sixties, however, changing university policy on adult education required the Maori Tutor-Organizers to develop more formal academic and specialized courses in the university centres, diminishing involvement in community education. These new-style courses proved comparatively unattractive to Maoris whose involvement in University Extension dropped off markedly. Only one Maori Leadership Conference has been held since 1965, at Auckland in 1970. Quite recently, however, the universities have shown signs of re-awakening interest in community development (see also Adult Education, National Council of, 1972).

The decrease in Maori participation in University Extension has been partially offset by an increase in Maori adults taking night classes at secondary schools and technical institutes. Fostered by the news media and the persuasive advocacy of John Waititi, Assistant Officer for Maori Education, a wave of enthusiasm for enrolling for School Certificate and University Entrance Examinations built up among Maoris in 1964–5, but it lost much of its impetus when John Waititi died late in 1965. Nevertheless, this proved the gateway to further academic success for a small but significant number of Maori adults, including the first Director of the Maori Research Centre in Hamilton.

### Other forms of education

For Maoris, as for most New Zealanders, learning outside the school system is largely informal, acquired through experience and in the context of inter-personal interaction in home and community, but from time to time Maori communities do also set up formal learning situations, mainly for instruction in traditional arts and crafts, tribal history and *marae* procedure.

For all sorts of reasons – because of paid employment and large families, because 'teaching is the schools' job', because the skills and knowledge they have to teach are devalued in contemporary society – Maori parents and grandparents have generally abandoned the methods of planned instruction of the young described by Buck (1949: 356–363). Maori children spend a large proportion of their time in association with, in the care of, or caring for other children. They are admitted to and often expected to be present at most adult activities from religious services to *tangihanga*, but how much they learn depends almost entirely on their own interest and attentiveness. Many Maori adults regret that they did not 'pay attention' as children to what was going on around them. However, unless their parents have completely lost contact with other Maoris, Maori children absorb more than they realize of Maori words, practices and especially attitudes and values. If and when interest in their own cultural background develops, as it often does in the middle years, they learn relatively quickly and effectively because they have a store of experience to re-interpret.

There is, however, much highly specialized and specific knowledge – family and tribal history, genealogies, *marae* and *hui* protocol, arts and crafts and song poems – that cannot be picked up merely by contact. For the last two or three generations at least many Maori elders have been reluctant to hand on this *tapu* knowledge lest it be treated with disrespect, with dangerous consequences to all concerned. Some have taken their knowledge to the grave with them. Others wait until they find a young relative, preferably, but not necessarily, male and a direct descendant, who has both interest and ability, and take him or her under their wing as an apprentice. In the last twenty years, a revival of interest in Maori ways on the part of many young people as well as the middle-aged has led to the holding of meetings described as *whare wānanga* in many parts of the country. These differ from the traditional schools of that name in several ways. They consist of comparatively short sessions of a few hours, one or two days, or (rarely) a week, are held at intervals, at *marae* used between sessions for other purposes, and are no longer restricted either to males or to the well-born. Sometimes admission is by invitation only, but often they are open to all tribal members interested enough to attend. The *tapus* observed are much less stringent than formerly, often limited to a ban on smoking and eating during sessions. Elders vary in their willingness to allow note-taking and tape-recorders.

While the arts of carving, *tukutuku* and *kōwhaiwhai* are increasingly taught at school, there is still scope for these skills to be acquired the old way, under experts commissioned to supervise the building of a meeting-house (see p. 275). Those who show a particular aptitude may develop their skill and reputation by working on similar projects in other communities or by attending the Maori Arts and Crafts Institute in Rotorua.

Finally, those who have not learnt *haka* and action-songs at school or want further experience usually join 'cultural clubs', which serve social as much as educational purposes (see p. 182). For many young Maoris, especially in urban areas, joining such clubs represents the first step towards developing pride in their cultural heritage.

## Centre for Maori Studies and Research

Opening the new University of Waikato at Hamilton in 1964 Sir Bernard Fergusson, then Governor-General, suggested that it was 'a proper centre for a Maori university within a university . . . not separate but part of the whole for Maori and European alike . . . and . . . a bright new dynamo for Maori education generally'. After delays due largely to economic difficulties, the university established a Centre for Maori Studies and Research on the university campus with the help of various organizations and individuals as well as the Government. Robert Mahuta M.A., a graduate of Auckland University, was appointed as Director late in 1972, and two further staff members in 1973.

To date, the Centre has given first priority to research objectives. In addition to membership of study groups on matters such as Maori education and *marae* subsidies, Mr Mahuta is involved in continuing research on the effect of the Huntly Power Station developments on Maori communities in the Waikato. Dr Jane Ritchie, post-doctoral fellow at the Centre, has been conducting an experimental pre-school project, while research fellow John Rangihau is engaged in the study of the urbanization process among the Tūhoe and the compilation of the records of the Ringatū Church. Staff also meet a continuing demand for *marae* seminars from communities within the university area, in conjunction with University Extension and the Department of Education. Within the limits imposed by a shortage of finance, shared at this time by all New Zealand university institutions, the Centre has in a few short years firmly established its worth as a vital link between the *whare wānanga* of the Pakeha world and the Maori communities of the central part of the North Island.

# chapter 13

# Association

While kinship and descent remain important bases of association, Maoris also associate with each other, and with Pakehas, in groups formed on other bases, chiefly age, sex, recreational interests, religion and politics. Like kin-groups, these may be informal – neighbourhood, peer and friendship groups – or they may be formally constituted, with a charter defining aims, membership and procedure. Some formal groups are legally registered as incorporated societies or educational and charitable bodies, but many are maintained only by agreement among members.

Maoris often describe their formal associations as *komiti*, a term we have already met in connection with *hapū* and large-families (pp. 135, 137). Since it occurs frequently in this chapter, let us begin by examining it more closely.

## Komiti

In form a transliteration of 'committee', the *komiti* is a good example of how Maoris modify not only the words but also the institutions and usages they borrow. Maoris use *komiti* to describe any Maori group that has a formal constitution with a *Haemana* (Chairman), *Hekeretari* (Secretary) and *Kai-tiaki-moni* (Treasurer – literally 'one who looks after the money'), regardless of aims, number of members, or legal status. In practice, the groups so described are of three distinct types: first, groups with a limited membership elected as an executive by members of a larger association; secondly, groups with a limited membership elected for special purposes by persons who may or may not belong to a formal association (e.g. School and Maori Committees); and, thirdly, groups whose membership is not limited in number, though it may be on other grounds (e.g. football and

171

family clubs, Maori Women's Welfare League branches). Groups of the first two types are committees, but those of the third are clubs. Confusion is compounded when Maoris render *komiti* in English as 'committee'. Thus a '*marae* committee' (for instance) may be either a small elected committee of six to ten members or a club with fifty subscribers!

Club or committee, *komiti* work in a distinctively Maori way. Their meetings are always open to the public, and non-members are allowed to take a full part in the discussions, provided they observe the rules of Maori debate. Holding secret meetings 'in committee' is foreign to Maori thought and practice. As a result, even special-purpose committees are well aware and act in the light of public opinion. Minutes are recorded in Maori or in Maori and English, subscriptions usually paid formally at monthly meetings, and money for special ventures raised by special levy or competitive giving. Meetings are opened and closed with prayer. Most speakers give a rounded speech, even when only registering assent. Women, 'immigrants' and young people wait for the 'big guns' to speak first, or brief a *kaumātua* to speak for them. Members prefer to talk their way round to unanimity rather than take a vote. Meetings tend to be lengthy, and several are required to settle important issues. But once a decision is taken, everyone is committed to its support.

### Age-grading

Maoris make a basic opposition between the categories 'old' and 'young'. The 'old' are identified collectively as *kaumātua* though in the singular this word is usually applied to a leading male and contrasted with *kuia* (old woman). The 'young' are subdivided into children (sing. *tamaiti*, pl. *tamariki*) and 'young people' in their teens and early twenties who in Maori terms have not reached full social maturity (*taitamariki*). The generations in between were formerly described as *taikaumātua* but this word has dropped from use. If necessary, the term *pakeke* is used to distinguish a mature, responsible adult from the *taitamariki*. *Pakeke* is also and most often used as a synonym for *kaumātua*.

In outlook, interests and choice of associates, Maoris do in fact tend to separate out into informal age-grades along the lines of this categorization. This is sometimes formalized in the establishment of youth clubs and the division of sports clubs into players, managers and supporters. It derives in part from traditional Maori society in which young people were expected to confine themselves to perfecting their crafts and enjoying themselves, the parental generations were occupied with household and community tasks, and authority and decision-making were concentrated in the hands of the elderly. But differences between the generations have also been intensified by rapid social change. Young people today become independent legally at twenty and financially and socially much earlier. Schools and mass media have displaced parents and elders as the main sources of knowledge and instruction. The young acquire as a matter of course knowledge and skills the elders do not possess.

The terms *kaumātua* and *kuia* are usually used to refer to people who are over fifty-five years, have grown-up grandchildren and show signs of age such as grey hair. However, they may also be allotted on the basis of role to someone younger, for instance a teacher in charge of a party of students. *Kaumātua* as a group are thought of as wise in personal and social relations, expert in Maori language, lore and custom, rather strait-laced and 'keen on the past and the old ways'. In fact only a proportion are truly expert in traditional lore; and these include many with wide-ranging interests and an open and positive attitude to the modern world. Younger Maoris regard the *kaumātua* with mingled exasperation, affection and respect, may brush aside their advice in some matters, but look to them for leadership in Maori situations and for comfort and support in trouble.

The 'young' are mostly under twenty-five either single or not long married. They are typically preoccupied with exploring new fields of experience and enjoying themselves. They insist on their independence, fiercely resenting any attempts to direct them, but are often reluctant to accept responsibility for running things for themselves. They like to be thought 'modern' and 'up-to-date', and are extremely knowledgeable about machines, radio, television and films. They are impatient of 'past history' and such 'old ways' as ceremonial speech-making and match-making. But they are usually enthusiastic about the distinctively Maori dances known as *haka* and action-songs, and they enjoy *hui*, cheerfully helping with the work at those sponsored by their kin or clubs and travelling long distances to attend the big ones. Though they covet the wealth and independence of the Pakehas, they are not usually prepared to cut themselves off from Maori friends to pursue them. The 'young' are sometimes referred to collectively as 'the *rangatahi*' (p. 204). As with *kaumātua*, this word is usually reserved in the singular for someone who has shown a capacity for leadership.

Members of the 'middle generations' are generally more stable and settled than the 'young', more liberal and adaptable than the 'old'. As they grow older, they become progressively more interested in family and community and in distinctively Maori ways of doing things. Most of the officers and really active members of *komiti* are drawn from their ranks.

Relations between these informal age-grades are complex and ambivalent, especially between 'old' and 'young'. Real and classificatory grandparents and grandchildren in many cases, they are bound by ties of personal affection, childhood intimacy, and Maoritanga; but their interests and aims are different and often contradictory. They spend little time together and less talking to each other. In each other's company, the 'young' are alternately silent and belligerent, the elders disapproving and indulgent. The 'old' criticize the 'young' for their instability, pleasure-seeking and impatience with the past, but accept such behaviour as normal for their age and status, secretly proud of their high spirits. They worry more over their insistence on self-determination, which they blame on 'Pakeha influence'. The 'young' criticize the 'old' as 'out-of-date old fogies whom the times have left behind', but they like to have them there in the background, because they represent dignity and stability.

The 'middle generations' get caught between 'young' and 'old'. The 'young', classing them with the 'old', rely on, but rebel against, their direction in sports, youth and *haka* clubs, and the 'old', classing them with the 'young', count on their support as 'workers', but resist their attempts to assume responsibility, especially when they try to modify traditional patterns. In many country communities, even the middle-aged are reluctant openly to challenge the elders, especially in public, preferring to persuade a liberal elder to present their views for them. But in other places, especially the city, they take a prominent part in the talking at club and committee meetings, and even at *hui*.

Though friction between the generations sometimes breaks into open conflict, breaches are usually resolved sooner or later, especially when a united front is required, to ensure the success of a *hui*, or in confrontation with the Pakeha.

### 'Gangs' and other youth movements

Young Maoris have always tended to associate with each other in informal groups of limited size and duration, like the group which set out to make the peace their elders had failed to make with hostile neighbours in 'The Story of Ponga and Puhihuia' (White, 1889, IV) or the friendship groups I found spending their spare time together in Auckland in the fifties (Metge, 1964a: 201–2). Since 1970, however, several new kinds of youth groups have come into prominence involving large numbers and often a strong element of protest against established society.

First there are a number of predominantly or exclusively Maori 'gangs' based mainly in urban areas. Membership is predominantly male, though the proportion of girls may be as high as 40 per cent.

Most 'gangs' involve young people in their late teens and twenties but some have been formed by thirteen- to sixteen-year-olds. Like comparable non-Maori groups, they favour dramatic names like 'Black Power' and 'the Mongrel Mob' and cultivate a distinctive appearance with long hair and jean-jackets decorated with paintings and badges.

These gangs first came to public notice in 1970 when members of one called the Stormtroopers were involved in a series of street brawls and later interviewed on a television public affairs programme. Viewers reacted with a sense of shock to their name, their Nazi insignia and their allegations of police harassment, but noted in extenuation the relative restraint of their leaders, the youthfulness of the rank and file, and their description of the lack of entertainment, meeting-places and adult concern in their home suburb of Otara in Auckland. The publicity brought practical help, especially from a Maori mother they nicknamed Mama Cass and members of the Auckland Maori District Council, Pat Hohepa and Rangi Walker. It also led to an influx of would-be members and dubious claims of membership. The Stormtroopers re-organized, revising their aims to emphasize community service and imposing membership limits. They had a friendly if wary meeting with the Minister of Maori Affairs and took a leading part in discussions at the Young Maori Leadership conference at Auckland University in August. Offered a hall as base, they initiated a weekly social programme for Otara youth and became involved in fund-raising for a *marae* and other projects, hitting the headlines again when they organized a two-day pop festival called 'The Love Affair' which raised $1,000 to help save Queen Victoria School for Maori Girls. They won the hearts of conservative Northland Maoris when they helped clean up the *marae* after the Waitangi Day gathering at Waitangi in 1971. Within a year they laid aside their 'colours' and became increasingly integrated into the developing Otara community they had helped stir into self-consciousness. Today most of the original members have married and settled down, but the gang's name and role has been assumed by their younger brothers who run a much patronized social centre in East Tamaki. Though they are jokingly referred to by other gangs as Otara Junior Rotary and accused of selling out, the Stormtroopers' story is important because it suggests that much of the gangs' apparent alienation is in reaction to a society they see as materialistic, selfish and uncaring.

Most of the gangs existing at a given time are in confrontation with the police and in open rebellion against the mores of the adult community. Many claim a membership of one or two hundred, but this usually involves a core of twenty to thirty and an amorphous circle of less involved members. Some, like the Stormtroopers, are essentially local groups, whose members live in a particular urban locality with parents or kin and spend their spare time together, perhaps with an old house as headquarters. Others are more self-contained, living together in flats and old houses often in the central city, moving frequently because of difficulties with landlords, and sometimes sleeping in public places like the railway station. Some of the older groups are 'bikies' building their lives round motor cycles, but most make do with old cars or public transport. Gang members are mostly, but not always, early school-leavers who disliked and acquired no qualifications at school. Living very much for the moment, they take mainly casual jobs, and those that have money share it with those who do not. Many have convictions and have served sentences in periodic detention and borstal mainly for theft and car conversion, and they are constantly watched, questioned and moved on by the police. Most of the gangs get involved in fights and feuds with other gangs.

At a Polynesian Youth Forum on The Gang held in Auckland by the Department of University Extension in 1972, participants, including many gang members, stressed the 'need for identity and a sense of group belonging' as the major reason for joining a gang. Whether they come to the city from the country or were brought up there, young Maoris (it was said) felt threatened by 'alien and unfriendly city folk': they banded together for comradeship and protection against both other gangs and the assimilative pressures of the Pakeha majority. Some complained of lack of interest from parents and other adults, some of unrealistic and hypocritical demands. The need for both parents to work to make ends meet, inexperience in exercising authority away from the supportive Maori community, and their own involvement with the pressures and attractions of the city are undoubtedly contributing causes. One ex-gang member said that most of his gang had joined for 'kicks': they had much spare time, plenty of money and found little to do even in the city. As the older people present commented, the motive was familiar: only the mode differed from their own youth. Maori communities have always encouraged young people to be active, strong and daring, qualities summed up in the adjective *toa* which as a noun means warrior, and have expected and tolerated a certain wildness and lack of judgment while they try their wings. The duplicative form of *toa* is *totoa* which means reckless. In the country, youthful energy can be directed into channels that either serve community purposes or at least do not disrupt them too much, but in the city where strangers with diverse life-styles live in close proximity and social control is exercised mainly by official agencies, young people are given less guidance and much less latitude. In reacting to the gangs with fear and distaste, the general public forgets that they are still growing up and as one put it, 'going through the toughest period of our lives'.

**11** The realm of Rongo: in the crowded meeting-house, body of the Whānau-ā-Apanui ancestor Tūkākī, hosts and guests come together in peace and friendship, at the Maori Artists and Writers Conference, Te Kaha *marae*, June 1973

**12** *Marae* ceremonial in the city: on a temporarily closed road, the challenger leads the guests of honour (Anglican Bishop of Waiapu Paul Reeves and Archdeacon of Kapiti Te Pura Pānapa, escorted by local elder Māui Pōmare) to their seats for the unveiling of a carved figure commemorating Te Rauparaha, warrior-chief of Ngāti Toa, at Plimmerton (Wellington); February 1975

Social workers, police officers and private citizens have tried to help the gangs with varying aims and degrees of understanding. The most successful are Maoris who, knowing what it is like to be members of a minority group, build on the gangs' assets of group pride and comradeship instead of trying to make them over in another image. Though they talk of 'society' as the enemy, the gangs themselves are not so alienated that they will not seek help even from the establishment. In 1974 a group who had been evicted from their house staged a sit-in in the foyer of Parliament until the Minister of Maori Affairs promised help in finding jobs and accommodation. In the nature of the case, the gang situation is constantly changing, with employment opportunities, the seasons (many leave town for the beaches in the summer), and the normal processes of maturation. Even when a name continues in use, a gang can change entirely in membership and leadership within a couple of years, as members approach twenty-five, marry and settle down.

## Ngā Tamatoa

While most gangs have a largely local reputation, the name of Ngā Tamatoa is known throughout New Zealand, because its members are articulate and skilled in the use of the news media. Ngā Tamatoa was formed in 1970 in Auckland as an action group to press for the preservation of Maoritanga, especially in urban areas, and the elimination of racial discrimination in New Zealand. The name, which can be translated as either 'the brave sons' or the 'young warriors', was chosen to emphasize action, courage and continuity with the ancestors. At least half the foundation members were university and teachers' college students and members with this background remain important in the group. Ages range from sixteen to the early thirties, including a number of married couples. Ngā Tamatoa groups were soon established in Wellington and Christchurch as well as Auckland. Though perceived by outsiders as a united radical movement, Ngā Tamatoa contains considerable diversity. The branches are completely independent in organization, policy and activities, though they keep in touch. Members are also divided on questions of political ideology and tactics and sometimes even on goals.

One of Ngā Tamatoa's first actions was to hold a ceremony in the grounds of Auckland University to 'rededicate' a memorial plaque on an old blockhouse wall after changing the wording from commemoration of 'the British soldiers and their Maori allies who died in the Maori Wars' to 'those Maoris who died during the Pakeha Wars'. In 1972 they organized a protest demonstration at the Waitangi Day observance at Waitangi to 'focus attention on Maori grievances';

177

later in the year they took a leading part in the establishment of a National Maori Language Day (14 September) and presented a petition with 30,000 signatures to Parliament on the teaching of Maori language in schools (see p. 99). The Auckland group organized seminars to train fluent Maori speakers in language-teaching methods in Auckland and the movement as a whole maintained pressure on the Government until special courses for this purpose were instituted at the teachers' colleges in 1974. They have made submissions and representations to Parliament on many issues particularly in relation to race relations, land, education and justice. Before the 1972 elections they set up a 'Maori Embassy', Te Whare o Te Iwi, on the steps of Parliament House. Operating entirely with voluntary workers and donations, both the Auckland and Wellington branches run advice bureaux and legal defence schemes in which members attend the Courts to advise Maoris charged with offences on their rights and how to obtain legal aid. In 1972 Ngā Tamatoa, along with the Polynesian Panthers, was awarded a Governor General's Youth Award for their work in these fields.

Thoroughly at home in what Maoris call 'the modern world', with strong personalities and the gift of trenchant expression, Nga Tamatoa leaders have attracted, and made effective use of, exposure in the news media, especially television. For a period the Aucklander Syd Jackson wrote the fortnightly Maori affairs commentary in the *New Zealand Listener*. They have also sought to rally Maori support by speaking at conferences and *hui*. Their speeches and actions have aroused mixed reactions among Maoris as among Pakehas. On the one hand, they have been criticized for trampling on Maori customs, using 'Pakeha' tactics such as heckling, and claiming to speak for Maoris generally. On the other hand they have been praised for voicing grievances and resentments which have been glossed over in the past on grounds of courtesy. As Ngā Tamatoa have learnt more about Maori custom and proved willing to work as well as talk (painting *marae* buildings, for instance) their acceptability has greatly increased, though they are periodically reminded that they do not speak for all Maoris.

As with all youth groups, the membership of Ngā Tamatoa has changed over time: most of the foundation members have by now decreased or withdrawn from involvement. In a few short years, however, they have achieved much. Building on foundations laid by previous generations, they have brought issues of concern to Maoris into the arena of public debate, and effectively pioneered new methods of dealing with them.

*Students' groups*

Maori clubs and societies have been a feature of the life of most universities and teachers' colleges since the early fifties, even those in the South Island. In their early years probably their most important function was to provide a familiar and supportive atmosphere for Maori students feeling isolated in an alien environment, a setting where they could work out together what being Maori meant to them (Williams, 1960). This often involved learning action-songs and *haka*, then the language and the skills of *whai-kōrero* (formal speech-making) and *waiata* (song-poems). Over the last ten years they have increasingly turned their attention outwards, to the task of educating Pakeha colleagues in Maori ways and to fighting for Maori causes, especially that of the language in schools. The work of Te Reo Maori Society (Victoria University of Wellington, 1972) in this regard has already been mentioned (p. 99). From its formation in 1959, the New Zealand Federation of Maori Students meeting in annual conference has made its voice heard on Maori issues. As with other student groups, its membership changes almost completely every three or four years.

*Te Huinga Rangatahi o Aotearoa*

In 1973, after a joint gathering at a *marae*, the New Zealand Federation of Maori Students, Ngā Tamatoa and several other groups amalgamated as Te Huinga Rangatahi o Aotearoa. It was this association which initiated and was mainly responsible for production of the first issue of a multi-language newspaper *Rongo* (p. 99). While they continue to meet once or twice a year in a *marae* setting, the constituent groups of Te Huinga Rangatahi largely go their ways between meetings and special projects like National Maori Language Week.

**Men, women and single-sex groupings**

As we have seen (p. 62), Maoris regard men and women as different in nature, roles and functions but united in a complementary relation. In Maori settings, men and women frequently associate in groups of predominantly one sex usually within sight of each other and engaged in complementary or associated tasks. At a *hui*, the younger men do the heavy work such as moving furniture, chopping wood and making the *hāngi*, and the older the formal speech-making, while the women work in the kitchen and dining-hall, prepare the meeting-house, call visitors on to the *marae* (*karanga*), wail in mourning for the dead (*tangi*) and support the speech-makers in singing *mōteatea*. This separate but complementary relation is also to be found in the household, where men work outside on the farm or in paid employment and lay the *hāngi* for special occasions, and women do the housework and normal cooking. Both work in the garden but often at different tasks. Especially in large households and when guests are present, the women often serve meals to the men and visitors first, and eat together afterwards. This practice should be interpreted not as an indication of inferiority, but in terms of the *tapu-noa* relation in which *noa* has its own value (see p. 60).

A comparison can also be made with the relation between hosts and guests at a *hui*; while the guests are *tapu* and honoured as such, the hosts also have a secure and *tapu* status as *tāngata whenua*. In both cases, the servers take pleasure in caring for (*manaaki*) those they serve and eat together afterwards in relaxed comradeship and pride in an important service well done. In country churches, men often sit together, on one side, the women and children on the other and young adults at the back. A similar separation may be observed at dances and football matches.

This particular patterning of sex roles does not in itself weaken the bond between husband and wife. On the contrary it often results in the development of a particularly strong relationship of interdependence. However, for spouses whose marriages are less than fully satisfactory, it provides ready access to companionship and support from friends of their own sex.

Single-sex *komiti* are common, especially in the country. The management of *marae* and/or *tangihanga* is often divided between a 'men's committee' or all-male '*komiti marae*' and a 'women's committee'. Many football clubs have a 'women's committee' to raise funds for the all-male management and players. In the fifties committees open to both sexes in theory were frequently regarded as a male sphere of influence and paired with women's organizations: the local Maori Committee (for instance) with the local branch of the Maori Women's Welfare League, the Anglican Church Committee with the Mothers' Union. This attitude has largely broken down in recent years, especially in urban areas.

Maori women belong to several women's organizations of Pakeha origin, notably the Country-Women's Institute and the Association of Anglican Women (formerly the Mothers' Union), and they have two large-scale associations of their own. In the case of the former, they often belong to Maori Branches established in days when they were sensitive of poorer housing and education and hesitant in English, and maintained because they still feel more at ease together. The Maori Health Leagues are mainly in the Rotorua area where they were set up in the 1930s at the suggestion of a District Nurse.

The Maori Women's Welfare League was founded in 1951 at a conference of delegates from women's welfare committees formed after the Second World War by Maori Welfare Officers. In 1974 it had 27,500 members belonging to 136 Independent Branches and 42 Branches grouped into eleven District Councils. Branch and Council delegates meet in conference annually as a Dominion Council, electing a Dominion Executive to run League affairs between conferences. The League operates mainly on the basis of funds raised by members, supplemented by a small annual grant from the Government. At present (1975) they have only one paid officer, a secretary stationed in Wellington. According to its Constitution, the main objects of the League are to promote fellowship and understanding between Maori and Pakeha, to instruct Maori women in the care of home and children, to encourage the practice of Maori arts, and generally to further the welfare of the Maori people. While branches vary in where they place their major emphasis, there is no doubt that the League has served a valuable function in helping Maori women, especially young wives and mothers, develop their abilities in organization and debate and their confidence in themselves. From the League as a base, many women have moved out to become effective leaders in general community and especially multi-cultural organizations. At the national level the League quickly established itself as a force to be reckoned with back in the fifties, expressing Maori views on a national basis years before the establishment of the New Zealand Maori Council. It is affiliated to the National Council of Women and the Pan Pacific Association and represented on the Maori Education Foundation and on the Advisory Committees on Maori Health and Education convened by the Government. Recommendations from Dominion Council have played a major part in securing (among other things) an increase in Maori housing assistance, the establishment of health clinics and pre-school facilities in predominantly Maori areas, and adoption of the anniversary of the signing of the Treaty of Waitangi (6 February) as New Zealand Day in 1974 – though they would have preferred it to be known as Waitangi Day.

## Sport

Like most New Zealanders, Maoris devote much of their leisure to playing and watching sport. In Kotare in 1955 70 per cent of those between fifteen and twenty-five belonged to sports clubs as players, and a third of those between twenty-five and fifty-five were involved in management and supporters' committees.

As players and spectators, Maoris show a decided preference for sports which involve team practice and bodily contact and are played in winter. They work best in a team and like to come to grips with the foe. They play less organized sport in summer because of seasonal employment (in shearing, harvesting and freezing works) and the counter-attraction of the seaside.

In the country Rugby football is undisputed king of sports. Every Maori community of any size has its own club and ground; players retire late, only to take up management and coaching; and all but the physically incapacitated turn out for matches on the home ground. The women play basketball and hockey – on Saturday morning to avoid clashing with football. Tennis and softball clubs are common but less well supported. Besides matches, sport involves many other activities: money-raising gatherings, feasts, dances and concerts to entertain visiting teams, 'away trips', and end-of-season parties.

In urban areas, Rugby and basketball are still favourites, but many Maoris also play Rugby League, indoor basketball and softball, and some have achieved prominence in tennis, table-tennis, boxing, wrestling, swimming and golf.

Clubs in predominantly Maori areas field predominantly Maori teams, but include any Pakehas who are available and good enough. But in areas where Maoris are in the minority, many Maoris play of choice in all-Maori teams, especially in basketball and softball. They say they like playing together because they have the same style. All-Maori teams are affiliated to ordinary regional Associations and so play regularly against all-Pakeha and mixed teams. There are a few Maori Associations, but these are either located in predominantly Maori areas or confine themselves to sponsoring annual matches and tournaments. In addition to the matches arranged by their Associations, Maori teams compete for a large variety of special Maori trophies. Periodically the selectors of the Rugby Football Union choose a New Zealand Maori representative team (the 'Maori All-Blacks') to play touring teams or tour Australia and the Pacific.

### Maori cultural clubs

Perhaps the most striking evidence for the vitality of Maoritanga is the continuing increase in size and number of Maori cultural clubs all over the country. Some of these have a long history, like the Rotorua clubs that provide concerts for tourists, Waihirere and Waipatu in Hawke's Bay, and Ngāti Pōneke founded in Wellington in the thirties; but probably a majority are a direct outcome of the urban migration, established in towns and cities by Maoris keeping alive their cultural heritage and identification for coming generations.

Though the learning of songs and dances for concert performances takes up much of the time at regular club meetings and often appears to be the primary purpose, the clubs are generally committed to a much wider view of Maori culture. Many run Maori language classes for members and arrange craft instruction so that they can make their own costumes, ornaments and weapons. Tribal traditions and rules of protocol are explicitly taught in preparation for, and absorbed during, frequent visits to *hui*, ranging from small ones on home *marae* to such large-scale *hui* as the Coronation Celebrations at Tūrangawaewae. In the absence of elders, younger men and women have to develop skills in speech-making and calling so that they can represent the group on the *marae*.

It is reliably estimated by informants involved as judges that there are upwards of three hundred cultural clubs in operation, of which at least a hundred have established reputations throughout New Zealand. Every urban area with a Maori population of any magnitude has at least one, and many rural communities are now forming formal clubs to meet the challenge from the city ones.

The increase in cultural clubs has been associated, as both cause and effect, with an increase in 'cultural competitions'. These have long been a feature of such large annual gatherings as the King Movement Coronation Celebrations (p. 197) and the Anglican *hui tōpū* and also of the Wellington City Competitions, but over the last ten years competitions have been increasingly organized on a regional basis, until now they are held annually in seven of the eight Maori Land Board Districts, using the same names. The leading teams from the District competitions win the right to participate along with groups from all over the Pacific in the biennial Polynesian Festival initiated with Government assistance in 1971. Year by year these competitions widen the number and scope of their classes: besides *haka*, *poi* and action-songs, they now include classes for *mōteatea* (traditional song-poems), choral performance, speech-making, and original compositions of varied types. Encouragement has also come from the New Zealand broadcasting services through the making of television series featuring Maori groups and the conducting of competitions for original Maori tunes and lyrics. The first of these was held in 1966, the second in conjunction with the Cook bicentennial celebrations in 1969. Now they have become an annual event, giving, with the District competitions, much needed encouragement to original composition.

### Religious groups

While Maoris generally share belief in supernatural beings which act in man's world, they vary widely in the patterns of belief and behaviour which they build on this foundation. To explore these variations is a major task, beyond my competence and the scope of this book. For the present I shall confine my attention largely to the most readily accessible aspect of the subject, membership of groups formed on a religious basis, recognizing however that the connection between group membership and understanding of, and adherence to, official doctrine and practice is by no means simple or complete.

Significantly, substantially higher proportions of Maoris than Pakehas 'object to state' or fail to specify religious profession on census schedules, a fact which makes comparison difficult. The reasons can only be guessed at: possible explanations include objection to the census as an invasion of privacy and/or a Pakeha imposition, and adherence to beliefs and groups that are not officially recognized. The statistics do however confirm the assertion that few Maoris openly repudiate religious belief: in 1971 only 1·2 per cent declared themselves to be atheists or to have 'no religion', compared with 2·8 per cent for the rest of the population. For the rest, the proportions of Maoris who belong to the Anglican, Roman Catholic and Methodist Churches are fairly close to the non-Maori proportions, but the Presbyterian Church, the second largest denomination for New Zealand as a whole, has very few Maoris, largely because of early concentration in the South Island. Significant proportions of Maoris also belong to the Ratana, Ringatū and Mormon Churches, all of which have relatively few Pakeha members.

Table 11    Religious Professions 1971

|  | Maoris % | Non-Maoris % |
|---|---|---|
| Anglican | 26·2 | 31·7 |
| Roman Catholic | 17·2 | 15·6 |
| Ratana | 12·1 | 0·1 |
| Latter Day Saints (Mormon) | 7·6 | 0·5 |
| Methodist | 7·1 | 6·3 |
| Presbyterian | 2·9 | 21·9 |
| Ringatū | 2·4 | 0·01 |
| Agnostic, atheist | 0·1 | 0·7 |
| No religion (so returned) | 1·1 | 2·1 |
| Object to state | 11·4 | 8·4 |
| Not specified | 7·1 | 3·3 |
| Other | 4·8 | 9·39 |
| Total | 100·0 | 100·00 |

*The major denominations*

The Anglican, Roman Catholic, Methodist and Presbyterian Churches minister to the majority of their Maori adherents through separately organized Maori divisions, while accepting those who wish to join as members of their general congregations. All have ordained Maori clergy, engaged mainly in ministering to Maoris. The Anglican Church has a Bishop of Aotearoa who serves Maoris throughout New Zealand and is also Assistant Bishop of Waiapu. The Churches run six boarding schools for Maori boys and five for girls, with State assistance on the educational side (see pp. 152–3).

The Anglican and Presbyterian Churches have both maintained separate Maori theological colleges at various times but now all candidates for the ministry train together at the same theological colleges. For many years the number of Maori candidates offering has been limited, possibly by the educational prerequisites and academic nature of the training. This problem is being partly overcome by accepting older men with long service as laymen for special shortened courses. Some provision is made for Maori language and studies in the colleges, for the sake of Pakeha as much as for Maori students.

Set up in the missionary period, the Maori divisions of the churches are maintained at the express wish of the Maoris served, who prefer to attend services conducted by Maori ministers in their own language among friends and relatives, and to receive pastoral care from Maoris who understand and share their basic concepts and life experience. Maori worship is characterized by informality, warmth and wholehearted participation. At Pakeha services (they say) Maoris feel conspicuous and unsure of themselves, and are either chilled by Pakeha formality or embarrassed by a special welcome. Used to singing unrestrainedly and without accompaniment, they are frustrated by differences in pitch and harmony and afraid to let themselves go.

The separate organization of Maori pastoral care was logical and easily arranged when most Maoris lived in predominantly Maori communities in the country, but urban migration and the decline in the proportion who speak Maori presents new problems. Usually the ratio of clergy to people is extremely poor and Maori clergy spend much time travelling between places of worship and parishioners' homes. The people too must often travel considerable distances to services; and there are many competing claims on their time and loyalty. Some Maoris join local congregations, but far more drop away from contact with the church except at life crises. Rarely self-supporting, Maori pastorates and parishes depend on subsidies from the wealthier Pakeha sector. In 1973 the Maori clergy and laymen argued in the Auckland Diocesan Synod that dependence and Pakeha oversight were factors contributing to the falling away of support and won agreement to the establishment for a trial period of an autonomous Maori Synod which can manage Maori affairs the

Maori way and deal with the Pakehas in the Diocesan Synod on an equal footing. This move was closely associated with endeavours by the Maori clergy to develop a Maori theology comparable with the Black theology of Africa and the United States of America and involving the synthesis of Christianity and traditional Maori religious concepts as handed down in the *whare wānanga*. Several Maori clergymen received training in the latter, sometimes before deciding to become ministers but often, if they came from Tai Tokerau or Tai Rawhiti, at the instance of their elders who had already chosen them for the ministry. It would seem that the experts of the *whare wānanga* were engaged in reconciling Christian and traditional theology long before the official theologians recognized the legitimacy of such an enterprise. A major contribution along these lines has recently been published by Rev. Maori Marsden in *Te Ao Hurihuri* (King, 1975; 191–219).

The Maori religious tradition past and present includes two kinds of religious experts, the priest trained in *whare wānanga* and/or theological college, and the prophet who is the channel for a direct revelation from God. Of the prophets who have arisen to help their people grapple with their problems over the last hundred years, two founded religious movements significant in a variety of ways.

*Ringatū*

The Ringatū Church, which takes its name from the 'upraised hand' used when praising God, was founded in the 1870s by Te Kooti, but not legally registered till 1938 (Greenwood, 1942). Its members live mainly in the eastern Bay of Plenty, the Urewera's and the East Coast. The Church derives its belief and ritual from both traditional and biblical, especially Old Testament, sources. Te Kooti (p. 34) is revered as saint and prophet and events in his life related to the history of Israel: his escape from the Chathams to the deliverance from Egypt, his fighting campaign to the wanderings in the wilderness, his pardon in 1883 and the subsequent consolidation of his church to the settlement in Canaan. Today the Church has a symbolic head (*poutikanga*) and an executive assembly of twelve, elected every two years at a general assembly; but in practice the congregations are largely autonomous, appointing their own ministers (*tohunga*) and 'policemen' (*pirihimana*). The ministers, who receive no payment, are of three kinds: ordinary *tohunga*, whose main duties are leading services, *tohunga ture*, legally authorized to perform marriages and burials, and *tohunga takuta*, healers. In addition to weekly Sabbaths, Ringatū keep holy day on the twelfth of each month on their own *marae* in commemoration of the reserving of the church's central *marae* at Wainui near Whakatane, and hold special festivals at Wainui on 1 January and June. At Ringatū gatherings the *marae* is closed at dusk, and smoking, drinking and eating are forbidden while successive services are held in the meeting-house. Worshippers recline on mattresses as at *hui*, the officiating *tohunga* distinguished from the others neither by place nor vestments. Together they chant hymns, prayers and *pānui* (medleys of Bible verses) in the traditional style, unaccompanied and from memory in Maori. In belief and worship the Church stresses continuity with the ancestors and the value of their Maori heritage. Far from being out-dated this is seen as a source of strength and peace in the turmoil of the modern world. As a leading *tohunga* explained: 'learn the prayers and you break the barrier between you and the elders – you can see into their world.' Though the Church was born in fighting, this was in defence of the land. Far from being a militant Church, Ringatū today is dedicated to the achieving of peace and harmony.

## The Ratana Movement

Members of the body legally registered as the Ratana Church prefer to identify themselves as belonging to a movement called *Te Maramatanga o Ihoa* (The Enlightenment or Revelation of Jehovah), but today it is commonly known and accepted as the Ratana Movement. The movement has two sides: a spiritual side and a secular. While the two sides are conceptually and organizationally separate, they are related as complementary halves of a single whole based on belief in God (*Ihoa*) as preached by the movement's founder, Tahupotiki Wiremu Ratana.

In 1918, when the economic status and health of the Maori people were at a low ebb, T. W. Ratana of Orakeinui near Wanganui received a vision from God in which he was commissioned to call the Maori people to repent their sinful ways and to heal their bodies and their divisions by turning them back to faith in the One True God. His preaching and healing attracted large numbers of Maoris to him on journeys through the country and at his home, where many stayed to form a unique non-tribal community known as Ratana Pa. Preaching faith in God (*Ihoa*) as the basis for peace and right living, Ratana directly attacked current beliefs in *atua* and *tapu* and the power held over the people by certain kinds of *tohunga*, proving the greater power of *Ihoa* by himself breaking tapus with impunity. He also instructed his followers to set aside their tribal allegiance and pride in *rangatira* descent to become the *mōrehu*, 'the faithful remnant'. In 1924 he made a world tour to acquaint the leaders of other countries with his mission. He presented the King of England with a petition asking for redress of Maori land grievances and formal recognition of the Treaty of Waitangi, but this was referred back to the New Zealand Government. In 1925, following growing misunderstanding from the other Churches and pressure from his followers, Ratana legally registered his movement as an independent Church and began building the Temple at Ratana Pa. With the establishment of the Church and completion of the Temple in 1928 Ratana set aside his spiritual works (*ture wairua*) and began works directed to the secular needs of his people (*ture tangata*). In this he chose to work through existing political institutions, sponsoring candidates for parliamentary seats. The Ratana Political Party won the Southern Maori seat in 1932 but went out of existence after making an alliance with the Labour Party in 1933. Since then candidates belonging to the movement have stood as members of the Labour Party. When Ratana died in 1939 three of the four Maori members of Parliament were members of both the Labour Party and the Ratana Movement, and as a result of legislation passed by the Labour Government all social welfare measures were available to Maoris equally with Pakehas.

Today the Ratana Movement has some 30,000 adherents living throughout New Zealand, looking to Ratana Pa as the movement's spiritual and administrative capital. Every year many thousands gather at Ratana Pa to commemorate the anniversaries of Ratana's original vision (on 8 November) and birthday (25 January).

The religious and secular sides of the movement are embodied in two parallel organizations which are linked through an elected President (*Tumuaki*) who is both spiritual and secular head of the movement. To date, all Presidents have been selected from Ratana's own family, the present President being his eldest daughter. The President is assisted in running church affairs on a national basis by a Church Executive consisting of members resident in or near Ratana. Both President and the Church Executive are elected by a *Hui Whakapūmau* (Conference of Confirmation), which consists of all members in good standing attending the January *hui* at Ratana Pa and discusses both general policy and specific issues. At the local level, the spiritual welfare of the *mōrehu* is cared for by *āpotoro* (apostles), who are nominated initially by the people themselves and receive training at an apostles' conference held every July at Ratana Pa. At present (1975), some 150 apostles are legally registered as ministers (*āpotoro rēhita*) empowered to perform marriages and burials, while several times that number serve as assistant preachers (*āpotoro wairua*). The *āpotoro* are assisted in their leadership of church life by local church committees (*komiti hahi*), lay-readers (*ākonga*), sisters (*awhina*), psalm singers (*rōpū raupo*), choirs (*nga koea*) and church wardens (*hahi watene*). Representatives of local church committees meet periodically in district councils. In the secular organization, auxiliary committees and councils match the church ones, their chairman corresponding to the *āpotoro*, helpers (*kai-awhina*) to the lay-readers and sisters, brass bands, youth and cultural groups to the choirs, and community wardens (*katipa*) to the church wardens. The bands also fulfil a religious function by leading the procession of worshippers to service in the Temple and playing hymns. Citing the eviction of the money-changers from the Temple as biblical warrant, the movement excludes money from its religious activities. *Āpotoro* receive no payment for their services. Fund-raising is the responsibility of the secular groups. The movement's newspaper, *Te Whētu Mārama*, publishes both church and secular news.

The religious teaching of the Church emphasizes the central importance of faith in God (*Ihoa*) and the special role of the Faithful Angels and the Mangai as links between God and men. God is sometimes referred to as Ihoa, but more often as the three persons of the Trinity: '*Te Matua, Te Tama, Te Wairua Tapu*'. This is invariably followed in prayers and hymns by reference to '*Nga Anahera Pono me Te Māngai*'. This practice has been the focus of much criticism and misunderstanding on the part of the other Churches. Official teaching however makes a clear distinction between the Trinity on the one hand and the Angels and the Mangai on the other. Because God is intensely holy and powerful He is reached or approached indirectly, and the Angels and the Mangai act as intermediaries between God and men. The movement bases its teachings about the Angels firmly on biblical sources as well as on their appearance to and assistance to Ratana. Ratana himself explicitly taught that the Angels were not to be worshipped, and removed a baptismal font held by an Angel from the Temple to the cemetery outside when people adopted worshipful attitudes to it during the earlier beginnings of the movement. The second person of the Trinity is identified with Jesus Christ but the latter name is rarely used, on the grounds that it is associated with the Son's earthly life and another time and place. Christ's death on the cross is hardly recognized because of its association with man's inhuman act to man. Rather, the emphasis is placed on his resurrection and promise of life after death. The title *Māngai*, which literally means 'a mouth', is applied to Ratana particularly in his role as intermediary between God and men. It could be interpreted as meaning the mouth-piece or spokesman of God: I have heard the word used in other contexts as a synonym for a *kai-kōrero* (orator) speaking as a representative of his people. However, a leading member of the Church insists that Te Māngai is 'God's own prophetic voice', which resided in and spoke through Ratana during the period of his spiritual works but was distinct from Ratana the man. When Ratana turned to secular works, he gave up the title of Mangai and called himself Piri-Wiri-Tua, 'Bill-the-gimlet-who-bores-right-through', emphasizing first his own reversion to ordinariness, Piri (Bill) being the familiar diminutive of Wiremu (William), and secondly his determination to penetrate all obstacles in order to attain equal social and economic opportunities for the Maori people.

Following Ratana's example, the Church rejects not the existence but the power of the old *tapus*, malignant spirits, ghosts and *tohunga*, and subordinates tribal loyalties and considerations of rank to membership in the *mōrehu*. Speakers at Ratana gatherings are chosen by the relevant committee on bases other than descent and the *kawa* (protocol) followed is highly flexible. At the same time, the movement is essentially Maori in action and orientation, using Maori language exclusively for church services and for most meetings, and working for mainly Maori ends in the political arena, with particular emphasis on the ratification of the Treaty of Waitangi.

Ratana was a past master in the art of conveying abstract ideas through concrete symbols meaningful to Maoris, and his followers have maintained this skill. The movement as a whole is distinguished by the symbol of the *whētu marama*, a crescent moon holding a five-pointed star, each point a different colour. The top three points of the star and their colours signify the three Persons of the Trinity, the lower two the Faithful Angels and the Mangai, while the symbol as a whole stands for the shining light shed by God's revelation through Ratana. The *āpotoro*, lay-readers and sisters, wear robes of various colours which have symbolic significance and are derived from those described in the Bible.

For many years after Ratana's death, the movement tended to avoid publicity in, and even contact with, the wider Pakeha world, but in recent years, as the economic circumstances of members have improved, as Ratana Pa has been almost entirely rebuilt, and as criticism from outside has moderated, it has begun to accept and even seek opportunities to dispel misunderstanding about its teaching and to re-establish former warm relations with other denominations.

## The Church of Latter Day Saints

The Mormon Church, as it is commonly known in New Zealand, began mission work among Maoris in the late nineteenth century, mainly in Northland and Hawke's Bay. In 1971 Maoris constituted 58 per cent of the Church's membership in New Zealand. The Church makes no administrative distinction between Maori and Pakeha members but stresses the study of Maori arts and crafts, history and genealogy. It also provides much encouragement, guidance and practical help to members to better their economic and educational status. However difficulties have arisen where Church elders have directed Maori members to abandon particular Maori customs perceived as inconsistent with Church beliefs, especially those of the *tangihanga* (Schwimmer, 1965). In the late fifties many Maori families moved to Hamilton to help build the central Temple at Tuhikaramea, and many settled there permanently.

### Interdenominational relations

Maoris pride themselves on overlooking denominational differences in the cause of community and Maori welfare. Besides working on common projects, they help each other raise money and stage church festivals. At the Anglican *hui tōpū* at Omahu Pa (Hastings) in 1959, the Ratana, Roman Catholic, Mormon and Methodist Churches each staffed a set of tables in the dining room.

At the same time, loyalty to the Church of one's forefathers is strong. Differences in denominational allegiance are the most common cause of opposition to marriages at *tomo*, and often divide large-families and *hapū*.

### Political association

At present in 1975 the Maori as a people are represented in Parliament by four Maori Members elected from four Maori electorates: Northern, Western, Eastern and Southern Maori. These four seats were established on the basis of male franchise in 1867 (p. 35). Maoris obtained full adult franchise along with Pakehas in 1893 but the secret ballot was applied to Maori electorates only in 1938 and compulsory registration in 1956. From 1956 to 1975 Maori electoral enrolments were governed by the Electoral Act 1956 which directed that adults who were more than half Maori must enrol on the Maori electoral roll but gave half-castes the choice of registering on either the Maori or the general roll. In 1975 the Government passed an Electoral Amendment Act which changed the definition of a Maori to that enacted in the Maori Affairs Amendment Act 1974 (namely, 'a person of the Maori Race of New Zealand, including any descendant of such a person') and gave all adult Maoris the right to choose whether they wished to vote on the Maori or the general electoral roll. It also makes provision for the number of Maori seats to be revised on the basis of the number of Maoris choosing to enrol on the Maori roll at the time of the previous census, but this will not take effect until after the 1975 election.

The majority of Maori electors support the same political parties as Pakehas: Labour, National and Social Credit. No Communist or Values Party candidate has stood for a Maori electorate as yet. Candidates standing independently or for other than the main parties poll very few votes. Since 1943 all four Maori seats have been held by Labour Members who command 80 per cent of the votes cast in their electorates and on several occasions have held the national balance of power in favour of Labour. The major parties each have national Maori executives and regional branches.

Although Pakehas widely credit the Ratana Church with domination of Maori politics, it is as we have seen (pp. 188–9) not the Church but the secular branch of the Ratana Movement which is involved in politics and this involvement is indirect, taking the form of support for the Labour Party. Since 1943 all four Maori Members of Parliament have in fact been members of the Movement, with the exception of Steve Watene, Member for Eastern Maori from 1963 to 1967.

From their establishment in 1867 to the passing of the Electoral Amendment Act 1975, the number of Maori seats remained fixed at four regardless of changes in the Maori population or the number of seats in Parliament. During that time the Maori electorates were specifically exempt from the provisions which governed and continually revised the number and boundaries of general electorates. The Maori electorates differed from other electorates in being much more extensive in territory, making it more difficult for Maori Members to meet their constituents and vice versa, and increasing travelling and campaign costs. Because of the provision for half-castes to choose between the Maori and general rolls, it was usual to measure the size of Maori electorates in terms of registered voters, and when this was done they proved to have proportionately fewer than the general electorates: an average of 13,600 in 1972 compared with 18,250. However, the size of general electorates was and is standardized in terms not of voters but of total population, which worked out at an average of 31,000 in 1972. If the problem of how many half-castes enrolled on the ordinary instead of the Maori roll is ignored as impossible to determine and the total Maori population (227,414 in 1971) divided by the four Maori seats, Maori Members of Parliament were representing approximately 56,000 adults and children.

To put it another way: the number of Maoris enrolled on the Maori roll has for many years been lower than the number of Maoris of voting age: 55,451 in December 1972 compared with 98,000 Maoris aged twenty years or over. Moreover proportionately fewer of the voters on the Maori roll recorded valid votes than of those on the general roll: 75 per cent compared with 85 per cent in 1972. Assuming that the missing 40,000 odd must have enrolled on the general roll, some commentators have interpreted these figures as indicating that Maoris are not particularly interested in national level politics nor concerned to support the principle of separate Maori representation. Others however dispute this interpretation. They point out first of all that an additional 9,871 Maoris cast special votes in the belief that they were on the Maori roll but had them disallowed either because they were not in fact on the Maori roll (8,106) or for other technical reasons. Thus the number of eligible Maoris who attempted to cast votes in the 1972 election on the Maori roll was over 65,322 or 66 per cent of those of voting age. From a background of first-hand experience, these commentators suggest that probably not more than a thousand Maoris were enrolled on the general roll in 1972 and that the large proportion of the 32,000 Maori voters thus left unaccounted for were not enrolled on either roll. Evidence in support of this view was provided by a study of the general roll for 1972 in a sample of electorates most likely to be affected by the enrolment of half-caste Maoris: the number of voters on the general roll was *not* significantly higher than the non-Maori population, allowing for the normal rate of increase since the 1971 Census. Maoris and others with experience of Maori politics attribute both non-enrolment and the lower proportion of valid votes cast in Maori electorates to the difficulties that have in the past faced Maoris endeavouring to enrol and vote on the Maori roll. The Maori roll itself, Maori enrolment forms and voting papers have typically been available only at certain centres whose location was often poorly publicized. If a polling booth did not have a Maori roll a voter registered on it had to cast a special vote, a daunting process involving complicated form-filling and the presence of witnesses. The special efforts made by the authorities and political associations to ensure enrolment and get people to the poll have not usually been effectively extended to the Maori people. Finally, enquiry among Maoris who have enrolled and voted on the general roll establishes that they do so, not because they reject identification as Maoris or the principle of separate Maori representation, but for practical, political reasons, because they feel they have readier access to the Member of a smaller, localized electorate especially in urban areas and/or that their votes are politically more useful where the contest between the parties is closer than in Maori electorates.

Separate Maori representation has long been the subject of recurring political debate. One school of thought, consisting mainly of Pakehas, argues for the abolition of the Maori seats on the grounds that they place Maoris in a favoured position and so are discriminatory. Most Maoris however strongly support the idea of Maori seats, arguing that they are necessary to ensure the presence of Maori representatives in Parliament. For a long time the two major parties made it a matter of policy to initiate no change until the Maoris asked for it. When the Labour Government set up a Committee to review the Electoral Act in 1973, the Maoris did just that, by strong submissions asking for an increase in the number of Maori seats. After hearing arguments on both sides, the Electoral Act Committee decided in favour not only of retaining separate Maori representation but also of increasing the number of Maori electorates in keeping with the size of the Maori population. In its Report (1975), the Committee recommended: that the definition of a Maori be changed to that enacted in the Maori Affairs Amendment Act 1974; that on the electoral form to be distributed with the census form at the time of every census, all adult Maoris be given the right to choose whether they wish to vote on the Maori or the general electoral roll; that the total number of those wishing to enrol on the Maori roll together with their children under eighteen be divided by the New Zealand quota (i.e. of voters per electorate) and the quotient thus obtained shall represent the number of Maori seats; that the Representation Committee shall determine the boundaries of the Maori seats using the same basic principles as used for determining those of general seats; and that no person shall be able to transfer from a Maori roll to a general roll except at the time of a census. These recommendations were incorporated in the Electoral Act of 1975. While the widening of the right to choose which roll to enrol on applies immediately, i.e. for the 1975 election, the other provisions will not be given effect until the census is taken in 1976. Meanwhile strenuous efforts are being made to ensure that enrolment and voting on the Maori roll are made easier and the proportion of enrolments and valid votes improved.

Given the overwhelming Maori vote for Labour it is a moot point whether the system of separate Maori representation operates to the advantage or disadvantage of the Maori people. As long as all the Maori Members are Labour, Maoris are virtually shorn of power and a share in political decision-making when a National Government is in power. On the other hand, the Labour Party has often tended to take Maori support for granted. Maori Members lack the power base within their own party which comes from the need to woo electors, and what influence they have depends on personal persuasiveness and the goodwill of colleagues. When Labour was in power 1972–5 Maoris commanded more political weight than they had for a very long time, with the first Maori Minister of Maori Affairs for forty years and two Maori Ministers in Cabinet, Matiu Rata being Minister of Lands as well as Maori Affairs and Whetū Tirikatene-Sullivan Minister of Tourism. Certainly this period has seen the passage of a substantial body of legislation which has gone a long way to meeting Maori wishes and aspirations. Nevertheless, Maoris have found the situation not without its drawbacks. As Cabinet Ministers, Maori Members have shouldered responsibilities to the people of New Zealand as a whole, responsibilities which have left them with less time for purely Maori concerns and have sometimes cut across their responsibilities as Maori representatives.

While neither party has yet chosen a Maori as a candidate for a safe seat Maoris won nomination as candidates in general electorates in the 1975 electorates and two were returned. There may well be a reawakening of Maori political interest and greater willingness to reconsider the prospect of integrated representation. It will be interesting to see how many Maoris decide to enrol on the general roll for the 1978 election under the new electoral rules. If they do so in any numbers, Maoris as a whole may actually increase their political influence, since more Maoris voting in general electorates will force Pakeha Members of Parliament to become more knowledgeable about and pay more attention to Maori views and interests.

(For discussion of Maori politics at both local and national levels and the relation between the two, see Jackson and Wood, 1964; Kernot, 1972; Pocock, 1963; Schwimmer, 1968: 382–50.)

## Kotahitanga and Kauhanganui

Besides the formal political parties there are two Maori movements whose primary aim is greater political autonomy for Maoris, Kotahitanga and Kauhanganui. Both are informal rather than formal organizations and attract support across tribal boundaries. Their spokesmen attend and speak at most important Maori gatherings, where they are listened to with respect and considerable sympathy, but the parliamentary candidates which they sponsor at most elections receive little support in the way of votes.

Kotahitanga claims continuity in name and aims with early Northland movements of protest against Pakeha domination (Hohepa, 1964: 23–9) and the Maori Parliament which met in the 1890s (see p. 36; also Williams, 1969). In the 1950s the northern Kotahitanga allied itself informally with like-minded groups in the Waikato, Bay of Plenty and East Coast, and now the movement has advocates in most tribes, though only loosely organized. Kotahitanga has always concentrated attention on the Treaty of Waitangi, pressing for it to be enacted as law, its provisions implemented, and past breaches investigated and remedied. Opinions vary about the degree of separatism which is desirable and necessary to achieve these ends.

Kauhanganui (the Maori Independent Movement) was established in 1949 and has sponsored candidates in several elections since without polling more than 500 votes. According to a spokesman, its adherents, who live mainly in Northland and the Waikato, seek the establishment of an independent Maori Federation headed by a chief's council, revision of the Treaty of Waitangi, just and honourable settlement of Maori land complaints and the founding of a New Zealand Kauhanganui Bank. As far as I know, there is no information about the movement available in print.

Closely associated with Kotahitanga is the Maori Organization On Human Rights (MOOHR). Formed in the first place in Wellington to fight the Maori Affairs Amendment Act 1967, the Organization has since widened its scope to the whole of New Zealand and the whole field of Maori grievances. A small, dedicated band of workers intermittently issues a magazine *Te Hokioi* which specializes in exposing 'Pakeha land grabs' and telling Maoris of their rights in relation to unclaimed monies held by the Maori Trustee. In 1974 it published a paperback *Te Karanga a Te Kotuku*, 'some records of the land struggles of Saana Murray and her people of Te Hiku o Te Ika, the Far North of New Zealand'. Like Kotahitanga, MOOHR speaks from and to a base of Maori values and experiences, evoking much sympathy and enjoyment of its exposures, but little active support.

## The King Movement

The King Movement (Kingitanga) is not primarily either a political, social, cultural or religious association but combines all these aspects in its own inimitable way. Its basic purpose is briefly summed up as 'the upholding of *te mana Maori motuhake*, the spiritual power, dignity and integrity of the Maori people in New Zealand society'. This aim is political in the broadest sense of the word, but it is pursued entirely by social and cultural means, informed by a religious awareness that makes prayers and hymns an integral part of all activities. Far from challenging their authority, the Movement accepts the Queen and Parliament of New Zealand as the constitutional framework within which it operates (see Pei Te Hurinui Jones's essay 'Maori Kings', in Schwimmer, 1968: 132–73).

The King Movement is centred on the person of Queen Te Atairangikaahu, its sixth head and direct descendant of the first King Potatau I, and on the *marae* of Tūrangawaewae on the banks of the Waikato River at Ngaruawahia. Its basic membership consists of the tribes of the Tainui canoe, occupying territory in the Waikato, King Country and Manawatu, and the related tribes of Ngāi Terangi and Ngāti Ranginui of Tauranga. Ngāti Tūwharetoa, Ngāti Pikiao of Arawa, Ngāti Tama and Te Ati Awa of northern Taranaki, and Ngāti Kahungunu have particularly close ties with the King Movement as supporters. The remaining tribes stand outside the Movement but accord Queen Te Ata-i-rangikaahu full honours as *ariki nui* (paramount chief) of one of the major sections of Maoridom.

Only child of late King Koroki, Queen Te Ata-i-rangikaahu was chosen to succeed her father by the Kingitanga tribes assembled at his *tangihanga* and crowned at Tūrangawaewae the day after his burial, on 22 May 1966. In the words of a Kingitanga spokesman, Queen Te Ata-i-rangikaahu stands as the embodiment of Maori ideals and cultural values. 'Her leadership is not one of active participation but rather one of symbolism – a symbol of the past glories of the Maori people – that reminds them of their heritage and status in the modern world and that guarantees the conservation of such values for the country as a whole.'

Next in rank to the Queen is the *Tumuaki* (President), an office held by the chief of the Waharoa family of Ngāti Hauā. The *Tumuaki* plays a key part at the Coronation and presides at table in the Queen's dining-hall. Members of the *Kāhui Ariki* (royal line) are also treated with deference and given places of honour at all King Movement gatherings. The Movement has two Councils: the *Tekaumarua* (Council of Twelve) and the *Rūnanganui* (Grand Council). The Twelve, chosen by the Queen herself from leading Tainui elders, advise the Queen personally, especially on matters of etiquette and procedure, supervise her Coronation, hold her seal, and publish the news-sheet, *Te Paki-o-Matariki*. The Grand Council consists of representatives elected by the *marae* and *hapū* committees of the King Movement area, and is the main governing body of the Movement. Its members express the views of their people, discuss matters of public concern, co-ordinate King Movement activities, and supervise the organization of *hui* at Tūrangawaewae. In addition, *kaumātua* from all parts of the Queen's territory help to hammer out policy in open discussions on King Movement *marae*. Both the Queen and her Councils strictly observe the traditional independence of the *hapū* within its own boundaries.

The main activities of the King Movement are a series of annual *poukai* (loyalty feasts) and the annual Coronation Celebrations. The *poukai* are held on fixed dates on twenty-eight *marae*, mainly in Tainui territory. Attended mainly by Maoris from local and adjacent communities, they are distinguished by the ceremonial entry of the Queen's party preceded by a brass band from Tūrangawaewae, the flying of the Queen's flag (a red cross on a white background), the making of loyal speeches, and the collecting of donations. The Coronation Celebrations are held at Tūrangawaewae on the anniversary of the Coronation of the head of the Movement, currently late in May. The *hui* usually lasts five days and attracts thousands of visitors. Sports and *haka* tournaments are held at the weekend, but the anniversary itself is observed soberly with religious services and *whai-kōrero* (speech-making).

Members of the King Movement pay no fixed dues: contributions are made voluntarily at *hui* in the Maori way. The Queen derives her personal income from private sources (chiefly land). *Poukai* committees send her a tenth of their gross takings, which are applied to the maintenance of *marae* buildings at Tūrangawaewae.

The official headquarters of the King Movement (though the Queen's own home is at Waahi near Huntly), the *marae* at Tūrangawaewae (Jones, 1971) was founded in the 1920s in fulfilment of a prophecy by King Tawhiao and developed under the direction of Princess Te Puea, who organized labour contracts, farming enterprises and concert party tours to raise the money. Today it is the largest and best equipped in the country. In addition to the carved meeting-house Mahinarangi and the Queen's dining-hall Turongo, it has three large sleeping houses (one double-storied) and a 'cultural complex' Kimiora, opened in 1974. A modern partly two-storied building embellished with fine wood carvings, Kimiora includes a dining-hall that seats a thousand and converts to a concert hall, numerous meeting-rooms, a sauna and workshops for carving and other crafts. The *marae* is used almost continuously for *hui* and conferences, not only by the Kingitanga itself but by other Maori bodies, churches, schools and universities. It is 'kept warm' (*whakamahanatia*) by the large community of *kai-tiaki* (caretakers in the full sense of the word) living on and around the *marae* reserve. For large *hui*, workers are supplied by all sectors of the Movement. The money to maintain and continually improve the *marae* comes from *poukai* tenths, donations from users and visitors, a *marae* store and temporary stalls erected during *hui*, and continuous money-raising by Tūrangawaewae clubs. Some subsidy moneys have also been used but for Kimiora the King Movement committed itself to raising the entire amount, in earnest of how much it meant to them.

Originally founded 'to stop bloodshed, to retain the land and to uphold the laws', the King Movement has changed its aims and its methods to meet changing circumstances. Today it seeks neither political independence nor a formal place in the political structure of the nation. Instead it aims to serve '*hei pou herenga waka, hei kanohi mō te iwi, hei pou herenga mō te whakaaro*' – 'as a post for tying the canoes together, a symbol (of their cultural aspirations) for the people, and a focus for discussion'. It also provides its followers with a social and cultural framework within which to live their lives. In the best sense of the word, the King Movement is a conservative institution, devoted to preserving and developing what is good and worthwhile both in the Maori heritage and in Maori-Pakeha relations. At the same time, it has shown itself highly adaptable and forward-looking, an attitude expressed in Kimiora with its combination of eminently functional design with the arts of the ancestors. For reasons of history and because the titles of King and Queen have political overtones for Pakehas, there has been, and is, much misunderstanding of the King Movement among Pakehas and among other Maori tribes. In recent years the Movement itself has taken the initiative in dispelling this misunderstanding and since Queen Elizabeth II made a short stop there during a royal tour in 1954 (after earnest representations from Movement spokesmen), relations have been cordial between the Move-and the Government. Queen Elizabeth II made Queen Te Ata-irangikaahu a Dame of the British Empire in 1970 (Jones, 1971: 53) and visited Tūrangawaewae again to open Kimiora in 1974. Governors-General and prominent overseas visitors also visit Tūrangawaewae as one of the major centres of Maoridom, and many Pakehas are welcomed there at every *hui*.

# chapter 14

# Leadership and social control

Maori communities today have more leaders and more kinds of leaders than in pre-European times. Except on the East Coast where women are equally eligible, rural Maoris still look to the first-born males in the senior lines of descent in the community as their 'proper' leaders, but they accept others for particular purposes and sometimes in general if the 'proper' leaders lack capacity or training. The cities offer plenty of opportunities for the able and well qualified to rise to the top, regardless of descent.

Leadership is associated with the idea of *mana*. This is used ambiguously to mean 'social and political standing' or 'supernatural power' or both. In Maori thinking the concepts are inextricably linked (pp. 63–5). The most important source of *mana* is inheritance from ancestors of superior descent, but it can also be acquired by special training or achievement, and it is increased or diminished by the possessor's behaviour. As one elder put it: 'Every leader has *mana* because he is a leader; and it is by having *mana* that a man gets to be a leader.'

## The traditional leaders

The traditional titles *kaumātua, rangatira, ariki* and *tohunga* are still in use, but there have been significant changes in the range of persons to whom they are applied, in the qualifications required, and in the holders' duties and power.

Of the four, the term *kaumātua* is far the most often heard. Usually translated as 'elder', it is invariably associated with advanced years – at least fifty-five and usually over sixty, an age when most Maoris have grand- or great-grandchildren. The term is applied, first, to the elderly as a group, regardless of sex and social standing, and secondly, in the singular, to elderly men. (Elderly women are *kuia*.) But *kaumātua* is also used, thirdly, in a specialized sense, for those elderly men who are distinguished as leaders by seniority of descent or by proficiency in Maori speech-making, *whakapapa*, history and ceremonial, and preferably by both. Such a *kaumātua* is usually head of a household and either sole head or one of the leading members of a large-family. (Now that the nuclear-family is the usual household unit, however, heads of households are not always *kaumātua*.) Country communities usually lay the primary stress on seniority of descent, conferring the title on younger sons or men from junior lines only if they are exceptionally gifted. In urban areas, however, where residents know little about each other's genealogies, it is commonly applied to any older man who is knowledgeable in traditional matters. Finally, *kaumātua* is often used as a synonym for *rangatira*, to describe traditional leaders at the *hapū* and even tribal level.

*Rangatira* is used as formerly to mean both 'chief' and 'aristocrat', but the distinction is becoming increasingly blurred. Many *hapū* appear to have not one undisputed chief but several of roughly equal standing. Because of past intermarriage between senior lines, even the experts cannot always agree which is the most senior, and when the hereditary chief lacks the required knowledge or ability some or all his duties are assumed by better-qualified relatives. It has become quite common to hear Maoris talk about the *rangatira* or chiefs of their *hapū* in the plural. These are mostly male. Maoris speaking Maori also use *rangatira* to describe leaders outside the *hapū* context, especially those who direct activities: the captain of a ship, those in charge of the various departments of work at *hui*, and, in the expression *hoa rangatira*, a man's wife.

In contrast, the use of *ariki* has been limited instead of extended. In Northland today it is practically unknown: since the missionaries used it to translate 'Lord' in the Bible, the northern tribes have ceased to apply it to men. Where it is used, *ariki* is reserved unequivocally for the paramount chief of a tribe. But by no means all tribes recognize a single head. Rarawa and Ngāpuhi, for instance, describe the *rangatira* of their various *hapū* collectively as *ngā rangatira o te iwi*, 'the *chiefs* of the *tribe*'; some *hapū* claim primacy for their *rangatira*, but the others dispute it. The tribes who do recognize an *ariki* usually choose a male. And they limit the power and publicity of his office, calling on him to take the lead only in a ceremonial capacity and at gatherings of a specifically tribal nature, or when it is especially important that the tribe speak with one voice, as in answer to an insult or challenge. They emphasize the status, and play down the personality of the incumbent. It is not uncommon to find members of such tribes who do not know the fore-name of their *ariki*, only the surname of the *ariki* family. Only the Tainui tribes and Tūwharetoa give their *ariki* an authority and honour comparable to that of former times. Queen Te Ata-i-rangikaahu of the Tainui and Hepi Te Heuheu of Tūwharetoa are known by name not only to the least of their own tribesmen but also to most members of other tribes.

The status of *kaumātua* in the limited sense is partly but not wholly hereditary. Unless their Maori is exceptionally poor, first-born sons of families of 'high' descent are accepted almost automatically when old enough, but younger sons and men of low rank can also win the title by displaying outstanding ability as Maori expert, orator or organizer. *Kaumātua* are not formally chosen or appointed at any point in time. As they near fifty-five, they engage increasingly in the activities expected of *kaumātua*, attending *hui* more often and staying longer, extending their knowledge of things Maori, and beginning to speak at public gatherings, briefly, and after those already accepted. As they become older and more skilled, they make more and longer speeches and slowly move up the speaking order. In my experience it takes a man about five years to become accepted as a *kaumātua*.

In the case of *rangatira* and *ariki*, it is accepted in principle that the title should pass on the holder's death to his eldest son. Being an important issue, the succession is usually discussed by the people at the *tangihanga*. Now that effective leadership on the battlefield or in the Maori Land Court is no longer required, the eldest son is usually accepted as long as he can perform the necessary ceremonial duties. Nevertheless it is not unknown for a *hapū* to reject the primary heir in favour of a better orator or organizer. Once recognized as *kaumātua*, *rangatira* or *ariki*, a man retains the title to his death, even when he can no longer perform the duties involved.

As we have seen, the term *tohunga* is commonly used to describe faith-healers, whose knowledge and practice is largely charismatic (p. 93). *Tohunga* of this kind may be male or female. They do not usually take an active part in community life, finding that a measure of withdrawal increases respect for their powers. Like prophets, they frequently secure greater belief and support from outsiders than from their own relatives. Some build up quite large followings, but their adherents are usually scattered residentially and disband after their death. In Maori, and occasionally when speaking English, Maoris also use *tohunga*, with or without qualification, in its original meaning of 'expert' – not only for a carver or master builder, but also for teachers, agricultural advisers, and sometimes the clergy of the orthodox denominations. The Ringatū Church applies it to all its ministers, whether they are faith-healers or not (p. 186).

*Kaumātua*, *rangatira* and *ariki* are first and foremost leaders of descent-groups: large-families, *hapū* and tribes. For their group they

are expected to perform or supervise ceremonial acts (making ceremonial speeches of welcome and farewell, imposing and lifting *tapu*,
'calling the flowers' at weddings); to take the lead in discussion and
decision making (speaking first, introducing new subjects, summing
up); and to speak as representatives in its relations with others.
Whether they are effective as initiators, organizers and policy-makers
as well depends on their personal capacity. Those who are wise or
forceful dominate the decisions of their group; the weak or retiring
act as ceremonial figureheads while others make the decisions.

In Maori communities, the *kaumātua* of the *tāngata whenua* families, including those who are also *rangatira* or *ariki*, are regarded as
the proper leaders of the community as a whole. Effective or not, they
are always given places of honour at community gatherings. The
strong wield great influence, and other leaders make little headway
without their approval even in non-kin associations. 'Immigrants' of
*kaumātua* status in their own descent-group are accorded the title but
not the standing nor privileges of those of local stock, except under
exceptional circumstances. In the early stages of urbanization, these
attitudes also obtain in towns and cities. Maoris living in Auckland
could not be organized to participate in the centennial celebrations in
1940 till the chief of the *tāngata whenua* assumed control (Sutherland,
1940: 169). But as 'immigrants' come to outnumber the *tāngata
whenua* and feel at home in the city, they form and run independent
associations. Usually they invite a *tangata whenua* to speak at any
gatherings they sponsor, but if one is not available they manage
without. When the Royal Tour was being planned in 1953, a group
of Auckland 'immigrants' formed a *haka* party and successfully
approached the City Council to give them a part in the civic reception,
without referring to or including the *tāngata whenua* (Metge, 1964a:
212).

Understandably, Pakehas assume that the recognized chiefs or
elders of a community are 'in charge' at every local gathering. At
those of large-families, *hapū* or clubs other than their own, they are
guests like everybody else. They can trade on their general status in
the community to advise or scold the sponsors, but they cannot usurp
the latter's right to make the final decisions.

## Specialists and sectional leaders

Maoris also accord respect to men and women with special knowledge and training and/or those with official positions in the wider
world: teachers, ministers of religion, nurses (especially District
Nurses), doctors and other professional workers, Members of Parliament, Government officials and local Councillors. At Maori gather-

ings, whether present in an official capacity or not, they are mentioned by name in welcome speeches and the call to the feast, and given places on the platform, in the front row and at the top table. Those who live in or visit a community regularly are looked to for example, advice, and instruction on all sorts of subjects, invited to act as Master of Ceremonies at dances, concerts and weddings, elected to club office, and even invited to speak on the *marae*. These attentions may be modified if they are relatively young, women, or poor Maori orators, but are nevertheless greater than they would otherwise receive.

There is a tendency among Maoris to regard these specialist leaders as non-traditional, opposed to and competing with the traditional leaders, but I see them as directly in the tradition of the old-time *tohunga*, who were essentially experts, whether in advanced religious knowledge or other valued crafts. The modern specialists differ from their predecessors in some of their fields of specialization, in their separation of secular and religious knowledge, and in recruitment from all levels of society. But like them they command respect because and so far as they use their knowledge for the benefit of the community. Many traditional leaders are also specialists, combining senior descent and Maori knowledge with a good education or public office. Provided they speak Maori, specialists are usually accorded the title of *kaumātua* when they become old enough, regardless of descent.

In addition to traditional leaders and specialists, Maori communities also accept certain individuals as leaders in limited spheres and for particular purposes only, as officers of clubs and committees and informal leaders of kin and peer groups. Such persons could be described as *sectional leaders*. They include both men and women and are mainly between twenty-five and fifty-five, old enough to have experience and know-how but too young for recognition as *kaumātua*. The most capable and assertive are leaders in several groups at once. Those who are knowledgeable in Maori matters usually develop into *kaumātua*, especially if their descent is good. Sectional leaders also had their counterpart in pre-European society, in the leaders of friendship, dance and minor work groups, but there are undoubtedly more openings for them today.

In recent years the term *rangatahi* has become increasingly popular. It derives from the proverb: '*Kā pū te ruha; kā hao te rangatahi*' ('the old net is cast aside; the new net goes fishing', Kohere: 1951: 36). This is frequently used to stress the need for leaders of a new kind, trained in modern skills, to help their people adjust to modern life. Since the leaders so equipped are likely to be comparatively young, the word for the 'new net' has come to be applied in the plural to the younger generations collectively and in the singular to those 'young people' who show capacity for leadership. In this context, 'young' usually means under about thirty, but may be widened to include all who are too young to be *kaumātua*. The *rangatahi* include most but not all of the specialists and sectional leaders. The *rangatahi* of today are likely to become the *kaumātua* of tomorrow.

### Women as leaders

Women are frequently recognized as *kaumātua* and *rangatira* in their own right among the East Coast tribes, but elsewhere only in outstanding cases. Those of an age with the *kaumātua* are called *kuia* and given complementary ceremonial duties: calling visitors on to the *marae* (*karanga*), leading songs of welcome (*pōwhiri*), supporting speakers in the singing of *waiata*, and wailing with the kinswomen of the deceased at *tangihanga*. As with the *kaumātua*, the order in which the *kuia* of a particular community are ranked depends partly on descent and partly on ability in the performance of their duties.

Among the tribes of the central North Island, women are normally barred from speaking on the open *marae* and from official leadership of descent-groups. Exceptions are however made in special cases: Mrs Iriaka Ratana for instance regularly spoke on Tainui *marae* as Member of Parliament for Western Maori. On the East Coast and to a lesser extent in Northland a number of gifted women engage in speech-making or are recognized as family or *hapū* leaders. But though most Maori women prefer not to compete with the men as speech-makers, they often provide the driving force in their descent-group and in community life. Te Puea Herangi of Waikato never spoke on a Waikato *marae* nor served on the King's Council, yet she is universally recognized as one of the outstanding Maori leaders of the twentieth century. Women usually figure prominently as sectional leaders, not only as secretaries and treasurers of family and *marae* committees, but also as members of Maori Committees, Trust Boards and incorporation Management Committees. And the Maori Women's Welfare League has established itself as a highly effective national organization, often the first in the field to press for important changes (pp. 180–1; see also Salmond, 1975).

### Members of Parliament

For over a hundred years Maoris have had four Maori representatives in Parliament. Until recently they were always men who had inherited great *mana* by descent or achieved it as orators in Maori. In 1949 however this male and *rangatira* monopoly was breached when Mrs Iriaka Ratana was elected to her husband's seat after his death; two of the new Members returned in 1963 were comparatively young men distinguished for their trade union activities; and another woman,

Mrs Whetū Tirikatene-Sullivan, was elected for her father's electorate of Southern Maori in 1969.

For nearly thirty years after Labour took all Maori seats in 1943, the Maori Members of Parliament worked quietly behind the scenes, speaking mainly on Maori topics in the House and establishing a reputation as loyal party members. Whichever party was in power, the portfolio of Maori Affairs was held by a Pakeha, though Sir Eruera Tirikatene served as Minister of Forests and Associate Minister of Maori Affairs from 1958 to 1960. But in the late sixties the Maori Members became more vocal, especially in opposition to the Maori Affairs Amendment Bill 1967, and when Labour swept into office in 1972 two were elected to Cabinet by the Labour caucus. In 1972-5 Matiu Rata held the portfolios of Maori Affairs and Lands and Mrs Whetū Tirikatene-Sullivan that of Tourism and after a Cabinet re-shuffle that of the Environment. With the assistance of Dr P. W. Hohepa, appointed joint adviser to the Ministers of Maori Affairs and Education for 1974 and 1975, Matiu Rata prepared a White Paper on Maori Affairs and a number of draft Bills. After much discussion and amendment most of his proposals were embodied in a new Maori Affairs Amendment Act 1974 and a Maori Purposes Act 1974. A Treaty of Waitangi Act was passed late in 1975. Between them these Acts have effected substantial changes in the status of Maoris and their language and culture, going a considerable way to meet Maori criticisms of previous legislation.

Maoris do not accept the Maori Members of Parliament singly or collectively as spokesmen for the whole race on every issue, any more than Pakehas accept their Members as such. They are elected only by those registered on the Maori roll, in arbitrarily defined electorates, and on the basis of party politics. Serving far-flung electorates comprising many tribes, they have greater difficulties than most MPs in keeping in touch with their electors, and are continually subjected to criticisms of remoteness on the one hand and favouring their own tribe on the other. Nevertheless, they are accorded high honour and respect at every Maori gathering they attend and all Maoris, including those who criticize and vote against them, express pride in 'our Members' and especially in the two Ministers whose prominence adds to the *mana* of the Maori people, as the achievements of the *rangatira* have always added to the *mana* of the tribe.

### Committee leadership

In recent years there has been a marked increase in the number and importance of elected committees operating in Maori communities (p. 171). The executive committees of clubs are formed primarily to carry out decisions made at general meetings; they may act independently only in emergencies and must refer all action back to the full membership for endorsement. But though their formal powers are limited, executive members usually play a decisive part in determining club policy by dominating plenary discussions. On the other hand, the special-purpose committees, which are in theory free to act independently during their term of office, in practice take account of community opinion, allowing visitors to attend and speak freely at their meetings. True, only committee members have the right to vote, but they prefer whenever possible to reach unanimity by discussion, so that a vote is not necessary.

## The Maori Committees and Councils

Of all forms of committee leadership, the Maori Committees and Maori Councils are the most important, because they are co-ordinated in a national system. The latest of several official attempts to give Maoris a degree of self-government, the present system was initiated with the establishment of two tiers of committees (by the Maori Social and Economic Advancement Act) in 1945 and completed by the addition of two upper tiers (by the Maori Welfare Act) in 1962.

The first tier consists of Maori Committees, each comprising seven members elected for a three-year term at a general meeting of Maoris living in a defined Maori Committee Area. There are at present (1975) approximately 400 Maori Committees throughout New Zealand. In the country, they coincide with local communities, which rarely comprise more than 500 Maoris. In cities, however, their arbitrarily defined Areas often include a thousand Maoris or more. Wellington in 1975 has 13 Maori Committees for a population approaching 30,000. The second tier consists of Maori Executive Committees which are made up of delegates from Maori Committees within a Maori Executive Area generally defined on a tribal and/or regional basis. Their size varies according to the number of Maori Committees involved. The third tier comprises 9 Maori District Councils. In 1969 an amendment to the Maori Welfare Act made it possible for Maori Committees to send delegates direct to their District Council if they wished, dispensing with the Executive Committee stage. This has been done mainly in the major cities, where the Maori Committees are physically much closer to each other than in the country.

When first set up in 1945, the Maori Committees and Maori Executive Committees were called 'Tribal Committees' and 'Tribal Executive Committees'. This use of 'tribal' cut right across Maori usage. 'Tribal Committee' Areas usually comprised the territory of a *hapū*, 'Tribal Executive' Districts part but rarely all of the territory of a tribe. Voting and candidature for 'Tribal Committees' were open to all adult Maoris living in its Area, not restricted to one tribe. Unsatisfactory as they were, however, the terms became familiar during seventeen years' use and are still occasionally heard.

Of the four tiers, only the Maori Committees are elective, directly responsible to and in touch with the people themselves. In country areas, half the members elected are usually *kaumātua*; most are over forty-five and of *tāngata whenua* stock; and nearly all are men. In urban areas, on the other hand, *kaumātua* are relatively less numerous; the average age is under rather than over forty-five; 'immigrants' outnumber *tāngata whenua*; and women are elected nearly as often as men.

Under the Maori Welfare Act 1962, Maori Committees have power to authorize summary proceedings against Maoris who commit specified offences (mainly involving disorderly behaviour in public places), or directly to impose penalties of up to £10, provided that the offender is given a reasonable opportunity to defend himself and does not elect summary proceedings. They are also authorized to issue permits (supplying a copy to the police) for the provision of liquor at gatherings (except dances) on the *marae*, on whatever conditions they see fit to impose. Maori Committee members are among those who may apply for a prohibition order against a Maori.

Maori Committees build up their funds as best they can from donations, fines and money-raising projects. On money spent on welfare, they can claim a pound for pound subsidy, both on their own behalf and for any local organization they endorse. On the other hand, they must contribute to the administrative costs of the higher Committees and Councils on which they are represented.

Maori Committees work best in communities with strong community feeling and good leaders – where they are least needed. Some have achieved improvements in community facilities and law observance, but many meet only when prodded into action by the Community Officers of the Department of Maori Affairs (formerly Maori Welfare Officers). By and large the system has not captured the imagination or the support of the people. Although Maoris played a major part in its planning, it is widely regarded as 'a Government plan'. In the confiscation areas, suspicion of Government directives delayed the establishment of Maori Committees into the mid-fifties. In the early days, many *rangatira* and *kaumātua* opposed the committees as a threat to their authority, refusing to 'belittle' their *mana* by submitting to a vote. While few now maintain this position, other problems arise when they are not elected or find themselves on an equality with persons of lesser rank. In many districts, the new Maori Committees found their prescribed duties being carried out by *marae*

**13** The *hākari* (feast), essential complement to the speech-making at a *hui*; held in this case in the old Ngāti Pōneke hall when Wellington Maori Anglicans welcomed Rev. Taki Marsden as their new Pastor, May 1975

14 Artist Rau Hōtere stands before his mural in the Rank-Xerox building, Auckland, 1973

and *hapū* committees, with the result that they either lapsed or engaged in a wasteful struggle for supremacy. Even under the most favourable conditions, Maori Committees are handicapped by limited funds and authority. In rural areas, in addition, both members' decisions and community support are affected by personal and group loyalties. In urban areas, Committee members do not know and are not known to most of those they are supposed to represent and control, elections are poorly attended, and most Maoris refuse to accept restraints that do not apply to Pakehas. In recent years, their right to 'try' and fine offenders for specified minor offences has been seriously questioned.

In the years since their establishment the District and New Zealand Maori Councils have faced many difficulties. To begin with, the original eight District Councils varied considerably in size because of wide variation in the number of constituent Committees. This was improved but not entirely overcome by re-organization and the creation of a ninth District Council. Finance has been a continuing problem. Trying to operate on levies from the district Councils (themselves financed by levies on Committees) plus a Government subsidy, the New Zealand Maori Council came near collapse in 1970. When the Government replaced its subsidy with a direct grant, the Council was able to maintain a full-time executive staff of three for nearly four years, with marked improvements in its effectiveness in research and public relations, but unfortunately inflation forced retrenchment in this direction in 1974. Because representation at the higher levels is indirect, by delegation, it has been alleged that Council members are out of touch with ordinary Maori opinion. Every Council member must also belong to a Maori Committee, and so has first-hand acquaintance with at least one local community. But having to attend meetings of Committees and Councils at different levels and places diminishes the time and energy Council members have to spend in informal contact with ordinary folk and often limits the range of candidates available to the retired, self-employed, or salaried workers rather than wage earners. In urban areas the Maori Committees themselves are not always representative of or closely in touch with the people living in their territory. As the system was originally constituted, communication between the Maori Committees at the base and the New Zealand Maori Council at the apex was indirect and slow. In 1969 the Act was amended to allow direct representation from Maori Committees to their District Council where desired, cutting out the intermediate Executive Committees. This provision has been most used in urban areas. The New Zealand Maori Council early adopted a policy of holding 'Meet the People' weekends at *marae* around the country, organizing them as *hui* with open invitations to the people to attend and participate in the discussions. Such weekends regularly

209

attract hundreds of participants. The Council published a newsletter covering its activities up to 1971 when it was converted into a quarterly journal, *Te Maori*, now published monthly.

With three delegates from each of nine District Maori Councils, the New Zealand Maori Council is a sizeable body drawing members from all parts of New Zealand and most tribes. It maintains a number of sub-committees on special topics with power to co-opt outside advisers, and over the years has made extensive and thoroughly researched submissions to Parliament on every issue of concern to Maoris, especially on the 1967 and 1974 Maori Affairs Amendment Acts, land, education, town and country planning, rating, the taking of land for public works, race relations, youth, and access to fishing resources. It has representatives on the Maori Education Foundation and the Maori Health and Education Advisory Committees, and close ties with the Maori Women's Welfare League.

Between 1962 and 1972 the National Party Government, which was responsible for establishing the upper tiers of the system and had no Maori Members in Parliament, publicly consulted and referred to the New Zealand Maori Council as representative of the Maori people, appearing on occasion to set it in opposition to the Maori Members of Parliament, who were all Labour. During this period, many younger Maoris criticized the Council as rurally oriented, tradition-bound and over-conciliatory towards the Government, mounting a particularly strong attack on the Council when it supported the 1970 All Black Tour of South Africa (p. 299). Certainly the Council tended to avoid publicity, putting its views forward in quiet representations to Ministers and Government Departments, but it was by no means a rubber stamp for Government policy. On the contrary many of its submissions were critical of existing and proposed legislation, so much so in the case of the 1967 Maori Affairs Amendment Act that the Council for once publicized its opposition in the news media. During the seventies, an increasing proportion of young outspoken leaders have been nominated to serve on the District and New Zealand Maori Councils, especially from the urban areas, changing the image and the practice of these bodies considerably. Since Labour came to power in 1972, the Maori Members of Parliament and the New Zealand Maori Council have developed a close and complementary association. All new legislation has been drafted and revised in consultation with the Council, and in addition to the MPs serving on the Council in their private capacity, the Minister of Maori Affairs has regularly attended the Council's quarterly meetings as a means of maintaining contact and co-operation. Already however there are signs that yet another generation is arising to challenge the current leadership.

## Bases of leadership

The bases on which leaders are chosen are many and complementary. Seniority of descent is a decided advantage in most situations, but rarely essential. It is never sufficient of itself, but needs to be supported, at least by proficiency in Maori knowledge and ceremonial. Education, wealth, personal charm and ability, and special knowledge and skills (both Maori and Pakeha) are all acceptable sources of *mana*, which not only enhance that derived from descent but can, under certain circumstances, make up for its lack.

Whatever their other qualifications, however, all leaders must identify themselves with the Maori group and show themselves in tune with Maori ways and ideals. Those who aspire to leadership not just at the sectional but at the community or supra-community level, must be able to make speeches in Maori and be tolerably well versed in Maori etiquette and history. Offered or thrust into sectional leadership because of their educational qualifications – and the personal drive that enabled them to finish their training – young Maori teachers, ministers and government officials – the *rangatahi* – generally improve their mastery first of the language and then of the art of oratory, until in their fifties they are accepted as *kaumātua*.

## Conclusion

It is often said that today's Maori leaders lack the stature of their great predecessors, Carroll, Pomare, Buck, Ngata and Te Puea. Like the latter, they will probably be judged greater by posterity than by their contemporaries. Whatever the verdict, leaders at the lower levels are both numerous and effective. As a Maori speaker put it: 'Instead of a few tall *kauri*, now we have a whole pine forest.' Like the great giants of New Zealand's native forest, much favoured as images for a chief in Maori poetry, the outstanding leaders of the past grew far above their contemporaries, sheltering and protecting them under far-reaching canopies but also limiting their access to light and air and stunting their growth. Today leaders are both more numerous and more of a size, so that they have more equal access to the experience needed for further development.

## Social control

### Official institutions

The responsibility for maintaining law and order in New Zealand is assumed by the State, working through the police force, law courts, probation, child welfare and prison services. Maoris are employed in all these services but records of their numbers and rank are not kept officially. Senior officials of the Police, Justice and Social Welfare Departments hold that professional qualifications and personal suitability are of primary importance in the appointment and promotion of staff, and race irrelevant. However, in view of the fact that separate records are kept on offenders and that these show an unduly high proportion of Maoris, it is I think reasonable to enquire into Maori involvement in the judicial system in other capacities. Informed estimates (supplied by senior departmental officers with the warning that they are based on general knowledge not self-declaration) indicate that in 1973 Maoris made up approximately 12 per cent of prison officers, 5–6 per cent of probation officers, 4·5 per cent of police officers and under 2 per cent of those on the magistrates' bench. There are no Maori judges outside the Maori Land Court. These percentages should be compared with the proportion of Maoris in the labour force (6·3 per cent in 1971), and both over- and under-representation related to the overall pattern of Maori occupational distribution (pp. 80–6). In some cases, recruitment is limited by minimum educational requirements, usually university entrance: the official attitude is that to introduce a double standard of qualification 'would surely be an offensive piece of patronizing '(Justice, 1974: 7). Many of these occupations are not particularly attractive to Maoris because they are seen as involving possible conflict with loyalties to kin and other Maoris. However, though in most cases still lower than is desirable, not only the number but also the proportion of Maoris in these services has increased considerably in recent years. The number of Maoris in the police force in 1973 (137) was three times higher than in 1961 (33), and as percentage they had improved their position from 1·5 per cent to 4·5 per cent. This included an increase in those above the rank of constable from two to sixteen. While overall figures are not available for 1974, it is known that 9·2 per cent of those recruited into the police force in that year were Maoris and other Polynesians. The comparatively recent entry of Maoris into these services in any numbers means that relatively few are to be found in the higher ranks, but the situation may be expected to improve with lengthening service. This is especially true of the legal profession from whose senior members magistrates and judges are drawn. The State also gives limited powers to Maori Committees and Maori Wardens. We have already discussed Maori Committees (pp. 207–9).

*Maori Wardens*

The role of Maori Warden was formally established in 1945 by the Maori Social and Economic Advancement Act. The relevant sections were later re-enacted in the Maori Welfare Act 1962. Far from being a Pakeha-imposed invention, the role was based on Maori precedents, the unofficial *pirihimana* (policeman) and *watene* (wardens) appointed to maintain law and order in Maori settlements and on *marae* by the King Movement, the Ringatū and Ratana Churches, and the original Maori Councils (p. 36). Under the 1962 legislation, Maori Wardens are appointed by the Minister of Maori Affairs on nomination by a Maori Committee, and their main duty is to prevent drunken and disorderly conduct at Maori gatherings and by Maoris in public places. To this end they have legal authority to warn a licensee not to sell liquor to a Maori who is or is likely to become drunk, violent, quarrelsome or disorderly, to order such a person to leave licensed premises, to enter any premises where Maoris are gathered to search for and remove unauthorized liquor without a warrant, to apply for a prohibition order against a Maori, to forbid an intoxicated Maori to drive and to take control of his keys or car. They have the same powers with regard to non-Maoris in or near a Maori meeting-place. They have no powers of arrest or restraint beyond those of the ordinary citizen.

Maori wardens work on an entirely voluntary and part-time basis. Most have received no specific training, learning the job by working in association with experienced wardens. Where possible, the Maori Committee or Council responsible for their appointment and supervision pays their expenses, but many meet costs out of their own pocket.

In rural areas the wardens' duties are relatively simple and straightforward, carried out in familiar and mainly Maori settings in local halls and hotels and on *marae*, and they need no identification beyond a badge worn on ordinary clothes. Nominated as wardens because they already have *mana* in the community on other counts, they generally receive both support and respect from local residents, who know them personally and to whom they are often related. Under urban conditions, however, their task is much more difficult. They must deal with Maoris of many different tribes, mostly strangers to them and to each other, in settings which involve non-Maoris in considerable numbers and numerous opportunities for breaches of the law. To meet the resulting problems, urban wardens developed a uniform as an aid to recognition and an unofficial ranking system based mainly on length of service. In some areas they set up their own local sub-associations to handle organizational matters such as rostering. A national Maori Wardens' Association was formed in 1968 and sponsors annual conferences.

Over the years a certain amount of criticism has been levelled at the Maori wardens by both Maoris and non-Maoris. Their very existence has been challenged as discriminatory, subjecting Maoris to controls not applied to non-Maoris. Urban wardens have been criticized for wearing uniforms and in particular cases and places for working too closely with the police and exceeding their authority. To improve supervision and overcome problems that arise when Maori Committees cease to function and experienced wardens move to other districts, the Maori Purposes Act 1969 transferred the control of wardens from Maori Committees to District Maori Councils with power to delegate to their constituent committees. Perceiving the dangers of wardens being identified with the police, the Department of Maori Affairs, the New Zealand Maori Council and the Maori Wardens' Association have entered into an on-going dialogue on the existing and future role of the warden system. As a result, they are endeavouring to play down the disciplinary aspect of the wardens' work and stress their role as voluntary social workers associated with and responsible to the Maori District Councils and Committees, representing and serving the Maori community. In the words of a statement issued by a meeting of the New Zealand Maori Council's Sub-Committee on Wardens and representatives of the Maori Wardens' Association in 1970,

> wardens help, lead, support and guide our people during a difficult period of transition and adjustment. . . . It is universally recognized that every cultural minority has the right to form voluntary associations to promote the well-being of its members and this ideally is the philosophy basic to the Maori Wardens' movement. There was never any intention to make it a secondary police force (*Te Maori*, December–January 1970–1: 29).

Reviewing the difficulties and achievements of the warden system, Rangi Walker of the Auckland District Maori Council concluded that 'Wardens operate within the social matrix of Maoritanga on the basis of *aroha* (compassion) for other Maoris' (*Te Maori*, July–August 1971: 33–7). In 1974 the Department of Maori Affairs set about correcting a major deficiency in the system by allocating places for wardens in newly instituted training courses for voluntary community workers. Currently both the official bodies concerned and the wardens themselves are seriously considering the need for changes in both the legal provisions governing wardens' duties and in prevailing practice, especially with regard to urban areas.

## On the other side of the law

There is no doubt that Maoris get into trouble with the forces of law and order on a scale that is seriously disproportionate to their representation in the total population. This emerges clearly from the statistics and research studies published by Government Departments and is highlighted periodically with varying degrees of balance, by the news media. (Justice, New Zealand Department of, 1968; Schumacher, 1971a and b; Roberts, 1972; Statistics, New Zealand Department of, 1972b and n.d.; Social Welfare, New Zealand Department of, 1973; Justice, New Zealand Department of, 1975.) In terms both of personal and social cost there are problems here which require careful assessment and interpretation of the evidence, exploration of all possible explanations and positive action.

As I have already emphasized (p. 75), statistics do not speak for themselves but must be interpreted, and that with the greatest care. Those published by the Statistics Department do *not* provide the basis for calculating rates of offending or law-breaking, as many people seem to assume: they deal only with cases brought to court and involving arrest. It is impossible to say whether Maoris offend against the law more or less often than non-Maoris, because an unknown number of offences go undetected. It has been argued with considerable cogency that Maoris end up in court relatively more often than Pakehas not because they offend more often but because they get caught more often. Besides being generally less sophisticated and well educated, they attract police attention by reason of high physical visibility, a reputation for offending, and congregation in certain places. Then there is the problem of identifying who is a Maori. The Justice Department itself is well aware that the number of defendants and offenders identified as Maori in justice statistics may be inflated compared with the census because identification is made by recording officials and not by self-declaration.

What the statistics give us then are not rates of offending but rates of conviction. On a population basis (i.e. the number of 'distinct cases' convicted reckoned as a percentage of total population) the Maori conviction rate is several times higher than the non-Maori rate: 3·1 per cent in 1971 compared with 0·6 per cent of the non-Maori population. This is true even when reckoned on an age-group basis. In 1971 when Maoris made up 7·9 per cent of the New Zealand population, they comprised 33 per cent of the distinct cases convicted in the Magistrates' Court, 27 per cent of those sentenced in the Supreme Court, 43 per cent of those dealt with in the Children's Court, and 40 per cent of the inmates in penal institutions. While conviction rates generally have been rising over the last ten years in New Zealand, Maori rates have risen faster than non-Maori ones.

When convictions are classified according to type of offence, further significant differences appear between Maoris and non-Maoris, with Maoris convicted of certain offences making up either a higher or lower percentage of total Maori convictions than the corresponding percentage for non-Maoris, and consequently a higher or lower proportion of the total convictions for each of the offences concerned. In 1972, when Maoris accounted for 32·2 per cent of the distinct cases convicted in the Magistrates' Court, they made up a higher proportion of those convicted of assault (37 per cent), robbery, burglary, breaking and entering (38 per cent), conversion of motor vehicles (51 per cent), breach of probation (49 per cent) and escaping custody (44 per cent), and a lower proportion of those convicted of indecency with males (18 per cent), fraud and false pretences (23·5 per cent), drunkenness (23·8 per cent) and breaches of the drug laws (8 per cent), although these latter percentages were with one exception still higher than warranted on a population basis. However, differences between Maori and non-Maori patterns of distribution among the various types of offences were less numerous and less marked than they were ten years before.

For several years the statistics have also shown a discrepancy between the proportion of Maoris and non-Maoris charged who are subsequently convicted: 88·8 per cent of the former in 1972 and 84·8 per cent of the latter. Among those convicted Maoris also appear to receive a higher proportion of heavy sentences: in 1972 14·2 per cent were sentenced to prison compared with 10·6 per cent of the non-Maoris convicted, and 10 per cent were sent to detention centre, borstal and periodic detention, compared with 8·5 per cent, while the percentage fined (49·6 per cent) fell below the non-Maori percentage (55·2 per cent). On the other hand, slightly higher percentages of Maoris were convicted without penalty (12·2 per cent compared with 11·2 per cent) or placed on probation (13·7 per cent compared with 11·8 per cent).

However they are analysed, the justice statistics clearly pose problems, and many attempts have been made to interpret and explain them, not least by the staff of the Justice Department itself in published and unpublished papers. The explanations advanced fall into four main groups stressing respectively, cultural differences, socio-economic factors, rapid social change associated with urbanization, and the structure and operation of the law enforcement and judicial systems. Particular commentators stress one, sometimes virtually to the exclusion of the others, but in my view all play a part, interacting in a complex way.

Explanations in terms of cultural difference involve recognizing that existing laws are based on Pakeha values and standards of behaviour, and while Maoris support these values and standards on many counts, in at least some respects they hold and act in terms of different ones. In the past it was assumed that the standards embodied in the laws were normal and necessary for life in a complex modern society, and that Maoris must adjust their behaviour accordingly or suffer the consequences. Today there is greater willingness to accept the proposition that the law should accommodate more than one system of values and behaviour.

The cultural difference explanation is most commonly raised in connection with Maori convictions for property offences, which it is suggested may arise in at least some cases from Maoris' communal approach to property. This is a concept about which there is much misunderstanding. Pakehas often seem to imagine it means dispensing with property rights and rules entirely in favour of a 'help yourself, free-for-all' philosophy. So too do some young Maoris who have seen the usefulness of a plea of 'Maori custom' in mitigation. But this is far from being a true picture of Maori views or practice with regard to property. Maoris do recognize individual rights of possession: where they differ from most Pakehas is in defining them less exclusively and placing an even higher value on sharing, especially in family, work and friendship circles. Likewise, they do distinguish between borrowing and theft, but they define borrowing more widely than most Pakehas do. As far as most Maoris are concerned, borrowing may include taking goods without the prior knowledge of the owner, but it should be done, like all borrowing, in the context of an on-going relation (that is, not from strangers), and according to unwritten rules which include the making of a return, whether by gift or reciprocal lending. It is true that Maori does not have a specific word that can translate 'borrowing' as an abstract concept. For what is common everyday practice, Maoris use common everyday verbs: *tango* (take), *tuku* (let go, give up, offer) and *whakahoki* (give back, replace). But these three verbs go together in a set, linked by the concept of *utu* – reciprocity (p. 67). To take secretly without return is unhesitatingly identified as theft (*tāhae, whānako*). Undoubtedly many Maoris have found themselves in court on theft charges when their only fault was lack of judgment in interpreting friendly relations with Pakeha mates as warrant for borrowing when the latter did not. Some were fortunate enough to have their defence accepted but not all. Some may have advanced no defence for reasons of *whakamā* (p. 65). Nowadays few Maoris are not aware that Pakehas have different standards in this regard, and a plea of Maori custom hardly applies in cases of burglary or breaking and entering. Nevertheless, cultural background remains relevant in that those who grow up in a Maori family setting typically do not develop, and are in fact discouraged from developing, a strong sense of individual property rights, and consequently also lack the strong inhibitions that would enable them to resist temptation when denied access to wanted goods.

217

In relation to crimes of violence, it has been pointed out that traditional Maori society gave individuals more scope for the legitimate exercise of physical force than is allowed by current laws (O'Malley, 1973: 389). Certainly force figured largely among the legitimate means of obtaining redress for wrongs either within the tribe by *muru* (p. 26) or between tribes by warfare, and the qualities of the warrior, strength, energy and daring, were valued and rewarded. While inter-tribal warfare and *muru* are no longer practised, Maoris still value strength, energy and daring in the young and able-bodied, even to the point of tolerating a certain excess (pp. 85 and 176). These same qualities are at a premium in the rural settings and occupations in which Maoris were so long concentrated. However, in the country older kinsmen are available to direct over-abundant energy and intervene before things get out of hand. In the crowded cities, on the other hand, people do not accept direction of that sort from strangers, nor do they accept responsibility for giving it. Both space and legitimate objects of aggression are in short supply, and occasions of frustration and conflict are correspondingly more common.

Maori attitudes to youth may well be relevant not just to crimes of violence but across the whole spectrum of offences. All generations, including the *taitamariki* (young adults) themselves, expect the latter to exhibit not only liveliness and enterprise but also a degree of rebelliousness and disrespect for established authority and custom. As a result, though they certainly do not condone offences against the law, Maori parents and grandparents accept them when they occur rather more philosophically than Pakehas. When they apply the old saying '*he tamaiti wāwāhi tahā*' ('a child who breaks calabashes') to a young person, behind the explicit rebuke there sounds a note of pride in his or her spiritedness. For the young themselves a run-in with the law increases rather than diminishes their *mana* with their age-mates, as tangible evidence that they are not afraid of anything or anybody. However, because such behaviour is seen as characteristic of the young, individuals are expected eventually to grow out of it and settle down to respectable and responsible married life. This is just what most young Maori offenders do. Over the age of thirty the proportion of Maori offenders drops dramatically to something close to the proportion of Maoris in the population as a whole.

There are also culturally patterned differences in reactions to authority and recognition of guilt. Maori defendants often appear unresponsive to attempts by lawyers, magistrates and probation officers to enquire into their circumstances and motivations, replying in monosyllables and making no apparent effort to raise a defence. Maoris charged with offences plead guilty much more often than non-Maoris: according to one study (Slater and Jensen, 1966) over 90 per cent of the Maori offenders interviewed had pleaded guilty and 70 per cent had signed admissions of guilt. Pakehas involved in legal aid schemes have attributed this high incidence of guilty pleas to pressure from the police and lack of faith in 'Pakeha courts' (Sutherland et al., 1973). Whether these explanations are valid or not – and they certainly call for investigation – I suggest that the possibility of *whakamā* being involved should also be examined. This is a complex syndrome of feelings and behaviour well-known in Maori settings which involves withdrawal from personal and social interaction for a variety of reasons, the common element being discomfort and confusion in the face of persons perceived as having superior social or moral status (p. 65). Pakehas commonly attribute the outward signs of *whakamā* – lowered eyes, monosyllabic answers or silence and general un-responsiveness – as indicating guilt, which may or may not be involved. Moreover, they usually react by trying to force response, thereby often with the best of intentions making matters worse. Maoris familiar with *whakamā* know that it can only be overcome by the removal of the discomforting presence, the reassurance of familiar faces and surroundings and an allowance of time. Members of voluntary legal advice groups are generally more successful in 'getting through' to Maori defendants than officials because they are closer in age and life-style and manifestly lack power in the judicial system.

In the case of Maori defendants who recognize themselves as guilty of an offence, readiness to confess may also derive from Maori social experience, where confession is regarded as part of the expiation that secures re-acceptance into the community, and lightens *whakamā*. Unfortunately, confession does not seem to be understood nor responded to in this light by the courts, and offenders may well feel that they are over-punished as a result. This is an area that as far as I know has not been explored. If Maori attitudes to confession were shown to be a factor in guilty pleas, then this should be taken into account by both magistrates and legal advisers.

Secondly, it has been suggested that Maori conviction rates are primarily or at least in part a function of Maori concentration in the lower educational and socio-economic sectors of the population. These sectors are generally characterized in Western societies by high overall conviction rates and especially high rates for certain crimes involving property and violence. In this case, the pattern of convictions is sometimes attributed to 'working-class values', especially those elevating physical strength and skill, and sometimes to bias in the various branches of the judicial system against those of limited educational and occupational status. Good prospects in a profession for instance may be used as an argument to secure a lighter sentence for a defendant with good educational qualifications, where a casual labourer lacking such qualifications is more likely to be sent to a penal institution for 'training'.

Thirdly, there are those who stress the role played by social and psychological disorientation consequent on rapid social change, especially as a result of urban migration. Prominent among these is Roy Te Punga, now Assistant Director of the Department of Social Welfare (McKean, 1971: 40–56). In the same vein, a senior police officer commenting on urban gangs wrote: 'These children cannot be described as emotionally disturbed but are rather the product of a "cultural void". They are children who have not been adequately socialized, either in Maori or in Pakeha cultures' (Vaughan, 1972: 51).

Fourthly, attention has been directed to the structure, operation and officers of the law enforcement and judicial systems. Over the years members of the Justice Department staff have themselves made scattered comments along these lines in print and rather more often in unpublished works. In 1973 particularly strong criticisms were voiced by Dr Oliver Sutherland in a paper read at the New Zealand Race Relations Conference (Sutherland et al., 1973). Speaking as a member of a committee formed to advise Maori defendants appearing in the Magistrates' Court in Nelson, Sutherland reported that in the first year of operation a marked increase in the proportion of Maori defendants who had legal representation (from 18 per cent in 1971 to 79 per cent in 1972) was accompanied by substantial increases in the proportions who pleaded not guilty, had their cases dismissed or were fined, while the proportions sentenced to probation and prison fell dramatically. On the basis of court experience as well as these statistics he asserted that Maoris and other Polynesians were severely disadvantaged in 'a purely Pakeha system', suffering not only through the lack of legal representation and knowledge of their rights but also from negative racial stereotyping on the part of officials and 'the complete failure of the courts to relate to non-Pakeha values'. This paper was followed by another on 'Maori participation in Pakeha justice' (Sutherland and Galbreath, 1974). Since 1973 critical submissions on existing and proposed laws as they affect minority groups have been made by a number of organizations including Nga Tamatoa and the Auckland Committee on Racism and Discrimination (ACORD), with regard for instance to the Police Offences Amendment Act and the Childrens' and Young Persons Act 1974.

While reacting defensively to such public criticism, the services concerned have shown increasing willingness in recent years to engage in self-examination and to contemplate the need for change. In a section on 'The administration of justice' in the Department's *Report* for 1973–4 (Justice, New Zealand Department of, 1974: 6–7), the

Secretary of Justice laid it down as 'only right that in a multicultural policy like New Zealand special care should be taken in framing and administering the law to ensure its just application to minority groups' and admitted that certain criminal law provisions did seem to conflict with Maori and other Polynesian values, notably parts of the vagrancy laws and the prosecution of men for sexual relations with girls approaching sixteen. Since 1973 police training programmes have included discussions with members of J-teams (see p. 223) and voluntary legal advice groups, and visits to *marae*. At the prestigious 16th triennial conference of the New Zealand Law Society in April 1975 lawyer Robert Ludbrook presented a commissioned paper on 'The Law and Polynesians' in which he criticized the lack of interest and concern shown by the legal profession in the plight of the Maori people throughout New Zealand's history and suggested that its 'slavish adherence to British traditions, unquestioning belief in the superiority of British laws, and cloistered camaraderie' had blinded the profession to the fact that the law as practised placed all but white middle-class males at a distinct disadvantage. The paper received powerful and general support, and although there was not time to debate its highly practical suggestions for improving the situation, their presentation in such a context should ensure they receive the attention they deserve.

*Research*

While many people have advanced general hypotheses under all four of these headings, comparatively little research has been undertaken to test them in depth and even less has been published. Jocelyn Roberts's *Self-image and Delinquency* (1972) is a sensitive exploration of the quasi-kinship relations established by girls in Borstal and the role they play in helping the girls develop understanding of themselves and their social role. All the other studies which I know are unpublished and available only to a restricted readership. Of these, two small-scale pilot studies are of particular interest. The first is an interview study on young Maori offenders carried out by the research officers of the Joint (inter-departmental) Committee on Young Offenders (Slater and Jensen, 1966). Interviewing a group of young Maori offenders, the research workers obtained details about their backgrounds which showed them to be 'highly disrupted and unstable by middle-class Pakeha standards', involving a high incidence of nuclear families disrupted by death or separation, upbringing in several different households, conditions of material poverty and overcrowding and frequent changes of school. However, they were jolted to find that interviews with a control group of young Maori national

221

servicemen without criminal records produced almost exactly the same pattern. The authors concluded that the factor that made the difference was the particular pattern of values, expectations and motivations built up by family interaction, and hypothesized that the 'more hierarchical, less parent-centred structure of the Maori nuclear family' and the social support available from the extended family and the wider community cushioned the effect of family disruptions for many young Maoris. They might have gone further and questioned the applicability of Pakeha middle-class ideas of what constitutes stability and disruption.

The second study examined the sentencing of first offenders, using a sample consisting of 137 non-Maori and 32 Maori males for whom a probation officer's report was prepared in the month of July 1973 (Gronfors, 1973; Gronfors and Mugford, 1973). After establishing that the Maori offenders in the sample received a higher proportion of heavier sentences, the research worker tested a range of possible explanations by examining the information, comments and recommendations made in the probation officers' reports. This procedure was chosen because in sentencing magistrates take into account all circumstances relating to both offence and offender, and because it has been shown that the recommendations in the reports are followed by the courts in sentencing in over 85 per cent of the cases where they are requested. Undertaken as a pilot for a larger project, this study produced results which suggest lines of further enquiry rather than providing answers. The research worker himself holds that the differences between Maori and non-Maori offenders on such counts as educational level reached, occupation, financial position and family background were not marked enough to account for the discrepancy in sentencing simply as a function of socio-economic status, while a colleague interpreted the findings in a radio interview as indicating 'it's a matter of class not race'. The study did however note that the writers of the reports included an explanation for the committing of the offence and attributed it to causes external to the offender more often in the case of non-Maori than Maori offenders; and that in describing personality they used psychological terminology (such as poor self-image) for non-Maoris but non-psychological terms (such as naïve, irresponsible) for Maoris. These findings are not easy to interpret. At least two possible explanations spring to my mind: first, that the writers of the reports were unconsciously more confident in their efforts to understand and explain the character and behaviour of non-Maori offenders and more at a loss with Maoris because of lack of familiarity with their background; and second, that their difficulties in understanding Maori offenders were compounded by the phenomenon of *whakamā*, especially where they did not recognize it as such. If discrimination is involved, it is in its proper, limited sense of 'making a difference', and is not conscious nor intended. Further research is clearly needed.

## *Action*

After the Hunn Report (1961) drew attention to the low proportion of Maori offenders with legal representation, the Department of Maori Affairs arranged for Maori Welfare Officers (since renamed Community Officers) to attend courts to advise them, but the staff available has never been sufficient to meet the need, competing duties preventing regular attendance at or complete coverage of the several courts especially in the main cities. While legal aid is available to those who cannot afford to engage lawyers under the Offenders' Legal Aid Act 1954 and Offenders' Legal Aid Regulations 1972, the real problem is that many defendants do not know what their rights are or how to ask for aid. To meet this problem, existing voluntary associations like Nga Tamatoa and others formed for the purpose set about placing representatives in the courts to advise unrepresented defendants and especially to help them get representation. Beginning in the early seventies the lawyers themselves set up voluntary 'duty solicitor' schemes in various centres and in 1974 these were integrated into an official, nation-wide scheme covering the magistrates' courts. Under this scheme, lawyers from a duty solicitors' roster take it in turns to attend the courts to give assistance free of charge to anyone charged with an offence carrying a possible prison sentence, whether in the form of advice – on matters of remand, bail, representation or pleas – or appearing in court on their behalf. Costs are met by the Justice Department and the operation of the scheme is supervised in each area by an informal Duty Solicitors' Committee which may include not only lawyers and official bodies but unofficial ones like Nga Tamatoa and interested private citizens.

Over the last few years the Police Department has increased its interest in preventive work by establishing a Youth Aid Section and co-operating with social workers in the formation of the so-called 'J-teams'. As a result of the work of Youth Aid about half the juvenile offenders apprehended are not prosecuted but are dealt with out of court either by a warning from the police or by a period of oversight by the Department of Social Welfare following consultation between the two services. However, it has been pointed out that the total number of youngsters prosecuted has continued to increase.

The J-teams were born in 1971 after discussions between the Police and Maori Affairs Departments: the 'J' stands for 'Joint'. The teams are made up of a police officer and two social workers. Present members are mainly Maori or other Polynesian and include a number of Maori ministers and women. They wear no uniforms, make no arrests and keep hours of their own choosing. The Police Department supplies them with a radio car for night patrols and refers cases to them for investigation and report, but otherwise they work on their own, supplying their Department with a monthly report. The J-teams' task is not to catch offenders but to prevent young Maoris and other Polynesians becoming offenders or moving from minor into more serious offending. They do this by meeting the youngsters where they congregate, talking to them, listening to their problems and frustrations, and advising them on how to handle them. They also contact and advise parents and visit schools to talk to teachers about dealing with members of minority groups. And they take every opportunity to establish links and improve communication between children, parents and schools. In the nature of the case, the success of the J-teams is hard to measure, but the Departments concerned are convinced that offences and general difficulties have been substantially reduced in the areas where they operate, and on the strength of this conviction plan to increase their number. At the beginning of 1975 there were three teams in Auckland, one in Wellington and one in Gisborne.

Another police innovation, a mobile Task Force set up to deal with increasing violence in the streets and hotels of the inner city in Auckland, has not been so well received: on the contrary, it has aroused strong expressions of protest and resentment from the Maoris and other Polynesians. Complaints centre around the disproportionately large number of young Polynesians arrested by the Task Force, the manner in which the arrests are made, the Task Force's alleged concentration on those streets and hotels most frequented by Polynesians, and the high proportion of arrests made not for violence but for relatively trivial offences against propriety such as drunkenness, offensive language and disorderly behaviour. Feeling ran so high in Auckland that the leaders of the Polynesian community set up their own unofficial tribunal, consisting of two Maoris, two other Polynesians and two Pakehas, to consider not only the activities of the Task Force but also other branches of the police force, the Police Offences Act, and the responsibilities of society at large. In its Report, which was read at a public meeting in October 1974 and later forwarded to the Prime Minister, the tribunal said that the evidence presented indicated that the actions of the Task Force were in fact heavily weighted against Maoris and other Polynesians, made little or no allowance for cultural differences, and produced scenes of tension and confrontation where its purpose was ostensibly to reduce them. The tribunal recommended the replacement of the

Task Force by more joint teams of police officers and social workers, 'revival' of the Maori warden system, greater use of the 'bobby on the beat', the up-dating of the Police Offences Act, and a greater sharing of the responsibility for remedying social ills by other sectors of the community, especially the brewery companies and industrial employers. Similarly critical views regarding the Task Force were aired by Maoris of all ages at a meeting with the Auckland Police Commissioner and senior police officers held on Maori initiative at the Mangere *marae*. When the Commissioner later expressed surprise and hurt at the vehemence and hostility of most of the Maori speakers, he revealed not only limited understanding of Maori ways of doing things but failure to appreciate that Maoris have different ways at all. As we shall see (p. 235), one of the chief functions of the *marae* is to provide a forum where hostilities and grievances can be fully expressed and worked out, so that they do not fester and turn inwards. Little progress will be made until more of 'the Pakehas in power' (to use Ngata's phrase – p. 48) recognize that their own paternalistic ethnocentrism itself is a major cause of disharmony.

*Informal controls*

Maoris still alive can remember the days when the elders took direct action to punish offenders against community norms, administering physical chastisement with a walking stick, shaming the culprit by a public tongue-lashing, or instigating a *muru* raid on his kinsfolk (p. 26). But today's elders lack the authority of their predecessors, because they lack the sanctions. The State not only forbids the use of force, but itself polices even the most isolated settlements. Control over land and their descendants' cash earnings has passed from their hands, and the young have many avenues of escape from their direction. The elders advise and scold, but cannot command. Their influence depends on personal affection and respect.

In Maori as in most rural communities, public opinion is an important control on behaviour. In cities it is easier to avoid critics. As Ritchie pointed out (1963: 145), Maoris spend a lot of their time talking about other people and their doings, exploring the limits of permissible behaviour. On the whole the strongest expressions of disapproval are directed against achievement above the ordinary rather than misdemeanours. To outsiders, Maoris appear extremely tolerant in their attitude to offenders against both the law and their own professed norms. Minor lapses, especially if they are funny and score off outsiders, are retailed with amusement. Whatever is said behind the culprit's back, disapproval is usually expressed to his face in jocular fashion. No action is taken unless the offender persists in behaving badly. Even then punishment is informal and indirect. Someone (usually an elder) administers a public rebuke or snub, and the community endorses it by withholding sympathy. The rebuke is directed at a particular offence but is more severe than the latter warrants on its own (Metge, 1964a: 90–2).

This toleration of offenders within the group has several causes. In country areas judgments are modified by ties of kinship and friendship. In situations of escalating depopulation, elders often hold their peace for 'fear of driving them away'. Maoris place a high value on *aroha* (peace and harmony, especially for kin). I have often heard them use the phrase 'I was sorry for him' to explain letting someone off a duty or a punishment, a phrase I eventually realized is used to translate a Maori one containing *aroha*. This tolerance often goes with lack of self-confidence: the ordinary Maori is sympathetic to the failure and the delinquent because he sees himself in them more readily than in the successful. 'Not being hard on people' bolsters self-esteem and the image of the self as a Maori. Finally, the fact that the State bears the responsibility for dealing with all serious offences allows the Maori community to stress its support and sympathy to its members in a way it could not afford to do in the past.

Once the judicial system has punished a Maori offender, his family and his home community normally accept him back sympathetically. Maoris released from gaol stand a good chance of rehabilitation if they can return to their own folk. Unfortunately this is impossible in many cases, because of lack of work in country areas. Most must go back to the towns and cities where they got into trouble, to the indifference and rejection of strangers. It is to cater for 'our children' in this situation among other reasons that elders and parents living in urban areas plan and work to develop urban *marae*.

# chapter 15

# The Marae

Speaking at Otaki in 1950, Sir Apirana Ngata said: 'The *marae*, buildings, such as meeting-houses and halls, with appurtenant amenities, have always been the chief preoccupation of a Maori community. Until these are provided the community will not seriously take up other problems, and will not freely contribute funds for these other affairs' (*Te Ao Hou*, Spring 1952: 23). As Maoris migrate in search of work, many older *marae* fall into disuse and dilapidation, but others are continually being built or renewed. In its Report of September 1974, the Committee on Marae Subsidies set up by the Government to review the situation indicated that under the current dollar for dollar subsidy scheme nearly three million dollars would be required to subsidize projects in hand or planned and brought down recommendations for revising the subsidy scheme and greatly extending the scope of Government help.

Today Maoris use the term *marae* in two related senses; first, for an open space reserved and used for Maori assembly, and secondly, for the combination of this open space with a set of communal buildings which normally includes a meeting-house. Their meaning is usually clear from the context. For our purposes, it is useful to distinguish the former as 'the *marae* proper'.

Since comparatively few Maoris now live in villages, most *marae* stand alone or with only two or three houses close at hand. Wherever they live, close to the *marae* or at a distance, Maoris occupy family houses with their own living-room, kitchen and toilet facilities. As a result, they no longer use the *marae* daily as an extension of their living quarters. Instead they use it 'occasionally', from time to time, for special purposes, for gathering in numbers the ordinary house cannot accommodate, and especially for entertaining guests. Under these circumstances, they have found it necessary to provide the

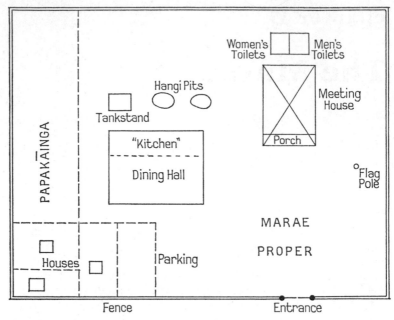

*Figure 5    Sketch plan of a typical marae*

*marae* with cooking and toilet facilities able to cope with large numbers and a hall for eating, recreation and money-making. Besides being required for sleeping and speech-making, the meeting-house is regarded as too *tapu* for such uses.

### Title

Most *marae* stand on land which has been legally declared a 'Maori reserve' by an Order-in-Council. Maoris call such *marae* 'legal' or 'official' *marae*. In each case the reserving Order sets the reserve aside 'for the use and benefit' of a specified Maori group, most commonly for a descent-group (a named *hapū* or tribe or 'the original owners and their descendants'), sometimes for a group defined by church membership or local residence, and occasionally for 'all Maoris'. In the case of *marae* reserved for a descent-group, members inherit 'rights *in* the *marae*' by virtue of their descent, from the owners at the time of reservation, but such rights cannot be attached to any particular part of the *marae* nor disposed of in any way, i.e. they are non-individualized and inalienable (p. 113). Each *marae* reserve is vested in trustees appointed from and by the 'owning' group. By law they cannot alienate it nor lease it for more than seven years at a time.

In most cases, the *marae* itself occupies only part of the *marae* reserve. In recent years the Maori Land Court has limited new reserves to under five acres, but most early ones, established when grazing had to be provided for visitors' horses, are much larger. The land not occupied by the reserve is usually leased for farming. Sometimes part of it is officially gazetted as *papakāinga* (housing land). Members of the 'owning' group may build houses on the *papakāinga*, but they cannot obtain sole title to their sites, and they cannot remove nor let the houses without the trustees' approval. Nowadays few *papakāinga* carry more than two or three houses. The chief exception is Tūrangawaewae, which has more than twenty.

*Marae* which have not been legally reserved are 'private' *marae*, held on ordinary Maori title by one or several related owners. The latter own individualized shares in the land. In theory, they can dispose of them independently, subject only to the approval of the Maori Land Court. In practice, this is rarely either sought or given.

**The parts of the marae**

Visitors to a *marae* pass through the main gateway directly on to the *marae* proper, across which they face the meeting-house (*whare hui*). The dining-hall (*whare kai*) is usually placed to one side, with the 'kitchen' (properly a cook-house) attached or in an adjoining building, and toilet blocks to the rear. Some *marae* also include a cemetery, church and sports' grounds. Small ones may have only one main building, large ones an extra hall or sleeping-house. Tūrangawaewae has a many-roomed 'cultural complex' with a dining-hall that seats a thousand and four sleeping-houses, besides the meeting-house and the Queen's dining-room and private suite.

Many *marae* have names of their own, attaching originally to the *marae* proper: e.g. Papa-i-o-uru in Ohinemutu (Rotorua) and Tūrangawaewae in Ngaruawahia. Meeting-houses are usually named after an ancestor, though sometimes their name recalls a significant event or has symbolic meaning, e.g. Hono-ki-Rarotonga at Tokomaru Bay, whose name commemorates the presence of a Rarotongan party at its opening. The ancestors who give their name to meeting-houses are mostly men, except on the East Coast where almost every second house is named for a woman. Sometimes dining-halls bear the name of the wife, sister or husband of the ancestor of the meeting-house, symbolizing the complementarity of the two buildings.

The *marae* proper may be any size or shape, and covered in grass, asphalt or concrete. Some are plain and bare, others have a carved flag pole and are bordered with flower-beds and shrubs. Usually they are quite flat.

The meeting-house is almost without exception traditional in form: a single-storeyed, rectangular building consisting of one large room, with a deep gabled porch across the front, and a single door and window in the front wall. Nearly all are built of modern materials, mainly timber weather-boards with corrugated-iron roofs. The older houses, dating from the late nineteenth century, are usually low on the ground, with low side walls, steeply pitched roofs and windows only in the front and occasionally rear walls. Those built this century are raised off the ground, with high side walls, electric lights, and often electric points for heaters and razors. While the conservative Arawa and Tūhoe resist such innovations, most other tribes now put windows in rear and side walls. The practical Ngāti Porou add extra doors, side porches and store-rooms wherever convenient. The façades and interiors of many meeting-houses are richly decorated with traditional carving, reed panelling (*tukutuku*) and rafter patterns (*kōwhaiwhai*). These are not, however, essential features. In Northland and Taranaki, only a few of the many houses are so adorned. Function, not appearance, is what distinguishes a meeting-house from a hall in the final analysis.

The meeting-house is not only named after an important ancestor: it is symbolically his or her body. Its ridgepole (*tāhuhu*) is his back-bone, a carved representation of his face (*koruru*) covers the junction of the two barge-boards (*maihi*) which are his arms, the front window (*mataaho*) is his eye, and the visitor steps through the door into his *poho* (chest), enclosed by the rafters (*heke*) which are his ribs. The central pillar supporting the ridgepole is the *poutokomanawa* or heart-post. When Maoris talk of the meeting-house they use a personal pronoun and refer to him (or her) thinking, feeling, speaking and acting as a living person contemporary with themselves. Providing a shelter for his descendants literally and figuratively, the meeting-house serves as a particularly potent symbol of their group identity.

Maoris see *marae* and meeting-house as 'going together' in many important ways. Spokesmen for visitors open their speeches by greeting them both: '*Te marae e takoto nei, tēna koe; te whare, e tū nei, tēna koe*' ('Marae lying here, I greet you; house standing here I greet you'). Spatially and in terms of function they are extensions one of the other. The *marae* proper is used for welcoming guests and speech-making during the day-time and fine weather, the meeting-house for sleeping in and for speech-making during the night-time and bad weather, and in some areas during *tangihanga* (p. 261). Because of their traditional origin and functions, both are *tapu* and must be treated with respect. Welcomes and speech-making are conducted according to basically traditional rules (pp. 250–9). Most tribes ban eating in the meeting-house, some even smoking. Water from the roof of the meeting-house (the ancestor's head) is not used but drained into the earth. On some counts, *marae* and meeting-house are seen as different and even set in opposition to each other, but their opposition is essentially complementary. It is often said: '*Ko Tū a waho, ko Rongo a roto*' ('Tū outside, Rongo inside'). Now Tū is Tū-matauenga, the god of mankind and of war: associating him with the *marae* is a symbolic way of referring to it as an arena where hostilities are worked out in the cut and thrust of debate and where men display their quality as leaders. Rongo on the other hand is the god of agriculture and the peaceful arts. The implication is that fighting should be confined to the *marae* proper while amity reigns inside the meeting-house. In my experience however some of the most heated and exciting debates take place inside the house in the early hours of the morning. A slightly different formulation names Tānewhakapiri-piri as the god presiding over the meeting-house and Tū-te-Ihiihi as the god of the *marae* proper. Tāne, as god of the forest, provides the materials of which the house is constructed, and the qualifying '*whaka-piripiri*' describes the way he brings people closer together by enclos-ing them within its shelter. *Tū-te-Ihiihi* is another name for Tū-matauenga. *Ihi* means 'essential force' and is virtually a synonym for *mana*. Its use in this context stresses the charismatic qualities of the orator, his ability to enthral his audience, inspiring awe and admira-tion. Tūhoe explain not allowing their women to speak on the *marae* on the grounds that it is a battleground where they might get hurt: they are needed to step in after the fighting is over to create an atmosphere of peace and friendliness. Whatever harsh things are said, whatever wounds are inflicted on the *marae*, in the end Tū gives way to Rongo: grievances must be left lying on the *marae* and not taken away to be talked about in the fields (*kōrero i te pārae*).

The porch of the meeting-house (*mahau*) is an intermediate area linking the *marae* proper and the inside of the meeting-house. Though physically part of the house it is open to and used as an extension of the *marae* proper. The *tāngata whenua* elders frequently sit there during welcomes and in some areas the coffin rests there during *tangihanga*. Outside and inside are both separated and linked by the doorway and its threshold (*paepae tapu*).

Compared with the meeting-house, the dining-hall is a utilitarian building lacking in *tapu*. Usually under the same roof as the cooking-area, with servery hatches along one side and a stage for concerts and dance-bands, it is used for feeding and entertaining guests and for all sorts of money-raising projects. In most cases it lacks adornment, but sometimes, especially on the East Coast, the people adorn the dining-hall with craft work while perfecting their skills in preparation for work on the meeting-house.

The capacity of a *marae* depends ultimately on its cookhouse. On many small *marae* cooking is done in open-air earth-ovens (*hāngi*) and in pots hanging over red-hot embers in vast corrugated-iron fireplaces. The *hāngi* is a good way of cooking for moderately large numbers, except in heavy rain, and the food is delicious, with its own distinctive flavour. More and more Maori communities are installing the most modern equipment on their *marae*: stainless steel cooking-coppers, concrete steam-boxes, electric and diesel stoves and boilers, refrigerated cool stores and even dishwashing machines. But for special occasions and for special guests a *hāngi* is still laid whenever possible because it is so distinctively Maori.

### Tapu and noa on the marae

*Marae* proper and meeting-house are often distinguished as the *tapu* parts of the *marae* complex, while the dining-hall and kitchen are described as *noa*. This comparison should be seen as a matter of relativity, not absolutes.

The *marae* complex is *tapu* as a whole in relation to the outside world. When a group of visitors arrive at a *marae* they remain outside until called to enter, and the invitation uses words that mean 'come up' rather than 'come in': '*Piki mai, kake mai, eke mai*'. Since most *marae* are flat, it is plain that the climbing is a symbolic movement from a *noa* realm to a *tapu* one.

Within its own boundaries, however, the *marae* is divided into a series of parts linked as *tapu* and *noa* in relation to each other. Thus *marae* proper and meeting-house are linked as a *tapu* sector in relation to the dining-hall and kitchen, but each is also internally differentiated into two parts which are *tapu* and *noa* in relation to each other. Probably the most *tapu* part of the *marae* is the central part of the *marae* proper, the area where visitors are welcomed and orators make their speeches. It is a serious breach of etiquette and of *tapu* to walk across this area during a welcome or speech, and even when it is not in use it should be skirted and not crossed. The surrounding fringe area where people sit and stand to listen to the speeches is by comparison *noa*, though still more *tapu* than (say) the dining-hall. Inside the meeting-house is likewise divided into two: the *tara whānui* (the 'big' side) and the *tara iti* (the 'little' side), which are related as *tapu* to *noa*. In most tribes, the *tara whānui* lies to the right of a person entering the meeting-house through the front door, the *tara iti* to the left, but in some communities the reverse applies. The *tara whānui* is reserved for the use of guests, while the *tāngata whenua* sleep on the *tara iti*. Formerly the places of honour occupied by those of highest rank on each side were at the front near the one door and

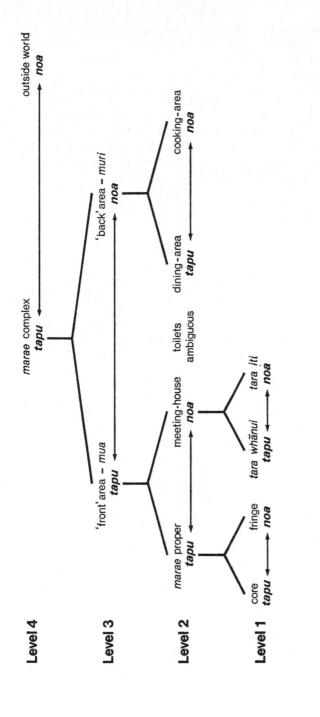

Level 4    outside world
           *noa*

           *marae* complex                                          outside world
           **tapu**                                                 *noa*

Level 3                        'back' area – *muri*
                               *noa*

           'front' area – *mua*
           **tapu**

                                          dining-area        cooking-area
                                          *tapu*             *noa*

Level 2    meeting-house
           *noa*

                               toilets
                               ambiguous

           *marae* proper
           **tapu**

                                          *tara whānui*      *tara iti*
                                          *tapu*             *noa*

Level 1    core          fringe
           *tapu*        *noa*

Key:    ←→  Relation of opposition on the same level

            ∨   Subdivision into parts
                Combination into unity at a higher level

*Figure 6   Opposition and unity: tapu and noa on the marae*

233

window, but nowadays they are usually placed at the rear under the windows that now ventilate that end, away from traffic in and out. The dining-hall is *tapu* in relation to the cooking area, which is the most *noa* part of the *marae*. In pre-Christian times the latrine was highly *tapu* and used for certain important rituals (Buck, 1949: 140–3). Today, when it is no longer so used, Maoris differ as to whether it should be classified as *tapu* or *noa*, and even if they settle for the latter they would regard it as a different kind of *noa* from that of the dining-hall and kitchen, which are warm and pleasant places to relax in. (For a discussion of *tapu* and *noa* in relation to the siting of pre-school centres on the *marae*, see McDonald in Bray and Hill, II, 1974: 74–8.)

The *tāngata whenua* of a *marae* complex are, like the *marae* itself, *tapu* to the outside world: they must be approached and treated with respect. The *kawa* (rules of protocol) followed at a *hui* is the *kawa* of the hosts, unless they expressly decree otherwise. In the process of caring for their guests, the *tāngata whenua* engage in a variety of tasks both *tapu* and *noa*. The *tapu* activities of calling, making speeches and wailing are carried out on the *marae* proper and inside the meeting-house, and those who carry them out, usually the *kaumātua*, are referred to as the *tāngata kei mua*, 'the people in front'. The rest of the *tāngata whenua* work behind the scenes at *noa* tasks in the dining-hall, kitchen and toilets: they are the *tāngata kei muri*, 'the people at the back'. In the meeting-house, the *tāngata whenua* sleep on the less *tapu* side. But engaging in activities that are *noa* does not diminish either the *mana* or the *tapu* of *tāngata whenua*: on the contrary, since they are done in the context of caring for visitors, they enhance it. Moreover, while *noa* activities are undramatic compared with *tapu* ones and do not attract the same public attention, they are valued as an essential contribution to the enterprise the community is engaged in. They are also greatly enjoyed by the participants, taking place in an atmosphere of warm relaxed comradeship and badinage. Well-schooled guests make a point of paying tribute before they leave to the *ringa wera* (literally, 'hot hands'), and the 'front men' are the first to acknowledge that all their fine words would go for nothing without the backing of the 'workers'.

Guests visiting a *marae* are also *tapu* to their hosts, especially those who have not been welcomed there before, who are described as *waewae tapu* ('sacred feet'). The welcome ceremony is designed among other things to modify this *tapu* and so make social contact possible and comfortable. Once welcomed, members of a visiting party may be asked to join the hosts in welcoming subsequent parties, but they are expected to keep to the more *tapu* parts of the *marae*.

It is often said that a meeting-house should be oriented to the rising sun, but many meeting-houses in fact face in other directions.

After looking at many *marae*, architect Michael Austin has suggested that they are almost invariably placed with hills or forest at their backs and open country in front, facing the direction from which visitors come, whether by road, river or sea. This reflects the relative positioning of the 'people behind' and the 'people in front', working together as hosts to receive and care for their *manuhiri* (Austin, personal communication, 1974).

### The uses of the marae

No longer a village living-room, the *marae* is used, firstly, for the same purposes as other local halls: for club and committee meetings, recreation and money-raising, for church meetings and services where there is no church, for political meetings, welcomes and farewells, and discussions of local issues. But it is also used for two distinctively Maori purposes: for staging gatherings that attract large numbers of visitors to stay for several days (*hui*), and for the temporary accommodation, between *hui*, of touring sports and concert parties, stranded strangers, and the temporarily homeless.

Of all the gatherings held at a *marae*, the *tangihanga* is the most important. Whenever possible, Maoris take their dead to a *marae* (preferably an ancestral one) to 'lie in state' for two or three days, while relatives and friends come 'to pay their respects'. Further, they consider it right and proper that *tangihanga* should take precedence over any other activity at a *marae*. Gatherings already in progress are curtailed, and imminent arrangements cancelled. Some communities keep the *marae* closed for one to four weeks after a *tangihanga* because of the *tapu* associated with death and as a mark of respect to the dead.

The *marae* also serves an important function as a community forum. Whenever Maoris gather at a *marae*, whether for purely local meetings or for *hui*, there is always plenty of speech-making. Speakers do not confine themselves to the ostensible object of the gathering, but take the opportunity to discuss any issue that is on their minds. At *tangihanga* and unveilings, when elders gather from far afield and the general mood is serious, discussions range very widely indeed. Plain-speaking rather than politeness is the rule. Maoris believe that grievances and disagreements should be brought into the open, and the *marae* is the proper place to do it. During *hui*, there are many elders present to arbitrate. The *marae* itself affords a sort of diplomatic privilege. People should not take offence at anything said on a *marae*, but should argue their differences through to an amicable conclusion. As we have seen, Rongo, not Tū-matauenga, should prevail in the end.

How often a *marae* is used depends on the size of the community it serves. In the Northland communities I know best, most *marae* are used once or twice a week for several hours at a time by up to fifty people, and for *hui* on an average of once a month, that is, for perhaps three *tangihanga*, five weddings, an unveiling, and three twenty-first birthday parties a year. Large *marae* like Tūrangawaewae, Papa-i-o-uru and Ōtiria (Northland) are in almost constant use. On the other hand, in areas affected by emigration, many *marae* (built in more populous times) come alive only once or twice a year. But though the buildings fall into disrepair, it is important to the emigrants that they should be there, when needed, for *tangihanga*.

### Rights on the marae

Well over 90 per cent of all *marae* belong, whether on group title by reservation or on multiple, individualized title, to a descent-group. This is usually a *hapū*, but some *marae* 'belong' to a large-family, and a few are reserved in the name of a whole tribe. With few exceptions, the descent-group involved has owned and occupied land in the district for generations. Provided that they live in the district, visit frequently and/or own 'Maori land' there, its members are recognized as *tāngata whenua*, possessing by virtue of descent both 'rights *in* the *marae*' (shares in the land) and 'rights *on* the *marae*' (privileges in its use) (pp. 107–9). In Northland, they are sometimes described as *tāngata marae*, a more precise term, particularly in communities where two or more *hapū* have separate *marae*.

A Maori describes the *marae* where he is *tangata whenua* as his *tūrangawaewae*, literally 'a standing-place for the feet' and figuratively a base and stronghold. On his *tūrangawaewae*, 'a Maori is king'; he 'may act as if he owned the place', and 'no-one can order him around'. In theory at least, he has four rights which others lack: the right to make a speech in public, on the *marae* proper or in the meeting-house, without asking anyone's permission; the right to share in its management; the right to use its facilities free of charge; and the right to invite and entertain guests there on his own initiative. In practice, however, the exercise of these rights is often limited by traditional rules and by practical considerations. Some tribes (chiefly Arawa) forbid speech-making on the *marae* proper to women and to men whose fathers are still alive. Men under *kaumātua* status and the landless usually speak only at local gatherings, leaving the leading elders to 'do the talking' when visitors are present. For convenience some groups hand the management of the *marae* over to an executive committee. *Tāngata whenua* usually agree to pay set charges to use the *marae* for recreational and money-raising purposes, in order to build up the maintenance fund, and they find it wise to book it beforehand to avoid clashes.

'Immigrants' use the *marae* only at the invitation of the *tāngata whenua*. In some communities, 'immigrants' never speak on the *marae* nor serve on the *marae* committee, no matter how high their rank in their own *hapū*. Today, however, these are exceptions to the rule. At least two-thirds of the *marae* committees I know include several 'immigrants', though usually excluding them from office, and many communities accept one or two among their regular spokesmen at *hui*.

Finally, a word about rights on *marae* which serve a major *hapū* or a tribe as well as a local community. Only members of the local *hapū* are *tāngata marae* in the fullest sense, but at *hui* sponsored by the large group the constituent *hapū* provide both speakers and workers, whether they have rights in land in the immediate vicinity or not. Sometimes the *marae* committee includes representatives of the other *hapū* as well as the local one.

### Marae management

The modern *marae* needs a lot of looking after. There are large, expensive buildings to maintain, grounds to keep clean and tidy, stores of bedding, crockery and other equipment to provide and keep ready for use, bookings to arrange, money to raise for expenses, and improvements to plan and pay for.

In most cases, the task of management is carried out not by the trustees but by a '*marae* committee' (*komiti marae*) set up for the purpose. *Marae* committees vary widely in size and membership. Some consist of a limited number of *tāngata marae*, often of one sex. Others comprise all the adult *hapū* members living in the district, some emigrant ones, and their spouses, a group of fifty people or more. The *marae* committee may do everything itself, but often it delegates tasks to sub-committees or other associations. For instance, the care of movable equipment (bedding, crockery, cutlery, pots and pans) is often entrusted to a 'women's committee' or the local Maori Women's Welfare League branch; the provision of fuel or hospitality between *hui* to a 'men's committee'. On the southern East Coast and in Wairoa, each local large-family is responsible for equipping several tables in the dining-hall. *Marae* committees do not usually run the *hui* held at *marae* except when opening new *marae* buildings. On other occasions, they simply hand over the keys of the *marae* to the *hui* sponsors, on the understanding that it will be left as found.

Maori Committees (p. 207) always have some connection with *marae* affairs, since their approval is required for the provision of liquor at the *marae* and applications for subsidy on improvements. Over much of Hawke's Bay and the Wairarapa and in many towns, they have taken over the actual management of the *marae* as well.

Finance is a perennial problem for most *marae* committees. Some lease part of the *marae* block or receive grants from tribal trust boards or incorporations, but most rely on subscriptions, donations, hiring fees and money-raising activities. It is an unwritten law that no charge is made for the use of the *marae* for *hui*. If they can afford it, the sponsors make a donation 'to the *marae*', passing on some of the gifts received from visitors (p. 259). Such donations rarely cover more than the cost of electricity and fuel used during the *hui*. Committees running large, well-equipped *marae* in well-populated areas, especially near towns, are able to let their dining-halls frequently and for high rents, to Pakehas as well as Maoris; but in remote country areas, where local Maoris are the only users, charges are sufficient only to meet expenses.

### The urban situation

*Marae* are to be found in their most typical and traditional form and in greatest number in the country. Twenty years ago there were very few in urban areas, most of them *tāngata whenua marae* built on ancestral land before the city grew up around them. Since then, more rural *marae* have been engulfed in the spread of urban settlement, and Maoris moving from rural areas into towns and cities where *marae* are few or lacking have established or are in the process of establishing numerous new *marae*, which often depart from the rural pattern in significant respects.

When they first settle in a town, 'immigrants' go home frequently and stage their *hui* on their home *marae*. But if home is more than fifty miles away – as in most cases it is – the cost in time and money soon reduces their visits. They join and form urban associations, and, as their circle of urban relatives and friends expands, begin holding weddings and twenty-first birthday parties in town. Usually the bereaved continue to take their dead home for a *tangihanga* on the home *marae*, but they find they must make provision for other urban residents to 'pay their respects' in town before they leave. Surrounded and outnumbered by Pakehas, they feel an increasing need for a place close at hand where they can relax in Maori company and 'do things the Maori way'.

If the *tāngata whenua* have a *marae* in or near the town, they usually issue a general invitation to 'immigrants' to use it, at least in the early stages of urbanization. Besides welcoming 'immigrants' to their own gatherings, they allow them to hire the *marae* when they are not using it themselves, and their elders call personally on the bereaved and invite them to take the body there. This arrangement works reasonably well while the number of 'immigrants' remains small, but difficulties arise as they come to outnumber the *tāngata whenua*, often many times over. The *marae* itself is not usually large enough for the demand. Afraid of 'being swamped on our own *marae*', the *tāngata whenua* limit their bereavement calls to those they know personally, and stand more firmly on their rights. The 'immigrants' on their side become increasingly impatient of their status as 'guests', unable to take the initiative. At any time their arrangements to use the *marae* may be upset by a death among the *tāngata whenua*, while the organization of their own *tangihanga* is often held up while they wait for an invitation to the *marae*.

If a local *marae* is lacking or not available, 'immigrants' must either use their home 'as a little *marae*' or hire public premises. The former course limits the guests they can cope with and alienates neighbours. Hired premises usually lack facilities for cooking meals for a crowd and are available only for a few hours at a time, so that they are forced to engage caterers, who are expensive and do not provide Maori foods, and to distribute their guests among many households for sleeping.

Confronted with these problems, Maoris living as 'immigrants' in urban areas commonly band together to work for a 'place of our own'. This is an undertaking of almost breathtaking proportions, for money must be raised for land as well as buildings and a site found which meets Maori requirements within terms set by zoning restrictions and by-laws. The site should be large enough to incorporate a reception area, facilities for cooking and serving meals to a crowd, and a hall suitable for a variety of purposes; the privacy of both the centre and its neighbours should be protected by walls or trees; and adequate parking space must be available. There are difficult decisions about the form the centre should take, who should be allowed to share in its management and use, and according to what rules. Sometimes there are objections to be met from surrounding residents, who have little understanding of what a *marae* is and how it is used. Finally, interest and support must be maintained over a period of years as the necessary tens of thousands of dollars are slowly accumulated and the building programme advances, usually in a series of stages. In spite of all the obstacles, enthusiasm is so great that every town and city with a sizeable Maori population has at least one and usually several such centres. Auckland, which has two *marae* on sites provided by *tāngata whenua*, has thirteen other Maori centres in 1975, while Wellington has three *tāngata whenua marae* and ten other centres.

### *'Community centres' and marae*

Some of the centres built in urban areas, especially in the fifties and sixties, are referred to as 'community centres', not *marae*. What is the difference? Maoris themselves often explain their choice of the term on the grounds that the centre concerned is not on a traditional *marae* site, does not have an open space, a meeting-house or Maori craft work, or is run by other than a descent-group. But these objections do not hold in every case, and they apply to some of the centres that *are* recognized as *marae*. The real reason why Maori community centres are not regarded as *marae* is because they are not available for *tangihanga* or the overnight accommodation of guests. 'There are two functions which delimit Maori complexes as *marae*, and which distinguish them from community centres . . . the importance of the *tangihanga*, and *manaaki i te manuhiri* (caring for visitors). . . . In the Maori view the *tangihanga* is not only essential to a *marae*, but has a pre-emptive right over every other activity' (*Report of the Committee on Marae Subsidies*, 1974: 20). The people who build and run Maori community centres place the major emphasis on providing recreational facilities for the young, who make up an exceptionally large proportion of most urban populations. On a *marae* the recreational function is subordinated to availability for *tangihanga*. In the country there is no difficulty about cancelling *marae* bookings when someone dies, because all the local residents know the bereaved family and therefore attend the *tangihanga*. But in towns where the Maori population is many times larger than in the average rural community, allowing people to use a centre for *hui* and especially *tangihanga* would cause frequent disruption of the recreational programme and leave the many patrons who did not know the deceased disappointed and resentful. The Maori Community Centre is a *marae manqué* – a *marae* without meeting-house or *marae* proper, which does not fulfil the definitive functions of the *marae*.

Finding that community centres leave important needs unsatisfied, urban Maoris have tended in recent years to concentrate their energies on working for *marae*. Far from diminishing, their need for somewhere to accommodate visitors overnight and hold *tangihanga* increases the longer they stay in town. Visitors come by the busload from the country and other towns for weddings, sports matches and concert tours. When a death occurs so many mourners come to pay their respects that the body must be kept in town for twenty-four hours and more. It becomes increasingly difficult to fit all the mourners into a private home and quite impossible to provide them with beds and meals as custom demands. Besides, the proximity of neighbours inhibits the *tangi* (wailing). Within a generation the city born want to

**15** Maori art forms in the fashion world: Mrs Whetū Tirikatene-Sullivan, Minister of Tourism and Publicity, wears a dress featuring a *kōwhaiwhai* design during the opening of a new dining-hall at Te Haukē, Hawke's Bay, October 1975

**16** Actor Josh Gardiner, playing Te Whiti in Te Reo Maori Society's production of the Dansey play *Te Raukura*, holds aloft the *raukura*, three white feathers signifying 'Glory to God in the highest; on earth, peace; goodwill towards men', Wellington, September 1975

bury their dead in cemeteries they can visit easily.

Over the years community centres can come to occupy a place of such importance and affection in the hearts of the people of a city that they eventually become *marae*. Ngāti Pōneke in Wellington is a case in point. Ngāti Pōneke is properly the name of an association of people who set out to create a place in the heart of the city where Maoris of different tribes and interested Pakehas could meet, learn from each other and do things together (Pōneke is the Maori name for Port Nicholson). Since the late thirties the name has been attached to a hall situated within a stone's throw of Parliament, tucked in behind a row of shops, with a carved gateway at its entrance but no courtyard. The hall has a kitchen and toilet facilities under the same roof and is invested with a Maori flavour by a few carvings, much *kōwhaiwhai* and a gallery of photographs. Partly because it lacks the facilities required by health and fire regulations, and partly because there is nowhere to serve food except in the hall itself, Ngāti Pōneke has not usually been used for *tangihanga*. A few people of special significance to the Wellington Maori Community have lain in state there for a few hours, only one for a night. Ngāti Pōneke is however widely known as the home of one of New Zealand's leading cultural clubs, a meeting-place for young and old, Maori and Pakeha, and the scene of innumerable welcomes and farewells to Maori individuals and groups travelling overseas. Now the site is scheduled for re-development, and Ngāti Pōneke have been given another small but valuable site in the vicinity. At first the Ngāti Pōneke Society planned to cover the site with one multi-storied, multi-purpose building, but after sounding community opinion they scrapped this plan in favour of a *marae*, with a carved meeting-house and open courtyard as well as a multi-purpose hall. Because of Ngāti Pōneke's centrality and national reputation, the Committee on Marae Subsidies has recommended that this new *marae* be designated a 'paramount *marae*', comparable with Orakei and Tūrangawaewae, and given special Government assistance.

### Kinds of urban marae

Where rural *marae* almost invariably belong to a descent-group, whether large-family, *hapū* or tribe, urban *marae* are established and supported by groups recruited on a variety of bases, including but not limited to descent. They are usually identified by the name of the suburb in which they are situated or by a name with symbolic significance, rather than the names of tribal ancestors: for instance, Te Unga Waka (The Landing-place of the Canoe) and Te Tira Hou (The New Company of Travellers). And especially when they are not

241

related by kinship, their supporters commonly form themselves into incorporated or friendly societies and associations both for legal purposes and to provide a corporate identity which continues in spite of the movement of individuals.

It is an indication of how numerous urban *marae* have become in the last ten years that it is possible to suggest a tentative classification. First there are the *tāngata whenua marae*, established on ancestral land by a *hapū* or tribe which occupied the area before the city was built. Some have been in use as *marae* for generations, others have been built quite recently. Examples are Takapuwahia in Porirua West, a Ngāti Toa *marae* which has a meeting-house built in 1900 and the Te Puea *marae* at Mangere in Auckland, opened in 1965 and widely known as a Waikato *marae*. Secondly, there are the 'immigrant' tribal *marae*, established and run by members of tribes whose territory lies elsewhere. Tūhoe have *marae* in Auckland (Te Tira Hou) and Rotorua (Mataatua) and plans for one in Wellington. A Ngāpuhi *hapū*, Mahurehure, is engaged in transforming land and buildings bought from a football club into a *marae* at Pt Chevalier in Auckland. Thirdly, there are *marae* supported and used by the Maori members of a particular church. The Roman Catholic church has *marae* in Auckland in Mt Eden (Te Unga Waka) and Otara (Whaiora), Hamilton (Hui te Rangiora), Wellington central (Te Kāinga) and Christchurch (Te Rangimarie), while the activities of the Auckland Anglican Maori Synod are centred on the Manu Ihaka Memorial Marae in Symonds St. Fourthly, there are the local-community *marae*, 'open' to all Maoris living in one town or one sector of a city regardless of tribal or church affiliation, and to any non-Maoris who wish to be involved. Thus Maraeroa, currently operating in an old building transported from another site, is *the* community *marae* for Porirua East, and the John Waititi Memorial Marae at present in the early stages of building will serve the same function for the western suburbs of Auckland. Finally, there are a few 'combination' *marae*, which though 'open' to the whole community have a particular association with one or more tribes. Poho-ō-Rawiri in Gisborne was built by the combined efforts of the three East Coast tribes Ngāti Porou, Rongowhakaata and Te Aitanga-ā-Mahaki in the days before members of other tribes settled in Gisborne in any numbers. It is incorporated in the names of the three tribes and vested in trustees appointed as their representatives, but its management committee is elected by a public meeting open to all Maoris living in Gisborne. The Orakei marae in Auckland is reserved for the benefit of all Maoris, but the Ngāti Whātua play an important role in relation to it as *kai-tiaki* (guardians). The site was given as a *marae* reserve as compensation for a traditional Ngāti Whātua site compulsorily taken by the City Council in

1953. Ngāti Whātua occupy a whole street of houses adjoining the *marae*, and four places on its Trust Board of fourteen members are reserved for Ngāti Whātua representatives. Of the remaining ten places four are held by members of the Auckland Maori District Council representing all the Maoris of Auckland, four by the Maori Members of Parliament representing all the Maoris of New Zealand, and two by representatives of non-Maori organizations, the Okahu Bay Progressive Association and the Auckland Rotary Clubs. Maoris and Pakehas from all over Auckland assist Ngāti Whātua in producing craft work both for the meeting-house and for sale and in other fund-raising activities, and speakers at *marae* functions always include both Ngāti Whātua and representatives of other tribes.

From time to time some Maori spokesmen put forward the view that a kinship base is essential to the definition and proper functioning of a *marae* and support the establishment of tribal or 'combination' *marae* in urban areas rather than those based on community or church congregation. Only tribal loyalty (it is suggested) is strong enough to hold people together in the face of the competing interests and personal ambitions characteristic of urban life and ensure that the *marae* is properly cared for (Kawharu in Schwimmer, 1968: 174–86). Also, differences in custom and *kawa* (protocol) present problems when members of different tribes try to work together, resulting in competition, uncertainty or unsatisfactory compromises (Rangihau in King, 1975: 226). Most urban Maoris however seem to accept inter-tribal co-operation on a local basis both as a practical necessity, given the cost of the enterprise, and a rewarding experience. In the city the *marae* is often less an expression of unity already achieved than the means to its development.

With the exception of those belonging to the *tāngata whenua*, urban *marae* are all built on non-traditional sites on land never before used for a *marae*. Many begin with old buildings already on the site or transported from another, making improvements in stages as they raise the money. Aware of the difficulties of providing for a variety of functions and protecting privacy on a small site, most *marae* associations commission architects to design not only the buildings but the total layout. As a result, urban *marae* vary quite widely in appearance and ground plan. Some have their reception area inside under cover: Te Unga Waka for instance, which occupies a converted factory. Some combine a hall for meeting and sleeping in under one roof with dining-room, kitchen and toilet facilities, for instance Arohanui-ki-te-Tangata at Waiwhetu (Wellington), which from the front looks like a conventional meeting-house. The complex planned for Wainui-o-Mata in Wellington has all the features of a traditional *marae* complex in separate buildings but linked with others in an enclosed

243

mall. The trustees and management committees of urban *marae* may be elected from a limited group – a descent-group, church congregation or subscribing members of an association – or at a public meeting. Sometimes places are reserved for representatives of particular organizations. At all events, the majority involve members of more than one tribe and not infrequently Pakehas and other Polynesians.

These urban *marae* represent a further stage in the creative adaptation of a traditional institution to changing circumstance and needs. They involve a radical modification in people's ideas about the form of *marae* buildings and the importance of inherited land ownership as the basis for status and authority on the *marae*. But they are true *marae* in the ways that matter most, that is, in function, providing their people with a place where they can accommodate large numbers of guests at *hui*, mourn their dead with due ceremony, and thrash out the problems that concern them as a group. As urban Maoris become more fully integrated into urban society, they will probably cease to want and build recreational centres of their own, preferring to share the same facilities as their Pakeha workmates and neighbours; but they will continue to need and work for *marae* as long as they remain Maoris with distinctive ways and values.

### The role of the marae in urban society

Pakehas sometimes raise objections to the building of *marae* in urban areas on the ground that they foster 'separatism' on the part of Maoris. But the *marae* is not an exclusive institution. It is built not for the sole use and enjoyment of its supporting community, as a Pakeha-style club is, but as a base, a *tūrangawaewae*, where those to whom it belongs can provide hospitality and entertainment for guests. As we saw above, *manaaki i te manuhiri* is one of the distinguishing features and main purposes of a *marae*. Like their country kin, urban Maoris usually issue open invitations to *hui* held at a *marae*, resorting to personal invitations only as a supplementary measure. They will and do welcome all comers, asking only one thing, that those they receive as guests should treat the *marae* and its people with respect, accepting and acting in accordance with their custom, and not rushing in, from ignorance or arrogance, where wise men would ask for guidance. As the number of urban *marae* increases, so does the proportion of non-Maoris involved not only as guests at functions held there but as members of the cultural clubs that meet there and as subscribing members of *marae* associations. Ngāti Pōneke is well known for the number of Pakehas who regularly attend cultural club practices and other gatherings, and its example is widely followed. The *marae* at Wainui-o-mata has been planned to serve the whole community of the valley and its *marae* association involves Maoris and non-Maoris in almost equal numbers.

Far from fostering separatism, urban *marae* have an invaluable contribution to make to the development of a truly multi-cultural society. In the first place, they provide a place where urban Maoris can relax, find release from the tensions of struggling to make their way in a predominantly Pakeha environment, and learn more about their identity and cultural heritage, by absorption as much as direct teaching. Secondly because of their tradition of hospitality, urban *marae* also provide a meeting-ground where people of different cultures, but especially Pakehas and Maoris, can get to know each other more readily than in situations ordered according to Pakeha rules, because there Maoris no longer feel at a disadvantage and on the defensive. On a *marae* Maoris walk tall, sure of the ground beneath their feet, organizers instead of organized, givers instead of receivers, hosts instead of immigrants in an alien world.

Thirdly, Maoris themselves see the *marae*, one of their most valued institutions, as a gift they have to offer the whole urban community. The publicity brochure put out by the Orakei Marae Development Council carries on its cover a photograph of a Maori girl and a Pakeha girl, obviously good friends, and the slogan 'Kia Kotahi', literally 'let us be one', which is translated 'Come Together'. 'Behind COME TOGETHER', it is explained inside, 'lies the thought of a community united in providing a Marae, a meeting-place for all people'. And the Council's outline of the functions the Orakei Marae will fulfil could readily serve as a charter for all urban *marae*:

To provide a place where all who live in New Zealand
can meet in a setting where racial harmony can be
established on the best basis of all – working together.

To provide a setting where youth can share the Maori
culture, where they can come as of right, the Marae
thus providing a catalyst in community stability.

To provide a place where those things which are Maori
can be conducted, taught and practised in a Maori way
in a Maori setting with fitting dignity.

To provide a fitting location for welcoming distinguished
visitors to this City.

# chapter 16

# Hui

Trying to explain the difference between the Maori way of life and the Pakeha, a Maori friend said: 'Well, for one thing, Maoris are always going off to *hui*, taking the whole family and staying there all together for days at a time.' While Maoris live most of the time in small family households as Pakehas do, they make a conscious effort to get together periodically in the old communal way.

A *hui* is a special sort of gathering. Properly, it takes place at a *marae*; it is open to everyone free of charge; it usually lasts more than one day; and visitors are provided throughout with meals and somewhere to sleep (for a detailed study see Salmond, 1975).

There are many kinds of *hui*. The most important is the *tangihanga* (often abbreviated to *tangi*), which takes precedence over all the others. Then there are weddings, twenty-first birthday parties, and 'unveilings'; 'openings' (of new buildings); church and other conferences (such as the annual *hui tōpū* of the Anglican Diocese of Waiapu); anniversary gatherings (such as the Coronation Celebrations of the King Movement); and gatherings to honour special visitors.

Everyone is welcome at a *hui*. General invitations (*pānui*) are sent to elders of other communities and tribes to pass on to their people, and the news is also broadcast by word of mouth and notices in local newspapers and shop-windows, and in the case of major *hui* on radio's Maori News. Individual invitations are issued only to Pakehas who are known to expect them.

All hospitality at a *hui* is free, though a charge may be made for special entertainments like dances and concerts. However, it is customary for visitors to give their hosts donations known variously as *koha*, *awhina* or *moni marae* ('*marae* money').

A *hui* attracts many visitors (*manuhiri*) from beyond the local community. Gatherings of five hundred to a thousand are common on even small country *marae*. Several thousand attend *tangihanga* for important persons and tribal or supra-tribal gatherings. Over five thousand mourners visited Tūrangawaewae during the *tangihanga* for Princess Te Puea in 1952; four thousand sat down to the feast at the opening of the meeting-house at Waiwhetu (Wellington) in 1960; and each year the hosts at Tūrangawaewae serve dinner to four or five thousand on Saturday and Sunday during the Coronation Celebrations. Often a whole field is needed to accommodate the cars, trucks and buses that converge on the *marae* for a *hui*.

Most modern *hui* last two or three days, few more than four. A *tangihanga* usually lasts three days, the burial taking place on the third. Other *hui* are usually arranged for a weekend, most of the guests arriving on Friday afternoon or evening and leaving on Sunday.

There is usually a great deal of coming and going at a *hui*. Local residents may go home to sleep, especially if there is a shortage of sleeping-room. Parties which have a long way to travel often arrive late and leave early. The longer the *hui*, the more people stay only part of the time. Yet in spite of this, the number of visitors fed and accommodated during *hui* is probably greater than in the past, for modern transport enables them to come from further away.

**Organization**

Staging a *hui* is a major enterprise in terms both of cost and organization. Far beyond the resources of the nuclear family, it is generally undertaken by a larger group: one or more large-families, a church congregation, a *hapū*, a local community, sometimes even a tribe or national movement. The hosts, identified during the *hui* as *tāngata whenua* or *iwi kāinga* ('the home folks') even if they include 'immigrants', underwrite the whole cost and do all the work. Maoris would not dream of hiring caterers for a *hui* on a *marae*, or even at an urban community centre. In their view work does not demean but dignifies those of high rank and low, especially if performed in the process of caring (*manaaki*) for guests. It is the supreme expression of *aroha*.

To make sure things run smoothly, the hosts usually hold a series of conferences before, during and after the *hui*. Sometimes they meet informally under the direction of an elder, but often they operate within the framework of a club (family, *hapū* or church) or set up a special '*hui* committee'.

*Finance*

Many large-families keep a *tangihanga* fund just for that contingency: otherwise the deceased's relatives pool what cash they have in hand to pay immediate expenses. Help may also be received from a local *hapū* or marae committee (pp. 135, 237). For other *hui*, the hosts establish a working fund by donation, levies or a money-raising campaign. Tribal trust boards and incorporations sometimes make special grants for *tangihanga*, 'openings', and anniversary *hui*.

In addition to cash, the hosts make generous contributions in kind: sacks of *kūmara*, potatoes, pumpkins, cabbages, watercress and *pūhā*, kits of shellfish, eel and crayfish, jars of preserved fruit, pickles and jam, cans of milk and cream, truckloads of firewood. Even animals for killing (cattle, sheep and pigs) are given free or for a fraction of their market value by farmers. The womenfolk lend table-cloths and tea-towels and supplement the *marae* stock of crockery and bedding. In the case of family *hui*, those most closely related to the person or persons being honoured make a point of contributing more than the others.

Because so much is given in kind, cash expenses are surprisingly low in relation to guests. In Kotare in the 1950s, payments made in connection with *hui* catering for between five hundred and a thousand guests rarely exceeded N.Z. $100.

While they should be prepared to meet all expenses, the hosts can count on receiving donations (*koha*) from many of their guests. These are usually in cash, but may sometimes include produce for which the donors are noted or which the hosts lack. At a *hui* near Taupo, I saw a truckload of eels (lacking in the pumice area) arrive as a present from relatives in Taumarunui. When the Anglican Diocese of Waiapu held a *hui tōpū* at Omahu Pa (Hastings) in 1959, Maori farmers throughout the diocese sent beef cattle to the Hastings freezing works to be killed and stored for the *hui*.

After the *hui* is over, the hosts auction or share out any leftover foodstuffs and hold one last meeting to settle the accounts. Any deficit they make up by further donations. If there is a credit balance, they make a donation 'to the *marae*' (i.e. to the *marae* committee), and either pay the rest into funds (if they have a club), divide it among the original contributors, or give it to an elder to bank against future needs.

*Allocation of duties*

Some groups allocate duties for each *hui* they hold at a formal meeting, but in most it is taken for granted that certain members of known ability and experience will take charge of certain departments:

tending the *hāngi*, cooking vegetables and puddings, preparing the meeting-house, laying and waiting at table. Ordinary members attach themselves to one of these 'chief helpers' according to preference and relationship, but work in other departments when extra help is needed. Frequently families specialize in certain tasks. The leading *kaumātua* of the group acts as general director (*kai-whakahaere-o-te-hui*) and supervises the ceremonial on the *marae*. In Northland an 'official list of workers' is often compiled, in a way that honours all the families involved with at least one office, and prominently displayed in kitchen or dining-hall. In actual fact, not everyone named on the list does the task assigned to him, and many not named also help. Frequently each table (seating twenty or more) is allotted to a particular sub-group to provide with waitresses: to a large-family, a minor *hapū*, or a denomination (p. 191).

At tribal *hui*, *hapū* often assume responsibility for different departments of the work. At the Coronation Celebrations at Tūranga-waewae during the sixties one of the dining-halls and the kitchen which served it were staffed entirely by Ngāti Koroki.

## The structure of the hui

As already pointed out (p. 69), *hui* are event-structured not time- or rather clock-structured. Events follow in an ordered sequence, each given whatever allowance of time is necessary for its proper performance. If times (that is, hours) are given for various activities in preliminary programmes, they are regarded as merely an approximate indication and no one worries if they are not adhered to. One can always 'tell the time' by the state that has been reached in the sequence of events.

### Arrival

Visitors to a *hui* usually arrive in the afternoon and evening of the first day. Some elders still insist on arriving before dusk, but parties coming a long way often arrive late. After midnight, however, their welcome is curtailed, and completed in the morning.

Only an ignorant man – or one of very high standing – would enter a *marae* alone during a *hui*: visitors normally do so in parties (*ope*). These vary in size from half a dozen to over a hundred. Visitors who arrive alone or in nuclear families, as increasing numbers do, wait outside until they can join forces with folk they know. Most parties come 'under' the name of a descent-group: that of their *hapū* if they are from the same tribe as their hosts, that of their tribe if from another. Busloads of visitors from urban areas present a problem, since they usually comprise members of several tribes. The host speakers may greet them by naming the tribes of those known to them, but this leads to embarrassment if they miss someone important. Often they address such parties by the name of their town with a tribal prefix, as (for instance) Ngāti Akarana (Auckland) (p. 134).

### The welcome ceremony (mihi)

The hosts welcome each party with a formal reception ceremony, the *mihi* or 'welcome'. This has two basic forms, that appropriate for the *tangihanga* when there is a *tūpāpaku* lying on the *marae*, and a general form used on other occasions. Both consist of a number of parts arranged, like the *hui* as a whole, in an ordered sequence. Some parts may be omitted or telescoped according to circumstances and sometimes they overlap or run into each other, but the basic structure is always there. Here I shall concentrate on the general form of *mihi*, leaving that associated with the *tangihanga* to be described later.

Amid the bustle of preparation on the *marae*, the elderly men and women sit chatting quietly on the porch of the meeting-house or on seats set to one side, holding themselves in readiness. When a party of visitors arrives, its members assemble in a more or less compact body outside the gate, ordering themselves according to one of several principles. Depending on tribal affiliation and the preferences of their leaders, some groups place the oldest and most important women in front, followed by the younger women, with the men to the rear, while others are led by the older, important members of both sexes, with the younger and less experienced behind. Sometimes the men who are to speak on behalf of the group lead it on to the *marae* a few steps ahead of the rest, sometimes the older women lead the advance with the speakers walking to the rear or side of the group and moving to the front at a later stage. When they are assembled ready to make their entry, the visitors usually wait for a signal from their hosts. A warden may be sent out to summon them personally by word or gesture, or one or more of the women by the meeting-house may simply begin to *karanga* (call). Occasionally one of the guest *kuia* may initiate proceedings by 'calling' to the hosts, but only if she is sure of her *mana* and that of her group.

If there is someone important in the party, the hosts will accord him the honour of a ceremonial challenge (*wero* in most areas, *taki* in Northland). A visitor of such status is always the first to approach the gateway and as he does so a young male challenger (*kai-wero*) wearing a flax kilt (*piupiu*) dances forward across the *marae*, executing a complicated drill with a *taiaha*, slowly kneels and taking a carved stick (*rākau*) from his waistband places it crosswise in the gateway at the visitor's feet, indicating that he is received in peace (to lay it pointing at him is a direct challenge to war). Properly speaking, the stick should not be picked up by the person challenged nor by a woman but by one of the other men in the party; this rule is however frequently breached today. Particularly distinguished visitors such as Queen Elizabeth II, her representative the Governor-General or visiting heads of state, are challenged three times by three separate challengers, presenting three sticks with different names, *taiaha* drills and significance: the *rākau whakaara* (warning stick), *rākau takoto* (stick laid down, the one which determines peace or war), and *rākau whakawaha* (the stick which clears the way). When the last stick is picked up, the challenger pivots to face the meeting-house, raising the *taiaha* high above his head with its blade facing forward, and leads the visitors on to the *marae*.

As soon as the visitors enter the *marae*, and even before if there is no *wero*, one or more of the host women starts a *karanga* (call) of welcome, standing on the right side (facing out) of the meeting-house, in or in front of the porch. The *karanga* is half-song, half-chant, words carried on a high flowing tide of sound ending on a dying fall. It is used in several contexts but reaches fullest development in the welcome ceremony. In a *karanga* of welcome, the callers first greet the visitors both in general and in particular terms, sometimes naming their tribe or *hapū*, their great ancestors and landmarks; then they invite them to 'come up' on to the *marae*, and invoke the dead of both sides, all in richly poetic language. Ideally some of the visiting women should answer the hosts' *karanga* in kind, picking up each call as it begins to fade, so that the *karanga* of the two groups alternate and mingle as counterpoint to each other. The beauty of words and sound evoke an atmosphere at once solemn and emotionally heightened, setting the scene for what is to follow.

As the visitors move across the *marae* with the *karanga* throbbing in the air, some of the women may also raise the *tangi*, the wailing cry of mourning. The *karanga* has called up the dead so that they are almost palpably present and reminded the living of the loved ones lost: hosts and guests join each other in honouring them with tears.

When the party includes persons of importance, as many hosts as possible come from behind the scenes to form ranks in front of the meeting-house. Following the *karanga* and sometimes overlapping with it they perform the *pōwhiri*, a sequence of *haka* and action-songs of welcome, the women gracefully waving pieces of greenery. The *pōwhiri* often incorporates old canoe-hauling songs, symbolically hauling the visitors' canoe on to the firm strand of the *marae*.

While *karanga*, *tangi* and *pōwhiri* run their course, the guests move slowly across the *marae* halting once or twice to stand with bowed heads in mourning for the dead, until they finally reach a station about half way across, where they take their place on seats or mats provided for them, the speakers and older women in front. These seats may be set so that they face the meeting-house full on or so that they parallel those occupied by the host speakers and *kuia*. The position of the latter varies not only between tribes but often between communities. They may be placed either to the left or to the right of the meeting-house, and at an angle of roughly 30 degrees or a full 90 degrees. Hosts and guests now face each other across about a half or third of the *marae*, which becomes the 'stamping ground' for speech-makers from both sides during the next phase of proceedings.

Now hosts and guests exchange speeches of greeting, a particular form of *whai-kōrero* (speech-making) known as *mihimihi*, and the origin of the term now commonly used in the singular for the welcome ceremony as a whole. This exchange is ordered according to one of two patterns: *pāeke*, in which the speakers of each side speak as a block, and *utu-utu* ot *tū-mai-tū-atu* in which they speak in alternation. *Pāeke* is the rule among the Northern, Mātaatua, East Coast, Tākitimu, Taranaki and Wanganui tribes, *utu-utu* among Arawa, Tūwharetoa and Tainui (comprising Waikato, Maniapoto, Ngāi-te-Rangi, and Ngāti Raukawa and Ngāti Toa of Manawatū) (see Figure 4). Normally the form used at a *hui* in this as in other respects is the *kawa* (protocol) of the hosts. On very rare occasions in some areas, notably Northland, the hosts may announce that they will observe their guests' *kawa*, a compliment of the highest order. In urban areas, where sponsors of a *hui* may have to hold it on a *marae* belonging to another tribe, or where members of many tribes combine to run a multi-tribal *marae*, difficulties and differences often arise over this and related issues of protocol. Gradually however experience is producing new sets of rules for particular urban *marae*, sometimes a compromise, sometimes an agreement to follow the *kawa* of either the owners or the sponsors. Whether *pāeke* or *utu-utu* is used, the hosts always open the speech-making, and in *utu-utu* they also close it. When the *pāeke* form is used, each side puts up as many speakers as they can muster and/or consider appropriate for the 'weight' of the occasion. An exact match is not considered essential, though to put up notably more or fewer speakers than the other side may affect a group's *mana* in complicated ways. When the *utu-utu* form is used, however, it is important to be able to match speaker for speaker, with the hosts needing one extra in order to have the last word.

Different tribes also have different ways of ordering speakers within each side. Sometimes the number and order of speakers is carefully prearranged; sometimes, speakers simply stand as they feel inspired; and sometimes the decisions are made actually on the *marae* in the light of the performance of the other side, either by the leading elder literally giving the nod to the others as he thinks fit or by brief whispered conferences. In some areas, the speaker with the most *mana* on grounds of descent and/or knowledge speaks first, so that he can identify individuals, trace links with the other side and generally set the tone for his colleagues, but in most he speaks last, summing up and providing the climax to his side's speeches.

Like all speeches, *mihimihi* begin with a warning shout (*whaka-ara*) such as '*Tihei mauri-ora!*', followed by a chanted introduction (*tauparapara*), and end with a traditional song-poem (*mōteatea* or *waiata*) but the body of the speeches are largely given to the expression of greetings and the search for and establishment of links between the two groups. This is in fact the *take* (main purpose) of such speeches. While orators of exceptional renown may sometimes introduce other topics, it is generally felt that these should be left to the later, freer debates that take place when the welcomes are over. Host speakers begin their *mihimihi* by directly addressing their visitors, identifying their tribes, *hapū* and leaders by name; guest speakers speak first to the *marae* and meeting-house, addressing them by name as living entities. After these introductions, both sides go on to pay their respects to the dead called to mind by the *karanga*, then address themselves to the living before them, greeting them personally, tracing out genealogical connections, working out appropriate kinship terms (p. 70), identifying other common interests, and if necessary mentioning and countering past conflicts by the expression of present goodwill.

When the last speaker has finished, hosts and earlier arrivals form a reception line across the front of the meeting-house and the visitors move along it to be greeted with handshake and often a *hongi* and a kiss as well. The *hongi* involves pressing noses, not 'rubbing' them as it is often incorrectly translated. There are several different styles of *hongi*, favoured by different tribes. Some press as much as possible of the nose and the forehead at the same time; others press only the right side of the nose just above the nostril, and some press first right side and then left side. The elders usually help the inexperienced make the right contact.

After the *hongi*, the visitors break ranks and stand chatting with friends among the hosts until they are called to the dining-hall for the meal which sets the final seal on their welcome and should, I believe, be regarded as an essential part of the welcome ceremony, backing up the fine words of the *mihimihi* with a practical demonstration of *manaaki*. To fail to provide food for newly welcomed visitors is an offence of the most serious kind to *kaumātua* of the old school and to all right-thinking moderns (see Witi Ihimaera's story, 'The Whale', in *Pounamu Pounamu*).

To Pakehas who see snippets of it – usually the dramatic *wero* – on television, the welcome ceremony often seems a matter of traditional form, colourful and entertaining to watch but largely lacking meaning in the present day, rather like the changing of the guard at Buckingham Palace. For those who take part in and experience it as a whole, however, the ceremony is very meaningful indeed at several different levels. As I have suggested elsewhere (p. 71) the welcome ceremony is a model par excellence of the way Maoris approach and handle the problem of difference and unity, first recognizing and even exaggerating difference and conflict, and then using a number of strategies to mediate them and bring the opposing 'sides' together.

The welcome ceremony begins with the relation between hosts and guests stated in terms of complete physical, social and ritual separation. The hosts are firmly entrenched on their home-ground, their *tūrangawaewae*, literally and symbolically under the shadow (*ata*) and protection of their ancestor and meeting-house, very much in control of the situation. It is they who initiate proceedings, and direct them according to their rules of protocol. They are *tapu* to their guests and so potentially threatening. The guests on the other hand are away from home, literally and symbolically on the outside, about to enter foreign territory, where other rules run and they can easily make mistakes with serious consequences. At the same time, they are guests, protected by the sacred duty hosts have to respect and care for (*manaaki*) guests; thus they too are *tapu* to their hosts and potentially threatening, especially if they are *waewae tapu* (sacred feet) visiting the *marae* for the first time. Once begun, the ceremony proceeds through a series of stages in each of which the separation and opposition of hosts and guests is progressively reduced. Stage by stage, the guests move physically closer to the hosts, their *tapu vis-à-vis* each other is lightened by ritual formulae and actions, and social links are sought and established in the form of genealogical connections, the shared experience of mourning for the dead, and common interest in the purpose of the *hui*. At each stage also, an exchange takes place: *karanga* for *karanga*, *mihi* for *mihi*, *hongi* for *hongi*, each signifying the desire to come together, an outflow of *aroha* towards the other. Even the *wero* and the *pōwhiri* can be seen in this light, the hosts giving the guests honour and peaceful entry, the guests showing their appreciation by acceptance. By the time the *hongi* is over, the distance between the two groups on all counts has been reduced to such manageable proportions (though never entirely eliminated) that members can mingle freely with little or no constraint, and the hosts can even invite the leading speakers among the guests to join them in welcoming subsequent parties.

The welcome ceremony, once begun, should be completed without interruption. Occasionally if one party arrives hard on the heels of another, the hosts will ask the earlier arrivals if they will let the later ones join in their welcome; but properly they should patiently wait their turn. If a party arrives late, when the *hui* has moved into a later phase, proceedings are held up while it is welcomed. In such cases the welcome may be foreshortened but nothing essential is omitted.

*Sleeping accommodation*

The visitors are given beds in the meeting-house or, if that is not big enough, in tents erected on the *marae*. In the meeting-house, mattresses are laid in rows on the floor at right angles to the side and rear walls, leaving central aisles covered with beautiful flax mats. The mattresses are covered with a sheet, with pillows in starched, embroidered pillowslips at their heads. Visitors bring their own blankets and rugs. Most prefer to change into night clothes and dressing-gowns. The guests are accommodated first on the *tara whānui*, the 'big' or *tapu* side, but if they are very numerous the hosts' side, the *tara iti*, is also given over to them (p. 232).

Everyone sleeps in the meeting-house, without distinction of age or sex. An elder commented: 'We like to put our visitors where we can see them all in one heap; then no one feels left out.' And another added: 'It is far too public for any nonsense – the lights stay on all night, and the elders are there to see that everything is done properly. This way everyone can see and hear everything that is going on.' For at night and in wet weather, the speech-makers move into the meeting-house, where until three or four o'clock in the morning they retell the stories of their ancestors, argue over present problems, and embellish their speeches with *haka* and songs.

*Speech-making*

From the time the first guests arrive until the last leave, speech-making (*whai-kōrero*) goes on intermittently all through a *hui*. In the earlier stages, as parties arrive hard on each other's heels, nearly all speeches fall into the category of *mihimihi*, but when all have been welcomed the character of the speeches changes and more general and often controversial topics are raised. In the daytime, if the weather is good, the listeners sit or stand in a large circle on the *marae* proper, with the elders on the porch of the meeting-house or the seats set to left or right (seats placed on the *marae* itself for visitors are removed when the welcomes are concluded). Beyond the circle, all is noise and movement, as workers hurry to and fro and friends exchange news. At night and if bad weather forces people to move into the meeting-house, the listeners recline on the beds, chatting and dozing between speeches and even through them. It is as if they challenge the speakers to command their full attention. According to the saying '*Tū-matauenga* outside, *Rongo* inside', 'fighting' debates should be confined to the *marae* proper, while speech-making inside the house should be peaceful and friendly. In practice, however, this ideal is as honoured in the breach as in the observance. Speech-making on the *marae* is a serious, *tapu* business, and though speakers use humour as a weapon, purely frivolous speeches are severely frowned upon and in fact are rare indeed. But debates full of fire and hostility occur in the meeting-house quite commonly, not only in bad weather but especially in the early hours of the morning.

The right to 'speak on the *marae*', that is to make a formal speech in Maori, is highly valued and hedged with restrictions (p. 236). It requires a thorough knowledge not only of everyday Maori but of its formal rhetoric, of myths and tribal history, of genealogies and *mōteatea*, and above all of the *marae* protocol (*kawa*) of many different tribes. A *kai-kōrero* (speech-maker) must also be a person of high *mana*, preferably by senior descent. Many tribes restrict the role to men and even in those which do not women speakers are a rarity these days, though some of the past, like Mihi Kotukutuku and Materoa Reedy of Ngāti Pōrou, are remembered with awe (Salmond, 1975: 150–2). Some, notably Tūhoe and Arawa, also hold to the rule that a family should have only one *kai-kōrero* at a time, which means that a man cannot speak as long as he has a father or older brother alive. This rule may be temporarily abrogated if the family speaker is absent on a particular occasion, and it is not uncommon for the eldest in the family to permanently give over his right to speak to a more gifted junior. Other tribes however give the right to speak to any who has the *mana* to claim and exercise it, though even they usually deprecate father and sons or brothers speaking on the same occasion. This opens the way to speakers whose *mana* derives from personal achievement rather than descent. Thus a number of civil servants and university and teachers' college lecturers regularly speak on the *marae* they visit, including their own home *marae*, regardless of their descent status.

During a welcome ceremony, speech-making is confined to representative speakers sitting on the hosts' or visitors' benches. At other times, speakers announce their intention to speak with a warning shout from anywhere in the circle of spectators around the *marae* or any part of the meeting-house. On the *marae* they then move forward on to the open space within the circle; in the meeting-house they usually speak from on or near the spot where they were sitting. Once a speaker has stepped on to the *marae* without being challenged, he is heard through without interruption, no matter how unacceptable his views. Listeners may express approval with calls (at half-power) of '*kia ora*', '*ka tika*' ('that's right'), '*tautoko*' ('I support that') or 'hear! hear!', but heckling and loud interjections are absolutely outlawed. Northland Maoris remain critical of Ngā Tamatoa because a Tamatoa member heckled the leading Government spokesman during a protest demonstration at the Waitangi Day celebrations in 1971, although in many ways they agreed with the protest itself. Disagreement is properly expressed by sitting in silence with eyes fixed on the ground.

Because the *marae* and what takes place on it are *tapu*, orators dress formally, preferably in a dark suit and tie, with hat and overcoat in cold weather, and on special occasions a traditional flax cloak, embellished with feathers, *taniko* or twisted black thrums (Mead, 1969).

Maori oratory is an essentially dramatic performance that uses the full resources of voice and body as well as language. Many of the most renowned speech-makers, following a traditional style, stride back and forth across the *marae*, establishing and changing the rhythm of their speech by their gait, stamping their feet and leaping or pivoting swiftly at the turns. In this case, host speakers move across the front of the meeting-house, taking care not to turn their back on their ancestor, while visiting speakers either move parallel to their hosts or charge directly at the meeting-house and then retreat, often backwards. Speakers with a less flamboyant personality or less confidence tend to restrict their movement to a few paces to right and left of a central position. On some *marae*, especially the larger ones, the introduction of microphones and amplifying systems have also tended to anchor speakers to one spot. Whether they move freely or not, most orators illustrate their words with a wealth of gesture, using not only their hands but the whole of their bodies and a carved walking stick (*tokotoko*) or hand weapon (*mere* or *kotiate*) as well.

Most speeches are relatively short, lasting between ten and fifteen minutes, though great orators can hold an audience enthralled for a couple of hours, especially on the subject of tribal history and inter-tribal connections. Speeches are properly opened (after the warning shout) with a fixed-form introduction (*tauparapara*) and closed with a song (*mōteatea* or *waiata*). *Haka* and *waiata* may also be included in the body of the speech at appropriate points. Each tribe has its own store of introductions, songs and *haka*, and a choice that is aptly related to topic and/or audience is greatly relished. Today however the repertoire of many speech-makers is more limited than it used to be and some particularly popular songs may be used by representatives of different tribes, even at the same *hui*. As we have seen, greetings – to the *marae* and meeting-house, the dead and the living, to hosts and guests – form the major substance of *mihimihi*. The first time orators speak in general debate they also devote some time to greeting those present and 'remembering' the dead, especially if they did not themselves deliver a *mihimihi*. But as the *hui* proceeds, speeches become increasingly devoted to special topics (*take*). These are by no means limited to the ostensible purpose of the *hui*, but range over a wide field. Where Pakehas call meetings for particular purposes and exclude discussion of other topics, Maoris attend *hui* on the understanding that many other topics will be discussed. In general discussion speeches fit into an overall pattern like a conversation, with many speakers speaking more than once. In cases where decision is required they sort themselves out ultimately into two main camps, and then the minority group 'gives in' and joins the majority in order that the decision may be unanimous. The best and most highly ranked speakers may not enter the fray till late in the piece, when they have had the chance to size up the general feeling and can use their *mana* either to clinch matters, or if necessary to swing it the other way. Most debates at *hui* however are open-ended, devoted to exploring all aspects of the issues concerned but leaving them to be continued at the next opportunity. While the *kai-kōrero* are greatly respected for their powers of expression, they cannot – or at least should not – commit their kinsfolk to a course of action without consultation. Women and younger men barred from speaking on the *marae* have and use the right to put their views strongly to the speaker representing them between *hui*, and even at *hui* between speeches. Besides, the very number of topics debated, often concurrently, precludes any one being pursued through to the end. And Maoris still hold to the principle that assent and support should be formally expressed, which takes time. To them indeed, silence is the sign not of assent but of dissent, a fact which has led to much misunderstanding in their relations with Pakehas (see especially Ritchie, 1956(b); Hilliard, 1969: 15–17). Once a speaker has recorded assent in a speech before an audience he cannot back out of its consequences.

Debates on the *marae* are debates in the fullest sense of the word: no attempt is made to avoid clashes. Speakers and listeners enjoy a good argument, for it calls forth the best oratory. As we saw in the last chapter, the *marae* is the proper place to air grievances, express hostilities and thrash out differences, provided it is done with the aim of achieving resolution and amity. Under certain conditions in fact, a 'fight' is almost obligatory. As Maoris see it, to argue with or over a person is a compliment of the highest order, because it indicates that he matters. 'A *rangatira* does not quarrel with a nobody.' An argument over the place of burial is a normal part of every *tangihanga*. Once, on the eve of a wedding, I heard the bride's aunt publicly

threaten to boycott the gathering unless one of the chosen groomsmen
was displaced in favour of her son. The family put up a vigorous
resistance but finally gave in, accepting her demand as an honour.

*The climax*

Each *hui* builds up to a climax ('the big day'), with a central ceremony
or series of ceremonies including speeches and followed by a feast
(*hākari*). Besides the church ceremony, weddings involve a formal
welcome to the newly married pair at the *marae*, the drinking of
toasts, the cutting of the wedding cake, in Northland the 'flower
ceremony', and an evening dance of which the highlight is a Grand
March led by the wedding party (p. 141). Twenty-first birthday parties
begin with a feast in the early evening followed by speeches and a
dance. At an 'unveiling', if there is a number of stones to be unveiled
in several cemeteries (as is common in Northland), the first ceremony
takes place soon after daybreak, in order that everyone can get back
to the *marae* for the midday feast. The 'opening' of a new building
begins with a dawn ceremony in which the elders lift the *tapu*; then
the Pakeha guests are welcomed, and the official dedication and opening take place about midday.

When the *hākari* is ready, a host elder calls the guests to the dining-
hall; the most important individually, then the various tribal and sub-
tribal parties. Usually two and sometimes three sittings are necessary.
The hosts do not eat till the guests have finished. The basic menu
consists of meat (beef, pork, mutton and chicken) and vegetables
(*kūmara*, potatoes and pumpkin) cooked in *hāngi* or steam box, with
boiled *pūhā*, watercress or cabbage, followed by plum pudding and
cream, trifles, jellies, fruit salad, cakes and fresh fruit. Individuality
derives from the number and variety of side dishes: eels, mutton,
birds, shell-fish, crayfish, seaweed, and that high-smelling Maori
delicacy, *kānga pirau* (fermented corn custard). Bottles of aerated
drinks add colour to the tables. Liquor can be served on a *marae* only
in limited quantities approved by the Maori Committee. *Hui* accounts
normally provide beer for the workers, but it should not be broached
till the feast is over.

*Presentation of koha*

Close relatives or neighbours of the hosts and visitors who come
singly or in families usually hand over their *koha* to an elder or
relative among the hosts. Sometimes they place them on the wedding-
cake or, at *tangihanga*, on the coffin. But, especially at the larger *hui*,
the leaders of parties from a distance present their gift publicly, on
arrival or departure or in a special ceremony. Each elder announces

the name of the donor group and sometimes the amount in a formal speech and literally lays the gift down on the *marae*, to be picked up by the hosts. Many older Maoris remember seeing banknotes tossed down loose, to be scattered by the wind, or presented pinned to branches like leaves, but the days of such ostentation are gone. Today the money is discreetly enclosed in an envelope, secured in a rubber band, or (if the sum is large) presented by cheque.

The amounts given range from one to several hundred dollars or more, depending on the importance of the occasion, the size and wealth of the donor group, and how much has been received from the hosts in the past. Large *koha* include contributions from people who could not come or derive from tribal trusts or incorporations. The hosts keep a record of the *koha* given, often by writing receipts. They take a pride in returning them with interest when next they attend a *hui* on the donors' *marae*.

*Koha* are not payments for hospitality but gifts given to the hosts to use as they choose, in return for previous assistance and expectation of more in the future. In actual fact, the hosts do use them to defray the expenses of the *hui*, if not directly then indirectly by banking them to replace money already spent. The system thus works to the mutual advantage of both hosts and guests, spreading the costs of their *hui* over time and many people.

On particularly important occasions and when particularly important individuals are involved, either the hosts or the guests or both may present the other side with more permanent gifts: greenstone weapons and ornaments with names and histories, *taiaha*, feather cloaks and fine flax mats. Such gifts may be kept for years, but are ultimately returned to the donors on a comparable occasion. The recipients hold them in trust: they do not 'own' them and should not dispose of them to anyone except a member of the donor group. Pakehas who are given such gifts as recognition of their social or political standing often offend in this respect out of ignorance. The Pakeha who knows enough of Maori custom to bide his time and return such gifts on an appropriate occasion greatly enhances his *mana* thereby. This was one of the reasons for the popularity of Duncan MacIntyre, Minister of Maori Affairs in the National Party Government from 1969 to 1972, among Maoris.

## The last phase

After the feast, the emphasis is on entertainment. In the afternoon, the guests disperse to watch football, visit the nearest beach, cinema or hotel, or catch up on their sleep. In the evening there is usually a dance or concert.

Guests may depart any time after the feast, but except at *tangihanga* the majority do not leave until the following morning. Before each party leaves hosts and guests exchange formal farewells (*poroporoaki*). These are initiated by the elders of each departing party; they may include presentation of the *koha* but always single out the *ringa wera* ('hot hands') from behind the scenes for special thanks, often calling them forth for the purpose.

The hosts speed each party on its way with a last gift of food loaded into the boot of car or bus for consumption on the way home. When all have gone, the clearing up begins. Within the next day or two, the hosts hold a final meeting to wind up the accounts.

### The tangihanga

As soon as possible after a death, friends and relatives visit the bereaved home where, gathered round the body, the women raise the *tangi* (a high-pitched stylized wailing performed only by women), prayers are said, and the men make speeches of farewell. From now on, the deceased's large-family takes over the organization of the *tangihanga*, relieving the bereaved nuclear family (*whānau pani*) of all work and worry. Conferring quickly its older members allocate the work and then disperse to notify the minister, undertaker and absent kin, collect stores and prepare the *marae*. The *whānau pani* (which contributes to the cost of hospitality as part of the large-family) usually insists on paying for the coffin and undertaker's services.

The body (*tūpāpaku*) is moved to the *marae* within a few hours in most areas. There it may be laid in a tent near the meeting-house (e.g. among the Mātaatua tribes), in the porch, or inside the meeting-house at right angles to the rear wall (in Northland) or against the fourth *poupou* (carved ancestor) on the 'home folks'' side to the right of the door looking in, among Arawa. Photographs of the deceased and his ancestors are hung on the wall behind the coffin and family heirlooms (*taonga*) such as feather or other flax cloaks, greenstone *mere* or *taiaha* are placed on top of it, expressing and reminding people of the continuity of living and dead. The close kinswomen of the deceased (wife, mother, sisters and daughters) recline on mattresses laid on either side of the coffin. Until the burial these 'chief mourners' leave their places only for the shortest of necessary breaks and never all at once. In some areas, they fast during the day. The close male relatives may sit with the women part of the time, but the younger ones at least find an approved outlet for their grief and honour the dead in hard work, chopping firewood, tending the *hāngi*, and later digging the grave.

The burial usually takes place on the third day after death, so that at a normal country *tangihanga* the body rests at the *marae* for two nights. Those living in the vicinity are expected to pay their respects within the first twenty-four hours, mourners from a distance as soon as they can. To turn up just in time for the funeral is considered extremely bad form. Only the very close kin, the chief workers and the elderly remain at the *marae* throughout the *tangihanga*. Other local residents often go off to work on the first and second day, returning to the *marae* at night and for the day of the funeral.

Mourners arrive in groups, the women wearing chaplets of greenery and the men sprigs stuck into black arm or hat bands as a sign of mourning. At the arrival of each party, the chief mourners renew their wailing and are answered by the women among the arrivals, the *karanga* becoming integrated with the *tangi*. Pausing at intervals, the visitors advance towards the coffin, while their spokesman, raising his voice above the wailing, delivers a *poroporoaki* (farewell), addressing himself directly to the deceased, whose *wairua* (spirit) lingers in the vicinity of the body it has so long inhabited and must be encouraged, by expressions of *aroha* and direct commands, to go to join the ancestors. Among the Northern tribes, the *poroporoaki* is quite a long speech in which the speaker chides the deceased for leaving his relatives and friends and recalls his character, achievements *and* failings. Elsewhere it is generally much shorter. The wailing goes on through the *poroporoaki* and continues perhaps for another ten minutes or so. Then at a Northland *tangihanga* all the visiting women go to *hōngi*, *tangi* and sit with the women by the coffin. Elsewhere only close kinswomen of the deceased do this. The rest of the party take their seats for the *mihimihi* (exchange of greeting speeches), moving forward for the *hōngi* only after these are finished. Neither *wero* nor *pōwhiri* are performed at a *tangihanga*: the *tūpāpaku* is the focus of attention and the chief recipient of honour. Even guests take second place. At *tangihanga* in the Wanganui area an interesting exception is made to the rule that hosts always speak first: when a body lies on the *marae*, the hosts wait for the visitors to open the speaking. Perhaps this, like the long Northern *poroporoaki*, is a way of paying special honour to the dead.

In the intervals between arrivals and deep into the night the speech-makers discuss the funeral arrangements, the future of the bereaved spouse and children, and a variety of other issues. There is usually a three- or four-sided argument over where the deceased is to be buried, each large-family and *hapū* to which he belonged asserting their claim to take the body away. A decision is not finally reached until the early hours of the burial morning. Members of the bereaved family take no part in the speech-making, leaving uncles and cousins to put their views. After the decision is made, however, they may pay a tribute to the deceased and thank those who shared their grief. It is in this way, under the stress of strong emotion, that many in their twenties and thirties make their maiden speech on the *marae*.

Early on the day of the funeral kinsmen of the deceased dig the grave, the women weep their final farewell and the coffin is closed. It may be moved to a church, or the funeral service may be held at the *marae*. After the service the pall-bearers (chosen in family conference as kinsmen, friends or representatives of the *hapū* of the deceased's tribe) carry the coffin in procession to the cemetery. In many cases, some or all of the deceased's clothes and his favourite possessions, rendered *tapu* by their association with death, are placed in the grave. On leaving the cemetery, most mourners ritually cleanse themselves by washing their hands with water or bread provided in basins for the purpose (p. 59). Back at the *marae*, the elders lift the *tapu* from the place where the dead lay by reciting *karakia* and consuming a token amount of food or liquor on the spot.

Before and after the funeral feast, the speech-making continues, but now the speakers deliberately introduce more cheerful themes. Soon the visitors who have far to go take their leave. Those that remain turn their attention to helping the bereaved shake off their grief. Liquor and musical instruments make their appearance. That night or next morning their relatives escort the bereaved family back to their home where the *tapu* is lifted first from the room the deceased occupied and then from the others. This is known as the *takahi* or trampling ceremony.

Within a few weeks, especially if the deceased was a person of importance, a group of his relatives carry out a *kawe mate* (literally 'carrying of the dead'), visiting all of the *hapū* represented at the *tangihanga* on their own *marae*. Visitors and hosts hold 'a little *tangi*', weeping together and making speeches in praise of the dead, and the visitors express their appreciation of the support given them in their grief. Sometimes they return the gifts given during the *tangihanga*. The *kawe mate* for Sir Apirana Ngata involved a party of a hundred strong.

In many areas, the mourning sequence is not completed until a year or two later, when the deceased's relatives sponsor another *hui* at which they ceremonially unveil a memorial gravestone (*hurahanga kōhatu*). The idea of unveiling monuments, borrowed originally from the Pakeha, has been developed into a ceremony which in function and importance recalls and perhaps replaces the pre-European ex-humation ceremony (p. 28).

Death is the occasion above all others which brings Maoris to-gether. They believe in sharing, not hiding, their grief. The close kinswomen of the dead are expected to weep aloud and in public for two days and two nights, expressing their grief in the stylized *tangi*. If they are still young, some related *kuia* may lead the wailing, but in the appropriate setting, under the stress of grief, most Maori women above thirty seem to find it a natural outlet. By the end of the *tangihanga*, they are emotionally and physically exhausted, but, purged of grief and actively encouraged by their kin, they are usually able to take up the threads of life again. Children of all ages are present at *tangihanga* as at all *hui*, sleeping in the meeting-house and witnessing every phase of the ritual. They learn to accept death as one of the realities of life at an early age, and in the emotionally charged atmosphere of the *tangihanga* they absorb more of their culture than they appreciate till many years later (see Ihimaera, 1973).

## Conclusion

*Hui* show no sign of diminishing either in size or frequency. Annual gatherings such as the Waiapu *hui tōpū*, the Ratana festivals and the Coronation Celebrations of the King Movement attract greater numbers year by year. Today Maoris travel a hundred miles to a *hui* as a matter of course, and three or four hundred to a major one.

Maoris enjoy *hui* for many reasons. They bring people together, enabling older folk to meet relatives and friends from whom they have been parted by circumstance and the young ones to make new friends. At *hui*, Maoris are able for a short time to live the old communal life, about which they have heard so much and for which they have a sentimental attachment. Most readily admit they would not like it all the time, but it is highly enjoyable for two or three days at a time. In particular, they enjoy working together in a large group. Everyone is cheerful and co-operative and determined to make the occasion a success. At *hui*, too, they can hear Maori spoken by masters and learn something of Maori history and poetry. They have an opportunity to hear what their leaders have to say on important issues and to express their own views. And last but not least, they can enjoy 'real Maori *kai*'.

# chapter 17

# Literature and art

While Maoris are proud of the literary and artistic forms handed down to them by their ancestors, they also take a lively interest in other forms, from the popular to the specialized. Defined in terms of 'what Maoris do often and enjoy doing' (p. 46), Maori literature and Maori art cover a wide spectrum of media and styles: oral literature and writing in Maori and English, arts and crafts based entirely on natural materials such as wood, flax and stone, and all the modern media including film.

In trying to deal with this diversity, I have found it necessary to make use of the word 'traditional' to describe those literary and artistic forms which are recognized as distinctively Maori. I should have liked to avoid it because so many people interpret it to mean 'unchanged since the coming of the Pakeha', but I could find no suitable alternative. The forms I wish to distinguish include some which are in fact of post-European development, for instance, action-songs, *piupiu* and possibly *tukutuku*, and they have definitely *not* stood still over the last two hundred years as many people assume. When I use the word 'traditional' I mean no more and no less than 'handed down through the generations from Maori ancestors', without any reference to 1769. Such transmission does not preclude change and development, but rather ensures it. The literary and artistic forms concerned were all developed in New Zealand out of earlier Polynesian forms in response to a challenging environment and the creative drives of gifted individuals. Good story-tellers and good artists always adapt their art to the needs and tastes of their audience, subtly up-dating and modifying inherited conventions in the process. The great ones break existing conventions creatively, blazing new trails for others to follow. One only has to compare the ornaments and weapons produced by the 'moahunters' of Wairau Bar (Duff, 1956), with those that Cook collected (Ryden, 1965) to appreciate how much Maori material culture had changed over the intervening centuries. It is high time we stopped identifying traditional Maori literature and art with the forms they assumed at a particular period, i.e. the late eighteenth century, and recognized that they are part of a dynamic on-going process of adaptation, innovation and development which continues to the present day, and hopefully into the future, alongside and in fruitful interaction with forms derived from the European tradition.

## Literature

As we saw in chapter 7, the Maori and English languages are both part of Maori culture, and Maoris use them both to express their experience of life.

### Maori literature in Maori

Maori literature in Maori is dominantly oral literature, composed for and presented before a live audience and relying on its hearers for preservation and transmission. Most Pakehas think of literature as synonymous with writing, especially publication in print, but it is defined by scholars in terms of quality of expression and significance of content. By such standards Maori oral literature unequivocally qualifies for the title.

Over the last hundred and fifty years a large body of Maori oral literature has been recorded, either during a performance or written down at leisure by literate Maoris, but oral transmission has continued alongside the recorded versions and it is still possible to hear pieces that have never been recorded.

Maori experts classify Maori literary forms into six major categories: *whai-kōrero* (speeches), *kōrero* (stories), *whakataukī* (proverbs), *mōteatea* (song-poems), *haka* (shouted exhortations with actions) and *waiata-ā-ringa* (action-songs). All these forms are 'traditional' in the sense discussed above. In the case of speeches and stories, every oral presentation is unique. The speech-maker or story-teller draws on a pool of stories, proverbs, poems and basic formulae for his (or less often her) material but uses individual skill in selecting and arranging the elements and expressing them in words. Maori listeners to a performance respond to the presentation as well as the content, which is usually familiar to them. The other four forms, once composed, are transmitted in fixed form, with only minor variations. On the whole, recorders have concentrated on stories, proverbs and poems and there are comparatively few verbatim records of speeches, which are only now being recognized by scholars as a major literary form, although always appreciated as such by Maoris.

The volume of this literature is substantial by any standards. To the full-length publications listed in the Bibliography (pp. 363–4) must be added numerous shorter pieces published in the *Transactions of the New Zealand Institute* (1869–1933), the *Journal of the Polynesian Society* (1891 to present), Museum Bulletins, the Maori periodicals referred to below (p. 269) and embedded in the works of Pakeha writers too numerous to mention. Yet the published material is far outweighed by the unpublished in various libraries and in private hands. For instance, Sir George Grey's collection of Maori material in the Auckland Public Library consists of 9,800 pages of manuscript, of which only 126 pages of prose and 500 pages of poetry have been published. In addition to manuscript, there are major collections of sound recordings held by the Alexander Turnbull Library, the New Zealand Broadcasting Services, the University of Auckland (in the Archive of Maori and Pacific Music) and Victoria University of Wellington. There is a certain degree of overlap, many pieces having been recorded in several places, but in view of the nature of oral literature, this is a positive advantage, making it possible to investigate the accuracy of transmission of fixed-form pieces and variations in the presentation of free-form pieces.

The stories that have been handed down by oral transmission cover a wide range, including myths couched in highly symbolic language dealing with the making of the world, the canoe migrations to New Zealand, the doings of the ancestors, right up to the present, and relations with Pakehas. However remote in time the events recounted, Maori story-tellers always make them live for their listeners, setting a story in their own natural and cultural landscape, and using modern colloquialisms. For this reason they remain for Maoris entirely relevant to their present concerns and not merely an echo from the past.

Maori oral literature includes a rich treasury of proverbs, the distilled wisdom of generations and an invaluable guide to the Maori philosophy of life. They demonstrate in highly concentrated form two features characteristic of Maori oral literature in general, strong rhythmical patterning and the use of concrete imagery to convey abstract meaning. Because the hearer is left to work out the reference for himself, they can be interpreted in a variety of ways and continue to be applicable in the modern world. A well-known example is the description '*he kōtuku rerenga tahi*' ('white heron of the single flight') applied to distinguished visitors such as the Queen. (The white heron rarely flies far from its breeding community and so is the sight of a lifetime.) Advice to a young girl to 'marry a man with calloused hands' is still figuratively sound, despite occupational changes. Many proverbs stress the importance of growth and change: '*Mate atu he tētēkura, whakaete mai he tētēkura*' ('One fernfrond dies, another pushes through in its place'). The human community is urged to co-operate with nature in this and other respects: '*Tūngia te ururua, kia tupu whakaritorito te tupu o harakeke*' ('Burn the overgrowth, so that the flax can put forth new sheets; get rid of outmoded habits and ideas and give the new ways a chance'). Laziness is deplored: a lazy man is '*he whiore tahutahu*', like a dog whose tail is singed from lying close to the fire. Industry and perseverance are praised. '*Mauri mahi, mauri ora; mauri noho, mauri mate*' ('An active man is a strong and healthy man; a man who sits around gets sick'). '*Kia mate ururoa, kei mate wheke*' ('Die like a shark, fighting to the last, don't give up limply like an octopus'). Because they draw on our own physical environment, the Maori proverbs have particular meaning to all New Zealanders.

*Mōteatea* are poems distinguished by being presented in a particular musical mode and with few or impromptu gestures. The music has a limited tonal range and makes little appeal to the uninitiated. The primary emphasis is however on the words. *Mōteatea* are typically non-narrative, 'occasional' poems composed on or for a particular occasion and full of references to particular people and places. Their average length is between twenty and thirty lines, though some approach a hundred. They are frequently identified by the name of a particular poet, often a woman. For these reasons their composition can be dated with some accuracy. While some have been handed down from pre-European times, the large majority can be dated to the late eighteenth and nineteenth centuries. Among them are a number which voice strong protest at the political and cultural imperialism of the Pakehas. In addition to allusion, *mōteatea* make powerful use of visual imagery. This includes many stylized images also used in speech-making and story-telling: for instance, forest trees, whales and stars are used to signify chiefs, while moving water – rain, rivers, waterfalls and the tides – signifies grief. However, though the connection is stylized, the wording is not, and the stylized images are matched by others of striking originality (see especially Papahia's Lament for Te Huhu, and Hariata Tangikuku's Lament for her Illness, nos 3 and 20 in *Nga Mōteatea*, vol. 1). In this century the composing as distinct from the re-presentation of *mōteatea* almost ceased for several decades, the rising generations preferring the modern *waiata-ā-ringa* form. In the last twenty years however a few new compositions of high quality have come to light and interest is reviving, especially with the development of university courses in Maori language and literature, the revival of tribal *whare wānanga*, and the institution of special sections for 'traditional songs' in several of the annual Maori cultural competitions (p. 183). *Mōteatea* continue to be sung today as a 'relish' (*kīnaki*) to speeches at Maori gatherings, the choice resting on kinship connection with the poet and the relevance of the topic to the occasion.

In contrast with *mōteatea*, *haka* and action-songs are associated with dancing. Although they are popular with non-speakers of Maori because of their aural and visual appeal, for Maoris their merit lies first in the words and secondly in the way words and actions are fitted together. The *haka* is, like *mōteatea*, a form of pre-European derivation but because its vigorous actions have kept it a favourite with Maori and Pakeha, the composition of new *haka* has never waned. The action-song is largely a twentieth-century development, characterized by bright catchy tunes and graceful movements, especially of arms and hands. The composition of action-songs proceeds apace, every major Maori occasion being marked by one or more new pieces and every group of performers composing at least some entirely their own. While most of the resulting hundreds are unexceptional, even banal, and borrow heavily from each other, the best have all the qualities of true literature and several action-song composers are recognized as poets through the Maori community, notably Tuini Ngawai and Henare Waitoa, both of Ngāti Porou. Indeed the latter has been the subject of an M.A. thesis (Dewes, 1974).

Having acquired the skill of writing, Maoris made use of it not only to record their oral traditions but to keep diaries, write letters to each other and the Government and to produce an impressive array of periodicals: *Te Hokio* and *Te Pihoihoi* (in the Waikato in the 1860s), *Te Waka Maori* (Napier and Wellington, 1863–84), *Te Wananga* (Napier, 1874–8, Wellington, 1928–30), *Te Paki-o-te-Matariki* (Waikato, 1890s–1928), *Te Puke ki Hikurangi* (1897–1906), *Pipiwhawauroa* (1898–1913), *Te Kopara* (1913–21), *Te Manukura* (Auckland, 1916–23), *Toa Takitini* (Hastings, 1921–30) and *Te Whētu-Mārama*, the newspaper of the Ratana Movement, which is still being published. As yet very little has been done to collect, edit and evaluate material of this sort, which could well prove a literary treasure. Sir Apirana Ngata's essay, *Te Tiriti-o-Waitangi* (1922), and electoral manifesto, *Pānui mo te pooti o te tau 1935* (1935), are already much used in advanced language classes for their literary merits as much as their political comment, but they are by no means the only pieces which deserve such recognition.

In general, Maoris have been slow to use writing to express themselves in Maori in new forms or on new topics, perhaps because of lack of outlets but also because they have continued to find satisfaction mainly in oral expression on the *marae* with its immediate feedback from an audience. In addition to Ngata, Reweti Kohere and Pei Te Hurinui Jones have a high reputation among Maoris for the quality of their writing in Maori and also for translations from English literature. Jones has rendered several of Shakespeare's plays and Fitzgerald's *Rubaiyat of Omar Khayyam* into Maori, while Kohere delighted in translating Robert Burns. Because of the problems associated with translating not only the language but the underlying cultural concepts, their renderings are (I am assured by those better able to judge) re-creations rather than translations. Over the last twenty years, the provision of outlets and literary prizes by *Te Ao Hou* and *Te Maori* and development of the series, *Te Whare Kura* and *Te Tautoko*, have encouraged the emergence of a number of writers in Maori. The most notable writers of prose are Pine Taiapa, Maharaia Winiata, Hirone Whikiriwhi, Hirini Moko (Sid Mead), Arapeta Awatere, Kataraina Mataira and Arapera Hineira Blank, while the last three and Hone Tuwhare have produced several Maori poems apiece written rather than composed orally. Their number is however discouragingly small, and as yet none has produced any substantial quantity of work in Maori.

*Maori writing in English*

Not surprisingly in view of the emphasis on oral literature, the first Maoris to write full-length works for publication in English concentrated on non-fictional narratives of the doings of their ancestors, either a particular tribe or the Maori people as a whole (see Bibliography E). Because of interest in the content, these works are not usually regarded from a literary point of view. In my opinion however, at least two of these writers, Peter Buck (*The Coming of the Maori* and *Vikings of the Sunrise*) and Pei Te Hurinui Jones (*King Potatau*) deserve recognition for their masterly and evocative style, so entirely suited and subordinated to their purpose, so flowing and effortless that it goes unnoticed by the absorbed reader. Reweti Kohere's writing in *The Story of a Maori Chief* and *The Autobiography of a Maori* also merits study from a literary viewpoint.

In his survey of 'The Maori and Literature 1938–65' (in Schwimmer, 1968: 217–56), Bill Pearson wrote: 'The body of imaginative work in English written by Maori is small: Hone Tuwhare's volume of verse and a handful of poems by others; and no more than one book and fifty short prose pieces, all of them, except for some by Rowley Habib, published in *Te Ao Hou* since 1955.' In the nine years since 1965, startling changes have occurred as Maori writers have established themselves on the national literary scene. The first sign of spring was a special prize for a short article awarded to Arapera Hineira Blank in the first Katherine Mansfield Memorial Award in 1959. The real breakthrough came in the late sixties when work by Maori writers began to appear outside *Te Ao Hou*, in the *New Zealand Listener*, the literary magazines, *Landfall* and *Mate*, and on NZBC radio. In 1970 Margaret Orbell edited a collection of short stories by Maori writers, *Contemporary Maori Writing*, which was placed second in the Wattie Book of the Year Award in 1971. Since then, things have happened fast. Hone Tuwhare, whose first volume of poems, *No Ordinary Sun*, appeared in 1964, was awarded a Robert Burns Fellowship at Otago University for six months in 1972 and a full year in 1974, and has produced three more volumes of poetry, *Come Rain, Hail* (1972), *Sapwood and Milk* (1973) and *Something Nothing* (1974), together with a long-playing record of *No Ordinary Sun*. Rowley Habib became the first Maori writer to win an award from the New Zealand Literary Fund in 1970 and has continued to publish poems and short stories in many magazines. In 1972 a play, *Te Raukura*, by Harry Dansey was produced at the Auckland Festival to critical acclaim. Based on the story of the prophets, Te Whiti and Tohu, *Te Raukura* was published simultaneously in hard and paper covers in 1974. The greatest impact however has undoubtedly been made by Witi Ihimaera, who published a collection of short stories, *Pounamu Pounamu*, in 1972, which was awarded third place in the Wattie Book of the Year Award in 1973, a novel, *Tangi*, which was placed first in 1974, and a second novel, *Whanau*, in 1974. With another collection of short stories and his third novel well under way he has a full working programme planned for 1975 which he is spending at Otago University as Robert Burns Fellow. In March 1975 Pat Heretaunga Baker made a stir with a novel set in pre-European times based on stories told him as a child by his grandfather, *Behind the Tattooed Face*. A collection of short stories by Patricia Grace, who has already won critical approval for those published in various magazines, was published later in the year under the title *Waiariki*. Harry Dansey and Arapera Hineira Blank are both preparing collections of their poems.

In his tentative but highly perceptive comments about Maori writing up to 1965, Bill Pearson noted 'a tone of belonging, of being an insider in the situation written about . . . sometimes a sense of responsibility as a Maori to other Maoris', the dominance of the theme of adaptation in a changing world, and the lyrical and sometimes passionate use of the English language. In Hone Tuwhare, whose work he considered the most impressive, he found 'a synthesis of European and Maori tradition that enables him to range in subjects that none of the Maori prose writers have attempted'.

A proper survey and evaluation of the achievements of Maori writers in the last nine years demands a companion piece to Pearson's essay and cannot be attempted here. I cannot however resist a few tentative comments. Maori writers in English have so greatly extended their range in a few short years that they cannot be dealt with as a single group. Nevertheless they have some qualities in common which

271

it seems to me are related to their Maoriness and show continuity with the literature of their forebears through the apparent differences. For one thing their writing has a vitally oral quality about it, fully appreciated only when read aloud. They have a typically unpretentious, unselfconscious, down-to-earth approach to life and writing which enables them to handle without mawkishness themes which Pakehas generally shy away from, especially the bonds of love – between friends, husband and wife, old and young – and mourning for the dead. Almost without exception they make vivid use of imagery, using things and relations in the concrete world to signify and express abstract ideas and relations. Far from being strained or obtrusive, this use of the figurative mode is so integral a part of their approach that its full richness is easily missed if not looked for (see especially Witi Ihimaera's short stories and novels). Pearson's prediction that 'Maori writing will be distinct in its passion, its lyricism and its unforced celebration of living' has been amply fulfilled. Maori writers have made their mark with both the general public and the critics. They are not only in use but among the most popular works in New Zealand schools, with Pakeha as well as Maori pupils. *No Ordinary Sun* is into its sixth printing, and printings of Witi Ihimaera's work have topped 30,000. Best of all, Maori writers are no longer dealt with by the critics as curiosities to be judged by special standards, but are named among New Zealand's leading writers on their own merits. Asked which writers she admired most, Phoebe Meikle, a leading editorial director, named Patricia Grace, whose short stories she considered 'the most beautiful since Janet Frame', Albert Wendt the Samoan novelist, Harry Dansey and Witi Ihimaera. The *Dominion* literary critic reviewing Ihimaera's second novel wrote:

> Witi Ihimaera has restored some much-needed balance to our literature. Just as his themes explore the roots of Maori culture, so his novels go back to the sources of all good novel writing: characterization, simplicity, dialogue, colour and readability. In the process without deliberately trying to do so he has written books that have the essential elements of true literature in them in that they can move people to sorrow, pleasure and anger.

### Bilingual writing

Beginning with Ngata, Buck and Kohere, a significant number of Maori writers have published worth-while work in both Maori and English, but usually they wrote any one piece wholly in one language or the other. At least two Maori writers are experimenting in using both languages at once. Arapera Hineira Blank writes poems in whichever language she feels like, then re-creates it in the other. The result is not one poem and a translation, but two variations on the same theme. In his early poetry, Harry Dansey experimented with working Maori words into English metrical rhythms, but latterly he has turned to composing poems that combine words, phrases and sentences from Maori and English in a single whole. To date (1974) he has used this technique mainly for humorous, bawdy ballads, but their popularity with mixed (Maori and Pakeha) audiences suggests a vein worth exploring. Many parts of his play, *Te Raukura*, were written first in Maori and re-cast in English. 'I would ask myself the question: "How would people say this?" And I found this best answered by letting them say it in Maori first.' Some of these passages have been left untranslated. 'It means a sharper definition here and there, a bonus as it were for those who understand Maori' (*Te Raukura*: x–xi).

## The visual arts and crafts

The term 'Maori arts and crafts' is commonly used in New Zealand to refer to the art forms developed as part of Classic Maori culture: *whakairo* (wood carving), *tukutuku* (lattice-work panels with stylized angular designs in cross-stitch), *kōwhaiwhai* (stylized and predominantly curvilinear designs painted in red, black and white, on narrow panels, often called 'rafter patterns' from their predominant use), and weaving, a term used to cover the different techniques of *taniko* and cloak making, and kit and mat making. In addition to these traditional forms however Maori artists are also involved in the practice of other art forms, to which they have been introduced by Pakehas but which they have made to varying degrees their own.

### The traditional art forms

The so-called 'traditional' Maori arts and crafts are all closely associated with the *marae*, especially the meeting-house, and with the activities that take place there. Ideally a meeting-house should be adorned with carvings on the barge-boards and their supports, the jambs, sills and lintels of the front door and window, panels (*poupou*) at intervals along the walls of the porch and interior, and at the bases of the pillars (*poutokomanawa*) which support the ridgepole, with *tukutuku* between the *poupou*, with *kōwhaiwhai* on the rafters and ridgepole, and with flax mats covering the floor. The skills of the weaver are also called upon to provide cloaks for major speakers, *taniko* bodices and *piupiu* (flax skirts) for the young people who welcome and entertain visitors. Not all *marae* are in fact so adorned

273

for reasons that range from lack of finance and skill to deliberate abandonment of forms regarded at one time as dangerous (because of *tapu*) or outmoded. When the decision is made to renovate or re-build, however, most communities favour the traditional, recogniz-ably Maori forms. Maoris also apply these forms with suitable modifications to other buildings which serve community purposes, to *marae* dining-halls, churches and school assembly halls.

Knowledge and practice of the traditional arts has passed through many vicissitudes over the last hundred and fifty years. In some parts they were virtually lost for a period but always somewhere, somehow, someone kept the knowledge alive. A major revival occurred in the 1920s stimulated largely by Apirana Ngata, then Minister of Maori Affairs, Peter Buck by his writing and lecturing, and Princess Te Puea in the Waikato. In 1926 a Maori Arts and Crafts School was established at Rotorua, where the noted carvers of the day trained some dozen young men and later sent them out in groups to build meeting-houses all over the country. Both the School and the carvers were financed by the Board of Maori Arts and Crafts, which was later merged in the Maori Purposes Fund Board and like it derived its income from profits on the investment of trust monies held by the Maori Land Boards. The School's graduates dominated *marae* build-ing for forty odd years, training another generation of carvers in their turn. In the 1950s Gordon Tovey as head of the Arts and Crafts Branch of the Education Department set out to establish Maori arts and crafts as an integral part of the school curriculum. Young Maoris with promise as artists were recruited into the Branch and trained for appointment as specialist art teachers; in-service training courses in Maori arts and crafts were instituted for teachers all over the country, often involving local Maoris as tutors and participants; and a set of instructional books and tapes of high quality were prepared and made available to the public through the Government Printer. (This support from within the school system was so greatly appreciated by Maoris that when Mr Tovey, a Pakeha, died in 1974 the Wellington Maori community farewelled him at his funeral with *tangi* and *poroporoaki* (p. 262).) In the fifties and early sixties, the University Extension Department in Auckland and Wellington also helped keep the Maori arts alive by paying the expenses of craftsmen and women to supervise particular *marae* projects. The house Parewahawaha at Bulls was built with this help under the supervision of Henare and Mere Toka. Unfortunately changes in policy caused the universities to withdraw from this work. In 1963 the Government established the New Zealand Maori Arts and Crafts Institute at Rotorua under the control of a board containing representatives of the Maori people, the Depart-ment of Maori Affairs, the Tourist and Publicity Department and the municipal authorities. The Institute occupies a specially designed complex on the edge of a thermal reserve to which it holds the freehold title, adjoining Whakarewarewa Maori Village. Operating with a staff of five, the Institute runs a full-time carving school and numerous short courses in women's crafts and takes part in demonstrations, arts festivals and educational conferences all over New Zealand. These activities are supported by income from the thermal reserve which the Institute operates as a tourist attraction, training local girls as guides, and from selling carvings and craft work in a souvenir shop or on order from cultural clubs. The carving training lasts three years: there are twelve boys in training with four coming in and four graduating each year. Besides carving for sale, the trainees have been engaged in the construction of a model *pa* on the reserve. Of those who have graduated from the school to date, two have joined the staff, several are working for private firms and a few have set up carving workshops of their own. As yet however they have not been involved in full-time *marae* building like their predecessors of the School.

In Maori eyes, the primary purpose of the traditional arts is still the embellishment of the meeting-house, the centre of Maori community life and *mana*, and it is in participation in the embellishment of one's own meeting-house, that the arts are best learnt and brought to perfection. Renovating or rebuilding a *marae* is a herculean task which requires the mobilization of the whole community to raise money, lay foundations and build the basic structure, gather materials and execute the art work, and cater throughout for the workers and then for the visitors bidden to the opening. As in the past, a community entrusts the oversight of the whole project to master craftsmen, normally a man to design and supervise the carving and *kōwhai-whai* and a woman to do likewise for the *tukutuku* and weaving, though some men are also *tukutuku* experts. The relatively few men and women of this status are widely sought after and often employed across tribal boundaries. Except when engaged in work for their own communities they are employed on a contractual basis, but their wages are amplified by farewell gifts and the *mana* that comes from being named in association with the house. While the responsibility for creating the designs and executing the major pieces rests with the master craftsmen, much of the art work is done by the people of the community under their instruction and supervision. The schools can teach forms and techniques only up to a certain point: in the *marae* context the learner imbibes all the associated traditions, attitudes and *tapus* that are of equal importance from the Maori point of view. It is in this way that the most promising in each generation receive the training and experience that enable them to emerge when the time is ripe as masters in their own turn. Thus Hapai Winiata who served his apprenticeship under Henare Toka during the building of Parewaha-waha is now seven years later supervising the building of the house Ngatokowaru at Hokio for a closely related *hapū* to which he also belongs.

As in language, there are distinct tribal and regional styles in carving and to a lesser extent in the other crafts. Some of these were lost for a period, for instance, in Northland where the tribes gave up the arts of peace for those of war in the 1820s and 1830s, and later, having forgotten their own patterns, adopted those of the East Coast craftsmen brought north through their campaigns. Where necessary the lost knowledge is now being regained with the help of old drawings and museums. The Maori Arts and Crafts School and the employment of experts across tribal boundaries from the twenties on, tended to break down some of the distinctions. For a period many houses were built in other than their own tribal style or contained *poupou* from every major tribal group. However some tribes have maintained an unbroken line of transmission of their own style from one generation to the next, often in one particular *hapū*, and currently there is a trend towards concentrating on the style appropriate to the community including just a few examples from other areas where justified by kinship connections.

All the traditional Maori art forms are governed, like all art forms, by their own conventions. These are not rigid prescriptions but a set of rules and symbolic meanings within which artists work and which the truly creative break or bend to their purposes. When the modification of a rule is effective and approved by the people it is worked into the tradition. In this way the so-called traditional forms have been and are continually and creatively developed. This characteristic willingness to experiment can be seen in the painted houses of the 1880s like Rongopai in Waituhi (Ihimaera, 1974: 121–4), the attempts to depict ancestors in *tukutuku* in many East Coast houses, and a carved panel in Otago museum depicting a horse race. Creativity was a marked characteristic of the work of Pine Taiapa, appearing clearly in Tukaki meeting-house at Te Kaha and Te Arohanui-ki-te-tangata meeting-house at Waiwhetū (Wellington), adorned under his direction. Currently it is to be seen in the work of Hapai Winiata for Ngatokowaru. Arguing that 'Maori history didn't stop with the coming of the Pakeha', Hapai has planned Ngatokowaru to depict the whole sweep of that history from Hawaiki to the present. In addition to the classic *tukutuku* patterns of *poutama* (ascending steps symbolizing aspiration), *pātiki* (the flounder symbolizing natural food resources) and *purapura whetū* (star seeds symbolizing the heavens), he has designed entirely new panels depicting the eight major canoes that brought the ancestors to New Zealand and illustrating Ngata's famous saying which begins '*E tipu, e rea*' (see p. 151). For the bargeboards he has chosen the theme of Ngāti Raukawa's migration to the Mana-watu from the Waikato in the 1820s. Inspired by a dream he has rendered this theme entirely by intertwined and highly stylized *manaia* figures, which are unequivocally traditional in execution and general effect, but to emphasize the sadness of leaving ancestral lands he has placed a round tear drop in the slanting eyes of those who look back over their shoulder.

Creativity is also evident in the way master craftsmen have adapted the traditional forms to meet new situations. This was earlier shown in the building of churches, where *poupou* depicting named ancestors were replaced by plain adzed slabs or repeated anonymous human figures, because a church is built to glorify God, not man. Later when embellishing dining-halls and school assembly halls, they began the craft work at shoulder height, gave more space and emphasis to *tukutuku* and *kōwhaiwhai,* and used anonymous figures instead of the highly *tapu* carvings of ancestors. Major modifications have followed the introduction of new building materials. In the twenties and thirties when building methods of Pakeha origin were adopted, the East Coast tribes greatly increased the size and height of their houses and added extra windows and side porches, and often a stage, embellishing the latter as if it were the façade of a meeting-house. When the Kawerau Maoris built a new community hall in 1964 with pre-stressed concrete arches instead of a ridgepole, they used *kōwhaiwhai* effectively on narrow rafters set lengthwise down instead of across the hall. Maori communities now frequently employ architects to design both *marae* and other community buildings. Not unexpectedly, some particularly fine designs have come from Maori architects, notably John Scott (Ngāti Kahungunu) and Bill Royal (Ngāti Raukawa), but others represent a fruitful co-operation between Pakeha architects and the Maori community, the entire new *marae* complex designed for the Orakei Marae Trust for instance, and the 'cultural complex' building, Kimiora, at Tūrangawaewae. The meeting-house at Orakei, at present in the process of construction, will be one of the largest houses in the country. To ensure adequate air and light, it has a side porch and narrow windows recessed behind the *poupou.* The carvings designed in the distinctive Ngāti Whātua style have been scaled up to fit panels twice the usual size with a skill that preserves the proportions perfectly.

Maori communities have also commissioned buildings that depart quite radically from the meeting-house model. John Scott's design for the Maori Battalion War Memorial Hall in Palmerston North is a two-storied building which uses raw concrete and a massive square shape to convey the rugged, rock-like character of the Battalion, and is embellished by carved *poupou* set like Greek columns across the upper storey. Kimiora, opened at Tūrangawaewae in 1974, is very much in contemporary style, built on two levels and containing many rooms of varying sizes and functions; but it is tied together and given a distinctive Maori identity by the use of carving on the edge and supporting pillars of a verandah along the two sides adjoining the *marae* proper.

An outstanding creative adaptation of traditional art forms to a new situation is Inia Te Wiata's *pou-ihi* which rises three storeys through the centre of New Zealand House in London, flanked with two canoe prows reminiscent of wings. When he died leaving one prow unfinished it was completed, by tribal decision, by his early teacher Piri Poutapu and Inia's two sons entirely in tune with Inia's vision.

Though the weaving crafts are taught in many schools to an elementary level, they require much patience, practice and advanced tuition for mastery and are not much practised in the home, even in rural areas. In most country communities however a few skilled women keep the knowledge alive, and the Maori Women's Welfare League has made a special effort to foster interest by running special courses and competitions, with the help in recent years of the NZ Maori Arts and Crafts Institute. It is mainly when their community decides to build a meeting-house that the women take steps to learn or revive the necessary skills, gaining encouragement from working together in groups. In general, the emphasis is on recapturing and practising the traditional techniques and patterns, but adaptation has also occurred within limits. Mat-plaiting techniques are used to make hats, and subtle modifications in kit-making have widened the range of shapes. *Taniko* was early applied to belts and bodices, impressive panels of it complement the carving on the pulpits of many Maori churches, and more recently it has been used to make small articles such as purses, serviette rings and ornamental medallions. Of all the women's arts *taniko* is probably the most widely practised because easily adapted to small articles of everyday use. However for the bodices which are part of concert party dress *taniko* mostly gives way to tapestry which is quicker and as effective at a distance. The importance of the work that has been done to preserve and creatively develop the weaving crafts was recently recognized by the Queen Elizabeth II Arts Council when it made an award including a cash grant to Rangimarie Hetet of Maniapoto for a lifetime devotion to the task.

The large majority of practitioners of these Maori arts are part-timers earning their living in other occupations but taking time out to execute a community commission whether as master craftsmen or under direction. Both Pine Taiapa and Henare Toka, well-known master carvers who died in 1973 and 1974 respectively, were farmers. A small number of teachers and apprentices are employed full-time at the Maori Arts and Crafts Institute, including John Taiapa as Master Carver. Because of reluctance to commercialize the arts of their ancestors and dislike of being tied down, Maori craftsmen and women have generally resisted the blandishments of entrepreneurs to supply tourist shops, but over the last few years several small carving workshops have been established in Auckland and Rotorua supplying the shops and executing commissions. To help finance their new *marae*, members of the Orakei community and supporters are producing an array of craft work on commission and for sale through a shop in the Auckland Museum. In the Maori way, these workshops are open to the public, and the workers take the opportunity to talk to visitors about what the pieces mean in the context of the culture as a whole.

## Modern developments

But Maoris do not limit their interest in art to forms inherited from their ancestors: they have always been eager to try out new ideas and media. By 1975 a significant number of Maoris – at least twenty-five and possibly more – have graduated from tertiary institutions with degrees or diplomas in fine arts. Most of these, along with some less formally trained, are practising artists, producing creative works for their own pleasure and for sale in a variety of media, as painters, print-makers, potters and sculptors in wood, stone, metal and synthetic materials. Recently a few have begun to explore the possibilities of photography as art form: for instance, Cliff Whiting as an adjunct to his sculptural work and John Miller who contributed most of the illustrations for this book and for *Te Ao Hurihuri* (King, 1975).

Like their forebears and most New Zealand artists, Maori artists generally engage in creative work on a part-time basis. However, many are employed in closely allied fields, mainly as art specialists in schools and teachers' colleges. Former teacher Rau Hōtere however has been working full-time for several years. In 1961 he took up a New Zealand Art Societies' Fellowship to study in Britain and a residential award at the Michael Karolyi Memorial Foundation at Vence in France. He spent 1966 at the University of Otago as Frances Hodgkins Fellow and later received a grant from the Queen Elizabeth II Arts Council to pursue special interests for four months. A retrospective exhibition of his work was shown in ten art galleries from Auckland to Invercargill during 1974 and early 1975.

As with Maori writers it is impossible to generalize about Maori artists, who are typically marked individualists. Many of them work effectively in more than one medium, especially painting and sculpture. Several combine art with writing: Kataraina Mataira for instance, and Harry Dansey, who illustrates his writing with vivid line drawings and watercolours and for some years produced political and humorous strip cartoons for a New Plymouth daily newspaper. Nearly all have a particular interest in Maori art forms and themes, but they use them mainly as a source of inspiration, rarely working within their conventions, and there are wide variations between artists and often within the work of one artist in the way their Maori background and interest comes to expression. Some draw directly on Maori myths and traditions for subjects, but they realize them in new ways, as in Fred Graham's wood sculptures *Rangi*, *Papa*, and *Maui Snaring the Sun*. Some have done work on commission for Maori communities: for instance, Arnold Wilson's statue commemorating Maharaia Winiata at Judea Pa (Tauranga), Muru Walters' carved gateway at Ahipara Primary School, and the mural *Te whanaketanga o Tainui* conceived by Para Matchitt and executed with the help of selected assistants for the hall in Kimiora at Tūrangawaewae (p. 278). But most of their work is designed for and appreciated by the wider New Zealand community, Maori and Pakeha. Their paintings and sculptures are to be found widely dispersed in art galleries, private homes and public situations like civic buildings, banks, hotels and public squares. Fred Graham for instance designed the fountain in the Rose Gardens in Te Awamutu, a flight of stainless steel birds rising through spray, and in 1975 executed a wood sculpture for Victoria University of Wellington depicting Tāne and Tupai with the baskets and stones of knowledge they obtained for man from Te Rangi. The Overseas Terminal building in Wellington has a mural painted by Selwyn Murupaenga, while Rank Xerox commissioned a mural from Rau Hōtere for their building in Auckland (Plate 14).

An even more recent development is the application of traditional art forms to fashion clothes. Maoris early adapted *taniko* patterns to men's and women's belts and occasionally to ties and knitting patterns, but on a private and non-commercial basis. As Member of Parliament Sir Eruera Tirikatene frequently wore a *taniko* waistcoat which was a gift from a Wanganui craftswoman. In the middle and late sixties several professional designers, prominent among whom was Reimana Adsett (Ngāti Kahungunu), began to produce hand-printed fabrics and knitwear using *taniko*, *kōwhaiwhai* and carving designs in new adventurous ways. This development received warm encouragement from Maori leaders, especially Queen Te Ata-i-rangikaahu and Mrs Whetū Tirikatene-Sullivan, who increasingly featured such garments in their wardrobes. On entering Parliament as Member for Southern Maori in 1967, Mrs Tirikatene-Sullivan sought and gained approval in principle and for specific designs by wearing a different sample to every *marae* in her electorate. In 1970 the New Zealand Maori Council sponsored a Maori Fashion Show in Wellington where it was warmly received. It was later shown also in Auckland and taken on tour to Australia under joint sponsorship with the New Zealand Wool Board. Since then garments incorporating Maori designs have become an integral part of the New Zealand fashion scene, available in boutiques in the main centres and regularly included in wardrobes supplied to girls representing New Zealand in overseas beauty contests. When Maori debutantes were presented to Queen Te Ata-i-rangikaahu at a coming-out ball in Wellington in 1973 all the girls wore full-length gowns and cloaks in plain fabrics strikingly embellished with *taniko* or *kōwhaiwhai* designs in traditional and non-traditional colours, while the Queen herself wore a regal gold gown with deep bands of *taniko* on sleeves and skirt (see Plate 15).

While clothes designers have so far used traditional patterns almost entirely for decorative effect, there is growing appreciation of their symbolic significance and potential, especially among church needlewomen. Patterns whose traditional meaning is easily re-interpreted in Christian terms are widely used to embellish liturgical vestments, altar clothes, hangings and kneelers, in particular *poutama* (ascent in search of truth), *pātiki* (the flounder i.e. a fish), *purapura whetū* (star seeds, symbolizing the heavens, God's creative power, and the company of saints) and *mangōpare* (the hammerhead shark, symbolizing the power and might of God). The Maori Division of the Methodist Church made a significant contribution to this development when it created a *kākahu* (robe) for Rev. Rua Rakena to wear for his induction as Moderator of the Methodist Church of New Zealand in 1975. Conceived as a 'synthesis of traditional Maori and Pakeha ecclesiastical dress', the *kākahu* is a seamless cloak the colour of worked flax, its front edges adorned with a *taniko* border and fastened with a plaited flax thong linking greenstone buttons. The *taniko* border is formed by two ascending zigzag white lines enclosing alternating red and black diamonds and themselves bordered on the outside by red and black zigzags. The white lines 'symbolize our continuing search for truth and enlightenment, a progressing forward towards wholeness', the red and black lines convey the ideas of 'integration and co-operation in the striving for wholeness', and the red and black diamonds recall the proverbial saying '*Mā pango mā whero, ka oti*': by black (commoners) and red (chiefs) working together the work gets done. The collar piece joining the two borders is worked with *purapura whetū* 'signifying the multitude of stars in the sky and the hope that those who profess Christ as Lord should likewise multiply and shine like stars in the world at large'. The greenstone buttons were the gift of church members from Te Waipounamu (the South Island, land of greenstone) and the flax thong indicates respect for the ways of the past.

Maori concert parties touring overseas typically equip their members with street and evening clothes incorporating Maori designs. Worn by men as well as women, such garments are now – in the mid seventies – a prominent feature of most Maori gatherings. Apart from the professional designers who are continually developing their ideas, increasing numbers of Maori women are designing and making garments with a Maori accent for themselves and their families.

## Music and dance

It should be clear by now that Maoris do not separate literary expression in words from music and dancing but see them as 'going together'. In the literary forms of pre-European origin, music though essential, is secondary to the words. In speech-making, story-telling, proverbs and *haka*, the mainly rhythmic musical elements underline and assist the sense, but in *mōteatea* the tune (*rangi*) seems to be mainly an identifying device related to the words only in a general way, slow and sad for laments and love songs, fast and forceful for poems refuting slander or instructing the young. Probably for this reason, composers of action-songs have not worried unduly about composing music that matches the words but have borrowed whatever catchy tune is to hand, modifying it to suit their purposes by altering time intervals and harmonies. Pakehas who do not understand the words often assume they are a translation of the English words of the tune but this is usually wide of the mark. The tune 'In the mood' for instance was used by Tuini Ngawai to carry a solemn and moving lament for the dead of the Maori Battalion.

Delighted and intrigued by European music with its different intervals and tonal range Maoris adopted what appealed to them, especially bright and varied melodies, the guitar and ukelele which were portable and good for singing to, and the idea of harmony; but they developed them in their own way. Maori harmonizing follows its own rules and includes plenty of extemporizing.

It is part of popular belief that Maoris are 'naturally' more musical than Pakehas. Certainly Maori children brought up surrounded by music-making sing unselfconsciously and with great verve, and play the guitar almost as a matter of course. 'For most Maoris singing is part of living. Some may aspire to the dizzy heights of the successful pop singer, but most are not concerned too much about fame and fortune. To sing is to be happy' (Mataira, in Schwimmer, 1968: 211).

Maoris are nearly always well represented in the field of popular entertainment in New Zealand both as aspirants in radio and television talent quests and as accepted 'names' in regular shows and on record. Some, like John Rowles and the Hi Fives, have achieved success overseas, encouraging the next generation. There is a predominance of vocalists, singing solo and in groups, but Maori instrumental groups are common and widely favoured for listening and dancing to.

In the field of middle- and high-brow music Maori participation is more restricted, but a few have won through to recognition as solo artists of standing, again mainly as singers. The names of Inia Te Wiata and Kiri Te Kanawa are internationally known, and the contralto Hannah Tatana is remembered warmly in New Zealand despite early retirement. In 1965 the New Zealand Opera Company recruited and trained a large Maori cast for a production of *Porgy and Bess*, with Inia Te Wiata as Porgy and black Americans in the other leading roles. A resounding success, the production toured both Australia and New Zealand. Some of the Maori singers continued with the New Zealand Opera Company for several years. One, George Henare, subsequently sang the title role in the musical *Mr King Hongi* at the Auckland Festival in 1973.

As regards composition, for reasons already explained, Maoris have tended mainly to adapt borrowed tunes. However, over the years some original melodies were produced and in the 1960s Arapeta Awatere, Kingi Ihaka, Bill Kerekere and Dovey Horvath-Katene began regularly to compose new melodies for their cultural groups and 'occasional' song-poems for *hui* such as the welcome to Queen Elizabeth II at Gisborne in 1972. This trend is gathering speed fostered by special classes for composition in competitions held at Maori gatherings and by the NZBC (see p. 183). The emphasis however continues to be on music to go with words, not on music as a separate form.

Most Maoris learn to dance as they learn to sing, at an early age and by participation, mainly Maori forms on the *marae* and at school and popular dance forms at public dances. In recent years a few Maoris have been involved in the creative dance movement, notably Matenga Kingi, who has created several dance sequences on Maori themes.

### Drama and film

A Maori elder once remarked to me that Maoris had not taken to the theatre because they already had access to drama in speech-making, story-telling and *haka* on the *marae*, drama that is close to and involves the audience physically and emotionally. By comparison

Pakeha-style drama seemed contrived and stagey. Now Maoris have established themselves successfully in this field also.

Maori involvement in stage presentation goes further back than is generally realized, but it was entirely on a small-scale, regional and amateur basis, as indeed was most indigenous drama in New Zealand at the time. In the twenties and thirties Maori actors like Paraire Tomoana were involved in amateur productions in Hawke's Bay in both Maori and Shakespearean roles, while poetry readings in Maori and English by Rev. Reweti Kohere, Dr Tutere Wirepa and lawyer Henare Poananga were highlights of concerts held up and down the East Coast to raise money for an X-ray unit for Te Puia Hospital.

In the thirties, a large number of Maoris appeared before the cameras in leading and supporting roles in Rudall Hayward's early classics, *Te Kooti's Trail* and *Rewi's Last Stand*, which have been periodically revived for nearly forty years. Unfortunately the Haywards went overseas, and up to about 1970, though some excellent documentaries were made on Maori subjects, the few feature films with Maori parts were made from a Pakeha point of view, and Maori actors were understandably stilted and uncomfortable in them.

On stage the way was opened by Bill Tawhai, whose performance as Othello for the Auckland University Drama Club in the late fifties sticks in the mind: besides an impressive physical presence, he brought to the part a rare depth of psychological and emotional understanding. Production of Bruce Mason's play, *The Pohutukawa Tree*, on stage and radio discovered four promising Maori actresses, but because of limited opportunities only Hira Tauwhare (Talfrey) continued acting, overseas. Then *Porgy and Bess* brought a large number of Maoris into the exciting world of theatre. Eager to build on that experience, members of the cast formed the New Zealand Maori Theatre Trust in 1966 with the express aim of developing professional standards in the presentation of Maori arts and culture, past and present, as a national art form. For several years the Trust provided an important training-ground and support for Maori actors, mainly co-operating with other groups in production. In 1970 the Trust sent a party of thirty on a world tour which included Expo 70 in Japan. Since then it has been inactive, but its work was done. Maoris actors are now integrated into existing drama groups.

For me the most memorable of the productions in which the Maori Theatre Trust was involved was *He Mana Toa*, presented in small theatres to small audiences in Hamilton and Wellington in 1967. It consisted of two acts, the first re-telling the Maori myths from the emergence of Rangi and Papa to the death of Maui, and the second the story of the warrior chief Te Rauparaha. Working with a script by James Ritchie which gave structure with room for improvisation, the Maori actors re-created the familiar stories in song, dance and occasional dialogue drawing out the relevance of the past for the Maori present. Integrating a variety of art forms, *He Mana Toa* was an exciting glimpse of what cross-fertilization of Maori and Pakeha dramatic modes could produce. It has since been produced by at least one secondary school with a large Maori roll.

In 1968 Bruce Mason again widened the demand for Maori actors with two radio plays, *Mr Hongi* and *Awatea*, centred on roles written for Inia Te Wiata. Downstage Theatre produced *Awatea* in the Wellington Town Hall in 1969 with Inia Te Wiata as the blind *kaumātua*, George Henare as his errant son and a large cast of Maoris, again mostly amateurs. Maoris were similarly involved in the Palmerston North centenary production, *Papa-i-oeia*, which covered the area's history from its Maori beginnings. In the early seventies the Waihirere Maori Club mounted a production of *The Taiaha and the Testament*, a play about Te Kooti by Pakeha novelist Leo Fowler, and took it on tour through Poverty Bay and later the South Island, playing mainly to Maori audiences. Using material from Maori sources and checked and approved by the Ringatū Church, the play was well received, and moves are afoot to produce it professionally.

Finally in 1973 came the first play written by a Maori, Harry Dansey's *Te Raukura*, produced at the Auckland Festival with nearly fifty Maoris in the cast, and passages of Maori dialogue. The play itself was about episodes in the history of Maori-Pakeha confrontation of which most Pakehas are totally ignorant. In form the play broke no theatrical conventions, but Dansey reported that 'the Maori actors, once the Maori sentences began flowing from their lips could seldom resist the temptation of carrying on in Maori – departures from the script which were to me sheer delight' (Dansey, 1974: xi).

While most of the Maoris who took part in these large productions were amateurs, a significant number have been laying the foundations of professional careers. For several years Maori students have been graduating from the National Drama School to places in New Zealand's small professional companies. Bruce Mason, reviewing Auckland Festival productions for 1974, praised two Maori players from the professional Mercury Theatre and reported that the Director of the Mercury 'regarded as his major achievement for 1973 the sudden great leap forward into stellar prominence of Maori performers'. Where Maori actors were once confined to roles as non or southern-Europeans, it is now taken for granted that they can transcend such limitation, and they have been seen in roles ranging from Mark Antony in Shakespeare's *Antony and Cleopatra* to both the boy and the psychiatrist in Peter Shaffer's *Equus*.

The seventies have also seen an increase in the number and quality of films for cinema and television involving Maoris both before and behind the cameras. Several television series have presented Maori cultural groups in action-songs and *haka*. These however made little impact. Pakeha producers attempted to introduce variety by 'getting rid of the straight lines' (as one put it) and moving performers around under changing lights, but failed to explore the meaning of the songs or put them into context. *Tihe Mauriora*, a series with a team of Maori scriptwriters and a broader view of Maori culture, proved disappointingly static in studio sets but came alive on the two occasions the camera moved into Maori settings, to film an evening of Maori poetry in Ngāti Pōneke hall and Maoris and Pakehas learning together on a *marae* in a country town. The breakthrough came with *Pukemanu*, a drama series set in a culturally diverse New Zealand timber town, written by Pakeha writers with Maori advice. Maoris filled a variety of the smaller roles, and several of those who appeared regularly became personal friends in thousands of New Zealand sitting-rooms. *Tangi*, with Harry Dansey telling the story of an old man's mourning and burial from a script by Ernie Leonard (a Maori who played a leading role in one of the *Pukemanu* episodes), was a finalist in the Feltex TV Awards in 1972. Maoris have also appeared in dramatized historical documentaries playing among others James Carroll, Apirana Ngata and the Hauhau leader Tito-kowaru, and in *Uenuku*, a re-creation of a Maori legend with dialogue entirely in Maori. As a NZBC staff member, Derek Fox of Aitanga-ā-Māhaki was involved in current affairs and documentary program-mes on television in a variety of roles, including interviewer and producer; early in 1975 he was appointed Wellington editor for TV2. Among the finest films screened on New Zealand television in 1974 were the six in the series *Tangata Whenua*, made by a team of private film-makers including a part-Maori director. Living, sleeping, and eating with Maori communities in many parts of the country, this team so won the confidence of the people that they became active participants in the making of the film, allowing viewers to share their most personal and sacred experiences and speaking in Maori and English with moving vividness and honesty.

## Conclusion

For Maoris, art – in the broadest sense of the word – was and is very much a community concern, its forms associated with community activities and expressing community values. Far from being lonely outsiders and rebels, Maori artists have always been full and valued members of the community in touch with and expressing both its actualities and its ideals. This remains true today, not only for the practitioners of the traditional Maori arts but also for the many Maori artists (including writers and musicians) who are at present making a name for themselves on the national scene. Though they differ widely in the art forms and styles they favour, Maori artists are nearly all deeply engaged in the life of both the Maori and the wider New Zealand community. Their art is born out of involvement rather than individual agony, busy schedules rather than isolated introspection. Many are active in sport, a combination Pakehas find surprising. With rare exceptions, they address themselves to a wide audience, to kinsmen, neighbours and workmates, to Maoris *and* Pakehas not the artistic or intellectual élite. Yet at the same time they are pioneers, ahead of the rest of the community, creatively exploring the ways in which the Maori and Pakeha cultural heritages can fertilize each other.

One other thing they have in common – a fine disregard for conventional categories and divisions within the arts. Just as a master carver like Pine Taiapa was also a master of *tukutuku*, speech-making and story-telling, so many younger artists range across several fields, combining not only (for instance) painting with sculpture, but writing with painting or music. And they are particularly conscious of what they have to offer each other. In 1973 Hone Tuwhare, poet, and Para Matchitt, painter and sculptor, took the initiative in calling a Maori Artists' and Writers' Conference at the Te Kaha *marae*. Another was held at Takitimu *marae* in Wairoa in 1974, and the third at the Waitara *marae* in Taranaki in 1975. It is now assumed it will be an annual event.

'Maori culture' has always been given a special place in the field of the arts in New Zealand, but it has often been as a museum exhibit and tourist attraction rather than as part of the mainstream. There are signs that this is changing. Increasingly Maori artists and writers are receiving assistance from general sources such as the Queen Elizabeth II Arts Council, for the traditional as well as the non-traditional arts. Realizing that Maori art is perceived overseas as distinctive of New Zealand as a whole, the Government now gives subsidies and often representative status to Maori groups travelling overseas on their own initiative, and frequently selects Maori groups for official tours both on their own, as on a visit to Papua-New Guinea, in 1974, and in conjunction with other groups, for instance with the New Zealand Silver Band on two tours of North America, and with the New Zealand National Orchestra at the opening of the Sydney Opera House. Increasingly also Maoris are now participating in bodies concerned with the arts in virtue of their own achievements and not as representatives of the Maori minority. In 1975 for instance

Witi Ihimaera was appointed to the general Queen Elizabeth II Arts Council and Mrs Mira Szaszy to the Broadcasting Council of New Zealand.

## Postscript

Since this chapter was completed, I have become aware of the exciting work that has been done by the artist Cliff Whiting of Whānau-ā-Apanui working with local Maori communities as District Adviser in Arts and Crafts for the Education Department and latterly from a teachers' college. In an attempt to overcome the high costs of traditional materials and methods, Whiting and his co-workers have developed the use of modern materials in the traditional arts, especially particle- and hard-boards. By exploiting the qualities of these materials, they have created a new style, continuous with but departing significantly from, the old, inter-mixing carving, *tukutuku* and *kōwhaiwhai* in one continuous panel extending horizontally, widening the range of colours and achieving dramatic new shapes in *tukutuku*.

These concepts and processes have been used in a number of *marae* projects, notably in the Wanganui and eastern Bay of Plenty areas and in the mural in Kimiora at Tūrangawaewae executed under the direction of Para Matchitt with Education Department assistance in 1975. Of key importance in this development and a powerful example of it is a mural illustrating the myth of the separation of the primal parents Ranginui (Sky) and Papatūānuku (Earth) by their sons, a subject of deep significance to all the Maori tribes and to other peoples of the Pacific. Conceived and begun by Cliff Whiting in 1969 and completed with family help, this mural has been displayed in several places as example and inspiration, showing what can be achieved with limited financial resources and group co-operation. The centre section of this mural appears on the jacket of this book, depicting the god Tāne, his head firmly planted against his mother's breast, thrusting his father upwards with his feet in order to let light into the world. I chose it for the cover not only for its artistic quality but for what it says about the vitality and adaptability of the Maori people, who hold fast to the treasures of their ancestors by making them at home in the modern world.

# chapter 18

# Maori and Pakeha

New Zealanders are extremely proud of their reputation for good race relations. In official publications and speeches, they tell the world that 'Maoris and Pakehas live on terms of complete unity and equality' and 'get on better together than any other two races in the world'. But an American sociologist has attacked this claim as 'unwarrantably sanguine and complacent' (Ausubel, 1960), and a leading New Zealand scholar writes that 'if one gets even a little beneath the surface a less happy situation reveals itself' (Sutherland, 1952: 149). Maori-Pakeha relations may be relatively good on a world-wide basis, but they are not nearly as good as we like to think.

Though there is a large body of writing on the subject, much of it is impressionistic. The number of well-documented research studies has increased substantially in recent years, but they are generally limited in scope in terms of population, area or aspects covered. The situation is changing so quickly in so many ways that attempts become quickly out-of-date. (Beaglehole, 1946; James Ritchie, 1956b; Pearson, 1958; Ausubel, 1960a; Geddes, 1961; James Ritchie, 1963, 1964a; Thompson, 1963, 1964; Mol, 1964; Vaughan, 1964; Mol, 1966; Harre, 1966; Hartley and Thompson, 1967; Archer, 1970; McKean, 1971; Vaughan, 1972; Tatz, 1972; St George, 1973: Murray, 1974; Kawharu, 1975.)

## The legal situation

As we have seen, Maoris have the same basic rights as other citizens, but are also distinguished in law for certain purposes (chapter 4, p. 43). The exact status of these differentiating provisions is a matter of debate. The Government views them as ameliorative measures necessary to remove disabilities, but many Pakehas argue that they place Maoris in a position of privilege and discriminate against Pakehas. The United Nations Convention of Elimination of All Forms of Racial Discrimination 1965, based on the work of a Sub-Committee of the Commission on Human Rights, provides that special measures shall not be deemed racial discrimination if they are designed to ensure equal enjoyment or exercise of human rights and fundamental freedoms for particular groups or individuals and provided that they are not continued after that objective has been achieved. The discrepancies that still exist between Maori and non-Maori in a number of relevant areas explored in earlier chapters would seem to meet the United Nations requirements. Indeed, one recent commentator criticizes existing measures as not nearly substantial or effective enough (Ryan in McKean, 1971: 105).

Up until 1971 New Zealand had no general legislation controlling race relations and only two specific provisions, one authorizing the prosecution of hotel licensees for refusing to supply accommodation, meals or liquor 'by reason only of . . . race, colour, nationality, beliefs or opinions', and the other voiding any provision in a property disposition which prohibited or restricted possession on the grounds of race. In 1971 the Government passed a Race Relations Act 'to affirm and promote racial equality in New Zealand and to implement the International Convention on the Elimination of All Forms of Racial Discrimination'. This came into effect in April 1972. Though it avoids defining the term discrimination its overall effect is to identify as unlawful and punishable certain acts or omissions which discriminate against a person on the grounds of race, colour or national or ethnic origin with regard to public access to places, vehicles and facilities, provision of goods and services, employment, land, housing and other accommodation, advertisements and the liability of principals and employers. Section 9 of the Act specifically provides that the Act is not breached when an act is done or omitted in good faith to assist persons or groups of a particular race, colour or ethnic or national origin and when the latter need such assistance to achieve an equal place with other members of the community. The Act created the position of Race Relations Conciliator whose main functions are to investigate breaches of the Act either on complaint or on his own motion and to endeavour to secure a settlement and satisfactory assurance of non-repetition. When conciliation fails, the Conciliator advises the Attorney-General who may then initiate civil proceedings in the Supreme Court, which is empowered to grant an injunction against the defendant, to void any contract involved and to award damages.

The Act has been criticized, not least by the first Conciliator (Race Relations Conciliator, 1973: 8–10), firstly, for relying on complaints as the main basis of investigation when they are known to be a poor guide to the actual incidence of discrimination, and secondly for taking a merely negative approach and failing actively to promote equality. 'It savours too much of the ambulance at the bottom of the cliff rather than the fence at the top' (ibid.: 8). In particular, much could and needs to be done by providing money and full-time staff to undertake public education on this issue, actively to develop harmonious community relations and to co-ordinate on a national basis what is being done by official and voluntary agencies.

A Race Relations Office was set up in Auckland in 1972 with a full-time Race Relations Executive Officer and secretary; an Assistant Executive Officer was added to the staff in 1974. The first Race Relations Conciliator, Sir Guy Powles, who operated on a part-time basis from an office in Wellington, resigned in March 1973 because of pressure of other duties as Ombudsman. For two years the work was supervised by the Deputy Race Relations Conciliator, an Auckland magistrate. Harry Dansey (p. 271) was appointed Race Relations Conciliator in 1975. He also lives in Auckland.

Laws lay down the basic principles and the limits of permissible behaviour: they cannot ensure that people will obey them, nor touch their feelings, beliefs and attitudes. How do Maoris and Pakehas feel about and act towards each other? How freely do they mix? How do they see New Zealand and its future development?

### Regional variations

Before attempting to answer these questions, it is important to stress that Maori-Pakeha relations vary widely in different parts of the country, with differences in population ratio, history of contact, occupational status, and relationship with the land. There is (for instance) a marked contrast between the western, central areas of the North Island, where civil war, confiscation and temporary withdrawal left Maoris distrustful, outnumbered, and almost landless, and the East Coast, where Maoris outnumbered Pakehas, in parts own most of the land, and are often prosperous farmers. Marked differences also occur between rural and urban areas, and between one city and another, especially between those where Maoris comprise a substantial proportion of the population, are predominantly *tāngata whenua* and have ready access to rural *marae*, as in Rotorua and Gisborne, and those where Maoris are very much in the minority, predominantly 'immigrants' and a long way from their community of origin, as in Auckland, Wellington and Christchurch. Finally, in a few places, relations are or have been undeniably poor, mainly in market-garden areas where Maori migrants are employed in seasonal labouring.

Regional variations are compounded by migration and rapid social change. Readers are therefore warned that every generalization in the following pages will have some if not many exceptions and will be wide of the mark in some places at some times.

## Attitudes and stereotypes

Maoris and Pakehas are clearly aware of each other as different in appearance, in many ways of doing things, and to varying degrees in aims and values, though Maoris are generally more aware of differences of the latter sort than most Pakehas. Each group includes some who are violently prejudiced against members of the other and their ways, some who champion and profess and prefer them, and some whose views are fairly objective. I doubt if any of these three categories claims more than 10 per cent of the total group. In each case, at least two-thirds can safely be characterized as mildly prejudiced, not so much against the other group, as in favour of the members, customs, norms and values of their own.

Most Pakehas deny believing in the innate superiority of a white skin, but their conversation and behaviour seem frequently to be based on the assumption that Pakeha ways are superior and Pakehas as a group and as individuals more likely to behave acceptably by their standards. If pressed they would probably admit this assumption and justify it on the basis of Pakehas' longer experience of 'civilization'. Because the majority of Maoris are employed in un- and semi-skilled occupations and fall below the national average in living standards (measured in terms of income and possessions), housing and education, Pakehas tend to see 'Maori ways' as causally connected and practically synonymous with lower socio-economic status. 'Pakeha ways' by contrast are equated with middle- and upper-class socio-economic status. What is more, their views of Maoris and the Maori way of life is a static one, slow to recognize and incorporate change. They judge Maoris by an out-dated assessment of the latter's actual achievement, compared against their own ideal standards. When Maoris do even moderately well in some field of endeavour, many Pakehas express surprise and gratification, as if the Maoris had overcome a handicap. They maintain that they accept Maoris as equals 'if they live up to our standards': any barrier that exists is 'a social or behaviour barrier, not a colour bar'. But because colour is for Pakehas the major index of membership in the Maori group, judging Maoris on group membership inevitably involves pre-judgment in terms of colour. But in general, colour prejudice is not so deeply internalized that it cannot be modified by favourable experiences.

Most Maoris regard Pakehas they do not know or meet occasionally in formal and public situations with a mixture of reserve, suspicion and wary respect. They tend to let the Pakehas make the running, responding rather than taking the initiative. In at least some cases, this arises from internal acceptance of the idea of Pakeha superiority, an attitude of *whakamā* towards the dominant group. In most others it is partly a matter of traditional courtesy, which disapproves of pushing oneself forward, and partly rooted in secure possession of a world of their own. Even when closely associated with Pakehas over a long period in some particular sector of life, as employers or employees, workmates, members of the same church, frequenters of the same hotel bar and so on, Maoris often succeed in keeping the personal and especially the Maori side of their life and feelings virtually hidden from view, by never volunteering information and evading questions on the subject. This is at one and the same time a defensive tactic protecting what is dear from possible ridicule, ignorance or patronage, and a form of one-upmanship maintaining areas of life where they alone have knowledge and power. If many Pakehas, especially those who 'grew up with Maoris', confidently and fallaciously believe that the latter do not know or care much about their cultural heritage, the Maoris themselves must bear part of the responsibility. Nevertheless, to those Pakehas who do not think they know everything and are prepared to listen, learn and refrain from hasty judgments, most Maoris will eventually open their hearts in unstinted and enriching friendship.

In areas where Maoris were defeated, lost land and/or were otherwise pushed around by Pakehas there is still a residue of mistrust and hostility reinforced by resentment at loss of *mana* and the need to regain it, though even there personal friendships occur bridging the gap. Recently also among the educated and/or urban Maoris of the younger generations individuals and groups have emerged who do not hesitate publicly to articulate their resentment of Pakeha domination and the limitation of Maori access to social and political power and status in New Zealand society (see pp. 174–9). Though they have attracted criticism and rebuke from the older generation for trampling on Maori custom in some respects, they have also received a good deal of support and approval for the general tenor of their protest and above all for attacking the idea of Maori inferiority wherever it occurs, in Maoris as well as Pakehas.

Both groups have built up a set of stereotyped ideas about the other. Like most stereotypes, these use emotive words, involve value judgments, and concentrate on differences and disapproved or envied traits. In 1973 the *New Zealand Methodist* compiled the following stereotype of the Maori from a range of interviews and presented it for comment as a 'fair summary of typical Pakeha attitudes':

> The Maori is by nature a warm and generous person. He has a happy-go-lucky approach to life, loves an excuse for a holiday and doesn't take responsibilities like work and finance as seriously as the pakeha.
>
> He's not really intellectual, usually leaves school early, and does better at manual jobs like freezing worker or shearer or driving heavy machinery. His good physical co-ordination also helps him in games like rugby. He's a great fighter and makes a fine soldier.
>
> Music and singing is his great love. He has a natural sense of rhythm and harmony and is good on the guitar. He likes bright colours too.
>
> The Maori loves his children and favours large families. He always seems to have lots of relatives about, especially older people. Has a great sense of hospitality as part of his tribal heritage.
>
> His understanding of the law is different from the pakeha, simpler, often childlike. This gets him into trouble, especially his 'what's yours is mine' attitude.
>
> He's inclined to be overweight. That's probably because he likes his beer and favours a diet of fatty foods.
>
> He's shy by nature, but a good bloke when you get to know him. By and large he fits in well to pakeha life.

In contrast the average mildly prejudiced Maori characterizes Pakehas as hard-working, individualistic, and go-ahead, cold and unemotional in personal relations, caring mainly about his immediate family and neglecting other kin, always in a hurry, two-faced (saying one thing and thinking another), preoccupied with the pursuit of wealth and social status.

> The Maori . . . when he draws his stereotype of the European . . . sees a man who is fish-eyed, with a dull mind, walking about the streets not communicating with anyone; a man who sits behind a desk with thoughts going round and round in his mind . . . too wrapped up in himself and his own interests to be worried about anyone else. He sits on an isolated island, sufficient to himself (*Te Ao Hou*, June 1962: 18).

It will be noted that both stereotypes use the singular, betraying the common tendency to recognize the diversity within one's own group but deny it to the other, seeing its members as all alike.

Those Maoris and Pakehas who are highly prejudiced against or prejudiced in favour of the other group hold the general stereotype but evaluate its elements in stronger or milder terms, 'lazy' (for instance) as 'bone-lazy' or 'contented', 'mean' as 'miserly' or 'thrifty'. Neither stereotype is wholly unfavourable, and disapproval is often ambivalent, masking suppressed envy. 'Maoris don't get ulcers and mental breakdowns; perhaps they have the right idea after all.' 'They certainly know how to enjoy life.' Similarly, Maoris envy Pakehas their perseverance and ability to 'get things done'.

These stereotyped attitudes find expression in, and are reinforced by, many colloquialisms: 'Maori physical training' (dozing in the sun), 'Maori time' (well past that arranged), 'Hori' (transliteration of 'George', used as a generic name for Maoris), 'a Maori job' or 'a Hori job' (something poorly done or looked after), 'go back to the mat' (return to a free-and-easy, supposedly 'Maori' way of life); and, on the Maori side, 'gone Pakeha' (become selfish and mean), and 'a Pakeha trick' (taking advantage of someone). Use of such expressions is not, however, invariably condemnatory. A lot depends on who uses them, in what context and in what tone of voice. Maoris use them frequently to make fun of themselves, and they figure largely in verbal by-play between friends and workmates.

When they meet members of the other group who do not conform to their stereotype, both Maoris and Pakehas tend to classify them as exceptions. 'The Pakehas at work think Maoris are happy-go-lucky and never worry, so when I have ups and downs like them they say I am not a Maori.' Pakehas often say of Maori friends: 'But we don't think of him as a Maori', or 'she is just like a Pakeha'. Ausubel interpreted this as indicative of Pakeha contempt for Maoris. But Maoris do exactly the same thing. In their view, to describe a Pakeha as a Maori is the highest compliment they can pay him. Expression of strong prejudice is by no means an infallible guide to practice. Many Pakehas who are critical of Maoris as a group have Maori friends, and Maoris who distrust Pakehas in the abstract frequently take their troubles to a Pakeha friend or official.

### Discrimination

According to the dictionaries, the word 'discrimination' can be used to mean making either a simple distinction or an accurate and discerning distinction, but in international usage the term has long been accepted as signifying any conduct which denies to individuals or groups wished-for equality with others because they possess a certain status, i.e. differential treatment that is unjustified, unwanted and invidious. Discrimination in this sense undoubtedly does occur in New Zealand perpetrated by members of both Maori and Pakeha groups, but it is officially disapproved and outlawed, and so its occurrence is essentially covert, sporadic and individual.

Discrimination against Maoris occurs mainly in areas of public contact – in housing, employment and certain types of commercial service – and in urban areas where people's dealings are so often with strangers. Pakehas rarely discriminate against Maoris at the personal level when they find themselves in the same company, but those who wish can easily avoid meeting Maoris in situations of personal intimacy.

The code of ethics of the New Zealand Real Estate Institute includes an article which forbids members 'to accept any instruction or listing from a client or customer which requires the member to discriminate against any purchaser or tenant or against any other member of the public by reason only of the race, colour or ethnic or national origins of that person or any member of his family'. The president of the Institute told the Race Relations Conciliator that a complaint of racial discrimination against an institute member would be treated as a disciplinary matter but to date no such complaint had been laid (Race Relations Conciliator, 1973: 13). However in 1974 the Conciliator reported that the largest proportion of complaints received continued to be concerned with accommodation and that from analysis of the cases and discussions between the Executive Officer and numerous real estate agents it appeared that discrimination by landlords was quite commonplace, at least in Auckland, and was being passively encouraged by a large number of real estate agents who accept discriminatory instructions despite their being prohibited under the Race Relations Act. Many landlords and real estate agents revealed in discussion that they do stereotype and discriminate in their selection of tenants on an ethnic basis. Small-scale tests of the way hotels responded to applications from people with Maori and English names in the middle sixties suggested that discrimination might have occurred in one case in six, but other explanations were possible and the differences not statistically significant (James Ritchie, 1964a: 85–99).

In the past certain life assurance offices offered Maoris less favourable terms in insurance contracts because of the lower life expectancy and higher disease incidence among Maoris as a group. The Race Relations Conciliator established that insurance companies operating overseas made no such distinctions. Though they protested before the Race Relations Act was passed, the life assurance companies have since eliminated the differential treatment of policy holders.

Even before the Race Relations Act prevented preferential advertisements, landlords and employers commonly masked discrimination by simply telling Maori applicants the place was taken. Many such instances never come to light, the victim either accepting the brush off at face value or not knowing how to counter it. On the other hand actions that appear discriminatory sometimes prove on investigation to involve co-incidental or complicating factors which either clear the alleged culprit or make interpretation difficult. Since landlords and employers who discriminate against Maoris mostly do so from stereotyped views about their capacity as tenants or employees, there is an urgent need for research on the actual record in these areas of the groups concerned. Pierce made a useful contribution with his study of Maori work attendance (1969), but much more is needed (Lee, 1974). In co-operation with the Auckland branch of the Real Estate Institute, the Race Relations Office is currently undertaking research aimed at 'establishing whether Polynesians are a greater risk factor in the accommodation business; if there is a greater risk then in what areas, e.g. prompt payment of rent, care of facilities etc.; and determining what steps our society should take to overcome these factors if they are present.'

In a survey of treatment of Maoris in the Press in the 1950s Richard Thompson (1953–5) found a tendency for news media to give disproportionate coverage to adverse news about members of minority groups and to specify the race of a group member when it had no bearing on the issue. Periodically since then the Press has resolved to discipline itself in this regard but after a spell the standards set imperceptibly relax and these tendencies reappear. Overall however improvement has been substantial. In the last few years as Maori individuals and groups have become more outspoken in their criticism of the Pakeha establishment, the news media have helped and been used by them to reach a wide audience. Many however complain that the media highlight the controversial and militant elements in their utterances and actions and underplay or completely ignore what is moderate and constructive. This treatment is not reserved for members of minority groups – most public figures complain of it – but it has tended to exacerbate rather than improve inter-group relations. The news media also lay themselves open to the charge that they devalue the interests and language of minority groups and the contribution they have to make to New Zealand society by inadequate allocation of space and expertise. Despite some notable exceptions, staff of newspapers and broadcasting services generally present inter-group relations from a dominantly Pakeha perspective.

In his 1973 *Report* the Race Relations Conciliator made a distinction between 'racism', defined as discriminatory practices which stem from belief in the biological hereditary moral superiority of one race over another, and 'racialism', which describes discriminatory actions resulting from stereotyping with the implication of inferiority in only particular areas with the possibility of change. He commented that the majority of cases handled by his office so far had involved racialism rather than racism. Rejecting the terms 'white racism' and 'white institutional racism' used by some commentators as inapplicable, he thought that

> there is no or little racist intent in New Zealand either among citizens or in the system or in the way of life. I do not think that institutions within the New Zealand system discriminate purposely against citizens upon the ground of their race or colour. The problem is that most institutions in New Zealand are derived from and orientated towards the economic, social and spiritual ideals and practices of the white Anglo-Saxon.

The Race Relations Conciliator noted a tendency for the alleged offenders he interviewed to disclaim discriminatory intention and/or plead mitigating or justifying circumstances. In general, conciliation was successful in the cases referred to him or the case was dropped as non-proven or because the complaint was withdrawn. There has been only one prosecution to date. It would however be dangerous to take this as indicating that discrimination is minimal, as overseas experience shows that those with the strongest cases rarely complain.

Even before the Race Relations Act prescribed legal penalties, discrimination attracted adverse publicity, disapproval and counter-action when exposed dramatically enough. When Dr Henry Bennett was refused service in the private bar of an Auckland hotel in 1959, the story appeared in newspapers throughout the country, followed by a flood of protest letters; the Prime Minister and Attorney General publicly affirmed Maori rights; and the restriction was immediately lifted by the hotel owners (Harre, 1962). Similarly, the principal of a small-town high school was widely reported when he complained that a pupil with excellent qualifications had been refused local employment because he was Maori. Questions were asked in Parliament, the employer concerned claimed it was all a misunderstanding, and the boy was offered several other local positions.

The decision of the New Zealand Rugby Union to omit Maoris from the team chosen to tour South Africa in 1960 provoked a storm of controversy (Thompson, 1964: 39–55). For over eighteen months, the newspapers reported a continual stream of protests from churches, trade unions, student, civic and professional bodies, and printed almost daily columns of letters. Local protest groups amalgamated into a national Citizens' All-Blacks Tour Association with the slogan 'No Maoris No Tour', and a deputation of leading citizens presented a petition to the Prime Minister. The NZRU would not debate the issue, maintaining that they were acting in the Maoris' own interests, to spare them embarrassment. The Government refused to interfere in the activities of a private sporting association, and the team departed without Maoris. In 1965, with another tour in view, the South African Government gave notice that a New Zealand team including Maoris would not be accepted. The NZRU then decided not to send a team on the terms indicated. In 1970 the South African Government accepted a completely representative New Zealand team, but though the tour took place the controversy continued, centring now on the non-representative nature of the South African team. The 1973 tour of New Zealand by the Springboks was cancelled on these grounds at the request of the Government. Throughout the debate Maoris like Pakehas have been divided on the issue, some supporting continuance of the tour exchange for reasons of courtesy, hospitality and love of the game, while others see it as part of the struggle to achieve equality for themselves and other non-whites.

As Maoris make accusations of discrimination more publicly, more often and less politely, there is a tendency for Pakehas, including some in official positions, to react defensively, making counter-accusations of exaggeration or trouble-making. Nevertheless the situation is probably healthier today in most ways than when such views did not come to expression.

Maoris have far fewer opportunities for discriminating against Pakehas than vice versa because they are in the minority and include comparatively few landlords and employers. Maoris can and do express resentment of Pakehas by withholding co-operation, talking Maori in their presence, and giving misleading information. Communities connected with the King Movement and the Ringatū Church excluded Pakehas entirely from their gatherings until fairly recently, but have now relaxed their guard. While they have no compunction in turning sightseers away from their gatherings, Maoris welcome Pakehas who are genuinely sympathetic. But they often treat them as guests of honour or elect them to office, consciously or unconsciously limiting intimacy by placing them in positions of superiority.

Racial abuse and name-calling is generally disapproved by Maori and Pakeha though not expressly included in the Race Relations Act. It does however occur in certain situations of extreme tension between members of the two groups, for instance in confrontation between young Maoris and the police and in the grounds of city schools with a high proportion of reluctant learners. It is used by Pakehas as a substitute for physical aggression, which however it frequently sparks off in the victims, and by Maoris as a response to feeling belittled and harassed by Pakehas in a stronger position, either individually or collectively. At present, since it is not expressly identified as an offence, the abused are likely to be charged with assault while the abuser goes unpunished, though the courts may accept abuse in extenuation.

### Social relations

Maoris and Pakehas mix fairly freely in a public and semi-public context: at school, at work, in clubs, at places of public entertainment, at church and community gatherings. However, in areas where they are in the minority, Maoris are commonly under-represented in local associations and often maintain separate Maori ones, feelings of *whakamā* – mingled shyness and resentment in the face of Pakeha pressure – combining with the greater comfort of 'being among your own'. However, in urban suburbs where Maoris form a significant proportion of a population of generally similar economic status, occupying State rental houses or homes of their own in the less expensive bracket, distinctions tend to break down as residents combine to counter adverse publicity and fight for public amenities.

At the informal, highly personal level, mixing is more limited, both Maoris and Pakehas tending to choose most of their friends from their own group. Over New Zealand as a whole, the substantial majority of Pakehas, especially in the middle and upper classes, have never had Maoris in their home or visited a Maori home or *marae*, and though Maoris are in the minority there are many who have never entertained or been entertained privately by Pakehas. However, relations are free and warm in many remote, back-country communities, church groups, and professional circles; and elsewhere inter-group friendship and home visiting are steadily increasing as Maoris move into residential areas and occupations that have hitherto been predominantly Pakeha preserves, and especially as they establish urban *marae* and Maori clubs as part of the urban scene. Without exception, these accept Pakehas as members on the basis of marriage to Maori members or of genuine interest in Maoritanga. On their side, more and more Pakehas are attracted to these centres for the interest and fellowship they afford.

Prejudice on both sides is undoubtedly a factor in limiting intimacy between Maoris and Pakehas; but it is only one of several. In many areas there are few Maoris and in some few Pakehas with whom to be on visiting terms. The concentration of Maoris in the lower socio-economic classes leads to differences in interests and patterns of behaviour. The Maoris themselves choose to withdraw periodically for gatherings organized 'the Maori way' for Maori ends, though always welcoming Pakehas prepared to participate. They prefer the company of other Maoris because they have known them longer, speak the same language literally and figuratively, and generally 'know where we are with them'. Both Maoris and Pakehas often hesitate to accept invitations from members of the other group for fear of 'intruding' or 'doing the wrong thing'.

## Intermarriage

One of the tests of the quality of inter-group relations is the proportion and fate of couples who intermarry. Since race is not recorded in the marriage register there is no direct measure of intermarriage but indirect evidence and observation suggest that it has increased substantially especially in the 1950s and 1960s. A continuing decrease in the proportion of persons who declare themselves as Maoris especially full Maoris on the census schedule may reflect increases in intermixing, but may also be the result of changes in self-identification. More useful figures are provided by the Statistics Department's survey of Maori children in the Auckland Province, which indicates an increase in the proportion of children of Maori descent who have one Pakeha parent from 13 per cent in 1956 to 25 per cent in 1966 (Statistics, New Zealand Department of, 1969: 19–20). Harre (1966) estimated that 42 per cent of the Maoris who married in Auckland in 1960 and 3·7 per cent of the Pakehas married members of the other group. Three out of five of these marriages were between Pakeha men and Maori women, two out of five between Maori men and Pakeha women. In the 1970s intermarriage has become so relatively common that it no longer attracts particular interest or public attention.

Several investigators have reported strong disapproval of intermarriage among Pakehas, mainly in terms of expressed views (Ausubel, 1960a; Beaglehole, 1946; James Ritchie, 1963, 1964a; Vaughan, 1964). Harre, working in the early 1960s, investigated not only attitudes but what happened in seventy-three actual cases. He found that most of the Pakeha and many of the Maori parents disapproved of the match when it was first proposed, the former because of an unfavourable stereotype of Maoris, the latter because they wanted their children to marry and remain Maoris; but their objections normally broke down when they got to know the chosen spouse personally. Few parents or kin did not attend the wedding. Both sets of parents exchanged visits, gifts and assistance with the couple involved as frequently as with their other children, and treated their grandchildren with the usual mixture of pride and indulgence. Half the couples had no problem of adjustment, either because they shared the same cultural pattern or because the Maori partner was at home in both cultures. Most of the rest worked out a satisfactory balance between conflicting cultural loyalties.

The mixed couples Harre studied did not retreat into special mixed groups but found a place either in completely integrated groups or in outrigger groups attached to predominantly Maori or Pakeha groups. Mixed couples who were culturally Pakeha stressed their children's Maori ancestry as a matter of pride, basing it, however, on Maori achievements in the past rather than the present. Children of mixed parentage endured some taunting at school but few showed signs of significant inner tensions over identification or abnormal tendencies to delinquency.

Harre studied only couples whose marriage had lasted. What proportion of inter-group marriages break down primarily because of the extra strains involved, and what changes have occurred in the last ten years or so it is impossible to guess.

### Models of Maori-Pakeha relations

In the history of Maori-Pakeha relations since the Treaty of Waitangi, a key part has been played by the models people have used to help them understand the current situation and to provide an ideal to work towards. A model is a construction made to reduce a complex reality to simpler, manageable proportions. The making of a model necessarily involves selectivity and interpretation: what features we select to emphasize and what we play down or leave out depends on our purpose, our basic assumptions and our general view of life. As a result people with different goals and values can develop different models of the same situation. This is what has happened in New Zealand race relations. Maoris and Pakehas have interpreted, and to a large extent still do interpret, the situation differently; and the policy of the Government and the theoretical formulations of the scholars have changed over time with changes both internally and on the wider world scene.

In this connection it can be useful to make a distinction between 'models of' the present and 'models for' the future, between a view of what is happening and a vision of what should be planned for. The two are always related, but the relation may be one of congruity or opposition. In some cases people's model for the future – what they want to see happen – affects their view of the present. Many New Zealanders, including most Pakehas, allow their desire for unity and harmonious race relations to persuade them that the latter already exist and this in turn leads them to reject any alternative view as 'rocking the boat' or 'creating divisions'. Others, including most Maoris, judge the present situation harshly by the light of their ideals.

An adequate study of the various models that have been and are being used in New Zealand would require a book of its own. Here I propose to concentrate on those which it seems to me are of major significance, either because they have been or are widely held or because they have had an important influence in stimulating or inhibiting action. In examining these models we are seeking not to identify them as right or wrong, but first to understand them in terms of the identity and aims of their makers and secondly to assess their usefulness in providing a stimulus and guide to effective action. Nor should it be assumed that they are mutually exclusive: some are obviously variations on a basic theme, and others have more in common than at first appears.

## Amalgamation

When Britain assumed sovereignty over New Zealand in 1840, the British administrators rejected proposals for confining Maoris to reserves beyond the settler pale and adopted a policy of amalgamation, which aimed to incorporate Maoris into one British-style state system on an equal footing with Pakeha settlers. However, ethnocentric assumptions of the superiority of British institutions and settler hostility combined to leave the Maori 'exposed to the impositions of state power without any share in the exercise of state power' (Ward, 1973, especially pp. 30–40). Amalgamation in practice meant assimilation.

## Assimilation

From the time that New Zealand became self-governing in 1952, until the Hunn Report was published in 1961, the Government, overwhelmingly Pakeha in membership and outlook, pursued an official policy of assimilation. Both in and outside the Government, most Pakehas took it for granted that their culture was more 'advanced' in every way, in economic organization and technology, in law, religion, art, manners etc., and that contact must inevitably result in the 'less advanced' giving way before the 'more advanced'. Land and educational policies were aimed at 'releasing' Maoris from attachment to their land, language and tribe and fitting them for full participation in New Zealand social and economic life. Maoris were perceived as progressively abandoning the ways of their ancestors, adopting Pakeha ones in their stead, and with intermarriage hastening the process, becoming physically and culturally more and more like Pakehas until New Zealanders were literally one people, all brown-eyed and faintly copper-coloured. Many Pakehas regretted the passing of a way of life that was colourful and had its own strengths, but saw it as a choice between assimilation and extinction. While these attitudes arose largely from the settlers' own background and experience, they chimed in with the social Darwinism which dominated social philosophy both in the universities and in government circles in Western countries until well into this century. Viewed from today's perspective, assimilation is easily interpreted as 'white racism', but it was relatively liberal in the context of its time in that it assumed at least in theory that Maoris had the intelligence and ability to make the transition to a more 'advanced' cultural level, and that culture not colour was the criterion of acceptability.

The first scholars to undertake fieldwork in Maori communities worked with scholarly variants of the assimilation model, based on theories of 'acculturation' currently being developed in United States universities. Harry Hawthorn's study of a Far North community (*The Maori: A Study in Acculturation*, 1944) was mainly descriptive and as a Memoir of the American Anthropological Association did not have a wide distribution in New Zealand. The work of Ernest and Pearl Beaglehole, *Some Modern Maoris* (1946), had greater impact for it was published in New Zealand and contained detailed recommendations for action. On the basis of fieldwork in Kowhai in the southern North Island, the Beagleholes suggested that Maori child-rearing practices and family life developed an adult 'character structure' which was maladapted to the dominantly Pakeha world in which their lives were set. Since this maladjustment caused personal unhappiness and tension and conflict between Maoris and Pakehas, they recommended extensive educational changes aimed at making Maori character-structure more congruent with the majority culture. Although their interpretation and conclusions have ultimately proved unacceptable, *Some Modern Maoris* was a major contribution to Pakeha understanding of the Maori way of life, for the Beagleholes recorded life in Kowhai in the late thirties with insight and sympathy.

In the middle fifties a group of Ernest Beaglehole's students led by James Ritchie made a field-study of personality development in Rakau in the Bay of Plenty and in presenting their results developed the concepts of an 'acculturation gradient' and an 'index of Maoriness'. The former was a unilineal continuum visualized as extending from Aboriginal Maori through stages characterized by progressive loss of Maori Culture to a final stage of Complete Assimilation. By investigating their attitudes and behaviour on a number of specific points such as ability to speak Maori and attendance at *tangihanga*, it was proposed that individual Maoris could be rated on an index of Maoriness and located as having advanced less or more along this one-way highroad (Jane Ritchie, 1964). This theory treated Maori and Pakeha cultures as static wholes, one located in the past and so essentially out-of-date and out-of-place in the modern world and the other located in the present and essentially modern. It assumed the dominance and historical if not moral superiority of Pakeha culture, and underrated the vitality and adaptability of Maori culture (Metge and Campbell, 1958). I have however presented the acculturation gradient theory in the past tense, for its two main exponents, James and Jane Ritchie, have moved progressively away from it in later writing to develop a sympathetic appreciation of the strengths and continuing viability of 'the Maori way'. (James Ritchie's text accompanying Ans Westra's photographs in *Maori* is a particularly sensitive and informative introduction to Maori life, and he fought untiringly for the establishment of the Maori Studies Research Centre at Waikato University.) Nevertheless, while the Ritchies should be valued primarily for their recent work, both their formulation of the acculturation gradient model and their ultimate abandonment of it were in their day useful contributions to the ongoing debate on Maori-Pakeha relations, which helped others develop their own stands on the matter, if only in opposition.

Though the word itself is less openly used, since the Government abandoned assimilation as official policy in 1961, many Pakehas still hold to the basic premises of the assimilation model. Over the years some Maoris accepted assimilation as a model for their own lives, sometimes finding advancement and satisfaction, sometimes disillusionment. But the large majority have resisted it strenuously, using strategies varying from withdrawal to 'beat them at their own game'.

'When Pakehas tell us we ought to assimilate', their speakers say, 'it is like a shark saying "let's assimilate" to a kahawai and then opening his mouth and swallowing him for breakfast.'

As this metaphor points out, the imagery of the assimilation model is that of the digestive tract, and it implies the inferiority of that which is ingested. Many experienced commentators, Maori and Pakeha, have suggested that continuing divergence from Pakeha patterns of educational achievement, occupational distribution and law observances may be interpreted as evidence of resentment, frustration and rejection of assimilative pressures from the Pakeha majority.

### Emergent development and cultural symbiosis

Maori aspirations to maintain their cultural identity found a champion in Ralph Piddington who arrived to fill the newly established Chair of Anthropology at the University of Auckland in 1950. On the basis of fieldwork in Australia and Canada and a solid theoretical training, Piddington rejected the view that acculturation was necessarily a one-way process and introduced two new concepts into the discussion.

The first was 'emergent development' which he defined as the positive and spontaneous emergence of new types of social institutions

305

within cultures undergoing change. The second, 'cultural symbiosis' borrowed a term used in biology to describe the co-existence of two organisms of different type in a relation of mutual helpfulness.

Applying these ideas to the Maori case, Piddington insisted that Maori culture was not a static harmonious whole belonging to the past and being eroded by acculturation, but a dynamic living organism continually developing by combining elements taken from both Maori and Pakeha cultures to produce new forms.

> We have here a people who under the impact of European culture have condensed centuries of material progress into a little over a hundred years. And they have done this without renouncing their cultural heritage, particularly so far as values and the organization of interpersonal relations are concerned. They may not have got the best of both worlds, but they have certainly acquired a substantial share of the advantage of each (Piddington in Schwimmer, 1968: 264).

At first inclined to feel that relatively low economic status was the social price that Maoris had to pay for 'mental integrity', Piddington later argued strongly that maintenance of Maori social values could be reconciled with the goals of material progress.

The terms 'emergent development' and 'cultural symbiosis' never caught on in New Zealand. Piddington published relatively little and late and failed to integrate the two ideas in a single theory or to test them against field data. The idea of symbiosis is a rather static concept that conflicts with the essential dynamism of emergent development and the term itself is rather too technical for most New Zealanders. Piddington's was nevertheless a highly significant contribution for he travelled and spoke widely, influencing and encouraging many students, officials and ordinary citizens, especially those who (like myself) reacted intuitively against the assimilation model and were looking for a theoretical base for an alternative.

*Integration*

As a result of representations from Maori leaders such as Ngata and scholars such as Piddington, increasing employment of Maoris in government departments, and a growing appreciation of the Maori point of view among senior officers, the Government gradually modified its policy of assimilation, introducing a system of local Maori Committees and introducing subsidies on *marae* building and improvement in the forties and fifties.

In 1961 after publication of the Hunn Report the Government

finally abandoned assimilation as its policy in favour of 'integration'. The Hunn report defined this as 'to combine (not fuse) the Maori and Pakeha elements to form one nation wherein Maori culture remains distinct' (Hunn, 1961: 15). A fuller statement (Hunn and Booth, 1962) did not greatly clarify the issue but speeches by Ministers of Maori Affairs and their departmental officers over the years suggest that the Government sees integration as involving two main aims and lines of attack: first the elimination of differences that involve inequality and discrimination, and second, helping Maoris retain their language and culture in so far as they wish to do so. The National Government which was in power from 1955 to 1972 laid the main stress on the first of these objectives and to that end stepped up the provision of housing, set up the Maori Education Foundation and the trade training schemes, and in 1967 passed an Amendment to the Maori Affairs Act aimed at reducing the restrictions on individual owners of Maori land (see p. 111).

With regard to the second aim, they introduced a scheme for subsidizing *marae* building and renovation (within limits) and established the Maori Arts and Crafts Institute at Rotorua; but in general they waited for the initiative to come from the Maori people before taking action. During its term in office 1972–5, the Labour Government introduced a considerable body of legislation relating to both aims, but it remains to be seen how effectively this is implemented in action.

Ordinary citizens, Maori and Pakeha, tend to have very confused and varying ideas on the meaning of integration, perhaps because it is widely used in other contexts. Academic attempts to give it precision are ignored (e.g. Metge in Brookes and Kawharu, 1967: 41–56). But varying meanings lead to a great deal of misunderstanding.

Most Pakehas do not seem to distinguish 'integration' very clearly from 'assimilation', using the former more because it has official endorsement. They generally place the primary emphasis on the need to improve Maori living standards, education and occupational range as the one essential condition of integration. Correct these discrepancies, they assume, and other problems, like high convictions and 'gangs' will be reduced to 'normal' i.e. Pakeha proportions. They talk about 'integrating the Maori into New Zealand society', a turn of phrase that equates New Zealand with Pakeha society and confirms Maori suspicions that they see integration as assimilation with a new name.

As far as Maori culture is concerned, Pakehas are happy for Maoris to maintain those aspects which have entertainment value, especially when they can be employed in the tourist industry and called upon to give New Zealand a distinctive image overseas, but they tend to assume that many other 'Maori ways' such as large families, hospitality and frequent attendance at *hui* are causally connected with lower socio-economic status and that improvement in the latter will automatically involve if not depend on their abandoning the former.

Maoris generally prefer 'integration' to 'assimilation' as a word and as a policy, but from time to time express serious doubts whether it is in fact any different, at least in terms of its implementation. In particular Maoris of all generations have criticized the 1967 Maori Affairs Amendment Act, the moving of country folk to the cities in relocation schemes, and the pepper-potting of Maori homes among Pakehas as assimilative in effect, and the aid given to encourage the preservation of Maori culture as too little and too late (Presbyterian Church, 1961).

### Inclusion and biculturalism

In his introduction to *The Maori People in the Nineteen Sixties*, editor Eric Schwimmer dismissed the term integration as ambiguous and tendentious and proposed replacing it by two more specific terms, 'inclusion' and 'biculturalism' (1968: 9–64).

'Inclusion' is a term first used by the American sociologist Talcott Parsons to refer to 'full membership in the societal community', the basic requirements for which are 'equal civil rights . . . a full sharing in the pursuit of the collective goals of the society – in the processes of government and the exercise of power . . . [and] equality of the resources and capacities necessary to make "equal rights" into fully equal opportunities.'

Inclusion does not imply assimilation but under inclusion 'allegiance to ethnic or religious groups will be one involvement which cuts across many other involvements of the same people'. By these criteria, the Maoris are not as yet fully 'included' in the New Zealand community: their inclusion is a goal that still has to be worked for.

However the Maoris do not simply wish to be included instead of rejected: they have a culture which they want to maintain and to have recognized as a contribution to the New Zealand culture as a whole. To meet these aspirations, Schwimmer proposes that the concept of 'inclusion' be complemented by that of 'biculturalism'. In the New Zealand situation, where everyone gives primary allegiance to one culture learnt in childhood, he defines biculturalism as meaning, in the first place, accepting the values of a second culture as legitimate, being to some extent familiar with them and being able to turn to them if necessary for subsidiary relations. Virtually all Maoris are bicultural in this sense, and some Pakehas. But Schwimmer widens the concept to include 'the ability to see two sides of the question', involving 'the conscious confrontation and reconciliation of two conflicting value systems, both of which are accepted as valid'. Bicultural individuals are continually faced with having to make a choice between two alternative correct ways of acting involving a value conflict. They may choose one or the other or they may work out a solution which keeps in check the contradiction between the patterns – a genuinely bicultural solution. 'In a bicultural society each society makes use of the other.'

At the present time New Zealand as a nation has achieved 'little more than a tentative biculturalism in principle . . . biculturalism is a Maori aspiration which is still – though to a diminishing extent – resisted by Europeans.' Genuine progress requires that biculturalism should become an accepted fact at the top administrative level and widely among Pakehas as well as Maoris in the country as a whole.

Schwimmer holds that biculturalism is compatible with inclusion as long as it is kept within certain limits. There must be an overcapping set of values common to both groups to which both are willing to give ultimate primacy. At the time of writing Schwimmer saw this overcapping set of values as derived almost entirely from Pakeha sources. While this was unlikely to change to a fundamental extent, he believed there was plenty of scope for the development and incorporation of Polynesian variants as integral parts of national institutions. The advantages of inclusion are obvious, and the Maoris themselves have shown that they want it by constantly making concessions in relation to land, social organization, education, economics and everyday behaviour. Biculturalism also should be deliberately fostered because it makes New Zealand culture richer and more stimulating and because the Maoris themselves have chosen and pursued this course with great tenacity.

Like Piddington's, Schwimmer's contribution has greatly stimulated discussion at the academic level, but the terms inclusion and biculturalism have hardly passed into general currency or displaced integration as he hoped. Schwimmer's definitions of these terms are perhaps rather too involved for easy handling. In the case of biculturalism in particular he fails to clarify the different values of the word when it occurs in the compounds 'bicultural individual', 'bicultural society', 'bicultural solution' and 'bicultural institution', or to show how these are related to each other. More importantly the concept has proved unnecessarily restrictive because of its stress on two main groups. Over the last few years, the word that has gained most ground in popular usage in New Zealand is 'multi-cultural', which is used on the one hand to describe New Zealand as a nation composed of several cultural groups, and on the other for events and institutions deliberately constructed out of elements from several cultures, such as the gathering at Waitangi to mark the first New Zealand Day in 1974 and the multi-cultural centres that are just getting off the ground in several cities.

### One people – but one culture or many?

When advocates of multi-culturalism champion the right of the Maoris and other minority groups to be actively assisted to maintain their cultural identity, many Pakehas react defensively, accusing them of creating divisions and disturbing national unity. They stress that we are 'one people', not Maori and Pakeha but 'all New Zealanders', sharing a common culture which binds together contributions from groups of diverse origins. For 'assimilation' this view substitutes the idea of 'fusion' in which elements from a variety of cultures are combined to form a new and distinctive whole, losing their identity in the process like the elements that are fused in a chemical compound or the making of a cake. This 'one people – one culture' model has been forcefully presented in print by two prominent New Zealanders, Ian Cross, Editor of the *New Zealand Listener*, and Robert Muldoon, who became Prime Minister late in 1975.

In a *New Zealand Listener* Editorial (24 September 1973), Ian Cross wrote:

> Some recent discussion about race relations is using 'Maori' and 'European' to mean distinct and separate peoples, and to suggest that each 'race' also has a 'culture'. . . . The amount of inter-marriage indicates that a high degree of physical and social compatibility exists between 'Maori' and 'European' peoples and makes nonsense of claims for a separation of racial identity. . . . There are differences among us, which reflect our heterogeneous origins. But what we have in common is overwhelmingly greater than what separates us. . . . We should take pride in things 'Maori' because of their great value, without believing they betoken anything apart and separate within New Zealand. . . . The New Zealand of the middle twenty first century will be equally as distant, socially and culturally, from the past of our 'Irish', 'Scots', 'English', 'Dutch', 'Jugoslav' and other races as it will be from our Maori past . . . we New Zealanders are one people together on a common voyage to an irresistible future.

Writing in his weekly column in the *Dominion* (16 November 1974) Robert Muldoon, then Leader of the Opposition, criticized the

Government for treating New Zealanders as 'two races, Maoris and others', and insisted that

> since the Treaty of Waitangi we have been . . . 'tatau-tatau' – one
> people. It is true that we are a multi-cultural race, and that is
> something which adds strength to the New Zealand character. We
> have the multi-culture of the British Isles . . . Maori culture, and
> this goes beyond the more obvious manifestations which we
> demonstrate to our visitors . . . our Chinese New Zealanders . . .
> the various Pacific Island communities, our Jugoslavs, the Indians
> and . . . the Dutch, each have brought their own cultural tradi-
> tions to add to the vital mixture that is the New Zealand people.
> We are not, in this country, Maoris and others. We are tatau-tatau
> – one people. It is our task to take what is good from the culture
> of each of our ethnic groups and reject what does not help New
> Zealanders to a fuller and better life.

This particular model is based on a high valuation of national unity and desire to recognize the contribution of other groups besides Maori and Pakeha, sentiments that are entirely laudable and shared by the advocates of multi-culturalism.

I personally have both sympathy and respect for the exponents of this model with their stress on unity and equality; but I cannot help feeling that their concern with unity blinds them to fallacies in their argument.

First, they seem to equate unity with absence of differences, that is, with uniformity and homogeneity. But there are other forms of unity which require and make use of differentiation and diversity. There is for instance the oneness of a rope woven out of several separate strands and, an even more powerful analogy, the oneness of the human body, which functions because it is made up of non-identical parts. Related to this definition of oneness as homogeneity is a ten-dency to interpret 'difference' as 'division'. But differences, whether in personality, abilities, or ways of doing things do not necessarily spell separation and hostility: they can equally well be the basis of co-operation and enrichment, stimulating creativity. In fact, co-operation cannot occur between individuals or groups unless they are different in at least some ways. Thirdly, however desirable the model is as a blueprint for the future, cultural differences do exist, or at the very least are believed to exist by many people, and refusing to see them won't make the differences, or people's perceptions of them, go away. Lastly, because existing institutions and laws are built on a Pakeha cultural base, the contribution of the minority groups is almost inevitably reduced to trimmings – the icing on, or the flavouring in, the cake – unless special steps are taken to redress the balance.

In New Zealand today Pakeha culture is what linguists call the 'un-marked category', the basis we take for granted as a fish takes water for granted. It is the other minority cultures we find remarkable. As a *Dominion* editorial put it (24 March 1970) 'the Pakeha takes it for granted his traditions will be accepted and even prevail, the Maori must fight to preserve his – let alone win Pakeha acceptance'.

There are I think very few Pakehas or Maoris who would reject 'one people' as a model of the present or of the future, though some prefer the wording 'one nation'. The debate really centres around the second half of the formula: whether to insist on 'one culture' as well or to recognize and encourage diversity of cultures within the national framework. Those who favour 'one culture' are afraid that recognizing many would be divisive. Those who favour recognizing and encouraging diversity of cultures argue that it is the best way to achieve a true unity, because only where we recognize that others see and do things differently can we set about listening to and learning from each other.

The translation of *tātau-tātau* as 'one people' fails to do justice to the subtle implications of that phrase. Where English has three plural pronouns, us, you and them, Maori has four: *mātau* or *mātou* (us here), *koutou* (you over there), *rātou* (them), and *tātau or tātou* (you-and-us-together as distinct from them). The significance of the usage is well exemplified on the *marae* where we the hosts (*mātau*) welcome you the guests (*koutou*) and then ask you to join us in an integrated group (*tātau*) to welcome the next group of visitors (pp. 250–4). The literal meaning of *tātau-tātau* is 'you and us – us and you'. It stresses oneness – but the oneness of a group made up of at least two constituent sub-groups.

## Maori models

As we have already seen, the assimilation model is completely un-acceptable to most Maoris. In the course of the last two hundred years Maoris have formulated and put into practice a variety of specific models at different times and places. Scholars are only now, with growing awareness of the importance of the Maori sources and ability to tap them, beginning to explore these models both as formu-lated and as worked out in practice, and I cannot possibly review them in detail. It has been suggested that they fall into two main groups, those which emphasize separation and Maori autonomy, and those which take the road of accommodation and co-operation with Pakehas. I personally feel that this sets up a false dichotomy and prefer to see them as ranged upon a continuum with the theoretical poles of complete separation from and rejection of the Pakeha at one end and

complete assimilation at the other. While admitting that my knowledge on this topic is far from complete, I would seriously suggest that
nearly all the really significant Maori models, including those which
Pakehas saw and see as separatist, fall into the middle sector of this
continuum, fairly close to one side or the other of a middle point. In
other words, they all contain elements of both separation and co-
operation, conservatism and adaptability, in varying proportions and
arrangements, and they all involve a strong desire to retain and not
lose a Maori identity. Those models which involved physical separation in communities composed of and run by Maoris like those in the
King Country, Parihaka, Maungapohatu and Ratana Pa, also involved the adaptation of many features borrowed from Pakeha culture: agricultural and industrial techniques, literacy, the Bible and
many Christian beliefs, bakeries, banks and judicial machinery, maintenance of economic and diplomatic relations with the Government
and continued allegiance to the Crown, perceived as above and beyond
the Government of the day. Those models which involved direct
participation in, for instance, the major Christian churches, the
schools, the employment system, and Parliament, very often did so at
their own express wish, through the medium of Maori sections and
Maori offices, and when 'Maori ways' appeared to lose ground it was
the leaders who were successful and at home in the Pakeha world who
led the Maori renaissance (Butterworth, 1972).

Today at Maori gatherings and in private conversations, it is impossible not to be struck by the frequency with which Maoris quote
two sayings: 'Hold fast to your Maoritanga', attributed to James
Carroll, and Ngata's poem, '*E tipu, e rea*', printed at the beginning of
chapter 12. The first is sometimes interpreted, mainly by Pakehas
taking it in isolation on face value, as a call to separatism, but it was
said and meant to be applied in the context of full involvement in a
social system embracing Maori and Pakeha. (Carroll was, let it not be
forgotten, MP for a non-Maori electorate for twenty-six years.) Carroll intended it as a counterweight not to considered but to uncritical
adoption of Pakeha ways, and he refused to indicate in detail how
it was to be done, leaving it to others to work out a variety of strategies.
In the poem, '*E tipu, e rea*', Ngata advised young Maoris to seek both
the cultural treasures of their ancestors which he associated as a
*tikitiki* (topknot) with the head, a very *tapu* part of the body, and the
technical skills of the Pakeha, to be grasped with the hands, representing the practical (*noa*) aspect of man; but he linked them in the context of a wider allegiance to God, who created all things – including
*both* Maori and Pakeha. Thus while Ngata contrasted Maori and
Pakeha ways and stressed the differences, he also saw them as comple-
ments of each other and capable of integration into a greater whole.

The popularity of these two sayings suggests that they correspond to or express the model held consciously or unconsciously by most Maoris.

Though aware of practical difficulties, most Maoris see no real conflict between maintenance of Maori identity and full participation in New Zealand society, no conflict, that is, except that created by Pakeha fears. As already suggested, Maoris are familiar with the idea that different and even opposing individuals and groups can be integrated into a unity by the processes of mediation and joint opposition to outsiders. Their conception of society – implicit in their behaviour but rarely explicitly formulated – is of a hierarchy of progressively broader unities: families united in a *hapū*, *hapū* in a tribe (*iwi*), local congregations in a church, churches in the community of all believers, Maoris of different tribes and churches in *te iwi Maori*. It is my belief that for most Maoris the process does not stop there but goes on to incorporate Maori and Pakeha (and other minorities) in one nation. Just as they expect Maoris of different tribes to meet and work together in amity for some common purpose without permanently discarding their own identity and *kawa* or Maoris of different churches to share in a *hui tōpū* without abandoning differences of doctrine and forms of worship, so they see no reason why unity between Maori and Pakeha should require them to cease being Maori.

In Maori, 'we are one people' is '*he iwi tahi tātau*'. Though *iwi* is most often used to refer to the tribe, its basic meaning is 'group of people linked by strong feeling of community': witness its use in the phrases *iwi kāinga* (home folks) and *te iwi Maori* (the Maori people)

The Maori spokesmen who express this Maori view in speeches and writing argue that true unity can only be achieved when the parts of the body politic are treated with equal dignity and given equal opportunities to contribute what they have to offer. Domination by one part over the others is in the long run more of a threat to national unity than cultural diversity. They also insist that maintaining and developing Maori identity and culture is of vital importance not only to the Maoris themselves but to New Zealand as a whole.

One of the best expositions of this Maori model I know is contained in the booklet, *A Maori View of the Hunn Report*, published in 1961 by the Maori Synod of the Presbyterian Church. Criticizing the Report for its definition of 'integration' the Synod presented its own definition in these terms:

> As we understand it, integration is the combination of the Maori and Pakeha peoples of the nation into one harmonious community in which each enjoys the privileges and accepts the responsibilities of their common citizenship, wherein there are no racial barriers

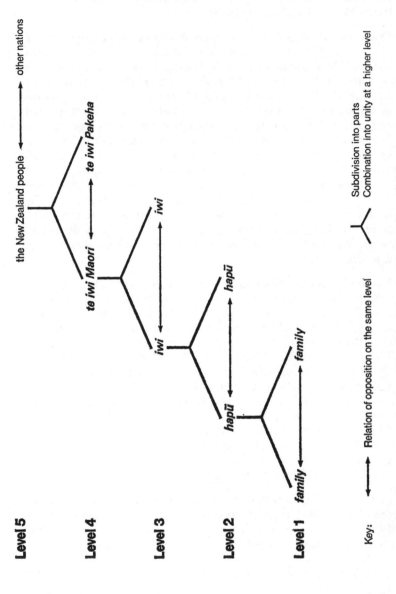

Figure 7  *Opposition and unity: Maori social organization through Maori eyes*

and wherein, with mutual understanding and respect, each race is free to cherish its cultural heritage, that in this way the best elements of both cultures may be united to form the pattern of future New Zealand society (p. 9).

In a sermon delivered at the opening of Kimiora at Tūrangawaewae in 1974 (see p. 198) Rev. Rua Rakena, Moderator of the Methodist Church of New Zealand for 1975–6, described Kimiora as embodying a particular kind of community and way of life based on both the biblical and the Maori understanding of the concept 'house' and thus involving an awareness of life as 'God-centred', an awareness that people matter more than things, and a deep community consciousness and solidarity. In such a community, each member is of value in his or her own right and made to feel significant and wanted, and differences between members are acknowledged, accepted and provided for. In Kimiora 'there will be a place for the old, the middle-aged and the young; for the *manuhiri* and the *tāngata whenua*; for the artist and craftsmen; for those pursuing sporting interests; and a place for the Pakeha.' But though Maoris created and will sustain Kimiora, it is not for themselves alone. Concluding his sermon, the Rev. Rakena said:

> The kind of community and life-style which I suggest is here represented in microcosm is one I would want to covet for our nation as a whole. Such moving events as the Commonwealth Games and last night's first official celebration of New Zealand Day suggest we have all the elements about us in embryonic form. . . . In the Old Testament the 'house of Israel' was often rebuked because of its tendency to insist on exclusiveness and exist only for itself. A basic and integral part of its covenant with God however was to 'exist for others' beyond the 'house of Israel'. . . . I believe we can make no greater act of dedication at this time than one in which we dedicate Kimiora and the life-style it represents, first to the wider community portrayed in last night's New Zealand Day celebration; and secondly to the wider community still represented by the recent Commonwealth Games held in Christchurch.

Certain Maori groups have made proposals that involve a greater degree of separation than at present obtains and/or predictions of conflict if Maoris are not accorded greater control over matters that vitally concern them. Kotahitanga and Kauhanganui have both proposed the idea of a separate Maori parliamentary chamber. But they have not made public any detailed plans, and the proposal can be interpreted as a primarily rhetorical expression of dissatisfaction with the present situation, an interpretation which does NOT diminish its significance. While Ngā Tamatoa have acquired a reputation for being 'radical' and even 'revolutionary' and themselves use these words, their public utterances, in print and on radio and television seem on analysis to be devoted mainly to attacking injustices and racism in New Zealand society as it is and pressing for improvements, making occasional rhetorical references to the racial strife which could arise if these are not effected but providing no detailed prescription that would warrant the charge of separatism. In this connection I cannot resist quoting in some detail from an article Harry Dansey wrote for the Auckland Star on 30 March 1971 in commentary on 'bitter criticism from young Maoris with, it would seem, chips on their shoulder, demonstrators at Waitangi and strong words from Maori conferences'.

Pointing out that 'there have always been Maoris who disliked Pakehas just as there have always been Maoris who liked them very much', Dansey asked:

How about Te Kemara speaking to Captain Hobson in the debate at Waitangi before the Treaty was signed: 'I shall never say yes to your staying. Were all to be on an equality, then perhaps Te Kemara would say yes. But for the Governor to be up and Te Kemara down – Governor high up, up, up and Te Kemara down low, small, a worm, a crawler? No, no, no, O Governor.' . . . How about Princess Te Puea, that wonderful woman who dominated the Maori people of the Waikato to their very great advantage for so long? So well known is her career of service that few now remember that it was she who led a passive resistance movement against conscription of Maoris towards the end of World War I, a courageous act that ended with the arrest of those who followed her. As demonstration against what they considered to be Pakeha injustice, it has no equivalent in modern times. Talk about rocking the boat! How about Sir Apirana Ngata, he who strides the Maori story of his times like a colossus? . . . Ngata was so repeatedly charged with hostility to the Pakeha that in a book dealing with Ngata's influence on Maori culture, Eric Ramsden felt obligated to devote a chapter to explain his attitude. One observation in it could well be applied to the so-called 'chip on the shoulder' people of today: 'Ngata is pro-Maori rather than anti-Pakeha' . . . We had better get used to the fact that we have Maori pressure groups. Their function is first to advance the cause of the group first and foremost though they might plead . . . and believe too – that their case is in the interests of all. . . . To overstate the case, to put forward only factors favourable to it, to press with dramatic gesture, even anger, this is standard procedure for your pressure group. We have learnt to interpret what pressure groups say. We know that some mean exactly what they say but that the majority will be happy with half a loaf. . . . A delegate to the N.Z. Race Relations Conference at Christchurch said that unless the Maori people were given a chance to put their views forward and to see that they were being recognized, not patronized, by Europeans, racial strife in New Zealand was inevitable. To me this seems classic overstatement of the kind which Federated Farmers and the teachers' organizations are masters at making. Most Maoris would subscribe to the general contention, few I think would support the conclusion. But in this day and age, when everyone else does, why shouldn't the Maori get in the act? When everyone else who has a cause to plead screams his head off, why should the Maori be expected to act with sweet reason as his guide? The old principle still holds good: The squeaking door gets the most oil. . . . Ngata wrote that he and Buck admired much about the British people. 'Our preference is for them above all other Pakehas we have met or read about . . . but we know groups and individuals among them prone to seize upon the weakness of our own people for their own advantage. I have been compelled all my life to fight for this weak element in the New Zealand population and so to appear anti-Pakeha. Should one always speak one's thoughts out loud in such a fight?' Should one indeed?

*My own views*

As a New Zealander born and bred I find it impossible to separate the personal and intuitive aspects of my understanding of Maori-Pakeha relations from the more objective and theoretical. I early reacted against the assimilation model and its patronizing view of Maori culture as a monolithic, inadaptable relic from the past, intuitively recognizing the strong drive to life and growth that has sustained Maoris through over a century of pressure to assimilate. While Piddington's concept of emergent development chimed in with and reinforced my own developing ideas, I did not use this or any other technical term nor develop a fully articulated theory of terminology of my own. Instead, speaking and writing mainly for ordinary New Zealanders, I made use of two very simple images, life in nature and a pair of overlapping circles.

In university extension classes and the first edition of this book which grew out of them, I insisted that Maori culture was neither dead nor dying nor a mere aggregate of survivals but a living organism made up of functionally interrelated and dynamically interacting parts. Like all living things, it was in a continual process of change and development in adaptation to a changing environment. I refused to talk of 'preserving Maori culture' because preservation implies either acceptance of death or a life-destroying effort to stop change. It is associated either with museums – or with the bottling of summer fruit. Though not explicit, this image of life in nature lies behind the following passage from the first edition of this book, to which I would still give assent, while going beyond it:

> The process [of Maori acculturation] is, I feel, much more complex . . . involving continual interaction, reaction and development. While the Maoris abandoned some of their ancestral ways (such as cannibalism and slavery) entirely, they have maintained many more by adapting them to changing circumstances, incorporating borrowed ideas into earlier patterns and where necessary developing new forms out of the old. They rarely adopt Pakeha ways without modifying them to some extent. Working from different values and experience, they perform the actions involved with a 'Maori accent', place the emphasis in different places, and subtly change form and function by re-orienting them to Maori ends. Nor is success in Pakeha terms – the achievement of wealth, advanced education and high-status occupations – invariably associated with loss or rejection of Maoritanga. On the contrary, Maoris in white-collar and professional positions pride themselves on keeping in touch with kin, attend major *hui* and include many leading experts in Maori language, history and art. Instead of a progressive abandonment of Maori ways, Maori acculturation (as I see it) involves Maoris taking the ways they borrow into their own culture, increasing the overlap with Pakeha culture and diminishing, but not eliminating, the differences (Metge, 1967: 213–14).

Taking the view that Maori culture and social life should first be studied as a working system in its own right and its own terms, I did not explore the relation between Maori and Pakeha in any depth in my own fieldwork. This too was a reaction against the prevalent tendency continually to measure Maoris and their culture against Pakeha standards, a practice which invariably found them wanting. These attitudes made good sense and were probably a necessary corrective at the time, but as the years have passed I have increasingly come to realize that the contemporary Maori way of life can only be understood in the context of its relation to the rest of the population, that for Maoris Pakehas are always there in the background as a reference group, and as such are as important, in a different way, as their ancestors. It was in contrast and reaction to Pakehas that Maoris first became aware of themselves as one people, as *tāngata maori* (pp. 29–31) and it is in contrast and reaction to Pakeha pressures that modern Maoris have rediscovered their Maoriness and continually define and re-define their idea of it.

Discussing the relation between Maori and Pakeha in the abstract I was from the beginning unhappy with the idea of symbiosis because it stressed the differences between Maori and Pakeha groups and cultures, seeing them as permanently discrete and different in kind, when experience and intuition indicated that they were intimately interrelated and continually being modified in their interaction. In an effort to accommodate what Maori and Pakeha shared as well as their differences, I used the image of overlapping circles.

> Instead of being discrete entities, Maori culture and Pakeha culture overlap, sharing a large common area. Within this common area, Maoris and Pakehas share the same experiences: but they approach them from different backgrounds or from different angles. . . . Outside this common area of culture, there are still sectors of Pakeha culture into which few Maoris venture . . . and sectors of Maori culture which most Pakehas know little about (Metge, 1967: 58).

I realize now that the image of the overlapping circles is static and two dimensional: by using it I evaded the real issues and failed to communicate a valid and necessary insight.

Today I continue to reject any formulation that sees Maori and Pakeha as separate entities, different in kind and mutually exclusive. There are many issues and experiences on which Maoris and Pakehas are united and others in which they are divided among themselves. I still find the image of the living organism useful but inadequate on its own. As I have explored the way Maoris order their experience of the world, I have become increasingly aware of the extent to which they make use of the concept of complementary opposition in which the two opposites are seen as mutually defining each other and united in a larger whole by shared characteristics and the process of mediation. All human beings and cultures use these ideas to some extent, as has been demonstrated by recent work in many disciplines under the title of 'structuralism', but the Maoris have developed them to a high degree. The more I explore the idea of complementary opposition, the more helpful I find it as a model for conceptualizing the relation between Maoris and Pakehas, and between Maori and Pakeha cultures. For the two sides of this opposition though differing in many ways are united by certain shared premises and experiences, by the function each performs in defining and giving value to the other, and by the activities of mediators who strive by many means to diminish misunderstanding and reconcile differences (Schwimmer, 1958; Kernot, 1964).

At the same time the ongoing relationship between the two sides is itself one of the generative factors in the continued development of the whole. As examples of complementary opposition, the models provided by the Maori concepts of *tapu* and *noa* and man and woman are particularly helpful; there is I feel poetic justice in using models taken from Maori culture when in the past we have invariably derived them from overseas (see pp. 303–9).

As I have already indicated, Maoris themselves often identify things and ways Maori as *tapu* in relation to things and ways Pakeha, which they thus identify as *noa* (p. 59). This formulation may well surprise Pakehas. In terms of 'power' and 'value' as commonly used by Pakehas, the Pakeha side would seem to have greater claim to be identified as the *tapu* one. But for Maoris 'power' is primarily spiritual power, and 'value' is interpreted in moral rather than economic terms. Identifying Maoritanga as *tapu* in relation to Pakehatanga stresses its sacredness for Maoris.

But the usefulness of the *tapu-noa* model lies especially in its stress on the complementary nature of the relationship. A true understanding of the *tapu-noa* relation involves seeing, first, that *tapu* has meaning *only in relation* to *noa* and vice versa, and secondly that both sides have value (or rather several values) on several counts. Neither side is wholly positive nor wholly negative, but each is positive on some counts and negative on others. Thus when Maoris identify Pakehatanga as *noa* in relation to Maoritanga, far from denigrating or rejecting it, they are accepting and giving it value as an essential part of their world, which both enhances the value of Maoritanga by contrast and provides relief from its demands. Where two categories of people are concerned, though Maoris typically express the *overall* relation between them by characterizing one as *tapu* and the other as *noa*, I am convinced that in fact they recognize a double *tapu-noa* relation, each group being *tapu* in relation to the other on some counts and for some purposes and therefore commanding at least a degree of respect. This is particularly clear in the case of *tāngata whenua* and *manuhiri* (pp. 250–4), but I believe it is also implicit in Maori views of the relation between men and women, old and young, themselves and Pakehas.

Importantly, the content of the opposing categories of *tapu* and *noa* is not fixed, but may change with changes in context, especially from one level of a hierarchical structure (whether of social organization or ideas) to another. Thus while Maoris identify Maoritanga as *tapu* at the level of its relation with Pakehatanga, they also make *tapu-noa* distinctions within Maoritanga at a variety of levels, e.g. between the *marae* complex and its activities (*tapu*) and the daily life of the home (*noa*), and between the different parts and activities of the *marae* (see

Figure 6). By the same token, given an appropriate context, Maori and Pakeha ways can be identified jointly as *tapu* in relation to a wider category such as Australian, American or 'overseas' ways. Whatever their referents, *tapu* and *noa* always constitute a unity, and both together are essential for the continued viability and distinctive character of the whole.

For me personally, and I like to think for most New Zealanders, the essential quality of New Zealand as a nation inheres in the relation between Maori and Pakeha, and without the Maori contribution it would not be the same country. While increasingly New Zealand is becoming a multi-cultural rather than a bicultural nation, it is the Maori-Pakeha relation which provides the master for all other inter-group relations. However, at present, while most Maoris are of necessity and choice bicultural in terms of Schwimmer's definition (p. 309), the majority of Pakehas are far from knowledgeable about any culture but their own, often afraid of confrontation with a different value system, and unaware of the enrichment that can result. If New Zealand is to realize its full potential as a rewarding and stimulating place to live, we must be more prepared to make the learning process a two-way affair. Our model for the future must include a concept of equality defined in terms not of sameness nor even equality of opportunity, but of equal rights to be valued and listened to, equal responsibilities to respect and learn from others. An understanding of the concept of complementary opposition suggests that this is best achieved, not by eliminating differences, but by mediating them and by emphasizing positive values instead of negative ones.

### A two-way process?

In the history of relations between Maoris and Pakehas, Maoris have unquestionably yielded, borrowed and changed more than Pakehas, not only in economic and technological respects but also in social organization and especially in ideology, with the adoption of Christianity and such ideas as monarchy, individual property title, adult franchise and representative government. In terms of Schwimmer's definition, most Maoris are bicultural, familiar with and able to operate in two cultural systems.

By comparison, acculturation in the opposite direction has been limited in quantity and fairly superficial. Pakehas adopted Maori names for places, plants and wildlife early and in large numbers. A limited number of other words have been assimilated into the New Zealand vocabulary, often so thoroughly their origin is forgotten. Generally the pronunciation of these Maori words is distorted by anglicization. Maori myths and history are taught in primary schools along with a restricted range of songs, dances, crafts and games; but the degree of appreciation and understanding achieved varies widely with the teachers' and students' interest. Pakehas not only rely heavily on Maoris and Maori arts as tourist attractions but they also turn to Maori sources for tangible symbols of national identity. Pakehas travelling overseas often make belated attempts to learn *haka* and action-songs. Traditional Maori art forms are incorporated into the design of public buildings and provide symbols and decor for (for instance) New Zealand's internal and overseas airlines. Modified Maori motifs figure prominently in commercial art. Of recent years there has been a noticeable increase in the use of Maori names and mottoes for new plants, pedigree stock, houses, schools and clubs.

There has always been a small number of Pakehas who have been interested and expert enough in Maori language and culture in their full complexity to be accepted by Maoris as participants in Maori activities. Some of these have attempted to communicate their understanding to other Pakehas through lectures and writing, but for too long the interest they aroused was academic and did not lead to personal encounter. In the late fifties and sixties however, as the country became increasingly aware of the consequences of Maori urbanization, increasing numbers of Pakehas sought to encounter Maoris and Maori culture directly and at a deeper level of reality. Enrolments in study courses in Maori language and culture at university and teachers' colleges rose rapidly with consequent increases in staff and comprehensiveness. Seeing the importance of introducing students to Maori culture as a living reality instead of an academic abstraction, the lecturers concerned, both Maoris and Pakehas, took their students on visits to *marae* especially during *hui*. Such groups usually included Maoris as members and spokesmen and observed all the requirements of Maori protocol including making speeches in Maori and giving *koha*. Enjoyable as well as educationally profitable, these visits increased annually in popularity and number. Former students turned teachers adapted the idea for use with school-children, and it was taken up by other bodies keen to improve relations with Maori communities, such as traffic officers, the police, Rotary and the churches. *Marae* visits with an educational aim still sometimes take place in the context of *hui* called for other purposes but increasingly they are arranged as special events. Frequently also, predominantly Pakeha organizations arrange to hold annual conferences at a *marae* venue.

The great popularity of *marae* visits among Pakehas is a good thing in so far as it reflects an awareness of the importance of the *marae* as an institution and a desire to experience Maori culture communicated by Maoris on their own ground. At the same time certain problems are involved. Firstly, there is the danger that focusing interest on the *marae* will reinforce the idea that Maori culture is limited to certain special areas set aside for the purpose, to the dramatic and occasional rather than the everyday, to observable patterns of behaviour rather than values that pervade all behaviour. Secondly, specially arranged visits and conferences place special strains on the Maori hosts. A visit planned to take place within the weekend from the visitors' point of view involves the hosts in a great deal of preparation beforehand. It is not uncommon for key workers to have to take time off their own employment in order to prepare the *marae* – reinforcing the stereotype of Maoris as unreliable workers. Though visitors give *koha*, these often do not cover the full costs, especially the hidden costs of labour and the activities hosts leave undone in order to attend the *marae*. Because most Pakehas have little facility in the Maori language, the procedure and speeches are simplified and English becomes the order of the day as soon as the welcome is over. While the Pakehas who take part derive both pleasure and knowledge from such visits, for the Maori hosts the returns are less obvious, especially in relation to costs. Unless relations with Pakehas in other contexts such as school or church improve noticeably as a result, they are likely to lose their enthusiasm and become *hōhā* about the idea. Even the presence of Pakehas as ordinary guests at Maori-originated *hui* can have a subtly inhibiting effect. There is a real danger that the intrusion of Pakehas into Maori situations in any but small numbers could itself change and even destroy the very qualities that attract them.

Aware of these dangers, those engaged in educating Pakehas in Maoritanga (which today includes ministers and social work trainers as well as teachers) now frequently arrange for students to attend *hui* as workers instead of guests and to set up on-going relations with particular communities between and apart from *hui* by working with them on *marae* maintenance and building programmes.

Over the years in particular places, Maoris and Pakehas have also come together in informal and formal associations to work for defined goals. A particularly good example of this co-operation was the public campaign to raise funds for the Maori Education Foundation in 1962, a goal which was represented as indirectly benefiting the whole community. Under the leadership of the late John Waititi (p. 158) local committees consisting of roughly equal numbers of Maoris and Pakehas were formed all over the country and worked together intensively over a period of several months. The friendships made and the respect for each other's ways developed in the course of this campaign were quite as important a contribution to the improvement of Maori-Pakeha relations as the money raised for the Foundation (p. 159). In 1973 the Pakehas of Khandallah combined with people of varied ethnic backgrounds to raise funds for Maraeroa, the *marae* planned for the predominantly State housing suburb of Porirua East. How much Pakeha participants gain from entering into such co-operation emerges clearly from the following article, which was contributed (unsolicited) to a daily newspaper under the heading 'An object lesson in race relations' (*Dominion*, 10 October 1972).

You know the saying – first the good news, then the bad.

Well, the news as far as race relations goes all seems to be bad these days. Reports from Africa of intolerance and violence, from Britain of racial apprehensions, and here in New Zealand news of impending racial problems in our cities.

Until a few months ago, I like most other Pakehas could only look on uncertainly at the racial situation unsure where we were all heading.

Like many other white, middle-class (WASP, they call us in the United States) New Zealanders, I had almost no contact with Maoris and other Polynesians living in my own city.

Sure I had worked with Maoris and Islanders during vacations in my youth, usually at menial or labouring jobs.

Sure, I recalled being at school with Maoris, and playing various sports with Maoris and Islanders.

I even had one or two Maori acquaintances who had made it in the middle-class professions.

But when I asked myself just how many Polynesian people I'd ever had into my own home here in Khandallah, I had to admit, none. You see, in this suburb of ours, there just aren't many Polynesians!

But in the past two months, all this has changed. I have made at least a dozen Maori and Polynesian friends: I've entertained them in my home, and been invited into theirs: and I've begun to learn something of the 'other half' of our New Zealand culture . . . the Polynesian half.

Other Pakehas in my suburb have shared the same experience.

It all began a couple of months ago when a local journalist became interested in the efforts of the Maraeroa Marae Association, which is raising money for a $100,000 multi-racial marae at Porirua.

The marae will fill an urgent social need by providing a community meeting place where Maori and Island people will be able to strengthen their own sense of identity and communal values.

The journalist could see that raising money in Porirua was difficult, with so many community projects struggling for limited finance. He suggested that the Maraeroa Association might be able to work in with Khandallah people to stage a Marae Day in Khandallah. This would draw on the resources of people in Wellington's northern suburbs with more spending power.

A school headmaster was consulted. He backed the idea, seeing its educational possibilities for local children.

The headmaster helped sell the idea to his Home and School Association.

The result: a combined Khandallah-Porirua committee was formed – Pakehas from Khandallah working with Maoris, Cook Islanders, Tokelauans, Niueans and Samoans from Porirua to organise a Marae Day, the 'Marae Roa O Khandallah', literally the 'Marae (at Porirua) is extended to Khandallah'.

I became a member of a multi-racial group in the truest sense for the first time.

Since then I've worked, eaten, talked, argued and laughed with people of different backgrounds to my own.

I've learned many things about the Maori and Island ways of doing things.

But I've had to 'unlearn' many more of my own ideas.

I'd always liked to really organize meetings so that everything was run with the greatest speed and efficiency. Now, at our meetings, European speed and efficiency takes second place to warmth and cordiality. Everyone in the 25-strong committee is part of the group – and all decisions must be very much a group affair.

Then there was the affair of the hangi. We're planning a massive hangi for the Marae Day on October 14.

Some of us Europeans suggested that, to get the right profit margin, the hangi portions could be reduced in size.

We found after a while that the Maori woman in charge of the hangi planning was clearly unhappy, though she was too shy to say why.

After some confusion, a Maori friend took me aside and said: 'Look, this just isn't the Maori way of doing things, and she's not happy, but she'd never tell you outright.

She just couldn't cut down the portions, and hand out small portions of food to the guests.

That isn't the Maori way of hospitality. It would be considered mean. And that's the worst insult a Maori can offer a guest.'

I took the point, and made sure the other Europeans did. The hangi portions will stay man-sized.

Another lesson came today when we talked about Press statements for the big day.

The journalist working on Marae Day publicity suggested that one or two of the Polynesian people could be featured in newspaper stories. It's well known among journalists, of course, that personality pieces like this can get the message across.

But we found the idea ran into a series of almost indefinable obstacles put up by the Maori members of the group. The puzzle was finally explained when my Maori friend once again took me aside and patiently explained that this isn't the Maori way of doing things.

If all the people are doing the work, then all the people should get the credit, he said. The publicity committee decided to lay less stress on individual achievement.

And so the education process continues. I know that in return the Maoris and Polynesians are learning techniques that we aren't even aware of, but which are part of our middle-class make-up.

We are, for instance, fairly expert at getting things done in a city environment. Most of the Khandallah people know how to use the resources of the business and professional community, of the media. And all this expertise has been of help to people who are mainly from Island or rural areas.

So the two-way learning process has gone on. At first I found (and was later told by some of the Maoris that they shared my feelings) that I was wary of, perhaps even a little frightened of, people from different races.

I've come to realise it's important to be sensitive, to be aware of nuances, but not to be over sensitive.

So the co-operation experiment may or may not have worked.

Certainly we hope the Marae Roa O Khandallah day on October 14 will raise a good sum for the urban marae at Porirua.

Certainly the Government is backing the idea. It is sending the Minister of Maori and Island Affairs, Mr McIntyre, to the day as its official representative.

But even if the money raised is insignificant, the Marae Day will have done something else.

It will have left me and I hope many others with the experience of having worked together voluntarily for a common cause.

By working together for a common good – and the urban *marae* will benefit all in our society by promoting community life – we have learned something about race relations.

Something worthwhile that can't be taught in text-books, can't be caught in protest marches, certainly can't be enforced by the Race Relations Council.

But it can be learned from people.

## Conclusion

When we New Zealanders claim that our race relations are 'good' and 'harmonious' we are making not an objective assessment of the situation, but a rhetorical statement expressing our ideals. The actuality is too complex, too varied, too much in a state of flux to be summed up so glibly. It is compounded of credits and debits, of shameful episodes and encouraging ones, of widely varying personal relations and social and economic forces beyond most participants' awareness.

In general the sanguine view we like to present to the world is a Pakeha view rather than a Maori one, developed over the long period between the armed conflict of the 1860s and the Second World War, a period when Maoris and Pakehas lived in different parts of the country pursuing different aims. Throughout the nineteenth century the Maori population diminished in numbers and though it began to increase again early in the twentieth it was several decades before the effects of this increase became apparent. During this time Maoris lived removed from the main concentrations of Pakeha population and did not compete with Pakehas on any significant scale for jobs, houses, spouses or wealth. When from time to time Maori groups, rallied by charismatic leaders like Te Whiti and Tohu, Te Kooti, Rua Kenana and Wiremu Ratana, articulated their own answers to the problems confronting them, often by founding special settlements, they were effectively limited and undermined by strong pressures from the State, often including removal of their leaders, and their story was either edited out of the historical record or interpreted from a Pakeha point of view as small-scale disaffection or 'rebellion'.

Since the Second World War however the situation has changed in many important ways. For thirty-five years Maoris have been increasing much faster than Pakehas, moving out of predominantly Maori areas into towns and cities, and exploring many new avenues of employment and recreation. While there have been general improvements and some notable individual achievements, as a group Maoris remain less favourably placed than non-Maoris with regard to educational attainment, occupational status, range and type of occupation, incomes and health standards. They make up a disproportionately high percentage of those charged, convicted and given heavy sentences for criminal offences. In urban as well as rural areas the middle and older generations maintain an interrelated set of Maori ways which involve formal membership and/or periodic congregation in predominantly Maori groups; but the proportion of Maoris who speak Maori fluently and frequently has declined markedly, and many city-born young people have had little or no opportunity to experience Maori culture continuously and at depth. Increased contact between Maoris and Pakehas does not always produce greater understanding and tolerance: in many cases it generates friction and self-protective discrimination as they compete directly for jobs, houses, spouses and wealth, experiencing at first-hand the inconveniences, misunderstandings and conflicts that can arise from differences in customs and values. As homegrown as well as visiting commentators frequently point out, far from presenting grounds for complacency, the present situation contains seeds of conflict and could easily deteriorate if the imbalances between Maoris and Pakehas remain uncorrected or are magnified by such factors as rising unemployment.

Perhaps the most striking feature of the last twenty years has been the way Maoris as a group have regained their pride in themselves and their culture, have become more articulate in expressing this pride, and have begun to protest publicly against discrimination, stereotyping and ethnocentrism on the part of Pakehas. Where formerly they voiced their views and resentments mainly in Maori in Maori settings in Maori ways such as *whai-kōrero*, *haka* and *waiata*, nowadays they are increasingly making use of the English language, the general communication media, literary forms like the novel, and administrative channels such as Parliament and the Race Relations Office. Some Pakehas see this as reflecting and contributing to a deterioration in Maori-Pakeha relations, but in my view it is one of the most exciting and hopeful developments of all. The open expression of criticism and resentment is always healthier than suppression: it prevents festering below the surface and opens the way to discussion, redress and renewed trust. A truly equal and fruitful relationship between groups as between individuals can be established only when they recognize and deal with each other as equals – equals not in actual achievement but in recognized rights to respect and self-determination. Most importantly resurgence of pride in Maori culture and in being Maori has been accompanied not by a decline but by a marked increase in inter-group friendship and intermarriage. As Maoris have gained confidence in themselves as Maoris they have become not less but more willing to admit Pakehas into Maori circles, to talk to and teach them about Maori ways and values, and to associate with them in pursuit of common interests and goals.

In response to the climate of world opinion, to growing disillusion with international culture built on the idea of 'progress', and the insistence of Maoris and other ethnic minorities on maintaining their identity, the Government and Pakehas generally are more open today than they used to be to the idea that the cultures of minority groups have a positive value, are worthy of respect and have a contribution to make to New Zealand as a nation. As yet however we have only begun to translate this idea into action, and it remains to be seen how effectively we can realize it.

### The Treaty of Waitangi

Whatever the objective state of Maori-Pakeha relations, the Treaty of Waitangi provides us with a potent symbol of our nationhood.

The Treaty itself is the focus of considerable uncertainty and academic dispute. There is some doubt over the exact text: the original English text has been lost, there are at least two slightly discrepant Maori versions and the adequacy of the words used in Maori to render (for instance) the highly abstract concept of sovereignty has been questioned (Ross in Victoria University of Wellington, 1972: 16–34). In the past many historians and lawyers held that it was not a valid treaty in international law because the chiefs who signed it were not the rulers of an independent state. Contemporary legal opinion rejects this reasoning and accepts the validity of the Treaty as an international instrument (McKean in Victoria University of Wellington, 1972: 35–48). But international law must be differentiated from domestic or internal law. The Treaty of Waitangi has never been incorporated in New Zealand's internal law. Over the years Maoris have invoked the Treaty on a number of occasions in support of claims especially to land, but their claims have nearly all been rejected none the less. Many Maori leaders and movements, notably Kotahitanga and Ratana, have pressed for its ratification or more precisely enactment as part of the law of the land. Since the Treaty is expressed in very general language, even if it were enacted special provisions in other legislation dealing in detail with the same issues would take effect in preference to the general provisions of the Treaty in the absence of a clear intention to the contrary. Other New Zealanders, both Maori and Pakeha, argue against incorporating the Treaty in state law. As Sir Eruera Tirikatene pointed out this would put it in the way of being amended or repealed: he considered it was 'best left to stand above the law as a guiding principle like Magna Carta' (New Zealand Parliamentary Debates, vol. 309: 1136–8). Many Maoris feel that parts of current law are in fact in clear contravention of the Treaty (Ngata in Victoria University of Wellington, 1972: 49–57), but this can be handled by working for changes in the particular laws concerned.

In an attempt to meet the objections of Maoris and to establish firmly the importance of the Treaty in New Zealand law, the Government passed the Treaty of Waitangi Act 1975 which establishes a Waitangi Tribunal to enquire into and make recommendations upon claims relating to the practical application of the principles of the Treaty and to report on proposed legislation referred to it by the House or any Minister of the Crown. The Tribunal is to consist of the Chief Judge of the Maori Land Court and two others appointed by the Governor General on the recommendation respectively of the Ministers of Justice and Maori Affairs; it will receive secretarial, recording and any other services it needs from the Department of Maori Affairs. In exercising its functions the Tribunal is to have regard to the English and Maori texts of the Treaty set out in a schedule to the Bill, and is to have exclusive authority to determine the meaning and effect of the Treaty as embodied in the texts and to decide issues raised by the differences between them. The Tribunal has jurisdiction to consider claims from any Maori or group of Maoris who consider that any current legislation, policy or practice or any act done or omitted by or on behalf of the Crown affects them prejudicially and is inconsistent with the principles of the Treaty of Waitangi.

Various objections have been raised to the Act as it stands, not least the fact that it does not provide for claims by non-Maoris.

Whether the Act stands or is amended, it is to be hoped that the Treaty of Waitangi will continue to act as it has in the past and as Sir Eruera Tirikatene suggested, as 'a guiding principle like Magna Carta'. The ideal set out in the Treaty of two races united in friendship and equality as one people is a great national myth which like all myths is concerned less with historical accuracy than with providing a charter for action and a standard of value against which particular actions and situations are to be judged. As such it does not apply only to Maoris and Pakehas but also provides a model for relations between all New Zealand's varied cultural groups, a sound foundation on which to build a truly multi-cultural society.

# Appendix

# Maori spelling and pronunciation

The Maori language, as rendered into writing by the early missionaries, comprises eight consonants (*h*, *k*, *m*, *n*, *p*, *r*, *t*, and *w*), two digraphs (*ng* and *wh*), and five vowels (*a, e, i, o, u*).

The consonants are pronounced approximately as in English, except for *r* which is never trilled. *ng* is pronounced as in si*ng*er (ŋ), *wh* either as in *wh*ere (ʍ) or as a lax *f* (f).

Each vowel has a single sound quality but occurs in both short and long forms, the difference in length being significant for meaning. Some writers indicate long vowels by doubling the vowel concerned (e.g. *paa*), others by placing a macron above it (e.g. *pā*). In this book the latter method has been used.

Every syllable in a Maori word ends in a vowel, never in a consonant.

When vowels occur together in the combinations *ae, ai, ao, au, ei, eu, oi*, and *ou*, each vowel is clearly sounded but Maori speakers glide from one to the other without a break in continuity.

The main stress in a word falls on the first syllable containing a long vowel or, if there is no long vowel, one of the eight vowel combinations listed above; otherwise it falls on the first syllable of the word, exclusive of unstressed prefixes such as *whaka-* and *kai-*. Accentuation is, however, much less obvious than in English.

*References*

Biggs, Bruce, *English-Maori Dictionary*, A. H. & A. W. Reed, Wellington, 1966.

Williams, Herbert W., *A Dictionary of the Maori Language*, 6th edn, Government Printer, Wellington, 1957.

## GUIDE TO THE PRONUNCIATION
## OF MAORI VOWELS

| Written Form | International Phonetic Symbol | Maori Example | Approximate Sound in an English Word |
|---|---|---|---|
| *a* | ɑ | *ha*k*a* | b*u*tter |
| *ā* | ɑ: | *p*ā | p*a*th |
| *e* | ɛ | *ma*t*e* | p*e*ck |
| *ē* | ɛ: | *k*ē*k*ē | p*ai*r |
| *i* | i | *i*w*i* | p*i*ck |
| *ī* | i: | *t*ī*t*ī | p*ee*k |
| *o* | ɔ | *k*o*ha* | c*o*lt |
| *ō* | ɔ: | *p*ō*whiri* | *o*rb |
| *u* | u | *m*u*ru* | p*u*t |
| *ū* | u: | *hap*ū | m*oo*n |

# Glossary

*action-songs* Dances with stylized actions illustrating songs sung in Maori mostly to popular modern melodies but not in most cases translating the original words; in Maori *waiata-ā-ringa*; p. 269.

*aituā* Misfortune, calamity; applied especially to death; pp. 60–1.

*ākara* Transliteration of 'uncle'; used for parent's brothers and male cousins and spouses of 'aunts'; p. 122.

*ao* Daytime as opposed to night; world; cloud. Te Ao-Marama, the world of light, enlightenment. Te Ao-Tū-Roa, the world of men and mortality; pp. 55–7.

*āpotoro* Apostle; minister of the Ratana Church; p. 188.

*ariki* Paramount chief; with a capital A, Lord (God); pp. 24, 55.

*aroha* Love, compassion, sympathy especially in grief, gratitude; p. 66.

*assimilation* Government policy until 1961, aiming at the complete absorption of Maoris and Maori culture into the dominant Pakeha way of life; pp. 303–5.

*āti* Transliteration of 'auntie', used for parent's sisters and female cousins and wives of 'uncles'; modern usage; p. 122.

*atua* Spirit, god; with capital A, God; p. 55.

*aukati*   Line which may not be passed; in particular, that drawn by King Tawhiao when he retired into Maniapoto territory after the 'Maori Wars'; p. 33.

*awhina*   Assistance, especially in tangible form of goods, money, personal attendance and labour; in some areas, e.g. Far North, donations given at *hui*; p. 67.

*bach*   N.Z. colloquialism: one- or two-roomed cottage not intended for permanent occupation.

*Classic Maori*   Maori culture and language in the late eighteenth century.

*communal ownership*   Ownership of 'Maori land' by a group without identification of individual owners; p. 113.

*confiscation*   Government confiscation of land from Maori tribes of central and western North Island after the 'Maori Wars'; p. 34.

*consolidation*   A legal process of exchanging 'Maori land' shares in order to concentrate each owner's shares in one block; pp. 37, 114.

*development scheme*   A block of 'Maori land' developed as a unit by the State for settlement by Maori farmers; pp. 37, 116.

*Far North*   The northern part of Northland, comprising roughly the counties of Mangonui, Whangaroa, Hokianga, and the Bay of Islands.

*flower ceremony*   A ceremony in which pieces of wedding cake and favours are distributed to representatives of tribes and sub-tribes present at a wedding; practised mainly by the northern tribes; p. 141.

*haka*   Rhythmically shouted chants of defiance accompanied by aggressive, stylized movements of hands and feet.

*hākari*   Feast; an essential feature of a Maori gathering, which usually follows the main ceremony; p. 259.

*hāngi*   'Earth oven', a pit full of fire-heated stones on which food is placed, splashed with water, covered with leaves and earth, and cooked for several hours.

335

*hapū*   Section of a tribe; pp. 5, 135.

*hē*   Adj. wrong; erring, mistaken, perplexed, at a loss; in trouble or difficulty; n. error, mistake, fault; p. 62.

*hinengaro*   One of the internal organs, probably the spleen; seat of the thoughts and emotions, mind, heart; desire; cf. *ngākau* and *manawa*.

*hīta*   Transliteration of 'sister'; also used for classificatory 'sister', i.e. female cousin of the same generation; p. 123.

*hoa*   Friend; spouse. *Hoa-riri*, literally 'angry friend', enemy.

*hōhā*   Wearied with expectation, importunity, anxiety etc., 'fed up', 'can't be bothered'.

*hokowhitu-a-Tūmatauenga*   Literally, the twenty times seven of the god of war; in pre-European times, the war-party raised by a *hapū*; used today for any body of fighting-men, but especially for the Maori Battalion; p. 27.

*hongi*   Pressing noses together; traditional Maori salute.

*hui*   A gathering for peaceful purposes, usually on a *marae*; pp. 27, 246.

*hui tōpū*   Gathering in a body; the annual conference of the Anglican Diocese of Waiapu.

*hunaonga*   Son-in-law, daughter-in-law; also in form *hunōnga*.

*hunarei*   Father-in-law, mother-in-law; also in forms *hunarere, hungarei, hungawai, hungoi*.

*hurahanga kōhatu*   Ceremonial unveiling of memorial gravestone.

*ihi*   Power, authority, essential force; close in meaning but not quite identical with *mana*; p. 231.

*'immigrants'*   Maoris who live in a place without being descended from the original owners or owning 'Maori land' there; p. 108.

*incorporation*   A special type of incorporated body formed by

Maoris owning shares in a block of 'Maori land' to facilitate development and administration; pp. 37, 116–19.

*individualization* The determination of individual shares in blocks of 'Maori land' owned by a group, carried out by the Maori Land Court; pp. 34, 113.

*integration* Government policy in Maori affairs, in force since 1961; p. 307.

*Io* Supreme Being whose existence and worship were revealed to initiates of the pre-European 'school of learning'; identified by many Maoris with the Supreme Being of Christianity and used instead of or in alternation with the name Jehovah; see Marsden in King, 1975; also p. 55.

*irāmutu* Nephew, niece.

*iwi* Tribe; pp. 4, 131; bone, often used in English to refer to fellow-tribesman or relative; people, as in *iwi Maori*, the Maori people, and *iwi kāinga*, the home folks or hosts.

*kahawai* *Arripis trutta*, a common New Zealand fish.

*kai* Food; 'Maori kai' = foods regarded as typically Maori, including many of post-European origin, such as porkbones-and-*pūhā*, *kānga pirau* and 'Maori bread'.

*kai-* Prefix meaning 'one who does something': e.g. *kai-kōrero* (orator, spokesman), *kai-mahi* (worker), *kai-tiaki*, guardian.

*kaihana* Transliteration of 'cousin'; p. 123.

*kāinga* Settlement; in modern usage, house or home; p. 9.

*kānga pirau* Literally, 'rotten corn'; a custard made of fermented corn.

*kaporeihana* Transliteration of 'corporation'; used in some areas for *hapū* or *marae* clubs.

*karakia* Ritual chant; in modern usage, prayers.

*karanga* To call; the stylized, chanted 'calling' of visitors to enter a *marae*, performed by women only.

*karanga rua* 'Double calling', used for a situation where two people are related in two ways; p. 123.

*karani* Transliteration of 'granny'; grandparent of either sex; *karanipā*, grandfather; *karanimā*, grandmother; used for grandparents' siblings, cousins, i.e. classificatory grandparents; p. 122.

*kaumātua* Patriarchal head of household in pre-European times, p. 6; today, an elder; p. 200.

*kauri* *Agathis australis*, a forest tree with a tall, well-shaped trunk, greatly prized in the nineteenth century for ships' masts and spars; found only in the northern North Island.

*kauri-gum* Solidified resin from the *kauri*, obtained mainly by digging in legally reserved 'kauri-gumfields'; important export in middle and late nineteenth century.

*kāuta* Cooking shelter or shed.

*kawa* *Karakia* or ceremonies performed for special purposes, e.g. completion of meeting-house or canoe; rules of protocol relating to the *marae* complex especially in relation to speech-making.

*kawe mate* Literally, 'carrying the dead'; a series of visits paid by relatives of deceased to the *marae* of those who attended the funeral wake; p. 263.

*kēhua* Ghost; p. 55.

*kēkē* Other, in a different line; used to distinguish classificatory kin from kin of primary and secondary degrees of relationships.

*kin-cluster* Groups of kin related by a variety of ties; Metge, 1964a: 166.

*King Country* The area associated with the Maniapoto tribe, where King Tawhiao and his followers lived for twenty years after the 'Maori Wars'; principal town, Te Kuiti.

*King Movement* (*Kingitanga*) The tribes who give allegiance to the Maori Queen; pp. 196–9.

*koha*   Gift, donation; especially that given by guests at a *hui* to their hosts; pp. 259–60.

*komiti*   Committee or club; pp. 171–2.

*kōrero*   Speak, talk; n. conversation; news; story, narrative, discussion; *whai-kōrero*, formal speech-making; pp. 255–9.

*koro*   Old man; a term of friendly address to an adult male.

*koroua*   Old man; *parāoa koroua*, baking powder bread.

*kotahitanga*   Word formed in post-European times by adding noun suffix to Maori word for 'one'; literally, oneness or unity; used in some areas as title of *hapū* clubs; with capital K, the name of the unofficial Maori Parliament (1894–1902), p. 36; and of a contemporary nationalist movement, p. 195.

*kōwhaiwhai*   Traditional patterns based on a scroll motif painted on meeting-house rafters in red, black and white; now applied to a variety of surfaces.

*kuia*   Elderly woman.

*kūmara*   *Ipomoea batatas*, sweet potato.

*large-family*   A group of kinsmen consisting of the descendants of a common recent ancestor and their spouses and adopted children, limited to some degree by residence, acting as a group for certain purposes; p. 136.

*mahi*   V.tr. work; make; do; n. work, occupation; activity, industriousness; doings; p. 84.

*mākutu*   Sorcery.

*māmā*   Mother, a borrowing from English; used for classificatory as well as own mother; p. 122.

*mana*   Power of supernatural origin; authority, influence, prestige; ability to do and get things done successfully; pp. 8, and 63–6.

*manaaki*   V.tr. show respect or kindness to; look after, care for, especially guests; n. 'caring' in the fullest sense of the word; p. 67.

*manawa*   Heart, both physical and as seat of affection; mind, spirit. *Manawa-nui*, stout-hearted; *manawa-rere*, impetuous; *manawa-roa*, persevering; cf. *ngākau* and *hinengaro*.

*māngai*   Mouth; spokesman; applied as title to Tahupotiki Wiremu Ratana; pp. 187–90.

*māngere*   Lazy.

*manuhiri*   Visitor, guest, person other than hosts at a *hui*.

*maori*   Normal, usual, ordinary.

*Maori(s)*   (a) the people occupying New Zealand when Europeans re-discovered it in the late eighteenth century; (b) the full-blooded descendants of the latter, together with those persons of mixed Maori-Pakeha descent who are identified as Maori by dusky skin colour and Polynesian features and/or choose to identify themselves as Maoris; pp. 31, 39–42.

*'Maori bread'*   Baking-powder bread; also bread made with home-made yeast.

*Maori Committees*, Maori Executive Committees, Maori District Councils and the New Zealand Maori Council: a hierarchy of committees and councils established by the Government, giving Maoris limited community self-government and national representation independent of party politics; pp. 207–10.

*Maori Community Centres*   Non-traditional Maori social centres established mainly in urban areas.

*Maori cousin*   Colloquial expression for distant relatives; p. 123.

*Maori Queen*   Paramount chief of the tribes supporting the King Movement; pp. 196–9.

*'Maori land'*   Land subject to special Maori land laws and handled by the Maori Land Court; p. 109.

*Maori marriage*   (a) marriage by mutual consent only, established prior to 1952 (legal definition); (b) *de facto* union commonly involving members legally married to someone else (popular usage); p. 139.

*Maori School*   School located in areas with high percentage of Maori residents and administered by the national Department of Education instead of regional Education Boards, prior to 1969; pp. 35, 152.

'*Maori time*'   A way of ordering time which gives priority to Maori values and pays little or no regard to the clock; pp. 68–9.

*Maori Trustee*   An office constituted and assigned functions under the Maori Trustee Act 1953; up to now (1975) the position has been held by the Secretary of the Department of Maori Affairs.

*Maori Wars*   Popular name for wars between the Government and Maori tribes protesting against loss of their lands mainly in the Waikato, King Country and Taranaki areas in the 1860s and 70s. Maoris refer to them as the Pakeha Wars or the Land Wars.

*Maoritanga*   'Maoriness', pride in being Maori, 'Maori ways'; pp. 48–52.

*marae*   Open space associated with a meeting-house and used for community assembly; also used for combination of open space, meeting-house, dining-hall etc, i.e. for the whole *marae* complex; pp. 227–45.

*marae money*   Donation given by guests at a *hui* to their hosts and/or by sponsors of a *hui* to *marae* committee.

*mātāmua*   First-born of siblings; head of a large-family.

*mate*   Sick, dead; *mate Maori*, 'Maori sickness' caused by breach of *tapu* or sorcery; p. 61.

*matua*, pl. *mātua*   Parent, own and classificatory, especially father.

*meeting-house*   Large rectangular house, usually of distinctive appearance, associated with a *marae* and used for discussions and accommodating guests; pp. 229–35.

*mere*   A short flat greenstone club formerly used in hand-to-hand fighting; nowadays treasured family heirlooms.

*mihimihi, mihi*   Formal speeches of greeting; in shortened form, the welcome ceremony; pp. 250–8.

*moa*   Extinct birds of the order Dinornithiformes.

*mokopuna*   Grandchild of either sex, classificatory (i.e. grandchild of siblings and cousins) as well as own; descendant; pp. 18–19.

*mōrehu*   Survivor, remnant; used especially by Ratana to describe those who followed his teaching; pp. 187–90.

*mōteatea*   Generic term for traditional orally transmitted song-poems, both sung *waiata* and chanted types; p. 268.

*mua*   (a) Of place, the front; in *marae* context, *marae* proper and meeting-house i.e. the *tapu* sector of the *marae*; (b) of time, the former time, the past; complementary opposite of *muri*; pp. 70, 234.

*multiple ownership*   Ownership of blocks of 'Maori land' by many owners jointly; pp. 113–14.

*muri*   (a) Of place, the rear. In *marae* context, the cooking quarters, 'behind the scenes', 'the back'; (b) of time, the sequel, the time to come, the future; complementary opposite of *mua*; pp. 70, 234.

*muru*   Legal plundering to take compensation for wrongdoing or injury; practice ceased thirty or more years ago; pp. 20, 225.

*ngākau*   Heart, not physical organ, but seat of affection and feelings, mind; *te ngākau Maori*, 'the Maori heart', pride in being Maori, sympathy for and understanding of 'Maori ways' and values; pp. 48, 67.

*noa*   Not under religious restriction; 'common', ordinary; relaxed; complementary opposite of *tapu*; pp. 58–60.

*ora*   Adj. alive, well, in health. n. well-being, life in all its fullness, eternal life; pp. 60–1.

*pā*   Fortified stronghold; p. 8; used colloquially today for an unfortified Maori settlement or village; p. 80.

*pāeke*   Method of ordering speeches during the welcome ceremony; host speakers speak en bloc, followed by visiting speakers en bloc; p. 252.

*Pakeha* (s)   Persons of European descent, more especially those born and/or brought up in New Zealand; p. 31.

*pānui*   (a) Proclamation or public notice usually announcing *hui*, p. 246; (b) medleys of Bible verses recited from memory during Ringatū church services.

*papa*   Anything broad, flat and hard; earth floor or site of house.

*pāpā*   Father, a borrowing from English; used for classificatory as well as own father; p. 122.

*papakāinga*   House or settlement site, especially part of a *marae* reserve set aside for housing.

*parāoa*   Transliteration of 'flour'; also used to mean 'bread'; p. 102.

*parata*   Transliteration of 'brother'; also used for classificatory 'brother', i.e. male cousin of same generation; p. 123.

*partition*   Division of a block of 'Maori land' by the Maori Land Court on application from the successors.

*pātaka*   Storehouse raised on piles; usually carved; p. 9.

*pātere*   Fast, vigorous chant with impromptu gestures composed in reply to slander.

*pirihimana*   Transliteration of 'policeman'; also applied to wardens appointed by Maori communities to keep order within their own boundaries; pp. 186, 213.

*piupiu*   A kilt of dried flax cylinders attached to a waistband, derived from pre-European kilt but developed in post-European times; part of standard dress of Maori concert parties.

*pō*   Night. Te Pō, Realm of Night and Death, place of departed spirits; pp. 28, 55–8.

*pōhutukawa*   *Metrosideros excelsa*, a tree with red blossoms.

*poi*   A light ball on a string swung rhythmically to a song; a dance performed with *poi*.

*poroporoaki*  Farewell; speech(es) given by visitors before departing, modern usage; reserved by elders for speech farewelling a person who has died and is lying in state prior to burial; p. 262.

*pōtiki*  Youngest of siblings.

*pou*  Post, pole; figuratively, support, teacher, expert.

*poukai*  Gatherings held annually by certain King Movement communities to express loyalty to the Maori Queen; p. 197.

*poupou*  Carved slabs placed at intervals along walls inside the meeting-house.

*poutokomanawa*  Free-standing heart-post supporting the ridge-pole of a meeting-house.

*pōwhiri*  Beckon to come on, welcome; action-song(s) or chant(s) of welcome; section of the welcome ceremony; p. 251.

*pūhā*  *Sonchus oleraceus*, sow thistle, cooked by boiling with meat.

*rākau*  Tree; wood, timber; stick; weapon; implement; the carved stick used in the challenge to visitors; pp. 151, 250.

*rangatahi*  A fishing net; the younger generations; young people with a capacity for leadership; pp. 173, 204.

*rangatira*  Aristocrat; chief, director of an enterprise; *hoa rangatira* = wife; pp. 7, 201.

*rangi*  Sky. Rangi, Sky Father of Maori mythology; Te Rangi, Heaven, the heavens, the abode in Classic Maori religious belief of the gods and especially of Io (in the topmost, most sacred heaven); pp. 23, 55–8.

*raro*  The bottom, the underside; down, downwards, down below; the underworld; the north; complementary opposite of *runga*.

*raupatu*  Conquest; confiscation of Maori land by the Government after the 'Maori Wars'.

*ringa wera*  Literally 'the hot hands'; the cooks behind the scenes especially at *hui*.

*runanga*   Assembly, council of sub-tribal or tribal elders; p. 25.

*runga*   The top, the upper part; up, upwards, up above; the south.

*sectional leaders*   Persons who act as leaders for sections of the community on limited occasions and for limited purposes; pp. 203–4.

*small-family*   Nuclear family of parents and children.

*surplus lands*   Lands which the Government retained after disallowing settlers' claims to have bought them from the Maoris; p. 32.

*tāhae*   V.tr. steal; n. thief; in some tribes, e.g. Tūhoe and Ngāti Porou, young fellow.

*tāhuhu*   Ridgepole of a meeting-house; figuratively the back-bone of the ancestor for whom the meeting-house is named; direct line of ancestry; eldest son of most senior branch of a family.

*taiaha*   A traditional weapon of hard wood with a blade for striking at one head and a carved head for stabbing at the other.

*taitamariki*   Youth; young adults not yet fully mature in Maori eyes; pp. 172, 218.

*takahi*   To stamp; a ceremony performed after a funeral to lift the *tapu* from the deceased's home.

*take*   Cause, reason; major subject of a speech.

*taki*   Challenge, Northern usage; cf. *wero*.

*tama*   Son; also classificatory 'son'.

*tamāhine*   Daughter; also classificatory 'daughter'.

*tāne*   Male; husband.

*tangata*, pl. *tāngata*   Human being; man; pl. people.

*tangata whenua*   A person connected with a place through a line of occupying ancestors and preferably also owning 'Maori land' there; pp. 107–9.

*tangi*  Weeping; stylized wailing performed over the dead by women; weeping together over recent dead when meeting after separation; a chanted lament for the dead.

*tangihanga*  A funeral wake lasting several days; pp. 261–4.

*taokete*  Brother-in-law of a male, sister-in-law of a female in Classic kinship terminology; now used for brother- and sister-in-law by persons of both sexes; pp. 18, 122.

*taonga*  Anything highly prized; treasure; heirloom.

*tapu*  Under religious restriction; sacred or unclean according to context; pp. 8, 58–60.

*tara*  Sidewall of a house.

*tara iti*  The floor space of a meeting-house occupied by the 'home folks', the complementary opposite of the *tara whānui*.

*tara whānui*  The floor space of a meeting-house reserved for guests, in most tribes to the right of the central alley-way on entering the house; pp. 232, 255.

*tātau, tātou*  Variant forms of the first person plural pronoun including the person or persons addressed; you-and-us; p. 312.

*taumau*  Betrothal, especially in infancy.

*tauparapara*  Prologue to a formal speech.

*taurekareka*  Slave.

*teina*, pl. *tēina*  Younger sibling of the same sex; cousin of the same sex and generation in a junior line.

*tika*  Straight, direct; right, correct; p. 62.

*tikanga*  Rule, plan, method; way of doing something, custom; *ngā tikanga Maori* 'Maori ways'; pp. 48, 62.

*tinana*  Body, trunk, the main part of anything; the physical aspect of man; p. 57.

*tipuna = tupuna.*

*toa*   Adj. male of animals; brave; boisterous, rough, stormy; n. brave man, warrior; bravery; roughness of sea. In duplicative form, *totoa*, impetuous, fierce; boisterous, stormy; reckless.

*tohi*   Pre-European rite performed by *tohunga* involving ritual cleansing and dedication of a child to a god; Buck, 1949: 353.

*tohunga*   Expert, specialist, followed in pre-European times by term indicating specialization, pp. 11, 24; popularly used today to describe a Maori healer; also used for ministers of the Ringatū Church, pp. 93, 186.

*tohunga ahurewa*   Pre-European specialist in religious knowledge, priest.

*tokotoko*   Walking-stick.

*tomo*   Formal meeting of kin to discuss a match and arrange a wedding; modern; p. 140.

*Treaty of Waitangi*   Treaty signed by Captain Hobson RN representing the Queen of England and various Maori chiefs at Waitangi, 6 February 1840; p. 31.

*tū*   V.tr. stand, be erect; also fight with. Adj. vehement, energetic.

*tū mai, tū atu*   Method of ordering speeches during welcome ceremony; hosts and guests speak alternately with hosts opening and closing sequence; p. 252.

*tūāahu*   A sacred place or altar consisting of one or more stones sometimes enclosed by poles or rods, always out of doors; pre-European.

*tuahine*, pl. *tuāhine*   Sister of a male, own and classificatory.

*tuakana*, pl. *tuākana*   Older sibling of the same sex; cousin of same sex and generation in a senior line; pp. 18, 122.

*tukutuku*   Latticework panels consisting of battens placed crosswise over reeds and secured by cross-stitches of flax and other natural materials in geometric patterns.

*tumuaki*  Crown of head; head, president; with capital T, a hereditary leader in the King Movement; p. 197.

*tungāne*  Brother of a female, classificatory 'brother' of a female.

*tūpāpaku*  Deceased person.

*tupuna*, pl. *tūpuna*  Grandparent of either sex, own and classificatory; ancestor.

*tūrangawaewae*  Literally, a standing-place for the feet; used to describe the *marae* and 'Maori land' shares, p. 109; with capital T, the Maori Queen's capital at Ngaruawahia.

'*unveiling*'  Ceremonial unveiling of memorial gravestone; *hurahanga kōhatu*; p. 259.

*utu*  Return for anything, good or bad; the principle of reciprocity; pp. 15, 67.

*utu-utu*  Method of ordering speeches during welcome ceremony = *tū mai, tū atu.*

*waewae tapu*  Literally sacred feet, guest(s) visiting a particular *marae* for the first time; p. 234.

*wahine*, pl. *wāhine*  Female, woman; wife.

*waiata*  Song-poem, especially those characterized by a melody, sung rather than chanted, i.e. *waiata tangi* (lament), *waiata aroha* (song of mourning, for loved ones lost), *oriori* (song for instructing children).

*waiata-ā-ringa*  Action-song; modern; see above.

*wairua*  Spirit, spiritual aspect of man, soul; p. 57.

*waka*  Canoe; loose association of tribes stemming from ancestors who came to New Zealand in the same canoe; p. 5.

*Warden, Maori*  Honorary wardens appointed by the Government with limited powers; p. 212.

*wero*  Ceremonial challenge; p. 250.

*whaea*   Mother; own and classificatory.

*whai-kōrero*   Formal speech-making, oratory, in Maori.

*whakahīhī*   Lofty; spirited, enterprising; vain, conceited, 'stuck-up'; p. 66.

*whakairo*   Carving in traditional style.

*whakaiti*   V.tr. belittle; adj. humble, modest (= self-belittling); p. 66.

*whakamā*   Conscious of being at a disadvantage; beset by feelings of inadequacy, discomfort, uncertainty, shyness, shame or guilt; a complex syndrome of feelings and behaviour involving withdrawal from personal and social interaction; pp. 65, 219.

*whakanoa*   To make common, available for use by lifting a *tapu* from.

*whakapapa*   Descent-lines and tables; pp. 127–8.

*whakataukī*   Proverbs and aphoristic sayings; p. 267.

*whāmere, whāmira*   Transliteration of 'family'; modern.

*whānako*   V.tr. steal; n. theft; thief; p. 217.

*whānau*   (a) extended family household in pre-European times; (b) a living elder and his descendants; p. 6.

*whānau pani*   Bereaved nuclear family.

*whanaunga, whanaungatanga*   Kinsman; kinship.

*whāngai*   Feed; nourish, bring up. *Matua whāngai*, adoptive parent; *tamaiti whāngai*, adopted child; pp. 22, 144.

*whare*   A rectangular one-roomed house; both pre-European and modern.

*whare hui*   Meeting-house; also sometimes called *whare nui* ('big-house') p. 230.

*whare kai* Modern dining-hall.

*whare wānanga* 'School of learning'; in pre-European times, restricted to selected male aristocrats; today often applied to the university.

*whētu* Star.

*Whētu Mārama* Identifying symbol and name of newspaper of the Ratana Church; pp. 189, 190.

*Young Maori Party* A group of young Maori professional men who worked for social and health reforms among Maoris in the 1890s and early twentieth century; p. 36.

# Bibliography

Maori writers marked*

*JPS* is the *Journal of the Polynesian Society*, published Wellington.

## A. The Maoris before 1880

Best, Elsdon (1924), *The Maori*, 2 vols, Wellington: Memoirs of the Polynesian Society no. 5.

Biggs, Bruce (1960), *Maori Marriage*, Wellington: Polynesian Society Maori Monographs no. 1.

*Buck, Peter (1949), *The Coming of the Maori*, Wellington: Maori Purposes Fund Board and Whitcombe and Tombs Ltd.

Duff, Roger (1956), *The Moahunter Period of Maori Culture*, Wellington: Government Printer.

Firth, Raymond (1957), 'A note on descent-groups in Polynesia', *Man*, 57: 4–8.

Firth, Raymond (1959), *Economics of the New Zealand Maori*, 2nd edn (1st edn, 1929), Wellington: Government Printer.

Firth, Raymond (1963), 'Bilateral descent groups: an operational viewpoint', in *Studies in Kinship and Marriage* (ed.) I. Schapera, RAI, Occasional Paper no. 16: 22–37.

Golson, Jack (1959), 'Culture change in prehistoric New Zealand', in *Anthropology in the South Seas* (ed.) J. D. Freeman and W. R. Geddes, New Plymouth: Avery: 29–74.

Golson, Jack (ed.) (1972), *Polynesian Navigation*, Wellington: Polynesian Society Memoir no. 34.

Green, Roger C. (1963), *A Review of the Prehistoric Sequence of the Auckland Province*, Auckland: N.Z. Archaeological Association no. 2.

Green, Roger C. (1974), 'Adaptation and change in Maori culture', in *Ecology and Biogeography in New Zealand* (ed.) G. Kuschel, The Hague: Dr W. Junk.

Groube, L. M. (1964), 'Settlement patterns in prehistoric New Zealand', M.A. thesis, University of Auckland.

351

Groube, L. M. (1967), 'Models in prehistory: a consideration of the New Zealand evidence', *Archaeology and Physical Anthropology in Oceania*, vol. 2 (1): 1–27.

Heuer, Berys (1972), *Maori Women*, Wellington: Polynesian Society Maori Monographs no. 3, A. H. & A. W. Reed.

Johansen, J. Prytz (1954), *The Maori and his Religion in its Non-Ritualistic Aspects*, Copenhagen: Ejnar Munksgaard.

Johansen, J. Prytz (1958), *Studies in Maori Rites and Myths*, Copenhagen: Ejnar Munksgaard.

Oppenheim, Roger (1973), *Maori Death Customs*, Wellington: A. H. & A. W. Reed.

Roberton, J. B. W. (1962), 'The evolution of Maori tribal tradition as history', *JPS*, 71 (3): 293–309.

Roberton, J. B. W. (1965), *Maori Settlement of the Waikato District*, Te Awamutu: Te Awamutu Historical Society Bulletin no. 2.

Scheffler, H. W. (1964), 'Descent concepts and descent groups: the Maori case', *JPS*, 73 (2): 126–32.

Sharp, Andrew (1959), 'Maori genealogies and the Fleet', *JPS*, 68: 12–13.

Sharp, Andrew (1963), *Ancient Voyagers in Polynesia*, Auckland: Paul's Book Arcade.

Shawcross, Kathleen (1967), 'Fern-root and the total scheme of 18th century Maori food production in agricultural areas', *JPS*, 78 (3): 330–52.

Simmons, D. R. (1969a), 'A New Zealand myth: Kupe, Toi and the Great Fleet', *N.Z. J. of History*, 3: 14–31.

Simmons, D. R. (1969b), 'Economic change in New Zealand prehistory', *JPS*, 78 (1): 3–34.

Smith, Jean (1974), 'Tapu removal in Maori religion', *JPS*, 83 (4): Polynesian Society Memoir Supplement no. 40.

Vayda, A. P. (1960), *Maori Warfare*, Wellington: Polynesian Society Maori Monographs no. 2, A. H. and A. W. Reed.

Yen, D. E. (1961), 'The adaptation of the *kumara* by the New Zealand Maori', *JPS*, 70 (3): 338–48.

## B. The years between

Barrington, J. M. and T. H. Beaglehole (1974), *Maori Schools in a Changing Society*, Wellington: N.Z. Council for Educational Research.

Binney, Judith (1966), 'Papahurihia: some thoughts on interpretation', *JPS*, 75: 321–31.

Binney, Judith (1967), *The Legacy of Guilt: a life of Thomas Kendall*, Auckland: Oxford University Press for University of Auckland.

Binney, Judith (1969), 'Christianity and the Maoris to 1840. A comment', *N.Z. J. of History*, 3: 43–65. Refers to J. M. R. Owen's article in *N.Z. J. of History*, 2: 18–40, 1968.

Butterworth, G. V. (1972), 'A rural Maori renaissance? Maori society and politics 1920–51', *JPS*, 81: 160–95.

Clark, Paul (1975), '*Hauhau*': *The Pai Marire search for Maori identity*, Auckland: Auckland University Press. Oxford: Oxford University Press.

Cumberland, Kenneth (1950), 'A land despoiled: New Zealand about 1838', *N.Z. Geographer*, 6: 13–34.

Cumberland, Kenneth (1954), ' "Jimmy Grants" and "Mihaneres": New Zealand about 1853', *Economic Geography*, 30: 70–89.

Dalton, B. J. (1967), *War and Politics in New Zealand 1855–1870*, Sydney: University Press.

Gadd, Bernard (1966), 'The teachings of Te Whiti O Rongomai', *JPS*, 75: 445–57.

Gorst, John (1864), *The Maori King*, reprinted 1959 Hamilton and Auckland: Paul's Book Arcade.

Hargreaves, R. P. (1959), 'Maori agriculture of the Auckland Province in the mid-nineteenth century', *JPS*, 68 (2): 61–79.

Hargreaves, R. P. (1960), 'Maori agriculture after the wars (1871–1886)', *JPS*, 69 (4): 354–67.

Hargreaves, R. P. (1963), 'Changing Maori agriculture in pre-Waitangi New Zealand', *JPS*, 72 (2): 101–17.

Holst, Halvor (1958), 'The Maori Schools in Maori education', *Education*, 7: 53–9, Wellington: Department of Education.

Miller, Harold (1966), *Race Conflict in New Zealand 1814–1865*, Auckland: Blackwood & Janet Paul.

Miller, John (1958), *Early Victorian New Zealand*, Oxford University Press.

Owens, J. M. R. (1968), 'Christianity and the Maoris to 1840', *N.Z. J. of History*, 2: 18–40.

Owens, J. M. R. (1974), *Prophets in the Wilderness: the Wesleyan Mission to New Zealand 1819–27*, Auckland: Auckland University Press.

Parr, C. J. (1961), 'A missionary library. Printed attempts to instruct the Maori 1815–45', *JPS*, 70 (4): 429–50.

Parr, C. J. (1963), 'Maori literacy 1843–67', *JPS*, 72: 211–34.

Rusden, G. W. (1888), *Aureretanga: groans of the Maoris*, London: William Ridgeway, reprinted Wellington: Hakaprint 1974.

Scott, R. G. (Dick) (1954), *The Parihaka Story*, Auckland: Southern Cross Books.

Scott, R. G. (1975), *Ask that Mountain*, Auckland: Heinemann-Southern Cross, revised and amplified version of *The Parihaka Story*.

Sinclair, Keith (1957), *The Origin of the Maori Wars*, Wellington: N.Z. University Press.

Sinclair, Keith (1959), *A History of New Zealand*, Harmondsworth: Penguin Books.

Sorrenson, M. P. K. (1956), 'Land purchase methods and their effect on Maori population 1865–1901', *JPS*, 65 (3): 183–99.

Sorrenson, M. P. K. (1963), 'The Maori King Movement 1858–1885', in *Studies of a Small Democracy* (ed.) Robert Chapman and Keith Sinclair, Auckland: Paul's Book Arcade for the University of Auckland.

Sorrenson, M. P. K. (1967), *Maori and European since 1870. A study in adaptation and adjustment*, London and Auckland: Heinemann.

Ward, Alan (1967), 'The origin of the Anglo–Maori Wars: a re-consideration', *N.Z. J. of History*,1 (2): 148–70.

Ward, Alan (1973), *A Show of Justice*, Auckland University Press/Oxford

University Press.

Wards, Ian (1968), *The Shadow of the Land*, Wellington: Government Printer.

Wilson, G. H. Ormond (1963), 'Maori and Pakeha', *JPS*, 72 (1): 11–20.

Wilson, G. H. Ormond (1965), 'Papahurihia, first Maori prophet', *JPS*, 74: 473–83.

Williams, J. A. (1969), *Politics of the New Zealand Maori: protest and co-operation 1891–1909*, Oxford University Press.

*Winiata, Maharaia (1967), *The Changing Role of the Leader in Maori Society*, Auckland: Blackwood & Janet Paul.

Wright, Harrison M. (1959), *New Zealand 1769–1840: the early years of Western contact*, Harvard University Press.


## C.   Maoris in the twentieth century

(General Bibliography chapters 4–18)

Adult Education, National Council of (1972), *Maori Adult Education*, Wellington: National Council of Adult Education.

Alexander, R. P. (1969), 'Stereotypes and Maori work attendance', *JPS*, 78: 127–9.

Archer, Dane and Mary (1970), 'Race, identity and the Maori people', *JPS*, 79: 201–18, reprinted in Webb and Collette (1973).

Archer, Dane and Mary (1971–2), 'Maoris in cities', *Race*, 13: 179–85.

Archer, D., R. S. Oppenheim, T. S. Karetu and R. St George (1971), 'Intelligence and the Pakeha child', *National Education*, 53: 258–60, reprinted in Webb and Collette (1973).

Ashton-Warner, Sylvia (1963), *Teacher*, London: Secker and Warburg.

Ausubel, David (1960a), *The Fern and the Tiki*, Sydney: Angus and Robertson.

Ausubel, David (1960b), 'Acculturative stress in modern Maori adolescence', *Child Development* (Baltimore), 31: 617–31.

Ausubel, David (1961a), *Maori Youth*, Wellington: Price Milburn.

Ausubel, David (1961b), 'The Maori: a study in resistive acculturation', *Social Forces*, 39: 218–27.

Barham, I. H. (1965), *The English Vocabulary and Sentence Structure of Maori Children*, Wellington: N.Z. Council for Educational Research. Reviewed by D. Walsh in *JPS*, 74: 129–30.

Barrington, J. M. (1966), 'Maori scholastic achievement: historical review of policies and provisions', *N.Z. J. of Educ. Studies*, 1: 1–14.

Barrington, J. M. (1971), 'Education, labour force and race in New Zealand', *Sociology and Social Research*, 55: 449–53.

Beaglehole, Ernest and Pearl (1946), *Some Modern Maoris*, Wellington: N.Z. Council for Educational Research.

Beaglehole, Ernest and James Ritchie (1958), 'The Rakau Maori studies', *JPS*, 67 (2): 132–54.

Bender, Byron, W. (1971), *Linguistic Factors in Maori Education*, Wellington: N.Z. Council for Educational Research.

Benton, R. A. (1965), *Research into the Language Difficulties of Maori School Children*, Wellington: Maori Education Foundation.

Blake-Palmer, G. (1954), 'Tohungaism and *makutu*', *JPS*, 63 (2): 147–63.

Blake-Palmer, G. (1956), 'Maori attitudes to sickness', *Med. J. Australia*, 2: 401–5.

Booth, John (1959), 'A modern Maori community,' in *Anthropology in the South Seas* (ed.) J. D. Freeman and W. R. Geddes: 235–45, New Plymouth: Avery.

Borrie, W. D. (1959), 'The Maori population: microcosm of a new world', in *Anthropology in the South Seas* (ed.) J. D. Freeman and W. R. Geddes: 247–63, New Plymouth: Avery.

Bray, D. H. (1970), 'Extent of future time orientation: a cross-ethnic study among N.Z. adolescents', *Brit. J. of Educ. Psychology*, 40: 200–8.

Bray, D. H. (1971), 'Maori adolescent temporal values: distance of goals perceived as important and of delayed gratification as compared with Pakehas', *N.Z. J. of Educ. Studies*, 6: 62–77.

Bray, Douglas and Clement Hill (1973), *Polynesian and Pakeha in New Zealand Education*, vol. I: *The Sharing of Cultures*, Heinemann Educational Books.

Bray, Douglas and Clement Hill (1974), *Polynesian and Pakeha in New Zealand Education*, vol. II: *Ethnic Difference and the School*, Heinemann Educational Books.

Brookes, R. H. and I. H. Kawharu (eds) (1967), *Administration in New Zealand's Multi-Racial Society*, Wellington: N.Z. Institute of Public Administration; also Oxford University Press.

Burch, William R. (1967), 'Cross-cultural dialogues: some trained incapacities of educators', *N.Z. J. of Educ. Studies*, 5: 142–52.

Burch, William R. (1973), 'Sectarian rhetoric and the survival of uniqueness', in *New Zealand Society: contemporary perspectives* (ed.) S. D. Webb and John Collette: 283–96. Sydney: John Wiley.

Butterworth, Graham V. (1974), *The Maori People in the New Zealand Economy*, Palmerston North: Massey University (Department of Social Anthropology and Maori Studies).

*Dansey, Harry (1963), *The New Zealand Maori in Colour*, with photographs by Kenneth and Jean Bigwood, Wellington: Reed.

*Dansey, Harry (1971), *Maori Custom Today*, Auckland: New Zealand Newspapers Ltd.

De Bres, Pieter (1970), *Religion in Atene: religious associations and the urban Maori*, Polynesian Society Memoir no. 37, supplement to vol. 79 (3 & 4).

Earle, Margaret (1958), *Rakau Children*, Wellington: Victoria University of Wellington Publications in Psychology no. 11.

Education in New Zealand, New Zealand Commission on (1962), 'Maori education', in *Report of the Commission on Education in New Zealand* (known as 'the Currie Report'): 401–37. Wellington: Government Printer.

Education, New Zealand Department of (1971), 'The education of Maori children: a review', *Education* (Wellington), 20 (4): 17–26.

Education, New Zealand Department of (School Publications) (1971), *Maori Children and the Teacher*, Wellington: Government Printer.

# Bibliography

Education, New Zealand Department of (1974), *Report of the Department of Education for the period ended 31 March 1974*. Wellington: Government Printer.

Ewing, John and Jack Shallcrass (1970), *Introduction to Maori Education*, Wellington: N.Z. University Press.

Fitzgerald, T. K. (1968), 'The social position of the Maori university graduate', *Polynesian Studies*, 7, Wellington: Wellington Teachers' College.

Fitzgerald, T. K. (1970), 'The first generation of Maori university graduates: a historical sketch,' *N.Z. J. of Educ. Studies*, 5: 47–62.

Forster, John (1969), 'Social development and labour force participation – the case of the Maori', *Pacific Viewpoint*, 10: 78–92.

Forster, John and P. D. K. Ramsay (1969), 'Migration, education and occupation', in *Social Process in New Zealand* (ed.) John Forster, Auckland: Longman Paul.

Foster, Frank H. (1962), *Maori Patients in Mental Hospitals*, New Zealand Department of Health Med. Stats Branch, Special Report 8, Wellington: Government Printer.

Foster, Frank H. (1965), *Maori Patients in Public Hospitals*, New Zealand Department of Health, Special Report 25, Wellington: Government Printer.

Geddes, W. R. (1961), 'Maori and Aborigine: a comparison of attitudes and policies', *The Australian J. of Science*, 24 (5): 217–25.

Greenwood, William (1942), *The Upraised Hand*, Wellington: Polynesian Society Memoir no. 21.

Gronfors, M. J. (1973), 'Give a dog a bad name', Victoria University of Wellington (Department of Anthropology), unpublished research paper.

Gronfors, M. J. and Mugford, S. K. (1973), 'Race justice or class justice? Some data from a pilot study on sentencing of first offenders', unpublished paper presented to the Third National Conference of the New Zealand Sociological Association, Wellington, November 1973.

Harker, R. K. (1970), 'Maori enrolment at N.Z. universities 1956–68', *N.Z. J. of Educ. Studies*, 5: 142–52.

Harker, R. K. (1971a), 'Socio-economic and cultural factors in Maori academic attainment', *JPS*, 80: 20–41.

Harker, R. K. (1971b), 'Social class factors in a New Zealand comprehensive school', *Educational Research*, 13 (2): 155–8; reprinted in *Schools in N.Z. Society* (ed.) G. H. Robinson and B. T. O'Rourke, Sydney: John Wiley.

Harre, John (1962), 'A case of racial discrimination in New Zealand', *JPS*, 71 (2): 257–60.

Harre, John (1965), 'The relevance of ancestry as a factor in social and cultural choice', *JPS*, 74 (1): 3–20.

Harre, John (1966), *Maori and Pakeha*, Wellington: Institute of Race Relations and Reed.

Hartley, Eugene L. and Richard Thompson (1967), 'Racial integration and role differentiation', *JPS*, 76: 427–43; reprinted in Webb and Collette (eds) 1968: 68–81.

Bibliography

Hawthorn, H. B. (1944), *The Maori: A study in acculturation*, American Anthropology Association Memoir 46.

Henderson, J. McLeod (1963), *Ratana: the origins and the story of the movement*, Wellington: Polynesian Society Memoir no. 36.

*Hohepa, P. W. (1964), *A Maori Community in Northland*, Auckland: University of Auckland; reprinted 1970, Wellington: Reed.

*Hohepa, P. W. (1972), 'Cultural minorities in Auckland', in *Equality of Opportunity through Education*: 16–24. Wellington: Association for the Study of Childhood.

Hunn, J. K. (1961), *Report on the Department of Maori Affairs 24 August 1960*, Wellington: Government Printer.

Hunn, J. K. and John Booth (1962), *Integration of Maori and Pakeha*, Wellington: Government Printer.

Jackson, W. K. and G. A. Wood (1964), 'The New Zealand Parliament and Maori representation', *Historical Studies: Australia and New Zealand* (University of Melbourne), 11: 383–96.

Johnson, J. Garfield (1973), 'A multi-racial college', in *Secondary Schools in Change* (ed.) J. Shallcrass: 16–17. Wellington: Price Milburn.

Johnson, J. Garfield (1974), 'A secondary school for a multi-ethnic suburb', in Bray and Hill, II: 148–59.

*Jones, Pei Te Hurinui (1971), *Turangawaewae Marae: Souvenir of the Golden Jubilee, 1921–1971*, Taumarunui: Pei Te Hurinui Jones.

Justice, New Zealand Department of (1968), *Crime in New Zealand*, Wellington: Government Printer. (See also Roberts, 1972; Schumacher, 1971a and b.)

Justice, New Zealand Department of (1974), *Report of the Department of Justice for the year ended 31 March 1974*, Wellington: Government Printer.

Justice, New Zealand Department of (1975), *Justice Department Penal Census 1972*, Justice Department Research Section, Wellington: Government Printer.

*Kawharu, I. H. (1973), 'Increasing the Maori contribution in manufacturing industry', in *Contemporary New Zealand* (ed.) K. W. Thomson and A. D. Trlin, 39–47, Wellington: Hicks Smith.

*Kawharu, I. H. (ed.) (1975a), *Conflict and Compromise: essays on the Maori since colonisation*, Wellington: Reed.

*Kawharu, I. H. (1975b), *Orakei: A Ngati Whatua Community*, Wellington: N.Z. Council for Educational Research.

Keesing, Felix (1928), *The Changing Maori*, New Plymouth: Board of Ethnological Research.

Keesing, Felix (1929), 'Maori progress on the East Coast', *Te Wananga* (Journal of the Board of Ethnological Research) 1: 10–56, 92–127.

Kelly, R. A. (1962), 'The politics of racial equality', *N.Z. J. Public Admin.*, 24 (2): 23–36.

Kernot, C. B. J. (1964), 'Maori-European relationships and the role of mediators', *JPS*, 73: 171–8.

Kernot, C. B. J. (1972), *People of the Four Winds*, Wellington: Hicks Smith.

King, Michael (1975), *Te Ao Hurihuri: The world moves on*, Wellington:

357

# Bibliography

Hicks Smith.

Labour, New Zealand Department of (1968), *Maori Employment and Unemployment*, Wellington: Government Printer.

Lee, Margaret (1974), *Nga Kai-Mahi*, Wellington: Government Printer.

Lovegrove, M. N. (1966), 'The scholastic achievements of European and Maori children', *N.Z. J. Educ. Studies*, 1: 15–39.

Ludbrook, R. (1975), 'The Law and Polynesians', *Proc. 16th Triennial Conference New Zealand Law Society:* 48–61. Wellington: N.Z. Law Society.

McCreary, John R. and John Rangihau, *Parents and Children of Ruatahuna*, Wellington: Victoria University of Wellington (School of Social Science).

McDonald, Geraldine (1970), 'The parent, the play-centre and the community', in *The Role of the Parent in the Education of his Child*, Wellington: Association for the Study of Childhood.

McDonald, Geraldine (1973), *Maori Mothers and Pre-School Education*, Wellington: N.Z. Council for Educational Research.

McDonald, Geraldine (1975a), 'A comment on some of the concepts and methods used in studies of Maoris and education', *N.Z. J. Educ. Studies*, 10 (1): 75–83.

McDonald, Geraldine (1975b), 'The categories "Maori" and "Pakeha" as defined by research workers and by self-report', *N.Z.J. Educ. Studies*, 11: 37–49.

McKean, W. A. (1971), *Essays on Race Relations and the Law in New Zealand*, Wellington: Sweet and Maxwell.

Mackenzie, Mary (1970), *Maori Education 1960–69: A bibliography*, Wellington: N.Z. Council for Educational Research.

Maori Affairs, New Zealand Department of (1964), *The Maori Today*, 3rd edn, Wellington: Government Printer.

Maori Affairs, New Zealand Department of (annually), *Report of the Department of Maori Affairs*, Wellington: Government Printer.

Maori Affairs, New Zealand Department of (quarterly since 1952), *Te Ao Hou*, Wellington: Department of Maori Affairs.

Maori Reserved Land, Commission of Inquiry into (1975), *Report*, Wellington: Government Printer.

Marae Subsidies, Committee on (1974), *Report of Committee on Marae Subsidies September 1974*, Wellington: Government Printer.

Maxwell, Gabrielle M. (1962), *Research Needed in the Education of Maori Children: proceedings of a conference 1961*, Wellington: N.Z. Council for Educational Research.

Metge, Joan (1964a), *A New Maori Migration: rural and urban relations in northern New Zealand*, London School of Economics Monographs in Social Anthropology no. 27, London and Melbourne: Athlone Press and Melbourne University Press.

Metge, Joan (1964b), 'Rural local savings associations (Maori *komiti*) in New Zealand's Far North', in *Capital, Saving and Credit in Peasant Societies* (ed.) Raymond Firth and B. S. Yamey, 207–29, London: Allen & Unwin.

Metge, Joan (1967), *The Maoris of New Zealand*, 1st edn, London: Routledge & Kegan Paul.

Metge, Joan (1970), 'The Maori family', in *Marriage and the Family in New Zealand* (ed.) S. Houston: 111–41, Wellington: Sweet & Maxwell.
Metge, Joan and Dugal Campbell (1958), 'The Rakau Maori Studies: A review article', *JPS*, 67 (4): 352–86.
Mol, J. J. (1964), 'Race relations with special reference to New Zealand: a theoretical discussion', *JPS*, 73 (4): 375–81.
Mol, J. J. (1966), *Religion and Race in New Zealand*, Christchurch: National Council of Churches in New Zealand.
Mulligan, D. G. (1957), *Maori Adolescence in Rakau*, Wellington: Victoria University of Wellington, Publications in Psychology no. 9.
*Murray, Saana (1974), *Te Karanga a te kotuku*, Wellington: Maori Organization On Human Rights, Box 19036, Wellington.
National Council of Churches in New Zealand (Women's Committee) (1964), *Maori and Pakeha: studies in Christian responsibility*, Christchurch: Presbyterian Bookroom.
New Zealand National Advisory Committee on Maori Education (1971), *Report on Maori Education*, Wellington: Government Printer.
New Zealand National Development Conference (1969), Maori education and training, section in the *Report of the Committee on education, training and research to the National Development Conference*, National Development Conference 12: 54–5, Wellington: Government Printer.
New Zealand Educational Development Conference (1974), Chapter 16: 'Maori education', in *Improving Learning and Teaching: report of the working party on improving learning and teaching:* 195–202, Wellington: Government Printer.
New Zealand Educational Institute (Maori Education Committee), (1967), *Report and Recommendations on Maori Education*, Wellington: N.Z. Educational Institute.
New Zealand Post Primary Teachers' Association (1970), *Maori Education: an interim report*. Wellington: N.Z. Post Primary Teachers' Association.
New Zealand Maori Council (monthly magazine), *Te Maori*, Wellington: N.Z. Maori Council.
Nield, P. G. (1971), 'Maori-non-Maori labour force participation in urban areas', *Pacific Viewpoint*, 12: 171–85.
O'Malley P. T. (1973) 'The influence of cultural factors on Maori crime rates' in *New Zealand Society: Contemporary Perspectives* (ed.) S. D. Webb and J. Collette: 386–96, Sydney: John Wiley.
Parent-School Communication, New Zealand Committee of Enquiry on (1973), *Report on Parent-School Communication*, Wellington: Government Printer.
Pearson, W. H. (1958), 'Attitudes to the Maori in some Pakeha fiction', *JPS*, 67 (3): 211–38. (See also Schwimmer, 1968: 217–56.)
Pierce, B. F. (1967), 'A case study of Maori work attendance', *JPS*, 76: 405–14. Also reply to criticism by R. P. Alexander, *JPS*, 78: 129–35.
Pocock, J. G. A. (1963), *The Maori and New Zealand Politics*, Auckland: Blackwood & Janet Paul.
Pool, Ian (1963), 'When is a Maori a "Maori"?', *JPS*, 72: 206–10.
Pool, Ian (1966), 'Rural-urban migration of Maoris: a demographic

analysis', *Pacific Viewpoint*, 7: 88–96.

Presbyterian Church of New Zealand (Maori Synod) (1961), *A Maori View of the Hunn Report*, Christchurch: Presbyterian Bookroom.

Prior, Ian (1962), 'A health survey in a rural Maori community', *N.Z. Medical J.*, 61: 333–48.

Pritchard, Ivor (Chairman) and Hemi Tono Waetford (1965), *Report of Committee of Enquiry into Laws Affecting Maori Land and Powers of the Maori Land Court*, Wellington: Department of Maori Affairs.

Race Relations Conciliator (1973), *Report for the Year ended 31 March 1973*, Wellington: Government Printer.

Race Relations Conciliator (1974), *Report for the Year ended 31 March 1974*. Wellington: Government Printer.

*Rakena, Rua (1971), *The Maori Response to the Gospel*, Auckland: Wesley Historical Society (New Zealand).

Ramsay, Peter (1972), 'Maori schooling', in *Issues in Special Education* (ed.) S. S. Havill and D. R. Mitchell: 60–77.

Richardson, Elwyn (1964), *In the Early World*, Wellington: N.Z. Council for Educational Research.

Ritchie, James (1956a), *Basic Personality in Rakau*, Wellington: Victoria University of Wellington Publications in Psychology no. 8.

Ritchie, James (1956b), 'Human problems and educational change in a Maori community', *JPS*, 65 (1): 13–34.

Ritchie, James (1963), *The Making of a Maori*, Wellington: Reed.

Ritchie, James (ed.) (1964a), *Race Relations: six New Zealand studies*, Wellington: Victoria University of Wellington Publications in Psychology no. 16.

Ritchie, James (1964b), 'The future of being a Maori', in *The future of New Zealand* (ed.) M. F. Lloyd-Pritchard, Christchurch: Whitcombe & Tombs.

Ritchie, Jane (1957), *Childhood in Rakau*, Wellington: Victoria University of Wellington Publications in Psychology no. 10.

Ritchie, Jane (1964), *Maori Families*, Wellington: Victoria University of Wellington Publications in Psychology no. 17.

Ritchie, Jane and James (1970), *Child-rearing Patterns in New Zealand*, Wellington: Reed.

Roberts, Jocelyn (1972), *Self-image and Delinquency*, Justice Department Research Series no. 3, Wellington: Government Printer.

Rose, B. S. (1962), 'Maori health and European culture', *N.Z. Medical J.*, 61: 491–5.

Rose, Richard J. (1960), *Maori-European Standards of Health*, New Zealand Department of Health Med. Stats Branch Special Report 1, Wellington: Government Printer.

Rose, Richard J. (1972), *Maori-European Comparisons of Mortality*, New Zealand Department of Health Special Report 37, Wellington: Government Printer.

St George, Ross (1973), 'Racial intolerance in New Zealand: a review of studies', in *Schools in New Zealand Society: a book of readings* (ed.) G. H. Robinson and B. T. O'Rourke, Sydney: John Wiley.

Salmond, Ann (1975), *Hui*, Wellington: Reed.

Schumacher, Mary (1971a), *Waipiata: a study of trainees in an open Borstal institution*, Justice Department Research Series no. 1, Wellington: Government Printer.

Schumacher, Mary (1971b), *Violent Offending*, Justice Department Research Series no. 2. Wellington: Government Printer.

Schwimmer, E. G. (1958), 'The mediator', *JPS*, 67: 335–50.

Schwimmer, E. G. (1963), 'Guardian animals of the Maori', *JPS*, 72: 397–410.

Schwimmer, E. G. (1965), 'The cognitive aspect of culture change', *JPS*, 74: 149–81.

Schwimmer, E. G. (1966a), *The World of the Maori*, Wellington: Reed.

Schwimmer, E. G. (1966b), 'Sense of belonging', *Education* (Wellington), 15 (1): 3–19.

Schwimmer, E. G. (ed.) (1968), *The Maori People in the Nineteen Sixties*, Auckland: Blackwood and Janet Paul.

Schwimmer, E. G. and James Ritchie (1964), 'The education of Maori children', in *The Currie Report: a critique*, 82–108, Wellington: Association for the Study of Childhood.

Slater, S. W. and J. Jensen (1966), 'Study of crime amongst Maoris: interview study. Preliminary report of results', unpublished report of the Joint Committee on Young Offenders Research Unit.

Social Welfare, New Zealand Department of (1973), *Juvenile Crime in New Zealand*, Wellington: Government Printer.

Statistics, New Zealand Department of (1969), 'Maori population and dwellings', *New Zealand Census of Population and Dwellings 1966*, 8, Wellington: Government Printer.

Statistics, New Zealand Department of (1972a), 'Increase and location of population', *New Zealand Census of Population and Dwellings 1971*, 1, Wellington: Government Printer.

Statistics, New Zealand Department of (1972b), *New Zealand Justice Statistics 1971*, Wellington: Government Printer.

Statistics, New Zealand Department of (n.d.), *New Zealand Justice Statistics 1972*, Wellington: Government Printer.

Statistics, New Zealand Department of (1974), *New Zealand Official Yearbook 1974*, Wellington: Government Printer.

Statistics, New Zealand Department of (1975), 'Maori population and dwellings', *New Zealand Census of Population and Dwellings 1971*, 8. Wellington: Government Printer.

Sutch, W. B. (1964), *The Maori Contribution Yesterday, Today and Tomorrow*, Wellington: Department of Industries and Commerce.

Sutherland, I. L. G. (ed.) (1940), *The Maori People Today*, Wellington: Whitcombe & Tombs.

Sutherland, I. L. G. (1952), 'Maori and European', *JPS*, 61 (1): 136–55.

Sutherland, O. R. W. and R. A. Galbreath (1974), *Maori Participation in Pakeha Justice*, Hamilton: N.Z. Race Relations Council.

Sutherland, O. R. W., J. T. Hippolite, A. M. Smith, R. A. Galbreath (1973), *Justice and Race: a monocultural system in a multi-cultural society*, Hamilton: N.Z. Race Relations Council.

# Bibliography

Tatz, Colin M. (1972), *Four Kinds of Dominion: comparative race politics in Australia, Canada, New Zealand and South Africa*, Armidale: University of New England.

Taylor, C. R. H. (1972), *A Bibliography of the New Zealand Maori and the Moriori of the Chatham Islands*, London: Oxford University Press.

Thompson, Richard H. T. (1953–5), 'Maori affairs and the New Zealand press', *JPS*, 62 (4): 366–83; 63 (1): 1–16; 63 (3 & 4): 216–27; 64 (1): 22–34.

Thompson, Richard H. T. (1963), *Race Relations in New Zealand*, Christchurch: National Council of Churches in New Zealand.

Thompson, Richard H. T. (1964), *Race and Sport*, Institute of Race Relations/Oxford University Press.

Thompson, Richard and Moke Couch (1966), 'Maoris and the urban churches I', *N.Z. Theological Review*, 2 (1): 56–62.

Thompson, Richard and Moke Couch (1967), 'Maoris and the urban churches II', *Colloquium* (formerly *N.Z. Theological Review*), 2 (2): 156–64.

Turner, Dennis Knight (1963), *Tangi*, Wellington: Reed.

University of Auckland (Department of University Extension), various dates, 'Data Papers and Reports on Maori Leadership Conferences': (a) Auckland 1939; (b) Auckland 1959; (c) Whangarei 1959; (d) Ngaruawahia 1960; (e) Whakatane 1960; (f) Gisborne 1960; (g) Kaitaia 1960; (h) Taupo 1961; (i) Rotorua 1961; (j) Wairoa 1961; (k) Ruatoria May 1962; (l) Tauranga 1962; (m) Ruatoria October 1962; (n) Taumarunui 1962; (o) Auckland 1963; (p) Murupara 1964; (q) Ruatoki 1964; (r) Auckland 1970. All cyclostyled and bound.

University of Auckland (Department of University Extension), Polynesian Youth Forum on 'The gang', cyclostyled.

Vaughan, Graham M. (1964), *Ethnic Awareness and Attitudes in New Zealand*, Wellington: Victoria University of Wellington Publications in Psychology no. 17.

Vaughan, Graham M. (1972), *Racial Issues in New England*, Auckland: Akarana Press.

Victoria University of Wellington (Department of University Extension) (1972), *The Treaty of Waitangi: its origins and significance*, Wellington: Victoria University of Wellington University Extension Publication no. 7.

Walsh, A. C. (1971), *More and More Maoris*, N.Z. Whitcombe & Tombs.

Watson, John (1967), *Horizons of Unknown Power*, Wellington: N.Z. Council of Educational Research.

Watson, John (1972), *Accommodating the Polynesian Heritage of the Maori Child*, Wellington: N.Z. Council of Educational Research.

Webb, S. D. and John Collette (1973), *New Zealand Society: contemporary perspectives*, Sydney: John Wiley.

Williams, John S. (1960), *Maori Achievement Motivation*, Wellington: Victoria University of Wellington Publications in Psychology no. 13.

## D. Language, literature and art

### (1) Maori language

Biggs, B. G. (1966), *English-Maori Dictionary*, Wellington: Reed.

*Hohepa, Patrick W. (1967), 'A profile generative grammar of Maori', *Inter. J. of Amer. Linguistics*, Memoir 20.

*Karetu, S. (1974), *Te reo rangatira: a course in Maori for sixth and seventh forms*, Wellington: Government Printer.

*Mahuika, A. (1974–5), *Te reo*, Books 1–3, Palmerston North: Massey University (Maori Studies).

*Paora, Roka (1971), *Learn Maori with Parehau and Sharon*, Books 1 and 2. Wellington: Whitcombe & Tombs.

*Waititi, Hoani (1962, 1964), *Te Rangatahi* 1 and 2, Wellington: Government Printer.

Williams, Herbert W. (1971), *A Dictionary of the Maori Language*, 7th edn, revised and augmented by the Advisory Committee on the Maori Language, Department of Education, Wellington: Government Printer.

### (2) Literature in or translated from Maori

Alpers, Antony (1964), *Maori Myths and Tribal Legends*, Auckland: Blackwood and Janet Paul.

Biggs, Bruce, *P. W. Hohepa and *S. M. Mead (eds) (1962), *Selected Readings in Maori*, Auckland: University of Auckland (Department of Anthropology).

Biggs, Bruce and *S. M. Mead (eds) (1964), *He kohikohinga aronui: selected readings in Maori*, Auckland: University of Auckland (Department of Anthropology).

Brougham, Aileen E. and A. W. Reed (1963), *Maori Proverbs*, Wellington: Reed.

Caselberg, John (ed.) (1975), *Maori is My Name*, Dunedin: John McIndoe Ltd.

Curnow, Allen and Roger Oppenheim (1960), Maori poetry, in *Penguin Book of New Zealand Verse* (ed.) Allen Curnow: 79–86.

Davis, C. O. B. (1855), *Maori Mementoes. A series of addresses by the native people to Sir George Grey . . . a small collection of laments*, Auckland: Williamson & Wilson.

*Dewes, Te Kapunga (1974), *Nga waiata haka a Henare Waitoa o Ngati Porou*, Wellington: Victoria University of Wellington.

Education, New Zealand Department of, *Te whare kura*, school bulletins published irregularly since 1960, Wellington: Government Printer.

Education, New Zealand Department of, *Te Tautoko*, school bulletins published irregularly since 1971, Wellington: Government Printer.

Grey, Sir George (1851), *Ko nga moteatea me nga hakirara o nga Maori*, 507 poems and 12 prose pieces, Wellington: Stokes.

Grey, Sir George (1854), *Mythology and Traditions of the New Zealanders. Ko nga mahinga a nga tupuna*, London: Willis. 3rd edn (ed.) H. W. Williams as *Nga mahi a nga tupuna*; reprinted 1971, Wellington: Reed.

Grey, Sir George (1885), *Polynesian Mythology and Ancient Traditional History of the New Zealand Race*, Auckland: Brett; reprinted 1961 as *Polynesian Mythology* (ed.) W. W. Bird, Wellington: Whitcombe & Tombs.

Grey, Sir George (1857), *Ko nga waiata Maori he mea kohikohi mai*, 48 songs, London: Trubner.

*Kohere, Reweti (ed.) (1951), *He konae aronui: Maori proverbs and sayings*, Wellington: Reed.

McGregor, John (1893), *Popular Maori songs as written by the Maoris of Waikato . . . 1864*, Auckland: Field. Plus four subsequent supplements.

Mitcalfe, Barry (1961), *Poetry of the Maori: translations*, Hamilton: Paul's Book Arcade.

Mitcalfe, Barry (1974), *Maori Poetry: the singing word*, Wellington: Price Milburn.

*Ngata, Sir Apirana (1935), *Panui mo te pooti o te tau* 1935, Wellington: H. H. Tombs.

*Ngata, Sir Apirana (1950), *The Treaty of Waitangi: an explanation. Te Tiriti-o-Waitangi: he Whakamarama*, Christchurch: Maori Purposes Fund Board/Pegasus Press. First published 1922.

*Ngata, Sir Apirana (ed.) (1958), *Nga moteatea*, I, Wellington: Polynesian Society.

*Ngata, Sir Apirana and *Pei Te Hurinui Jones (eds) (1963, 1970), *Nga moteatea*, II and III, Wellington: Polynesian Society.

Orbell, Margaret R. (ed.) (1968), *Maori Folktales in Maori and English*, Auckland: Blackwood and Janet Paul.

Reed, A. W. (1963), *Treasury of Maori Folklore*, Wellington: Reed.

Smith, S. Percy (1913–15), *The Lore of the Whare Wananga*, 2 vols, New Plymouth: Polynesian Society Memoirs 3 and 4.

White, John (1887–90), *The Ancient History of the Maori*, 6 vols, Wellington: Government Printer.

(3)   *Critical studies in Maori literature*

Jackson, Michael (1968), 'Some structural considerations of Maori myth', *JPS*, 77: 147–62.

*Mead, S. M. (1969), 'Imagery, symbolism and social values in Maori chants', *JPS*, 78: 378–404.

Rhodes, H. Winston (1973), 'Race relations and literature', *Meanjin Quarterly*, 32: 260–7.

Simmons, D. R. (1966), 'The sources of Sir George Grey's *Nga mahi a nga tupuna*', *JPS*, 75 (2): 177–88.

Simmons, D. R. and B. C. Biggs (1970), 'The sources of *The Lore of the Whare Wananga*', *JPS*, 79 (1): 22–42.

*Walker, Rangi (1969), 'Proper names in Maori myth and tradition', *JPS*, 78: 405–16.

(4)  *Literature in English*

Audley, E. H. (1963), *No Boots for Mr Moehau*, London: Hodder & Stoughton.
*Baker, Heretaunga Pat (1975), *Behind the Tattooed Face*, Wellington: Cole Catley.
Brathwaite, Errol (1964), *The Flying Fish*, London: Collins.
Brathwaite, Errol (1965), *The Needle's Eye*, London: Collins.
Brathwaite, Errol (1967), *The Evil Day*, London: Collins.
*Dansey, Harry (1974), *Te Raukura: the feathers of the albatross. A narrative play in two acts*, Auckland: Longman Paul.
Finlayson, Roderick (1938), *Brown Man's Burden*, Auckland: Unicorn Press.
Finlayson, Roderick (1965), *The Springing Fern*, Wellington: Whitcombe & Tombs.
Fowler, Leo (1959), *Brown Conflict*, Wellington: Reed.
*Grace, Patricia (1975), *Waiariki*, London: Heinemann.
Hill, Bernie and Jane (1961), *Hey Boy!*, Christchurch: Whitcombe & Tombs.
Hilliard, Noel (1960), *Maori Girl*, London: Heinemann.
Hilliard, Noel (1963), *A Piece of Land*, London: Robert Hale.
Hilliard, Noel (1969), *Night at Green River*, London: Robert Hale.
Hilliard, Noel (1974), *Maori Woman*, London: Robert Hale/N.Z. edition Whitcombe & Tombs.
*Ihimaera, Witi (1972), *Pounamu Pounamu*, London: Heinemann.
*Ihimaera, Witi (1973), *Tangi*, London: Heinemann.
*Ihimaera, Witi (1974), *Whanau*, London: Heinemann.
*Jones, Pei Te Hurinui (1961), *Puhiwahine Maori Poetess*, Christchurch: Pegasus Press.
*Kereama, Matire (1968). *The Tail of the Fish: Maori memories of the Far North*. Auckland: Oswald-Sealy,
*Kohere, Reweti (1949), *Story of a Maori Chief* (Mokena Kohere), Wellington: Reed.
*Kohere, Reweti (1951), *The Autobiography of a Maori*, Wellington: Reed.
Morrice, Stella (1958), *The Story of Wiremu*, Hamilton: Paul's Book Arcade; and London: Phoenix House.
Orbell, Margaret (1970), *Contemporary Maori Writing*, Wellington: Reed.
Powell, Lesley Cameron (1963), *Turi*, with photographs by Pius Blank, Hamilton: Paul's Book Arcade.
Satchell, William (1938), *The Greenstone Door*, Auckland: Whitcombe & Tombs.
*Tuwhare, Hone (1964), *No Ordinary Sun*, Hamilton: Paul's Book Arcade.
*Tuwhare, Hone (1970), *Come Rain, Hail*, Dunedin: University of Otago (Department of English); 2nd edn 1973, Dunedin: Caveman Press.
*Tuwhare, Hone (1973), *Sapwood and Milk*, Dunedin: Caveman Press.
*Tuwhare, Hone (1974), *Something Nothing*, Dunedin: Caveman Press.

Bibliography

## E. Regional history

Best, Elsdon (1925), *Tuhoe Children of the Mist*, New Plymouth: Board of Maori Ethnological research, Avery.

Buick, T. Lindsay (1903), *Old Manawatu*, Palmerston North: Buick & Young.

*Carkeek, W. C. (1966), *The Kapiti Coast*, Wellington: Reed.

Campbell, John Logan (1952), *Poenamo*, 1st edn 1881; N.Z. edn: Whitcombe & Tombs.

Elvy, W. J. (1957), *Kei puta te wairau: a history of Marlborough in Maori times*, Christchurch: Whitcombe & Tombs.

*Grace, John Te H. (1959), *Tuwharetoa*, Wellington: Reed.

Hammond, T. G. (1924), *The Story of Aotea*, Christchurch: Lyttleton Times.

Houston, John (1965), *Maori Life in old Taranaki*, Wellington: Reed.

*Jones, Pei Te Hurinui (1960), *King Potatau*, Wellington: Polynesian Society.

*Kelly, Leslie (1949), *Tainui*, Wellington: Polynesian Society.

McKay, J. A. (1966), *Historic Poverty Bay and the East Coast, North Island, New Zealand*, 2nd edn, Gisborne: J. G. McKay.

Maning, F. E. (1863), *Old New Zealand*, Auckland: Creighton & Scales. Also Whitcombe & Tombs, 1948.

*Mitchell, J. H. (1944, 1973), *Takitimu*, Wellington: Reed.

Oliver, W. H. (1971), *Challenge and Response: a study of the development of the Gisborne-East Coast Region*, Gisborne: East Coast Development Research Association.

Rickard, L. S. (1963), *Tamihana the King-maker*, Wellington: Reed.

Smart, M. J. G. and A. P. Bates (1972), *The Wanganui Story*, Wanganui: Wanganui Newspapers.

Stafford, Donald M. (1969), *Te Arawa*, Wellington: Reed.

## F. Art, music and dance

Archey, Gilbert (1955), *Sculpture and Design: an outline of Maori art*, Auckland: Auckland War Memorial Museum.

Armstrong, Alan (1964), *Maori Games and Hakas: instructions words and actions*, Wellington: Reed.

Armstrong, Alan and *Reupena Ngata (1960), *Maori Action Songs*, Wellington: Reed.

Barrow, T. (1964), *The Decorative Arts of the New Zealand Maori*, Wellington: Reed.

Barrow, T. (1969), *Maori Wood Sculpture*, Wellington: Reed.

Buck, Peter (1949), *The Coming of the Maori*, Wellington: Maori Purposes Fund Board.

Education, New Zealand Department of (Art and Craft Branch) (1961), *The Arts of the Maori*, Wellington: Department of Education, Government Printer.

Education, New Zealand Department of (Art and Craft Branch) (1963),

*The Arts of the Maori Instructional Booklets*, a series published irregularly, Wellington: Department of Education, Government Printer.

Fowler, Leo (1974), *Te Mana o Turanga*, Auckland: Historic Places Trust.

Hopa, N. K. (1971), *The Art of Piupiu Making*, Wellington: Reed.

Jackson, Michael (1972), 'Aspects of symbolism and composition in Maori art', *Bijdragen tot de taal-, land-, en Volkenkunde Deel*, 128: 33–80.

King, Michael (1972), *Moko: Maori tattooing in the twentieth century.* Wellington: Alister Taylor.

McEwen, J. M. (1966), 'Maori Art', in *An Encyclopaedia of New Zealand*, 2: 408–29, Wellington: Government Printer.

McLean, Mervyn (1964–6), 'Can Maori chant survive?' 'Music of Maori chant.' 'Transcriptions of authentic Maori chants'. *Te Ao Hou* passim nos. 47–57.

McLean, Mervyn (1970), 'The music of Maori chant'. Preface to *Nga moteatea* III (eds. A. T. Ngata and Pei Te Hurinui). Wellington: Polynesian Society.

McLean, Mervyn (1971), *Maori music. A bulletin for schools*, Wellington: Department of Education (School Publications).

*Mead, S. M. (1961), *The Art of Maori Carving*, Wellington: Reed.

*Mead, S. M. (1968), *The Art of Taniko Weaving*, Wellington: Reed.

*Mead, S. M. (1969), *Traditional Maori Clothing*, Wellington: Reed.

Phillipps, W. J. (1955), *Carved Houses of Western and Northern Areas of New Zealand*, Wellington: Government Printer.

Phillips, W. J. (1944), *Carved Maori Houses of the Eastern Districts of the North Island*, Wellington: Records of Dominion Museum, 1: 69–119.

Phillips, W. J. (1952), *Maori Houses and Food Stores*, Wellington: Dominion Museum Monograph 8.

Ryden, S. (1965), *The Banks Collection*, Stockholm: The Ethnographical Museum of Sweden Monograph Series Publication no. 8.

Skinner, H. D. (1974), *Comparative Speaking*, selected works (ed.) Peter Gathercole, Foss and Helen Leach, Dunedin: John McIndoe for Otago University Press.

Trotter, Michael and Beverley McCulloch (1971), *Prehistoric Rock Art of New Zealand*, Wellington: Reed.

# Index

Index

370

# Index

Index

377

Index

Poutapu, Piri, 278
Pouwer, Jan, xv
*pōwhiri*, 251, 344
prayer, 162, 172, Plate 1
pre-employment courses, 83
pre-school education, 159, 160–2,
170
prejudice, 292, 300; colour, 292–3
Presbyterian Church, 184–5, 308;
Maori Synod, 314, 316, 360
Press, Maoris and, 297, 362
pride in being Maori, 48, 51; *see*
identity
priest, 64; *see also* minister(s),
Christian, *tohunga ahurewa*
primary production, 81–2
prison officers, 212
probation officers, 212, 222
professions, professional workers,
81–2, 203–4
property: attitudes to, 217;
offences against, 217
prophet(s), 64, 186–8
protest, 177–8, 317–18, 329
proverbs, 13, 61, 63, 72, 204, 218,
266, **267–8**, 364
psychologists, 142
public opinion, 25, 26, 225
*puhi*, 20
Puketapu IIIA, 117, 118
*purapura whetū*, 276, 281
*pure*, 28
Puriri, Brownie, xiv

Queen Elizabeth II, 199, 251, 267,
283
Queen Elizabeth II Arts Council,
278, 279, 287–8
Queen Te Ata-i-rangikaahu,
196–9, 202, 280, 281

race relations, 289–93
Race Relations Act 1971, 290–1,
296, 299
Race Relations Conciliator,
290–1, 296, 297–8, 360

Race Relations Office, 291, 297,
329
radio, 98, 99
*rāhui*, 12
*rākau*, 151, 250–1, 344
Rakau Studies, 142
Rakena, Rev. Rua, 281, 316, 360
Ranapia, Mrs Beth, 100
*rangatahi*, 173, 204–5, 211, 344
*rangatira*, aristocrats, **7–8**, 201,
258; chiefs, 24–5, 65, 133,
**201–3**, 205, 208, 344; *see also*
aristocrats, chief(s)
Rangi (Sky), 23, 280, 288, 344;
*see also* Te Rangi
Rangihau, John, xv, 170, 243
Rangiihu, Rev. Samuel, 49
Rarawa (tribe), 129–30, 201
*raro*, 57, 344
Rata, Matiu, 194, 206
Ratana, Mrs Iriaka, 205
Ratana: festivals, 188, 264;
Labour alliance, 188, 192;
Movement, 187–90, 213, 357;
Pa, 187
Ratana, Tahupotiki Wiremu, 37,
94, 187–90, 328, 357
reciprocity (*utu*), 67–8
recordings, sound, 267
Reedy, Tamati, xiv
religion, religious view of the
world, 22, 23–4, 49, **54–62**
religious groups, 183–91
relocation schemes, 308
rental housing, state, 88
representation, parliamentary,
191–5
research: on education, 161–2,
166; on language, 95, 98, 166;
on Maori Studies, etc., 170; on
offenders, 221–3
Reserved Lands, 115
*ringa wera*, 234, 261, 344
Ringatū Church, **186–7**, 213, 285,
299
Ritchie, James, 84, 142, 258,
284–5, 304–5, 360
Ritchie, Jane, 142, 170, 304–5, 360

378

Index